A Man's Reach

A Man's Reach

ELMER L. ANDERSEN

Edited by Lori Sturdevant

University of Minnesota Press
Minneapolis • London

Published by the University of Minnesota Press
111 Third Avenue South, Suite 290
Minneapolis, MN 55401-2520
http://www.upress.umn.edu

Printed in the United States of America on acid-free paper

Library of Congress Cataloging-in-Publication Data

Andersen, Elmer L., 1909–
    A man's reach / Elmer L. Andersen ; edited by Lori Sturdevant.
        p.   cm.
    Includes index.
    ISBN 0-8166-3738-5 (alk. paper) — ISBN 0-8166-3739-3 (pbk. : alk. paper)
    1. Andersen, Elmer L., 1909–   2. Governors—Minnesota—Biography.
3. Legislators—Minnesota—Biography.   4. Minnesota—Politics and government—
1951–   5. Businessmen—Minnesota—Saint Paul—Biography.   6. Saint Paul
(Minn.)—Biography.   7. Muskegon (Mich.)—Biography.   I. Title.
    F610.3 .A54 A3 2000
    977.6'05'092—dc21

                                                                00-008891

11 10 09 08 07 06 05 04 03 02 01 00   10 9 8 7 6 5 4 3 2 1

Dedicated to
Tony, Julian, and Emily
who give us
joy and love

Ah, but a man's reach should exceed his grasp, or what's a heaven for?
                    —Robert Browning, "Andrea del Sarto," 1855

Contents

Preface

ON JULY 4, 1928, I was in Cheyenne, Wyoming. I had finished a three-week trial sales trip for E. H. Sheldon and Company of Muskegon, Michigan, and was awaiting further instructions. Alone and far from home, I passed the holiday by attending a rodeo at Frontier Days, an annual festival that Cheyenne claims is "the daddy of them all." When I returned to the hotel, a telegram was waiting for me. It contained orders to proceed to Minneapolis and take over the Minnesota sales territory.

My chance had come—a chance for a life beyond my imagining on that day. I only knew then that the job I wanted was mine. E. H. Sheldon and Company was a nationally known manufacturer of school furniture for specialized courses, such as manual training, home economics, physics, and chemistry. On graduating from Muskegon Junior College in June 1928, I asked Mr. Sheldon, the company's owner, for a sales position. He agreed to give me a trial, though he thought I was rather young. I had just passed my nineteenth birthday, but I had worked in the Sheldon factory since I was fourteen, and I knew the product line well. He sent me through Minnesota, North Dakota, Montana, and Wyoming. I must have performed reasonably well, because there was the crucial telegram that would change my life. It brought me to Minnesota, where, for more than seventy years, I have had a family, business, political, and community life that has been richly rewarding.

Now, in my ninety-first year, the time has come to tell my story. I do so at the urging of my family and the suggestion of many people through the years. At first I thought it might be rather self-serving to write an autobiography. But my children, especially my elder son, Tony, pushed me to tell my story myself, in my own way, while I am here to do it! My longtime friend and colleague Tom Swain also encouraged me. He sounded out the person I wanted as my interviewer, editor, and partner on the project, Lori Sturdevant of the *Star Tribune*. It was a most fortunate choice. Lori's enthusiasm, dedication, and skill have been an incredible help. She in turn made an all-important connection with our exceptionally skillful transcriber, Beverly Hermes.

Lori and I benefited greatly from the scrapbooks kept through the years by my loyal secretary, Donna Petersen. We called on the fine memories and editing skills of Russell Fridley, Tom Swain, and Gene Lahammer. Editing help also came from my sons, Tony and Julian, and Lori's friend Martin Vos. We had transportation help from our family aide, Randy Christenson.

Lori found facts that my memory did not readily supply from many sources: H. B. Fuller Company, the Minnesota Historical Society, the Bush Foundation, the University of Minnesota Foundation, the University of Minnesota Landscape Arboretum, the Andersen Horticultural Library, the Minnesota Legislative Reference Library, Sugarloaf Interpretive Center Association, the *Star Tribune,* the Charles Lindbergh Foundation, the Norwegian Consulate General, the Child Welfare League of America, the National Council on Foundations, the office of Sen. Paul Wellstone, the University of Minnesota Board of Regents, former Minneapolis City Council member Gladys Brooks, former Gov. Arne Carlson, Tom Roeser's book about the 1962 gubernatorial campaign, *Ingenious Deceit,* and A. Scott Berg's biography, *Lindbergh.*

And, as in all things, I relied on Eleanor. I thank them all.

Over the years, I have developed certain theories about human relationships, business management, good government, and more. I am convinced that these theories raised the level of my efforts in business and government from what they might otherwise have been. As I report the events of my life in the following chapters, I relay many of my ideas, in the hope that readers may find them of some use.

Editor's Note

ELMER L. ANDERSEN HAS DRAWN a lifetime of inspiration and assurance from the Robert Browning line his college literature teacher loved: "Ah, but a man's reach should exceed his grasp, or what's a heaven for?" It is a fitting source for the title of his autobiography. This is the story of a man who found life's greatest satisfaction when he was launching a project, advancing a cause, or working toward a goal. He aimed first for a better life for himself and his family. But while he was still a young man, he was already reaching beyond his immediate grasp, to build a better community, state, and nation.

Nevertheless, another title would have fit this book as well. Elmer said it often as he related the saga of his ninety years: "You never lose." Nothing done to advance a good cause can ever be counted as a loss, no matter the outcome, he said. If a goal has merit, an effort to pursue it is worthwhile, if only to show those who come later how not to proceed.

"You never lose" is not an obvious truth, coming from the politician Minnesotans may remember best as the loser of the closest gubernatorial election in state history. A mere 91 votes out of more than 1.2 million cast ended Andersen's governorship in 1963 after the excruciating drama of a four-and-a-half-month recount. Then, as before, when faced with circumstances that would crush many a spirit, Andersen willed himself to overcome. He would never again hold elective office, but his leadership for his state was far from over.

By the time Andersen reached adulthood, he knew adversity well. The child of an immigrant father and first-generation American mother, he was raised in poverty. When he was six, his parents separated, and his father's presence and support ended. Polio left its physical and psychological mark. His education was pinched by his need to work. He was orphaned at age fifteen. Today he would qualify for the label "at risk." But Elmer refused to let himself fall into despair. Somehow, he accepted his lot and looked ahead.

Adulthood brought Andersen more than his share of setbacks, because he was more than usually active in business, politics, and civic affairs. Firm in the faith that even unsuccessful efforts in pursuit of a good cause are worthwhile, he persisted—and through persistence, he achieved much. Keeping on in the face of doubts and reversals are what built H. B. Fuller Company and ECM Publishers, Inc. Not letting opponents have the final word produced Voyageurs National Park, pioneering civil rights guarantees, and the constitutional amendment that led to the development of Minnesota's taconite industry. Refusing to let a good idea die created the Metropolitan Planning Commission, an independent school district for St. Paul, and improved care for the mentally ill.

Those are only some of the achievements that can be traced to this one man. His record is the antidote to any doubt that one life can make a difference, and the joy he derived along the way belies any claim that hard work yields only headaches, or public service, only sorrow.

Where did it come from, this unflagging will to persevere? Elmer himself is hard pressed to identify its source. He tells of taking inspiration from many people—parents, siblings, teachers, mentors, friends, heroes both living and in literature. The steady devotion of a quietly remarkable spouse certainly contributed greatly to the man he became. So did a desire to make a better life for his children, grandchildren, and great-grandchildren.

But after spending many enthralled hours listening to the memories recorded in the pages that follow, I can only conclude that Elmer L. Andersen's undefeated spirit is a gift beyond human giving—given to him for us all.

Lori Sturdevant
September 1999

Part I

THE EARLY YEARS

Boyhood

I WAS BORN IN CHICAGO, ILLINOIS, on June 17, 1909. My arrival was carelessly recorded, which came to my attention years later, when I sought a passport. I needed a birth certificate, and when I inquired of Cook County for the document, they produced the certificate of a baby Anderson, spelled *son* instead of *sen,* born June 17, 1909, but a girl, not a boy. Affidavits were supplied by my brothers that, indeed, I was that child, that I was a boy, and that my name was spelled *sen.* Cook County issued a modified birth certificate, which satisfied the passport authorities, and I was finally recorded properly as having arrived.

My father was Arne Andersen, an immigrant from Solør, Norway. As a young man, he left his parents and siblings behind on a modest farm and came to the United States, looking for opportunity. He was so anxious to be Americanized that he changed his name from Kjelsberg to the more American-sounding Andersen. He settled in Chicago, where some distant kinsfolk had preceded him.

My mother was Jennie Olivia Johnson Andersen, of North Muskegon, Michigan. Her father was a seaman from Lulea, in northern Sweden, who came to America as a young man and worked in the timbering business. That was what brought him to Muskegon, where he met my grandmother. She was born in the Christiania area, which is Oslo today, and came to the United States as a young girl.

My father was a streetcar motorman in Chicago, operating on the Halsted streetcar line out of the Ashland Avenue car barns. My earliest memory is of riding with him on the streetcar and being permitted to clang the bell as we came to street crossings. The bell was a foot-driven device in the floor of the driving area. Stepping on it sounded a bell below the floor that rang loudly in the street.

Another early memory is of my mother taking me, at about age six, and my infant sister, Caroline, early one morning to the Lake Michigan boat docks. We were on our way to Muskegon—not for a visit, but a permanent move. My mother was taking two of her four children and leaving Chicago for an uncertain future. I remember going down to the big boat dock at dawn, my sister a baby in my mother's arms, I a small boy trudging beside them. It was my first trip on a big boat, my first trip to my mother's home in Muskegon. It was a momentous day for me, but the only memory I retain is of that early morning walk to the dock.

In those days, ferryboats carried automobiles. It was a common thing to go from one Lake Michigan city to another via car-transporting boats. Those vessels spared drivers a long trip around the lake. Of course, the ferries also served people who did not have a car—including us.

Just what were the circumstances of my parents' separation, or what provoked it, I have never known. There was no divorce. Efforts at reconciliation, if there were any, were not successful. It was never discussed among the family—or, at least, not with me. It was just accepted that there had been a change, and we went on.

Going to Muskegon was going home for my mother. She was seeking refuge in the home of her two unmarried sisters, Lillian, a teacher, and Eleanor, a receptionist at Shaw Walker Company, a manufacturer of office furniture. Aunt Lillian was older than my mother; Aunt Eleanor was younger. They were living together when we arrived, in a small house on Houston Street. Aunt Lillian may have been the first person to inspire in me a love of books and a desire to collect them. She lived to be nearly one hundred. Aunt Eleanor married eventually, but she had no children.

Not long after we arrived in Muskegon, we rented and later purchased a tiny house at 86 Smith Street, on what was then the edge of town. My two older brothers, then in their teens, soon joined us there. That little house was the first home I remember well, the home of my boyhood.

My recollections of Muskegon are happy ones. We worked hard, but we survived and even flourished.

Muskegon's economic foundation was timber. It is located on Lake Muskegon, which empties into Lake Michigan and is fed by the Muskegon River. The plain around Muskegon has sandy soil, ideal for the pine trees that once grew in abundance. The town got its start in the nineteenth century as a center for processing and distributing those pine trees after they were cut. Loggers used to run logs down the river to Muskegon.

But, as was so often the case, the early settlers cut the lumber, took the wealth, and abandoned the city—all except one lumber baron, Charles Hackley. He stayed in Muskegon, built a luxurious home, and became a local philanthropist. There was a Hackley Public Library, a Hackley Art

Museum, and a Hackley School. He provided a manual training school building for use in vocational education. His generosity was a great boon to the city during its transition from lumbering to more diverse modern industry.

Several industries related to the automobile developed in Muskegon. Continental Motors, one of the first automobile motor manufacturers, was located there. The Campbell, Wyant and Cannon Foundry made parts for the auto industry. A man named Charles Johnson invented the piston ring and founded the Muskegon Piston Ring Company, a flourishing concern. We called him "Piston Ring Johnson." His wife had been a classmate of my mother. During our early years on Smith Street, Mrs. Johnson would come with her chauffeured limousine at Christmas time, and the chauffeur would bring in bags of goodies. They would always include oranges. Having an orange—that was a big deal. When Mrs. "Piston Ring Johnson" came, we thought she was a saint.

Furniture manufacturing was also important to Muskegon. E. H. Sheldon and Company produced specialty school furniture. The Shaw Walker Company made office equipment, at first wooden, later steel. They were a progressive, fine company. My Aunt Eleanor worked there and also met her husband there. Eventually, Shaw Walker was taken over by Herman Miller and Knoll. I was so impressed by the first Herman Miller L-shaped desk I saw that, many years later, I designed my own desk after that pattern.

The household furniture industry was well established in nearby Grand Rapids, and spilled over to Muskegon. The towns are about forty-five miles apart, and though Grand Rapids was larger, the two were rivals. In 1920, Muskegon was home to about 36,000 people, compared with nearly 140,000 in Grand Rapids. The area had a diverse population that included a large contingent of Dutch immigrants. That explains the name of the city fifty miles south of Muskegon—Holland—and its tulip industry. Tulip Days in Holland are still celebrated.

Between Holland and Muskegon was Grand Haven, a stopover point for the boats that went from Muskegon to Chicago. Young people in Muskegon used to do something we called "loop the loop." A group of young people would get on the boat to Grand Haven, while one of the number, chosen by drawing straws, would drive a car the fifteen miles there to meet the group arriving by boat and drive them home. It was quite a lark to "loop the loop" to Grand Haven. Boating was popular, as was ice-boating in the winter. Ice-boating was a daring activity. As cold weather set in, boats from Chicago and Milwaukee plowed through ice as long as they could. When the ice got too thick, they had to give up. Early in winter, the large vessels could plow through two or three inches of ice to get to the dock. After a big boat passed, young ice-boaters would scoot up and down parallel to the channel the big boats made and then attempt to jump across it, often on only a fraction of an inch of ice. They flew across, hardly making contact with the surface. Now and then, an ice-boater failed to make the jump, and either lost his life or was badly hurt. A great excitement was watching the ice-boaters try to jump the channel.

I watched occasionally, but I did not try it myself. I did not play very much. I was always working. I am afraid I never learned to play with a clear conscience. I am reminded of a woman who said that she enjoyed something so much, it must be a sin. I know the feeling.

I had a great drive to work, even as a young boy. All of the Andersens did. Practically from the time we could walk, all of Arne and Jennie Andersen's children did something to help the family survive. Work consumed my father. He did everything to save money, get ahead, and give his children an education. He repaired shoes for the family with his own equipment. When I was small, I liked to watch him put shoes on a form and tap in the nails to resole them.

My father was what one might call a hard man. Not only did he work hard himself, but he was hard on others too. I have reflected often on something that occurred when I was four or five. I had been at Ogden Park, near our home in Chicago, with my mother. I was not allowed to go into the wading pool where all the other children were. But it was a hot day, and just to get a little taste of it, I put my feet in the water. That night, my father examined my shoes, as he frequently did to see how careful we had been with his work. He saw the marks of water on my shoes. He was so angry, he threw a shoe at me. I felt so rejected. I think this experience at an early age may have been responsible for my determination to win other people's approval. It may even have helped me in politics!

Our parents' drive was not unusual among immigrants to the United States. They all struggled to learn a new language, to find employment, to make it. Life was serious for them. In the early twentieth century, employees had little protection. Unions had difficulty getting established. Some workers were grossly exploited. Many people simply got buried. Yet the country was growing and expanding so rapidly that in spite of all the greed, enough prosperity spilled over so life eventually became tolerably good for everybody.

After our parents' separation, our father wrote to us occasionally. He would always close his letters with the same words: "Am well and working." That was his test of life. If you were well and working, you were succeeding. He infused in all of us a belief that work was not just duty. It was a privilege and an opportunity. As a result, we liked work. We liked projects. We liked to do things that showed results.

Muskegon was a bustling town, a good place for a young family that had more ambition than means. Yet, the city did not provide public support for people facing difficulty. If people were impoverished when they reached old age, they went to the poor house. There was no provision for emotionally disturbed or eccentric people. Those poor souls wandered about and sometimes faced cruel abuse. We children were terribly unkind to a fellow we called "Crazy Carlson" because he liked to dress in women's clothes. I do not look back on those incidents with pride.

Otherwise, it seemed that almost everybody in Muskegon was on a par. There were a few really rich people, but we had little association with them. There were not many black people in town. I had one black classmate in high school.

At 86 Smith Street, we all pitched in to make ends meet. Both of my brothers started work at E. H. Sheldon and Company, and the owner, Mr. Sheldon, took an interest in the Andersen family. He had been a vocational teacher in Chicago when he invented a rapid-acting vice. Lifting a lever would make the vice slide back and forth. It was a variation on the longer screw-type vice that had to be turned up to contact its contents. With some success with the vice, he began to manufacture manual training benches, and then moved the business to Muskegon. It grew rapidly as specialized vocational education took hold in the country's schools.

My eldest brother, Arnold, went to work in the glue room and was quickly promoted to foreman. The glue room was an important part of Sheldon's factory. Most of the furniture was made of wood harvested at a Sheldon-owned lumber camp in Upper Michigan and assembled with glue. Marvin, my second brother, started as a salesman for Sheldon and worked in the southeastern United States, calling on school boards, colleges, and other institutions of vocational training.

During our first years in Muskegon, I was too young to work at a factory. My first job was to help my mother. She took in washing. My job was to haul the washing to and from her customers, back and forth in my coaster wagon. One load of laundry would fill a giant reed hamper. She was paid a dollar for laundering that whole load. I can still see my mother rubbing wet clothes by hand on a corrugated metal washboard. It was hard, hard work.

Initially, the lady we washed for provided the washing powder. It was a blow when I came home one day with the news that from now on, the lady said, we would have to supply the washing powder. So, we got Fels Naptha soap, in big, strong-smelling bars.

I had a strange feeling once while walking through an antique shop and seeing an old washboard with a high price on it. I thought, boy! I would not pay two cents for a galvanized iron washboard. To me, it is a symbol of my mother's toilsome labor, trying to keep our family afloat.

I was about nine years old when I began to sell newspapers on the streets of Muskegon. I bought the papers each day for two cents apiece and sold them for three cents. Sales volume was usually high, because in those years newspapers were the primary means of communication for the general public. I looked forward to big breaking news stories, because they would trigger the publication of extra editions. An extra was a made-over front page, wrapped around the most recent regular edition. Like other editions, extras cost me two cents apiece, but they caused such excitement that customers would frequently give me a nickel, a dime, or even a quarter, and say, "Keep the change, buddy." The two biggest days for extras stand out in my mind. One was Armistice Day, 1918, the end of World War I. There was enormous excitement when the extra came out with the banner headline: "War Ends; Peace Declared." That was a wonderful day for tips. But one extra even exceeded Armistice Day, and no one has ever been able to guess what day that was. The closest was a woman who said, "It must have been an athletic event." Indeed, it was. It was on July 4, 1919, when Jack Dempsey knocked out Jess Willard for boxing's heavyweight championship. The young Manassa Mauler had attracted the interest of the entire nation, so there was enormous excitement over the fight between Dempsey and Willard, who had dominated the field until then. Dempsey was declared the winner when the much larger Willard failed to answer the bell at the start of the fourth round.

Selling newspapers on the street in winter was a cold occupation. I regularly visited two places when the temperature dropped. One was Poirer's Restaurant, where the proprietor kindly let me go through the dining room. I was allowed to offer newspapers to the diners, but I was not to tarry or make a nuisance of myself. That little trip served to warm and bolster me for a return to the street. Another favorite stop was at the vendor of Coney Island red-hot hot dogs. They were served in a fluffed-up bun that was delicious on a cold night. But they cost a nickel—a major part of my day's earnings—so it was an indulgence not often taken.

I enjoyed selling newspapers, even on cold days. I never felt abused or disadvantaged in any way about work. I learned early that success in any activity often depends on staying power—the ability to stay calm, avoid discouragement, and press on. I often tell audiences, "You never lose. Every effort you make is a contribution to success." The work you start may be completed at some other time and by some other people. But when you make sincere effort toward a good end, you contribute to its ultimate attainment. When you understand that, you never fail. That truth served me well much later, when my setbacks were measured not in unsold newspapers but in votes.

Soon I was selling vegetables as well as newspapers. Farms in the lowlands along the Muskegon River grew celery and other produce. It was customary for vendors to go to a farm early in the morning, load a wagon, and go from house to house selling fresh vegetables. My brothers would take turns going to the farms early to load my coaster wagon so I could spend the morning selling door-to-door.

I made it my daily challenge to keep selling until my wagon was empty. One day I had some beets left that were not tied in bundles. I was eager to unload them. I told my customer, "I'll sell you all the beets I have left for fifteen cents." She asked, "What's your regular price?" I told her a nickel for six. She counted the remaining beets. "You're charging me more for these last ones than you were charging for your regular beets," she said. "I hadn't figured all that out," I admitted. She talked me down to a fairer price.

Next, I added a line of extracts and specialty products distributed by a company in California, similar to the Watkins line in Minnesota. The line included items for ladies, such as little disposable papers coated with face powder. There were some accessories for women that I knew little about. I would show the catalog, people would place their orders, and I would send the order to California without ever learning much about the products I sold.

Since those preteen years, selling has been an important part of my life. I love selling. I love the interchange with people. A good salesman gains influence on another person's mind. That makes selling quite a serious undertaking. I like the challenge of selling. I used to tell myself that every call brought me closer to a sale. If I could make enough calls, I was bound to succeed.

A belief that success is inevitable has proven very powerful in my life. In politics, it takes enormous conviction to be a successful candidate. You have to believe in yourself and in what you are trying to do. You have to believe that you are going to win. That is crucial in politics and fundamental to most walks of life.

Even as a boy, I loved dealing with people. I kept observing and gathering impressions. At Christmas time, I gave my newspaper route customers a calendar that the newspaper supplied. The calendars were a kind of bait, to remind your customers that maybe they would like to do something for you. I noticed that the lower-income people were more apt to be generous than those with larger means, who were busy looking out for themselves. I told myself: If you ever are fortunate enough to have some means, be generous with it. Remember that a little generosity makes a big difference to people who do not have much. Just a little caring goes a long way.

People want to be loved. I have come to think that the greatest force in life is love—not sexual love but love of humanity. If people will believe in the power of love and let it work, it can do wonders. That philosophy has been at the core of all my efforts in business and government.

I had other odd jobs in my early teen years. Along with other boys in their young teens, I often went to the Muskegon boat docks to see whether I could earn a few coins by carrying travelers' baggage to the nearby railroad station. This was pure entrepreneurship, learned by watching and listening to the older boys. They would approach heavily burdened travelers and say, "Carry your grips, Mister?" My listening was not as good as my watching. When I tried it, I thought I was supposed to ask, "Carry your drips, Mister?" I got some odd looks, but people in need of help still obliged me.

I also joined several other boys in selling candy bars and soft drinks aboard trains during their Muskegon stops. We would board the trains at the Muskegon station. The first stop for trains after leaving the station was only a mile away. That meant we could sell not only during the stop but also during the first short leg of a train's journey, before we had to jump off the train. I was fortunate to get off the train on time, every time.

Jobs like those kept my pockets jingling until I was fourteen—the minimum age for full-time work at that time in Michigan—and could join my two older brothers at the Sheldon furniture factory.

I started out in the blueprint room, working nights after school and full-time during the summers, making twenty-five cents per hour. I ran the blueprint machine. Others at Sheldon would prepare glassine drawings of classrooms and the equipment to go in them, for architects to use. My job was to make copies of those drawings. The blueprint machine was a large device with a bright light on it. I put paper under a canvas cover, inserted the glassine original, and, magically, it would print.

I worked fifty-four hours a week during the summer. The day started at 7 A.M., when the whistle blew. I had twenty minutes for lunch. The closing whistle blew at 5:20. There were short breaks for morning and afternoon coffee. That added up to ten hours a day. I also worked four hours on Saturday. The factory whistle guided life. My coworkers and I got to work on time, because we were docked if we were late. In fact, we got there early. We sat around chatting until the whistle blew, then got to work.

I felt enormous pride as I turned over to my mother my first weekly pay-check—$13.50. That was a lot of money. I told my mother, "You really shouldn't take in washing anymore." Even as a boy, I badly wanted to relieve her from the tedious washing, drying, ironing, and folding that produced such small reward.

Later, I was placed in Sheldon's trimming room, where workers were paid by production for piecework. Installing a lock in a drawer paid one and a quarter cents. It took four screws to fasten the lock in place, and a staple to put a set of keys on the inside of the drawer. Another worker and I would race. We would produce so many units that we would not turn them all in, for fear the rate per lock would be cut. We did some work for nothing, just for the fun of comparing skills.

I found a little time for fun outside the factory, too. I had a school friend named Leroy Thomas Olson—a dear fellow who, sadly, died rather early in life. We had a mutual interest in nature. On Saturdays, when I was through with work at the factory, we went to Lake Mona on nature hikes. It was a tiny lake, separate from Muskegon Lake. It had wetlands around it and a floating bridge that let us get close to the water. In the spring, we went to note the arrival of birds from their winter homes to the south, and to observe flowers as they appeared. We became serious students of nature, keeping logs and reading to learn more about what we saw.

We decided to develop a balanced aquarium, one that produced enough natural oxygen to support what we put into it. Our aquarium was an old, galvanized, round washtub, about a yard in diameter, filled with specimens we collected on our hikes. We soon learned that clams use a lot of oxygen! Algae grew on the washtub's sides, to our parents' dismay. They thought we ought to clean it up. We begged, "We can't clean that up. That gives oxygen. That helps support life. Just let it grow, and after awhile the water will get real nice and clean. You'll see." We were teaching a little science to my mother and his parents.

Once I received a gift of roller skates that almost caused a rift between Leroy and me. Leroy complained that if I wore my skates on our walks to school, he could not hear the birds. I had to give up skating to save our friendship. That is how much he enjoyed birds.

His interest was contagious—and lucrative for me. I took to writing short essays about the birds we saw. I had graduated from selling the *Muskegon Chronicle* on the street to having a paper route. One day I asked my circulation manager if I could meet the editor and show him my essays. He arranged for me to meet Archie McCray. Mr. McCray was kind to an aspiring young writer. He read a couple of the essays and asked how many I could write. I told him I could write a great many. He said that the *Chronicle* would begin to print them, one a week, and pay me $1.50 an essay. At the time, $1.50 was about what I was paid to deliver more than one hundred newspapers five days a week. I certainly could see the advantage of a writing career! I was fourteen at the time the *Chronicle* began publishing my bird stories. They were first labeled "Birds of Muskegon," then, later, "Birds of Michigan." The thrill I had seeing those columns in print was the start of an abiding attraction to the newspaper business.

Setbacks and Survival

Polio—or infantile paralysis, as it was called when I was young—greatly affected my early life and continues to affect me today. I was stricken with the illness when I was nine years old. I am not sure how I contracted it. No one else in our neighborhood or in my circle of friends had the disease, to my knowledge. Shortly after falling ill, I lost all use of my limbs and was confined to bed. My vivid recollection is being in bed, helpless, and having to be fed. I do not remember being afraid—which probably only indicates that I was too sick to think deeply about the long-range implications of my illness.

My mother told me later about a doctor's dire prediction: there would be atrophy of muscles that would lead to infirmity. With braces, I might be able to walk some, but I was likely to spend my life in a wheelchair. But Mother would have none of that. She had faith in an osteopathic physician who believed in exercise and the possibility of recuperation, and her confidence made me believe that I would get well. In later years, scientists learned that there are many kinds of polio. Some are recoverable, and some not. Apparently, I had a milder form, for either because of the osteopath or in spite of him, I walked again. Ultimately, I regained use of all my muscles with only minor exceptions.

It was summertime when I fell ill. I was not well enough to return to school immediately in the fall. When I first resumed school attendance, I could walk, but if I tripped and fell, I had difficulty getting back on my feet. I had to crawl to something that could support me and pull myself up. Some of my classmates enjoyed watching me struggle, so they would trip me and laugh as I crawled and strained to get up. I felt humiliated doing that.

Fortunately, I was without the use of my limbs for a relatively short time. At the urging of the osteopathic physician, we put some exercise equipment in the house. By regularly using it, I regained strength quickly.

One effect of polio lingered longer than the paralysis. I developed a speech problem—not stuttering but an impasse. I could not get out some words starting with certain letters—*P* was one of them. That was awkward. Eventually, the problem faded away—but not before I tried to overcome it by taking a speech class in high school. The instructor took an interest in my problem and suggested I take up debate and extemporaneous speaking. She may have sensed that I had an argumentative bent, too. Through those activities, I learned to give a decent speech without using a manuscript. I learned to watch the audience and read their faces for clues about their interests and reactions. It could be said that polio made me a better speaker— and a better politician.

Beginning at about age eighty, I began to lose muscle strength again. I suffer from post-polio syndrome. Certain types of polio, while recoverable in youth, come back later in life, causing muscle mass to disappear and leaving their victims with impaired movement. That has happened to me. Though my health is good, my strength and mobility are lacking.

Despite my continuing struggle with polio, I believe that the disease's psychological impact on me has been positive. An ill child puts great focus on recovery. I noticed it when visiting children who have a physical infirmity at the Gillette Hospital in St. Paul. They were the brightest, happiest children, determined that they were going to recover and do well. A major illness when one is young has the effect of increasing one's determination. Once the obstacle of illness is overcome, it puts all of life's later obstacles into perspective. Polio was not a deterrent in my life. It might have given my life more vigor, by convincing me that whatever happened could be overcome.

One of the sermons preached in the Nazarene church our family attended at about that time was titled "*Dis*appointment Is *His* Appointment." The pastor said that whatever happens is God's will, and he would not will anything to permanently harm you. Some good will come of adversity. That thought stayed with me as I recovered, and much longer. When disappointments came to me later in life, I would say, "There must be something good to be found in this somewhere. Let's see if we can't turn this to an advantage." Battling disease also gave me empathy with others who suffer impairment. My experience with polio could be at the root of my desire to improve education for children with disabilities when I became a state senator.

The little house at 86 Smith Street, later renumbered to 1764 Smith Street, was the setting of the daily dramas of living and growing and is still vivid in my memory today. All of us—mother and four children—pitched in to make it a snug, cozy shelter. For example, all five of us had a hand in digging out a big tree that was growing alongside the house, so close that it threatened the foundation. What a big job that was!

Neighbors were important to us. Across the street lived a buxom, outgoing woman named Mrs. Karnowski, who was kind to us. She was a big woman with a big husband. I admired their bountiful approach to life. We Scandinavians are more restrained, less flamboyant and expressive. Our next-door neighbors were named Sheldon—not related to E. H. Sheldon—and they had two daughters, Grace and Alice. There was a little neighborhood grocery store nearby where a young fellow worked who dated the Sheldon girls. The whole neighborhood would take note of relationships like that. It was that kind of close-knit place.

One year, my brother Marvin contracted tuberculosis and lived in a tent, as prescribed by "the fresh air treatment" that was in favor then. He also had to eat raw eggs. We had a little chicken coop out in the back where we raised our own chickens to eat and gathered our own eggs. Marvin ate plenty of raw eggs and slept in a tent for some time. Remarkably, given that harsh regimen, he did recover and went on to a healthy life.

By the time I reached my teenage years, the Andersens were a busy, happy family. Our home life was pleasant. Somehow, we had acquired a player piano—how in the world we could afford it, I will never know. It was great fun to play its rolls and bring music into our home. I loved the march "American Patrol" and always worked the piano's controls with great vigor when I played it.

My mother was musical. She had a lovely, natural solo voice and was invited to sing at weddings, funerals, and other occasions. She also played the piano, and, somehow, she saw to it that we children had music lessons.

I was not as musical as my mother and brother Marvin. When I played violin with a school orchestra, someone inquired, "Who is that little boy playing second violin so vigorously?" I did things with vigor. I did not always do them well. Later on, when our son Tony began to play the clarinet, I took clarinet lessons with him. I did not do as well as he did.

Music came into our lives at home and at church. During our first years on Smith Street, we attended a little neighborhood Nazarene church because the Lutheran church was far away, and we had no means of transportation other than walking. The members of the Nazarene church were outgoing people. It was customary when they felt inspired for them to call out "Hallelujah" or "Amen" during a church service. The hymnal used in Sunday school was full of peppy tunes that I used to accompany with the violin.

Finally, after one of my older brothers got a car, we became members of Our Savior's Lutheran Church. That is where I was confirmed and where we attended Sunday school and church. When we joined, worship services were conducted in Norwegian. I even sang hymns in Norwegian in the choir, without the slightest notion of what I was singing. The church went through months of discussion before deciding, in my teenage years, to switch to Sunday morning services in English and Sunday night services in Norwegian.

I was a little bit of a singer—enough so that the pastor once called on me for a solo when I came back for a visit after moving to Minnesota. "We're so glad to see our friend Elmer Andersen in church this morning, and I wonder if he wouldn't take a few minutes to find one of the hymns that he would sing for us," the pastor said. That was all the warning I had. I scrambled through the hymnal and found something suitable. It might have been the old evangelistic tune "Brighten the Corner Where You Are," for I have always been partial to it. I appreciate its message, that there is something that everyone can do to make life a little better for himself and those around him. I wrote that in an editorial not long ago, and a reader responded that he expected the editorial to say, "If you brighten the corner where you are, you'll soon have more territory."

My confirmation class at Our Savior's Lutheran consisted of three boys and three girls, and we became a close-knit group. I still hear from Lucille Olson. She married Charles Silky, a junior college friend of mine, who went on to become a judge. I may have introduced them, though I used to date Lucille myself. We were fond of each other but not too much! I had a fine friend in Cully Otterson, a straightforward, decent, kind fellow. Mary Meyers was a girl with a fascinating hairdo, featuring a big puff on each side of her ears. With no sister close in age to ask, it took me a while to learn that her hairdo was the product of an artificial device under the puff. The third girl was Ardys Ramberg, who was rather snippy and flippant. I was nevertheless interested in her because of my admiration for her father, who was a builder. Even as a youngster, I thought highly of people who built things.

On Sunday evenings, a group often met at our home after church services for coffee and a songfest. My mother would play the piano, my older brother Marvin would play the violin, and the rest of us would sing or chime in as best we could.

It was a happy time. We did not feel the least bit sorry for ourselves—although our lifestyle was certainly modest. We were over the hump of polio, tuberculosis, and hard times. We were making it.

Then our mother died.

Our mother was dedicated to church work. She saw to it that we went to Sunday school and church on Sunday mornings, back to church Sunday evening, then to prayer meetings on Wednesday or Thursday evening. In addition, she spent a good deal of time going house to house looking for unchurched children to invite to Sunday school, in the hope that they might come and then draw their parents into a church relationship also. It was during one such excursion in bad weather in the winter of 1925 that she contracted a cold and then developed pneumonia.

My brother Arnold was at college, and my brother Marvin was selling on the road. I was fifteen and at home with mother and my little sister, who was nine.

Children take mothers for granted. Mothers are always well and strong, and they can do everything. Children are generally not aware of the problems of parents. When our mother contracted a cold and was sick in bed, I did not comprehend the gravity of her illness. It did not occur to me that she might die. She called a doctor to come, and he said that she had pneumonia, a bad case. But he did not talk to me in terms of imminent death.

She died at home on March 3, 1925. I was at her bedside. That experience has largely fled my memory, except for one moment. She seemed to want to talk to somebody about her children, but no one was at hand but me. She looked up. She said, "You take care of my children." She was praying to God, asking him to take care of her children.

We were alone when her breathing stopped. Then I called her sisters, and the adults took over. I had not notified her sisters about her illness. They scolded me pretty hard for not calling them earlier. It was a sad, difficult time.

Yet, it is a strange thing: I never really lost my mother. Almost immediately, I had a sense that she was still there. She is above me, a little to the right, always watching, caring, nudging, and consoling. She is always there. I suppose that, psychologically, that sensation would be considered an hallucination. At times it has been very real to me. I will go some time without thinking of her, but then comes some tight moment or some strain or some decision to be made, and there she is. Perhaps that sense only shows what a powerful influence she was in my life.

The days right after her death are vague in my memory. A loss of memory is fairly common when a person suffers a severe trauma. Nature blots out our recollection of the worst experiences, to protect us from them. I learned later that the human body produces natural substances called endorphins that are more powerful painkillers than any drug. They come into play when a person suffers a physical trauma, and I suspect they are present when emotional trauma strikes, too. When my mother died, I was numb for days, perhaps weeks.

Within twelve months of our mother's death, our father had a sudden heart attack on the street in Chicago. He dropped and was gone. I had seen little of him in the years before his death. He had come to Muskegon a few times to take my brothers fishing, but I was not included in those trips. He had not been supporting us financially. In fact, he had been investing money in Norway, where his family lived. After his death, his brother, Martin Kjelsberg, refused to send that money to us, on the grounds that when my mother left him, her children lost all claim on his assets. We had to press the matter and make clear that under U.S. law, we children were entitled to inherit anything he had. That episode chilled our relationship with our Norwegian relatives.

When our father died, we certainly were alone. But my two older brothers were reliable and resourceful and a stabilizing influence on the two younger children. Arnold was nine years older than I was. He was a father figure to Caroline and me. He had our father's determination to work hard and get ahead. What he decided, we accepted, because we trusted his judgment. He went on to buy an industrial supply corporation and become a successful businessman and a leading citizen of Muskegon. He was a natural leader.

Marvin was more of a brother and a companion to me. He was seven years my senior. He was gentle, kind, a very humane person. He once asked me to travel with him when he was selling for Sheldon. We called on a purchasing agent who was terribly discourteous to my brother. He was so rude that I was appalled. But Marvin just took his abuse as part of the conversation. Even when we got back to the car, he said nothing about it. "Marvin," I said, "you must have some reaction to the way that fellow acted toward you." He said, "Elmer, I don't think he's well."

What a compassionate and perceptive comment that was. So frequently, when people act in ways they should not, they are not well. They deserve compassion and rehabilitation, not punishment. That understanding is sorely lacking in today's trend of getting tough on crime. Society should not be tough on the perpetrators of crime. We should have mechanisms for finding out what is afflicting them and exert the effort to salvage their lives in some way.

Marvin sold for Sheldon and attended Kalamazoo College in Kalamazoo, Michigan. Eventually he left Michigan to join Central Scientific Company in Chicago, a producer of scientific equipment for laboratories—not furniture, but test tubes, beakers, Bunsen burners, and other gear for chemistry laboratories. He did so well that they cut his commission rate. Marvin was so gentle that when people took advantage of him, he would go along. He had a lovely wife, Ella Boucher, as sweet and loving a person as Marvin himself. I think Marvin was as much like our mother as Arnold was like our father. We four siblings wound up with distinctly different temperaments.

Somehow, I accepted everything that came our way, without anger or depression. I did not think that the loss of my parents was awful or a tragedy. It was something that happened that I had to accept. I did not dwell on problems. Somehow, I believed, there would always be solutions.

I recognize now that you lose something important when you lose the love and guidance of a mother and a father at a young age. There were some things I never learned, some things I did not do very well as an adult, because my parents' deaths made a gap in my training. Later on, I felt a void, a lacking in my life. It was filled when I met my wife-to-be, Eleanor, and her parents. They gave me the support and encouragement that I had missed.

Our little family of four siblings—two young men, a teenage boy, and a young girl—resolved to stay together. For awhile, I was chief cook and bottle washer. One time I tried to bake a cake and left out the baking powder or whatever it is that causes cakes to rise. It fell flat and hard and was really inedible. I was not hurt when the family refused to eat it, but when I threw it in the chicken coop and even the chickens would not eat it, I felt offended!

Marvin once inquired about my method of making coffee. "Elmer, the coffee seems to get stronger and stronger. What do you do?" "I just keep adding coffee and adding water." He looked in the coffeepot and discovered that it was half full of coffee grounds! Whenever we needed more coffee, I would just toss some grounds in the pot, add water, and heat it. I never emptied the pot. As a result, each potful was stronger and more bitter than the last. "Elmer, you've got to start fresh each time," Marvin advised. Then I learned how to make really good coffee. We had chickens, so we had eggs. I would put the grounds in a little bowl, put an egg in the grounds, stir up the grounds and the egg, then put that in the coffeepot. That method made the clearest, finest coffee that anybody ever tasted. There is no coffee quite like it. Marvin said, "Son, you've really learned how to make coffee."

Before long we abandoned the little house on Smith Street. With the help of Mr. Sheldon, we relocated to a house in North Muskegon. Mr.

Sheldon was key in the development of a residential area called Interlaken, a beautiful area on a peninsula between Lake Muskegon and Bear Lake, a little bit to the north. Bear Lake was a smaller lake that emptied into Lake Muskegon. Interlaken homes were not selling as fast as Mr. Sheldon expected. He had a little Dutch Colonial home that had not sold. Mr. Sheldon settled us four children there.

That move introduced us to a new level of life. With all three of us boys working and saving and doing pretty well, we were able to afford a housekeeper. We hired Anna Munson, the widowed mother of two grown sons, Harry and Knute Munson, who were friends of Arnold and Marvin. They used to drop by at our house on Smith Street. So when Mrs. Munson became our housekeeper, we were kind of a family getting together.

Mrs. Munson was a devout, lovely lady who helped us a great deal. But she had her own ideas about things, including whom I ought to date. She favored girls who attended her church. They were decent girls but not the sort for whom I had any particular fondness. Mrs. Munson had an irritating way of making her wishes known. Often, after I took a girl to a movie or for a walk, we stopped at home for some coffee or other refreshment. I could not afford to take a date to a restaurant. Mrs. Munson was good about having some refreshments ready, but she would also remove any photos of my friends that I had placed on the piano or the Victrola and put up pictures of the girls she liked. I thought that was unkind.

Another time, she thought I had stayed out too late. When I came home, the door was locked. I did not have my key with me, so I had to crawl into the house through a basement window. I thought, she is going too far. She was trying to be the boss, and I did not want a boss anymore.

Nevertheless, Mrs. Munson was a fine woman who meant well. She helped watch over our sister, Caroline—though shortly after our move to North Muskegon, Arnold married a wonderful woman named Eunice Northrop, and they invited Caroline to live in the home they bought in Interlaken, not far from our Dutch Colonial. Eunice was a lovely woman who had been on the music faculty at the University of Michigan when Arnold arrived on campus as an older student. She was a gifted singer and violinist. She came from a marvelous farm family in Lawrence, Michigan, whom we came to know and occasionally visit. We Andersens were most impressed with the Northrop's walk-in freezer, stocked with a variety of homemade pies, ready for the oven. Guests were asked what kind of pie was their favorite. Often, that pie was fresh from the oven after dinner that night.

Caroline's high school days were spent in Arnold and Eunice's home. But she pretty much took care of herself. Little tyke that she was when our mother died, she became self-reliant and resourceful. I marvel at what she undertook. When she finished high school, she wanted to be a nurse. We thought she ought to go to the finest nurse's training school there was, and somehow it came out that Presbyterian Hospital in New York City was *the* place to get a fine nurse's training. It never occurred to us that we were proposing quite a challenge for a young girl, to go live in New York all by herself and find her way in a great big institution. Off she went to New York as a young high school graduate. When she became a nurse, she entered the University of Michigan, studied public health, and got a degree. She was a public health nurse official until she married a labor lawyer, Charles Marston. That provided a new experience for us. For the first time, we had Democrats in the family.

Our arrangement with Mrs. Munson, followed by Arnold's welcome of Caroline, freed me of some of the obligations I might have otherwise had at home. They made it possible for me to concentrate on work, school, and growing up.

Learning

OUR FATHER AND MOTHER both imbued in us the idea that a good education was vital to our success. When they were gone, we four children saw to it that each of us went to high school, then to college, and earned a degree.

My love of learning goes way back. As a grade school student, I was much influenced by the principal of my school, Mabel E. Seeley. I was coming out of my bout with polio when she befriended me. I must have appeared rather undernourished or underdeveloped, because she would invite me into her office in the middle of the morning and ask me to lie down on a mat for a short nap. I would get a little rest. When I awoke, she would have waiting for me a half-pint of milk to drink. I thought that was so nice of her. I think she knew that we were a struggling family. Miss Seeley and I became great friends. I visited her at her home in North Muskegon when I was picking cherries in an orchard nearby.

Miss Seeley knew that I was interested in nature. Once some schoolchildren saw a screech owl in the school's belfry and threw rocks at it. Down it fell. A maintenance man rescued it and brought it to the principal. She gave it to me to nurse back to health and release. I learned a little bit about screech owls and also discovered how rewarding it is to enjoy the confidence of someone like Miss Seeley.

Two discussions we had stay with me. I came from a fundamentalist Christian family, where not only the spirit but sometimes the letter of biblical law was upheld. For example, my mother believed that people not only should not work on Sunday, but also should not do anything that required anybody else to work. It was not enough to do the right thing themselves. I admired the consideration of others that my mother was showing, but I did have some questions about how far she carried her convictions. I questioned her idea that using what she called saloon cards—playing cards—was a sin because they came from bad places. I also balked at the notion that it was sinful to go to a movie. I asked Miss Seeley if she thought going to a movie was a sin. She replied, "I don't know that it's a sin, Elmer, but there are better ways of using your time." She was so wise not to undermine whoever had influenced me and to make me think about using time well.

That lesson stuck, maybe too well. I never did become much of a card player. My brother-in-law, former Minnesota Senate Majority Leader Stanley Holmquist, loves to play cards—gin rummy, bridge, cribbage, any game of chance. When we had adjacent cabins during the summer, I would play a little. But after about one hand, my conscience would begin to bother me, and I would start thinking that I ought to be doing something a little more productive.

Miss Seeley and I talked about religion more than once, because it was so much on my mind. Once when I told Miss Seeley some thought I had about a religious subject, she said, "I can understand how you have that feeling, Elmer, but keep your mind open, because maybe a greater truth will come to you someday." She was always trying to stimulate me to keep thinking. She must have felt there was a germ of greater ideas growing in me that someday could come to something.

She was a single lady, quite large, hearty, and outgoing. She lived alone and, as far as I know, never married. She engaged life and lived it abundantly. Friedrich Nietzsche once said that a secret to a happy life is to live moderately but not to miss anything. I think Miss Seeley did not miss very much. I never knew whether she gave other children as much attention as she gave me. I felt specially privileged. I certainly respected her open, full-life vigor. I thought, that is the kind of life I want to lead.

I must confess that I was more worker than scholar during high school. My focus was on my work at the Sheldon plant, my newspaper columns, and any other moneymaking enterprise I could find. After polio, I lacked the physical ability for athletics, and I had little time for many parties or other extracurricular activities.

Some days, I had little time for study, either. I hurried to Sheldon's every night after school and on Saturdays. My two brothers attended Muskegon High School before me as nontraditional, older students, and performed well. I remember one day being upbraided by a Miss Carpenter: "You know, Elmer, you can't live on the reputation of your brothers forever." That hurt, because I thought I was working pretty hard. After all these years, her remark still stings.

One high school teacher who left a more positive impression on me was Ebba Bedker. She took an interest in me and thought I might have the talent to write poetry. She had me writing a good deal of verse, and she arranged for the publication of one of my poems. It was about a friend who proves unfaithful, and how one should respond when such betrayal occurs.

Always, my mind then was testing, reaching, searching. I admire the fable of the blind man and the elephant. People can be positive they are right, and indeed be right, but still not have the whole truth.

Particular people would capture my attention periodically when I was young. I would single them out, study them for a few weeks or months, and try to live like them. For a time, I was fascinated with John Craig, my high school principal. He was a dignified, scholarly person, a fine educator, and good model for children. I liked to watch Ben Oosterbaan. He was a wonderful athlete with an appealing style. As a forward in basketball, he glided around the court. Spectators doubted he would make it across the court fast enough, but he always did. You would think he was not quite positioned to make the basket, but he always did. He was an end in football and had that same leisurely grace of play. He went on to be a star athlete at the University of Michigan and eventually was athletic director there, living up to his early promise. I much admire people who do things with grace and style. When someone can make a skill look effortless, it is generally the result of a great deal of effort.

I was never able to acquire that kind of ability in any athletic endeavor. The lingering effects of polio limited my ability. I have a tremor now, which people assume is a sign of my advancing years, but I already had a tremor in high school, because of polio. I gave it little thought; it just happened. I took things as they came, without allowing myself any great emotional distress over it.

I played a little tennis for a time. I made money shagging balls at a tennis court, and I watched and learned the game. Later, I played golf, but it took a lot of time. I remember well when I quit playing golf. I had hit a ball off the fairway, and it hit a tree and bounced back behind me. I thought, if you cannot make more headway than this, you had better quit!

When I finished high school in 1926, I asked Mr. Sheldon for a sales position. He said, "You're very young, Elmer, and you've had no sales experience, so we really couldn't send you out as a Sheldon salesman." He discounted all my years selling door to door and on city streets. "Well," I said, "I won't get any sales experience working in the plant, so I'd better leave the Sheldon Company and go where I can get some." But, I assured him, "I'll be back."

Leaving the Sheldon plant was a little bit like leaving home. I had a kinship with people in the plant. They were friends who took an interest in me, particularly in the lonely time after my mother died. Henry Barkel was a fellow who made crates. Every night, as he left the plant, he would say, "Well, fellows, another day, another dollar. A million days, a million dollars." I think he eventually dropped that last line when somebody pointed out to him that a million days was about three hundred years.

Another memorable character was John Stoppels. He had a routine in the company lunchroom, where lunch was served family style, at big tables. Heaping bowls of meat and mashed potatoes would be on each table when the workers were seated. Most workers would sit down and dive in, but John always paused, bowed his head, and prayed. That meant that by the time he got around to reaching for the serving bowls, they were nearly empty.

One day, he surprised us by skipping his prayer and filling his plate along with everybody else. I was curious about the change, so I kept an eye on him. As soon as he had filled his plate with everything he wanted, he bowed his head as usual.

John Rood was a superintendent at the plant. He was a red-haired, red-bearded, gentle fellow who kept the peace. The factory was the workplace of rugged men who worked hard and would sometimes get mad. He kept things calm. He also had a nice way of keeping people in line. For example, if someone was habitually taking long breaks, he would tell that person, "A break is a nice thing. If we abuse it, we might lose it. So please, shape up a little."

Those factory workers were dear to me. They worked so hard. They were genuine. Knowing them was a factor in my desire as a businessman and a politician to be considerate of working people.

Fortuitously, it was just as I was leaving Sheldon in 1926 that a new junior college was being established in Muskegon, on the top floor of the senior high school. It occurred to me that I could combine an additional two years of education with a sales job. Hence, I became a member of the first class of Muskegon Junior College, now a flourishing community college. Two years later, I was one of twenty-six members of the first graduating class. Because my name started with *A,* I got the first diploma to be issued by the new educational institution—something that has brought me some recognition when the college celebrates its anniversaries. I am also one of only two graduates in that first class still living, as far as they know.

The sales job I found was with J. J. Fagan and Company, then the leading real estate firm in Muskegon. Its owners, partners named Fagan and Larson, were very generous to a kid just out of high school. They put me to work selling real estate. Fagan specialized in forming syndicates to sell Lake Michigan frontage. Their slogan was, "Water, Sand, and Sunshine." I did not get in on the big deals, but I sold farms and houses and gathered the mature sales experience Mr. Sheldon wanted me to have.

I am not sure how we sandwiched it in, but not long afterward my brothers and I started a little company of our own, the Muskegon Realty Company. We had a small office in the Lyman Block, an inexpensive office building on Western Avenue in downtown Muskegon. We also sold the casualty insurance line of the Mercury Insurance Company, which I later learned was one of the St. Paul Companies of St. Paul, Minnesota.

Junior college was a time when I began to blossom. I found new interest in things intellectual and new satisfaction in things social. I began to initiate things, rather than being guided and directed through life. My two years at junior college went by quickly and happily.

One teacher, Caroline Barber, impressed me very much. She was rapturous about English literature. She encouraged in me an interest in literature and books. I grew to love books in junior college. It may be due to Miss Barber and her enthusiasm for English literature that I have come to feel a debt of gratitude to England as the source of much of the tradition, history, laws, and culture of our own country. This nation is truly fortunate to have had English roots and to have inherited the English ideas about freedom and governance that originated with the Magna Carta.

In one course, Miss Barber focused on Robert Browning. She emphasized a famous line from his poem "Andrea del Sarto": "A man's reach should exceed his grasp, or what's a heaven for?" That line has stayed with me all my life. I find myself recalling it often and pondering its meaning. What does a man's reach entail? Where, what, who is heaven, and how is it attained?

I had a little more time for socializing in junior college—or perhaps it was that I had a little more desire to be sociable, after the wound of my mother's death began to heal. I was part of a group that called itself "Eight Brothers," after a brand of chewing tobacco that was then popular. We were buddies who shared experiences and helped each other in many ways.

Several of us took part in an event called a "Roof Raising," a student vaudeville show performed for a paying audience. We had talent, but it was undeveloped and unguided. Our program sprang from a zest for life and from the lively music of the Roaring Twenties. The show's instigator was Ken Gottschalk, a talented musician who played the piano and the saxophone. Later, he headed a professional dance band that won quite a bit of renown. The Roof Raising was great fun. In one number, we sang and danced to the popular tune "Rain." We devised a way for a column of water to come down behind us as we sang. In another number, performed in black face, I played the tambourine. As usual, I was rather vigorous. I hit the fellow next to me in the head, and the tambourine's metal edge cut him. "We'd better go into the washroom," I said to him when the number ended, without telling him why. When we got there and he saw the gush of blood on his head, he fainted. We had action in our show!

In another number, I played the ukulele while I sang. My friend Olive McCray, the daughter of newspaper editor Archie McCray, said afterwards that my performance had not fooled her. I knew only two chords on the ukulele, and when those two chords were not appropriate, I simply did not play.

I became the stringer for the *Muskegon Chronicle* covering the junior college, and that experience led to one interesting episode. We were conscious that it was up to us to establish traditions for this new college. One we settled on was that freshman men should wear green hats, called pots. We thought freshman women should be identified in some way, and with tongues in our cheeks, we decided they should wear green cotton hose during their freshman year. Of course, this went over like a lead balloon. But I persuaded Olive to cooperate with us for the sake of a news story and come, at least one day, in green cotton hose. We wanted her to let us take some pictures. She was a good sport and did it. Not only did Olive and her green legs make a feature for the *Muskegon Chronicle,* but the *Detroit Free Press* also picked it up. That was about as far as the idea went—just far enough to bring me a check from Detroit.

Olive was a special friend to me then, partly because of my connection to the *Chronicle* and my admiration for her father. She was a nice young lady. We dated somewhat, but it was a low-key relationship, more of a friendship than any deep emotional involvement. I knew a few other girls, too, very casually. But romance was not part of my life then.

I saw Olive in 1978, on the fiftieth anniversary of our junior college graduation, when I was the commencement speaker. She married a fellow from southern Michigan and built a good life there. Seeing her again made me even more conscious of the kindness her father had shown me. I had thought for years about doing something special for Muskegon Community College, as it is now called. It occurred to me then to do something to honor the memory of Archie McCray. I asked if anyone had ever done anything at the college in his name. No one had, I was told. I contacted the president of the college and said I would like to endow a scholarship in journalism in the name of Archie McCray. The scholarship was first available in 1999. It is to go to a community college graduate, chosen on the basis of merit, who has been admitted to an accredited school of journalism at a university. It has a $5,000 stipend per year.

In my junior college years I felt torn between a career in business and in journalism. My bent toward newspapering inspired me to start a newspaper for the junior college. I chose the name—the *Bay Window*—because it implied an ability to see in all directions. I was the *Bay Window's* first editor. We had no money or support from the administration, but we were determined, and we got a little better each week. We sold subscriptions. We tried to sell copies to the high school students, because our college enrollment was small. Our method of distribution was to go into the high school cafeteria, drop a tray to cause enough clatter to bring everyone to attention, and then shout that it was publication day for the *Bay Window* and copies were now available.

Junior college widened my world. For example, it exposed me to ballet. The Denishawn Dancers, a touring ballet company led by Ruth St. Denis and Ted Shawn, came to perform at the school auditorium. I was an usher, so I had free admission. I had no concept whatever of ballet dancing before I saw that performance. I thought it was the most beautiful thing I had ever seen. The dancers' grace and style were awesome. I have loved the ballet ever since.

I matured fast in those years. I was selling homes and farms. I was selling insurance. I was editing a college newspaper and stringing for a daily newspaper. I was studying and learning about things I had never known existed. It was almost an incredible time.

Money was scarce, but tuition was free and books were not very expensive. Somehow, we managed. Never have I worried about money. I insist that money has to take care of itself. Somehow, there is usually enough. I learned early that other things in life are more important. Money is merely an instrument, a means of conveyance and communication. It should never be the basis for important decisions. Life is so wonderful, so promising, that it should not be limited by an overemphasis on money.

I continued to be a regular in the pews at Our Savior's Lutheran Church. Going to church had always been a part of our life, and prayer was always part of our home life. My mother's death did not change that. When I was a little boy, I knelt beside my bed at bedtime to pray. We read the Bible. We said grace at meals. I still do. It is a habit that reminds me to be thankful.

One hymn begins, "Prayer is the soul's sincere desire." That is how I think about prayer.

The Bible says, "Teach children in the way they should go, and they will not depart from it." It is so true. I learned conventional Lutheran theology, the stuff of confirmation class and the catechism. The lessons were simple: faith, trust, service to others. Those ideas have affected my whole life. I trust people, and when I find people I cannot trust, I do not react against them. I just avoid them. I learned at church that every human being has great potential. There is a great deal of good in everybody, and there is potential for evil in everybody. What makes the difference is the environment in which people are placed. In all my relationships, particularly in business, I have tried to place people in situations in which it is easy for them to be at their best.

To me, religious faith is the marching song of life. It is what appeals to something deep within you that you do not quite fully understand but that holds the potential of making something finer or nobler of you.

The Lutheran Church taught more than theology. From it I learned a way of life that has stayed with me longer than some church doctrines have. It was a life that required a great deal of people. One was always to be honest, decent, kind, generous, civil. Those strictures were so imbedded in me that I did not think of behaving any other way. Obedience to parents was a commandment. I did not think of doing anything but what my mother thought I should do. I never thought of smoking when she was alive. I never tried any type of illicit drug—it never occurred to me to want to. I am not totally lacking in adventure. I have been innovative in a lot of other ways. But in those areas of conduct, no way other than the way I was taught had any appeal.

I learned early that a good way to stay out of trouble is to go to places where the police do not go. There are not many police around churches. There are not many police around libraries or concert halls. Those are places I like to go, and I have never had any encounter with the police.

A pastor who became a dear friend in Minnesota, the Rev. C. A. Wendell, suggested that I should think about a career in the church. He said, "I don't know, Elmer, what constitutes a call to the ministry, but I really think you should consider that as a calling for yourself." I did this much about it: I decided to get professional vocational counseling. I went to the psychology department at the university and took some tests. They advised that I would do well at anything that related to people, that I had strong indications of leading people, and that I had a high correlation with the ministry.

Those results made me think a little more about becoming a minister, but I concluded I lacked the commitment that the ministry requires.

Still, I was convinced then and still believe today that faith in something beyond ourselves is fundamental in life. There is potential in the human mind—the human soul—far beyond our concept today. That unrealized potential is part of the sense that there must be something more, somewhere beyond our consciousness. There is some greater power that we seek, some higher influence that we want to bring to bear in our lives. The church can put that longing in terms that are meaningful to many people, but that other people have trouble accepting. But even agnostics share a sense that there is something beyond humanity's reach today. They are searching. They desire. They cannot quite bridge the gap between here and there. I am like that. I keep searching.

Traveling Salesman

I GRADUATED FROM JUNIOR COLLEGE in the spring of 1928. It was time to go back to E. H. Sheldon and ask one more time for the sales job I had dreamed of for years. I sought him out weeks before commencement. I wanted to get going.

"I'm two years older," I reported to Mr. Sheldon. "I've had two years of sales experience. I've had two years of college. Now will you give me a chance to sell?" He said, "Elmer, you're still pretty young."

He was right. I was nineteen. But I had worked in his factory for three years. I had two years of nearly full-time sales experience, selling real estate and insurance. I had advanced my education. For more than three years, I had largely supported myself and helped to support my sister. I did not need to relate all of that to Mr. Sheldon. He was familiar with the Andersen family story. "I'll tell you what we'll do," he said. "We'll send you out on a trip and see how you get along. Then we'll decide."

Within a week of college graduation, I was on a train, heading west for a three-week trial. I dealt with school supply outlets—jobbers, we called them. The factory man was the expert on school furniture installations. On contracts for new buildings, where there was spotting of footings and electrical outlets and drain systems to be done, the factory man participated in the sales. But the jobber handled smaller sales, ones that involved existing buildings. The jobber in Minneapolis was the Minneapolis School Supply Company. In Fargo, it was the Northern School Supply Company, a firm with a branch in Montana, too. I was assigned to visit these jobbers and ask whether they had any clients with furniture problems that needed solving, or with a desire to see some drawings of Sheldon's furniture line. I was prepared to make sketches and to send them back to the plant, where blueprints could be prepared.

I approached my trial venture with a good deal of excitement and care—care because I was doing so many things for the first time. I was not fearful. In fact, I think there has never been a time when I was afraid in business.

But I was cautious, because I knew that one could make mistakes, and those mistakes would have to be overcome by even harder work. So, on the train, I mulled over all the possibilities I thought I might face.

Just traveling so far by train was new to me. Not every train I took was a sleek modern model. Some were mixed trains—part freight, part passenger. Some had only one coach car. In North Dakota, my fellow passengers included Native Americans who would not sit with other passengers in the coach car. They opted for the baggage car.

I observed everything. I was eager to learn new things, have new experiences, eat and sleep at new places. On my very first day in Minnesota, when I arrived in St. Paul, I went immediately to visit the St. Paul Cathedral. I had heard that it was the most important building in town, and that made me want to see it right away. I must say, I was impressed.

Then I went to Minneapolis, to call on the Minneapolis School Supply Company. My next stop was Fargo, then on to Montana. I landed in Cheyenne, Wyoming, on the Fourth of July. I went to a rodeo, the main attraction in Cheyenne's annual Frontier Days celebration. When I returned from the rodeo to my hotel room, a telegram was waiting for me. It was from E. H. Sheldon. I was to return to Minneapolis to take charge of the Minnesota sales territory. I had landed the job.

Ed Sheridan was Sheldon's sales manager and my boss. He liked the Curtis Hotel in downtown Minneapolis, so I stayed at the Curtis. I had an arrangement to have the same room every time I was there, room 1205. It had two closets, one of them with a plugged key so that no other key would work in it. I would arrive in town and go straight to the Curtis Hotel. The hotel staff would have room 1205 ready for me. I would go to 1205, open my private closet, haul out my things, and settle in. When I was leaving for another sales trip, my gear would go back into the closet behind the locked door. The Curtis could then rent the room to other customers while I was gone. I paid for that service, $2.50 a night for the nights I was there.

The Curtis Hotel was a place of quiet, soothing charm. It was retirement headquarters for a lot of schoolteachers. They liked its calm atmosphere. In the dining room, Dick Long and his orchestra never got much louder than moderately soft. The atmosphere would have been too sedate for some nineteen-year-olds. But for me, alone in the big city for the first time, it was quite satisfactory.

I made my home in the Curtis Hotel for a little more than a year, from the summer of 1928 to the fall of 1929. It was a year of learning. I learned a lot about business competition. Sheldon's principal competitor was the

Kewaunee Company of Kewaunee, Wisconsin. Their representative in Minnesota was a man named Langley—I am not sure I ever knew his first name. I did not want to honor him by knowing his first name. He was about fifty years old and had been working the territory for many years. He seemed to know all the tricks of the trade.

One of his tricks was in his manner of presenting bids to school boards. The boards would open the bids for school furniture at a public meeting, read them aloud, and give the sales representatives a chance to justify a higher price if they had not submitted the low bid. Langley developed the tactic of presenting "alternates" within a single bid. The bid would specify that if this or that variation could be made in the plans, he would deduct so much from the bid. Some of his alternates were superior. We used to say of Langley that he could move a gooseneck lamp from one end of a table to another with a bigger deduction than anybody in the business.

Learning how to work that tactic to my advantage was a hard lesson for me. The Great Depression was approaching, and school boards were quick to take advantage of any opportunity to cut costs. They would call me and say, "Your competitor is willing to do this or that for less money. Have you any alternates we ought to consider?"

I could not always accommodate them. For example, I went as low as I dared go in the fall of 1929 on a bid to the school board in North Branch, Minnesota. The board members indicated that they wanted to give me their business, but they felt they had to go with the low bid. The stock market crash had just occurred, and things were already disastrous in the farm economy. The night of the board meeting that would choose between Kewaunee and Sheldon, Langley and I were called in and out of the meeting room several times. When the school board called me back one more time, I said, "I just can't do anything more. I've gone the limit. I guess you're going to have to give the contract to my competitor. But why don't you do this? Offer it to him for $50 less than his last offer." It was about $900, a little order.

Langley was called in again, and a few minutes later, the school board president came out, chuckling. "Elmer," he said, "that last little talk of yours just cost your competitor $50."

Langley got back at me, plenty of times. We were heavy rivals for the business of the Fargo Agricultural College—now North Dakota State University—as it planned a new science laboratory. I worked hard on the plans, met with the architects and the teachers, and thought I had presented the low bid. I was sure I would get that business. Yet somehow Langley outsmarted me and got it. I was so depressed and angry with myself that I wrote a long report back to Sheldon, filled with remorseful analysis of where I had gone wrong. I received a letter back from E. H. Sheldon himself. It was one of the nicest letters I ever received. It was just two sentences: "Dear Elmer: I have been reviewing your report on the Fargo A.C. Just remember, you don't learn much from the jobs you get."

I cried when I first read it. I almost do today when I think of what that letter meant to me. What a thoughtful man Mr. Sheldon was, to pay attention to my performance and offer me that encouragement.

Langley had another trick that was particularly galling. He would call my office in Muskegon or one of the jobbers' offices. He would not identify himself. He would only say, "It's very important for us to get a hold of Andersen. Do you know where he is or where he can be reached?" "Oh, he's on a special call in Starbuck, Minnesota," the innocent phone receptionist would say. "If you'll call the school board in Starbuck, you'll find him." He would be off to Starbuck to find out whether they had an order he could get for Kewaunee. Tricks like that shocked me at first. I thought, if I make my living as a salesman, am I going to become that kind of person?

That concern was on my mind one day as I drove to Belle Plain, Minnesota, for a bid-letting. I said to myself, "I've got to come to some decision here. Either I'm going to be a martyr to what I believe and lose my job, or I'm going to have to play it the way they're playing this game, and beat them at it." I decided on that ride to Belle Plain that I was going to play the way the rules were being played, but that I would be as honest and aboveboard as the situation allowed. That resolve eased my conscience a little.

After that, I went after Langley, hard. I was driven by the thought that I simply had to succeed. This was my big opportunity. If I failed, I did not know what the alternative would be. I became so good at beating Langley that he even objected to my sales manager once, claiming that I was too ruthless a competitor. My manager told Langley that his complaint was the best recommendation of my work he had heard yet!

I discovered that I could be a little mean to Langley, if that is what it took, to land a sale. But I never tried to be mean to the customer. I always wanted the deal to be good for the buyer as well as for me. I would try to find out what customers would like to have, and then I would try to get it for them, while keeping the terms advantageous to me. I decided that it was not incumbent on me to tell customers what they ought to be seeking. Knowing their desires was their responsibility. I was fair with them in helping them get what they wanted and not taking advantage of them, but I did not have to do their thinking for them.

In a matter of months, I was doing well. I was making it. I was doing so well that I felt justified in asking the Sheldon Company for a raise. The reply from Sheldon was that "in salaries, we have to take into consideration times of poorer performance as well as good performance." They recognized my success but suggested that it might not last. I thought, "My gosh! You're certainly not going to give a raise to someone who is not selling. If you can't reward the good times, when *is* there going to be a raise around here?" I was beginning to formulate some lasting ideas about employee compensation.

My work at Sheldon was full of lessons. I was struck by how Sheldon handled customers' requests for adjustments if an order was damaged or was not quite satisfying them. We were dealing in wooden furniture, and sometimes, in shipping, little nicks would occur or a joint would split a bit. Joe Horness handled those cases. He could never get quite enough information. Whenever he received a complaint, he would write a polite letter right away expressing the company's concern that something had gone wrong. He would say it would aid the Sheldon Company very much in setting things right if the customer could provide complete details about the problem. Then, he would ask a great many questions. In due course, the customer would respond, and Joe would reply again, thanking them profusely for their cooperation and asking a few more questions. He would wear the customers out. Only those with the most serious complaints would stay the course with Joe, and get a financial adjustment.

Mr. Sheldon showed me the importance of being a considerate, caring, respectful boss. He was more than a boss to me—he was a mentor. He paid attention to even the lowliest workers in his plant—and we sure noticed!

I tried to be like him years later, when I was the boss at H. B. Fuller. The meanest, dirtiest job in the plant was what we called "boiling out the drums," the fifty-five-gallon drums that went out with glue and came back smelly and dirty. They had to be cleaned for reuse with steam and hot water. In the summertime especially, it was a terrible job.

A retired fireman, about fifty years old, applied for a job one day. He wanted a job badly. I said, "Ed, all we have in the plant right now is a beginning job, and it's a dirty job. You can try it, and if you want to keep it, you can stay." He tried and he stayed.

One hot summer day I spotted Ed, stripped to the waist, sweat pouring from his body, boiling drums. I stopped long enough to say, "Ed, do you know this is one of the most important jobs in the plant?" He said, "Elmer, I like my job. But please don't tell me it's an important job, when you yourself said it's the dirtiest, stinkiest job in the place." "I know it is, Ed," I said. "But think of this. We spend a lot of money on research to develop a good product, and we have process men who try to make the product absolutely according to formula. If it went into a dirty drum, all that effort would be lost. I know it's dirty and stinky, but you've got to believe it's important." He paused for a moment to let that sink in. I am sure what I said gave him a new feeling of satisfaction.

I believe that every employer owes it to the people associated with him to convey to them a sense of importance, a sense that they are growing and developing and doing something of real value. Greatness lies not in doing big things but in doing well whatever you are doing. Any job can be done superlatively. Any job is entitled to respect.

I am sure that just as often I have failed to be as considerate as I could be. Isaac Stern, the great violinist, once said he never played anything completely to his satisfaction. I know exactly what he meant. Whenever I make a speech, write a column, or do anything, I always analyze it to the nth degree, and I find it falls short.

My first year in Minnesota also taught me about life in a big city, something I had not experienced since I was a little tyke in Chicago. In 1928, Minneapolis was as much into the Roaring Twenties as its Scandinavian temperament would permit. I remember attending the dedication of the Foshay Tower, a wonderful new building, the tallest in Minneapolis. John Philip Sousa's band came to play and Secretary of the Navy Curtis Wilbur came to speak. It was a high day—but unbeknownst to the crowd, the seeds of financial destruction had already been planted. Wilbur B. Foshay was already overextended and in rocky financial condition at the time the Foshay Tower was being built. He never paid Sousa for his band's performance at the dedication.

A big treat in downtown Minneapolis was a night at the Minnesota Theater. The Minnesota Theater was *the* entertainment center downtown. It had wonderful entertainment, first-run movies, newsreels, and special events. But what really made it special was the stage show. It featured music by Lou Breeze and his orchestra, Gertrude Lutzi, a marvelous soprano who also sang on WCCO radio, and Eddie Dunstedter at the tremendous Wurlitzer theater organ. Dunstedter later went to California and became one of the leading theater organists in the country. The Minnesota Theater building eventually became the headquarters of WCCO-TV.

There were also stage shows at the Orpheum Theater—in fact, it was the last theater in the Twin Cities to have vaudeville entertainment. I saw Jimmy Durante there. His act was full of slapstick comedy, which ended with him sliding off the stage and landing in the orchestra pit. After the crowd quieted down, he would climb out of the pit and back on stage, looking begrimed and saggy. "What the hell do you want me to do next?" he would ask. The crowd would just roar.

I used to frequent a little café on Hennepin Avenue that had a downstairs ice cream soda parlor. A man of color played jazz piano there, and he was very good. After taking in a show at the Minnesota Theater, I would go to this café and have a chocolate ice cream soda, my favorite confection, and listen to jazz. It was such innocent entertainment, yet it was wonderful.

Life in Minneapolis was high-spirited. For a young man with a few dollars in his pocket, there was a lot of joy in living. Things were going well. People were happy. Popular pastimes were fishing, hunting, concerts, and baseball. I would only rarely see a game by the old Minneapolis Millers, at their stadium at Nicollet and Lake. I cannot stand to sit still through a whole nine-inning game. But I followed the Millers' performance and rooted for them to do well.

Dance halls—the Rosebud in Minneapolis, the Prom in St. Paul—were gathering spots for many young people, but not me. Even as a young man, I was not a party person. I never enjoyed being at a large gathering nearly as much as being with one, two, or three other people, double-dating, enjoying quiet entertainment and conversation.

At the Curtis Hotel, I met another young single fellow, named Lawrence B. Slater, who became a good friend. His job was to organize Lions Clubs in the area. He was a Baptist, so we went to the First Baptist Church on Sundays. This was a new church experience for me—a big downtown congregation with a nationally known pastor, W. B. Riley. He was a famous orator within the American Baptist Church. He had flowing white hair and a big voice that filled that temple. I enjoyed his sermons very much, so much so that Larry and I went to First Baptist every Sunday while I lived downtown.

Larry needed a friend. I guess I did too, but he seemed the more needy because he was infatuated with a woman who worked in the circulation department at the *Minneapolis Star*. She was Doris Wilke, from Hettinger, North Dakota. She was a lovely young woman, but she was enamored, to some degree, with the circulation department manager, and my friend was as jealous as he could be. He could not stand it when she had a date with her boss. Larry was so emotional, he would be sick to his stomach. I would have to nurse him through lovesickness.

Finally, he won his lady fair. I was in their wedding party in North Dakota. He eventually became a secretary to a congressman, and she a publicist for the Chain Store Association, and they moved to Washington, D.C. Larry is gone now, but we still hear from Doris at anniversary and birthday times. I think she feels that she and Larry might never have married if I had not kept him bolstered during the times in their courtship when he felt so discouraged.

As warmer weather arrived in 1929, Larry and I decided it would be fun to spend the summer on Lake Calhoun, one of Minneapolis's premier city lakes. We thought the Curtis Hotel was getting a little confining. We rented a room in a boardinghouse, but that adventure did not work out well. We were accustomed to the housekeeping services we had at the hotel, and not ready for the lesser standards of the boardinghouse manager. I can still see the cream pitcher at the boardinghouse. It had been repeatedly refilled without being washed, until ugly dark cream was encrusted on its sides. It was not for us. We went back to the Curtis.

I did not do any dating that first year in Minneapolis. I did not really know what it was like to be in love, and I could not quite understand the way Larry felt. But I was soon going to find out.

University Student

A YEAR IN MINNEAPOLIS left me convinced that I wanted something more. I wanted to enroll at the University of Minnesota.

I usually approach a new venture with specific objectives. In aiming for the University of Minnesota, I had three: I wanted to get a degree for reasons of job protection. I did not want somebody to push ahead of me because he had a degree and I did not.

Another objective was to meet a woman whom I might marry. I was beginning to long for a home life and a family. I was lonely. I discovered that being a traveling salesman, on the road all the time, was no way to meet the kind of women I wanted to meet. From my twelfth-floor room at the Curtis, I would eye the university and think, there must be all kinds of wonderful young women on that campus.

My third objective was to have a good time! I had been a fairly successful salesman and quite frugal with my earnings. I had accumulated a little money, and I was willing to spend it to have some fun. I thought it might be nice to join a fraternity.

So, having fun, finding a girl, getting a degree—those were my objectives. If I was able to learn anything along the way, that would be purely incidental!

I did not have to leave the Sheldon Company to go to the university. E. H. Sheldon was a former teacher who believed in education. He believed in building up his employees. And, by then, I think he also believed in the Andersen brothers. He wanted to help me. I arranged with Mr. Sheldon to cut back on my work load and be paid a flat sum of $50 a month—enough, I thought, to see me through to a bachelor's degree in two years.

Enrolling at the university did mean leaving the comforts of the Curtis Hotel. I had to find something more affordable. A friend from Muskegon Junior College, Malcolm Hoos, decided to come to Minneapolis and join me when I entered the university. We agreed to room together. We found a room at a dwelling in southeast Minneapolis, an upstairs room in a private home. We lived there together until Malcolm decided to leave the university, before the first year was out. From then on I rented what rooms I could find and afford.

We did not cook for ourselves, but our budget was too tight to allow us to dine out in style. We would often go to the Bridge Café at Fourth Street and Fifteenth Avenue Southeast, just a block off campus. We would order one dinner and split it, and then ask for extra rolls.

Times were changing fast in the fall of 1929. The stock market crashed a month after I enrolled in the School of Business Administration. It was a frightening time for many people, but for me, it was fascinating. I had entered a wonderful place from which to analyze what was happening to the world economy.

I entered as a junior, having received credit for my work at Muskegon Junior College. I undertook to complete a degree in five quarters instead of six, which meant I had to take eighteen credits each quarter. That is more than the usual full-time load.

The School of Business—now the Carlson School of Management, named for its benefactor, and my friend, Curtis Carlson—may have been at a peak during the late 1920s and early 1930s. It was populated with professors who were leaders in their field. One fine professor was Alvin H. Hansen. He was a Keynesian economist who went on to be an adviser to Franklin Roosevelt, and a professor at Harvard University. He wrote the book *Economic Stabilization in an Unbalanced World*—a wonderful title. He taught the course titled "Business Cycles." His theory was that about every three years, business would experience a setback; about every 12 years, it would have a more significant recession; and about every 50 years, the top would blow off. He used that theory in a class in 1930 to predict that the crisis in the financial markets just then was the beginning of a deep depression.

Another fine professor was a man from Germany, Robert M. Weidenhammer. He was an expert on the stock market. He taught me one lesson I have never forgotten: People who speculate in the stock market on short terms, buying and selling frequently, only benefit the broker. In the long haul, they will not make much for themselves. Investing, if it is to be successful, must involve picking good stocks and staying with them. That lesson was much on my mind years later, when I served on the board of the First Trust Company of St. Paul, examining people's trusts. I saw that those who bought IBM and 3M and stayed with them got rich, and people who were constantly in and out of the market did not do very well.

Arthur Marget was the professor who taught banking. I had no intention of going into banking, but I thought Marget was such an intellectual giant that I took every one of his courses that I could. Frederick B. Garver was another of the great ones. He and Hansen collaborated on an economics textbook called *Principles of Economics,* published in 1928, that became a standard of basic economics.

I tremendously enjoyed my classes, though at times, I was a little frustrated. I was annoyed by the requirement that I take a class called "Analysis of Financial Statements." I thought, what a ridiculous class for a salesman to be taking! As it turned out, no course I took had more practical application for my future than that one did.

Almost as valuable were the classes I took on business law. Everett Fraser, the legendary dean of the Law School, taught the one on contracts. He used a great big textbook, Samuel Williston's *A Selection of Cases on the Law of Contracts.* Whether or not I appreciated it at the time, I was getting terrific preparation for a career as a business executive.

Early on, I became acquainted with the dean of the school, Russell A. Stevenson. He was a former Muskegonite. His mother had been a principal of one of the city's elementary schools. Dean Stevenson and I had many encounters during my student days, and became friends. I think he ran a splendid school—one that succeeded despite terrible physical facilities at that time. It was not until the 1990s that the university finally gave its fine business school the top-notch facilities it deserves.

My classes were good, but my life was hectic. I was not working many hours each week, but when I was working, I was traveling. I had to miss class quite a bit. I took an 8:30 A.M. class from a professor named Jack Reighard. My attendance record in that class was not good. Once at midterm, Professor Reighard looked at me with a half-smile and said, "We're honored to have Mr. Andersen with us this morning."

I had no choice but to attend to my responsibilities for Sheldon. Losing that job would mean the end of my studies—and given the state of the economy, it might mean the end of my eating for a while. Moreover, the job was not getting any easier. School construction fell off during the depression, making what business there was to be had exceedingly competitive. I worked hard on a new science building at Yankton College in Yankton, South Dakota. I felt assured of getting the business because I had worked closely with the two main professors involved, Greg Evans in the physical sciences and Austin P. Larrabee in the natural sciences. We prepared the specifications and figured the job carefully. Langley, of course, was also invited to bid. His bid came in higher than ours. But then the president of the college, Dr. George Nash, told me that he had received a communication from the president of the Kewaunee Company. It said that they were so interested in Yankton College and felt it was doing such a beautiful job that they wanted to make a gift to the college, in the form of a reduction in their bid of $3,000. That was enough to give Kewaunee the low bid. I managed to convince Nash that this was simply a device to take the bid away from the legitimate low bidder, and that he should stay with Sheldon. He did, and we outfitted Forbes Hall of Science. It was one of the larger jobs during that period. I was so grateful to Professors Larrabee and Evans that I wanted to do something for them that they would not forget; so, at Thanksgiving time, I sent them each a live turkey. Dealing with a live turkey may have been more of a problem than a joy. But if they were around today, they would still remember my gift!

My need to focus on my work—and the pleasant distraction of a lady I had met—kept my grades rather mixed. I took statistics from a brilliant fellow, Richard Kozelka. I got an A one quarter, but the next quarter, I got a C or a D. I was working for Sheldon awfully hard just then. "You know, Andersen, you can do it if you study," he said to me. That stung—probably because I knew he was right.

I got one failing grade, in a transportation class that I thought was a poorly designed course—the only bad course that I had. I just could not stand it, and I flunked. I went to see the professor, and I said, "I have to do something about this. I just can't flunk. I have to have all my credits in order to graduate." I proposed to do a paper for him on transportation in business, using the Sheldon Company's practices as my example. He agreed, and when the paper was written, he changed my grade from an F to a C.

I was frustrated, too, by the lack of opportunity to range very far into the liberal arts while I was pursuing a business degree. I wanted to take classes in literature, history, and geography, but the required program in the business school allowed little time for those subjects.

I was able to participate in debate. Through that activity I met Philip Dybvig, a graduate student who was aiming for a career in the ministry. Philip was brilliant, a deeply thoughtful, serious, well-organized person who could argue with great persuasion. He held his own once in a debate with a University of Oxford team from England. He went on to be an official in church administration, and an active force at Luther Theological Seminary. We remained friends throughout his life, and we miss him now that he is gone.

Debate kept me in touch with current events. I participated in a debate with a University of Puerto Rico team on the question of U.S. intervention in Central America or the Caribbean in the event that the Panama Canal's security were threatened. Our position was that any situation that affected the security and safety of the United States was our nation's responsibility to address. But the Puerto Rican team argued vigorously about imperialism and respect for the sovereignty of other nations. They won over the audience and the judges. That single debate provided a good course for me in international relations. I gained an appreciation for how difficult it is for the United States to maintain its position in the world while giving due respect to others. It was a lesson that would come back to me often in the 1960s.

Of course, the big news story in 1930 and 1931 was the rapid tailspin of the economy. It is hard for people who did not live through the depression to realize how serious it was. Banks closed. Businesses failed. People's life savings were lost. To add to the trouble, the 1930s brought drought and infestations of grasshoppers to Minnesota farms. The depression was catastrophic for many, many families.

Minnesota had been the center of a populist movement for some time, but it gathered force in the depression and led to the heyday of the Farmer Labor Party, under the leadership of Floyd B. Olson. In 1930, he was county attorney for Hennepin County. The Democratic Party was weak then, and the Republicans had been the dominant force in Minnesota for some time. But, in 1930, Floyd B. Olson was elected governor as the champion of the Farmer Labor Party. He had difficulty making much headway against the depression. When he ran for reelection in 1932, it was on a platform some people considered even more radical than the program of government intervention in the economy that the Farmer Labor Party embraced in 1930.

Much later, when I was a state senator, I heard about an incident that reveals much about Olson. In his inaugural address in 1933, Olson called for production for use, not profit. That was then considered a basic tenet of socialism. After his inauguration, he went to his office and sent for state Sen. A. J. Rockne of Zumbrota, the staid, conservative watchdog of the state treasury and chairman of the Senate Finance Committee. Rockne wondered what the governor wanted with him. Olson explained: "I wanted to know what you thought of my inaugural address." Rockne paused for a moment, and then answered, "I'd have to tell you, Governor, that if we did one half of the things you proposed, we'd drive this state into bankruptcy." Olson leaned back in his chair and laughed heartily and said, "That's why I've sent for you, Senator. If you let me make the speeches, and you keep the state finances sound, we'll get along just fine." That was part of the secret of

Olson's success. He knew where the people were and how to appeal to them, but he also had a pragmatic sense of what was possible and what was in the state's best interest in the long run.

Olson made a notable contribution to the welfare of the state when he proposed an income tax, not a sales tax, to correct the shortfall in property tax receipts that the depression was producing. He recommended that a state income tax be imposed and dedicated to education. That move led Minnesota to develop strong public schools in spite of the depression, something that became a hallmark of the culture of this state.

All the economic and political change swirling around me could not help but heighten my interest in politics. I maintained a little correspondence with Floyd B. Olson. I was involved in the formation of the Liberal Republican Club of Minnesota. I was a member of something called the G. P. Club, which was a little political. I even tried my hand in politics myself—on a purely local level, one might say. The university had a Board of Associated Students, and I ran for that. In my senior year, I was chairman of the board. I was also elected president of the senior class of the business school.

Busy as I was, I made time to achieve my third objective—having fun. I joined a fraternity. Most of the social fraternities tended to pledge freshmen, not juniors. But professional fraternities did not invite a student to join until he was in a professional school. There were two professional business fraternities, Alpha Kappa Psi and Delta Sigma Pi. I was courted by both, but when I was offered a pledgeship at Alpha Kappa Psi, I opted for that one. The offer was extended by Valard Lufi, a native of Isanti, Minnesota, who went on to become a leading accountant for the Dayton Company. He was a friend, and when he said, "Elmer, the fellows would like to pledge you," that hooked me.

Hell Week soon followed, leading up to full membership in the fraternity. These fellows really had some wild ideas for initiating new fraternity brothers. I enjoyed Hell Week, but I found it strenuous. Staying awake all night was part of the exercise, and given my schedule, I was already tired. One event involved sending all of the pledges out at midnight with orders to accomplish a specified mission and return before 6 A.M. My mission was to bring back at least two white rats—live. I was dumped out of a car somewhere around Shakopee at midnight. At that time, I had a company car that Sheldon had provided me, a Model A Ford. As soon as I knew where I was, I hiked to where my car was parked. Then I was mobile. I went to one of the science buildings at the university and sought the mercy of a night watchman or maintenance fellow. I pleaded, "There must be a store of white rats that aren't in an active experiment, maybe ones that are being bred. Can't you get me a couple of white rats?" The kindly soul did. It may not have been his first exposure to a desperate Hell Week participant. I went back with my mission accomplished. I remember that when I got back to the fraternity house, the housemother was terribly excited because one of the fellows had a mission to bring back twelve cockroaches. She dreaded the thought of getting cockroaches in the fraternity house.

I lived at the fraternity house in my senior year. There, I met Vernon Bauman from Le Sueur, Minnesota. His father was a grocer, and his mother was a German cook par excellence. He invited me to spend several weekends in Le Sueur, where I got a pleasant taste of small-town life in Minnesota. Bauman went on to be a distributor of Lazy Boy chairs in California, and a lasting friend.

The university touched me in so many ways. While I was there, I subjected myself to an inventory of my muscles, to better understand the lasting effects of polio. The only atrophy that remained was in the muscles that allow one to put weight on one's heels and lift one's feet. I could not walk on my heels then, and I still cannot lift my feet very well off the floor and balance on my heels. One little muscle in my foot never became normally functional after polio, but it was a trivial handicap. I was encouraged about entering adulthood with so little lasting damage from the most serious illness of my childhood. I thought I was in pretty good shape.

But the legendary Dr. Louis Cooke, for whom Cooke Hall at the university is named, apparently thought differently. Seniors then were provided a free physical examination before graduation. Dr. Cooke performed the examination on me. I was just under 6 feet tall, and weighed 132 pounds. I was plainly exhausted, worn to a frazzle by my schedule. I must not have looked very well. He said, "What grade are you in?" I said, "I'm a graduating senior." He said, "It's a good thing you're going out instead of coming in."

I graduated in 1931 with a Bachelor of Business Administration degree and great appreciation for all I had been given during my time at the University of Minnesota. I had been taught by a remarkable faculty and exposed to a wider world. But the greatest gift I derived from those years was not found in any classroom.

Eleanor

I FOUND ELEANOR ANNE JOHNSON at Grace University Lutheran Church. Before I describe how we met, she deserves an introduction.

Eleanor was the oldest of three children born to Gustaf and Elizabeth Anderson Johnson of southeast Minneapolis. Her father was a lumber and coal dealer, the owner of Gust Johnson Lumber Company on Como Avenue Southeast. Both of Eleanor's parents were natives of Sweden.

Gustaf Johnson was one of six children. He was the only one of his family who came to the United States and stayed here. One older brother came too, but he went back. Interestingly, Gustaf was also the only child in that big family to marry and have children. The rest, four brothers and a sister, lived together their whole lives on their family farm, a small dairy operation in a forest in Dalsjöfors, near Göteborg. They were still living when we visited there in 1963.

Gustaf was about twenty when he left home. He lived for a time in Philadelphia, where many Swedes settled, and found work in a lumberyard. When he sailed home for a visit, he met another immigrant aboard ship, also making a return visit to her homeland, Elizabeth Anderson. She had come to America from Sweden as a household worker, as many Scandinavian girls did in the late nineteenth and early twentieth centuries. Elizabeth's family was also centered around Göteborg. She had six siblings, and all but one of them came to the United States eventually.

Grandma and Grandpa Johnson were married in Philadelphia, but they moved to Minneapolis within a year of their wedding. Before long, the Johnsons became the keystones of an extended family. They frequently housed other Swedish immigrants, both relatives and friends, when they first came to this country. Their generosity is what brought so many of Elizabeth's relatives to Minneapolis. Beda Anderson Ekstrom, a sister, married and settled next door to the Johnsons in southeast Minneapolis. Another sister, Olga, married Arvid K. Carlstrom and lived across the street from them.

Two incidents indicate the kind of businessman Gustaf Johnson was. For years, he drove an old Buick touring car. It became dilapidated, and the family pestered him to get a new car. Finally he did, but he kept the old Buick. I asked, "Grandpa, why did you keep that old Buick when you have a nice new car now?" He replied, "Elmer, I couldn't drive that new car up to Rose Hill to make collections." That is how much he cared about his customers' feelings. He supplied one of the necessities of life in Minnesota— coal for home heating. In the 1930s, he knew people had a hard time paying him. He carried many of his customers on credit for a long time.

On another occasion, I watched him as he worked on his accounts receivable. He had little stickers made to put on the bills he sent his customers: "Anything you can do to pay on this would be appreciated," and "Please, this account is overdue." I said, "Grandpa, I notice you spend a lot of time on accounts receivable, but I don't recall seeing you work on accounts payable." He said, "Well, Elmer, we deal with so many fine firms, Weyerhaeuser and other fine lumber companies and big coal companies, and they have such wonderful accounting systems, I let them look after accounts payable."

Eleanor was born March 28, 1911, at St. Andrews Hospital in Minneapolis and grew up in a bustling, busy household in the shadow of the campus of the University of Minnesota. Her aunt and uncle next door had a daughter Eleanor's age, Olga. Eleanor and Olga used to get into mischief, either deliberately or accidentally. They once frightened Eleanor's mother by putting the cat in the oven. When Elizabeth turned on the oven, a terrible howling started that Elizabeth could not identify until she opened the oven, and a terrified cat came flying out!

Eleanor attended Tuttle Grade School, where she developed a close friendship with a girl who lived nearby, Margaret Keefe. Ironically, Margaret Keefe married a close friend of mine, E. A. "Al" Vigard, and I was best man at their wedding. I was best man at the wedding of Eleanor's best friend. He eventually came into the H. B. Fuller Company, and while I was governor, he was the company's interim president. Margaret is now his widow, living in Illinois.

After Tuttle School, Eleanor went to Minnesota College, an interesting school operated by the Augustana Synod of the Swedish Lutheran Church. It had nothing to do with the university, but it was located on what is now the university campus, in the block where Pioneer Hall dormitory now stands. Minnesota College's principal was Dr. Frank Nelson, a venerable, saintly scholar. Eleanor was raised in the Swedish Lutheran Church; I was raised in the Norwegian Lutheran Church. We were a little involved in bringing about the combination of those two churches in the 1970s into what is today the Evangelical Lutheran Church of America.

Eleanor had a talent for music. She studied piano, and as a fairly young girl in high school, she taught piano lessons to small children. She thought being a music teacher would be her life's work. When she entered the university, she majored in history and minored in music. In the fall of 1929, she was an entering freshman; I was an entering junior.

When I went to the university to register, I stopped at the YMCA on the corner of Fifteenth and University Avenues to ask whether there were any Lutheran churches near the campus. There were two: Grace Church and Hope Church. Hope was predominantly Norwegian, while Grace was more Swedish. The people at the YMCA took my name and phone number. That very evening, I got a call from Pastor C. A. Wendell. He called to say that the young people of his church, Grace University Lutheran Church, were having a welcoming party for new students, and he invited me to join them. I thought that would be fun, so I went for the first time to the brick church at Harvard and Delaware Streets. Early in the evening, I noticed a beautiful blonde girl in a blue polka-dot dress. I can still see her. I was just smitten. She was not a sophisticated, enhanced beauty. She had a pristine, natural Scandinavian beauty. It was almost as if a vision had come true.

I kept my eye on that girl all night. I wondered what was going to happen to her, who she was with, what her situation was. I waited around till the party was over, and learned that she was a member of the church. She was on the party committee. She was out in the kitchen, washing dishes. In a flash, I was in the kitchen, wiping dishes.

That was how we met, washing and wiping dishes. I did not ask her out right away. I do not remember that we talked much. I just wanted to be with her, to observe her, to drink in my first impressions of her. I do not remember how she got home that night, but I know it was not with me. I learned right away that first evening that she was reserved and deliberate. I knew it was going to take me quite a while to attract her interest.

But I found out that she loved music, and that gave me an idea. I called her a few days later and invited her to go to a Minneapolis Symphony series with me. Now, I had always enjoyed classical music, but the main reason I extended that particular invitation was that a symphony series involved about twelve concerts. I was asking her not just for one date but for twelve dates over a period of time.

The symphony was then at Northrop Auditorium on the university campus, and it was playing under its second conductor, Henri Verbruggen. He was a dynamic, small man and a vigorous conductor, so much so that a rail was placed around the rostrum so that he would not fly off.

We continued as season ticket holders for the orchestra under every conductor thereafter, until Eiji Oue. We have heard every Minnesota Orchestra conductor's work except the first one, Emil Oberholtzer, who had retired by the time we started attending concerts. The orchestra became a treasured part of our lives. Watching Eugene Ormandy conduct Hungarian dances was something to remember. For years I considered Ormandy my favorite conductor, but when Klaus Tennstedt arrived, I rated him superlative. I was disappointed he did not stay longer.

Theater, too, has been important to us. When the Guthrie Theater came to Minnesota, we were original subscribers, and season ticket holders through the decades. We cannot see or hear well enough to go now, but we relish our memories of Guthrie plays and of Tyrone Guthrie. There was great richness of life in his ideas.

Eventually, I served on the Minnesota Orchestra board. I always find a personal project to pursue when I become involved in an organization. My idea for the orchestra was that it could serve more people if it offered more variety. I thought the orchestra ought to have a string quartet, a brass ensemble, a woodwind quintet, and other small performing groups that could tour the state, bringing lovely music to more Minnesotans. My idea was not well received. The orchestra is an inflexible organization, and the conductor is a czar. Conductors pass their batons to one another in what strikes me as a rather inbred, closed society. There was no swaying them with new ideas from outside their circle.

Music was part of the magic that slowly, so very slowly developed between Eleanor and me. She was the only girl I dated while I was at the university. I was sure she was the one for me. Her feelings developed more slowly, and that gave me some moments of discouragement, when I was not sure I was making much headway with her. On one occasion, Margaret Keefe, my roommate Malcolm Hoos, and Eleanor and I went out as a foursome. It got back to me later that Eleanor favored "the shorter one," meaning Malcolm. That hurt. But I told myself that I was a new experience for her, and that courting her was going to take time.

Eleanor is not as outgoing as I am. She is not as spontaneous. I think she is wiser, because she takes more time with important decisions. I am more instinctive and more wary of delay, for fear I will go wrong or lose an opportunity. I often act on intuitive judgments. My feelings for her were strong from the start and never wavered. They never have.

I have come to think that life is made up not of weeks and months and years but of vignettes, little captured moments, and I treasure those. Hearing Handel's *Messiah* in London was one such glorious moment. Seeing Laurence Olivier playing *Hamlet* in a movie was another. It was so moving that I was in tears when I left the theater. Eleanor and I had a long courtship, but in memory now it is a series of such vignettes, each one precious.

We developed a pattern of communication that first year at the university that lasted through our student days. Each student had a post office box for campus mail. We used to write notes to each other, to schedule times and places of meetings, and leave the notes in each other's post office boxes. Those notes became a lot of fun and are the stuff of memory today.

We would also see each other regularly at Grace Church. She taught Sunday school, so I became a Sunday school teacher. She would volunteer for committees; so would I. I became active at Grace Church—and it was not just to pursue Eleanor. I enjoyed that church. I enjoyed Pastor Wendell's broad-minded thinking. He was a gentle man. He did not spell out harsh facts of life or issue harsh warnings about sin and damnation. He took life as a continuum and an experience. His sermons always began with his relating an incident that was current, often something in the news. He always wound up on a hopeful note, lifting up some sign or possible solution that would help us live better lives.

Early in our dating days, I wondered whether Eleanor danced. She seemed to be a rather strict Lutheran, so I was not sure. I had strayed from the rigid strictures of my youth in this respect. I had done a little dancing. I was not a very good dancer—I never advanced far beyond the fox trot—but I loved the rhythm and the music. I decided to invite Eleanor to dinner at the Curtis Hotel, where Dick Long was holding forth. Between the main dish and dessert, I asked her if she would care to dance. She said she would, and we danced together for the first time. I thought it was glorious. I was so drawn to her.

I had a car, a Model A Ford provided by Sheldon so I could get around the state more easily. That car provided an episode. I frequently drove her home from church or an activity. Sometimes, particularly in the winter, when it was going to be just a short goodnight, and she was not inviting me in for coffee, I would leave the car running so it would be warm when I got back. Once when I did that, the car took off without me. It was stolen. Somebody jumped in and drove off in the car, leaving me hollering in front of Eleanor's house. The thief or thieves went for a joy ride, then left the car somewhere. To my great relief, I got it back in a day or two.

The big party of the college year was the prom. For my senior prom, Eleanor ordered a special dress from Dayton's. When the day of the party arrived, the dress had not come. Her father called the store and asked for Mr. Dayton. He was put on the line with the store's venerable founder, David Draper Dayton. Gustaf said that he had been a customer of Dayton's for years, and that he thought their policies were good, and that they really cared about their customers. But, he said, "Somebody has to find my daughter's dress and get it out here right now." Dayton's did it. They found the dress and got it to her in time for her to wear it that night. It was a long beige dress that was so suited to her. She looked beautiful.

The prom was spread over two ballrooms in the Lowry Hotel, with an orchestra performing in each one. When the first orchestra took a break, we strolled over to the other ballroom. The orchestra in the second ballroom was Jimmy Joy's Orchestra. It was just beginning to play, and we found ourselves alone on the dance floor. Jimmy Joy's Orchestra played "Stardust" just for us. I remember the music. I remember the dance. Wow!

Later that night, we joined another couple, Eleanor's sorority sister Karen Daniels and her date, a man named Peterson whom she later married. She eventually became a noted nature writer and an Indian scholar. The four of us planned to have a little refreshment after the dance. We stayed for the whole dance, so it was about midnight—or maybe later— when we left. We dawdled over ice cream until 2 or 3 A.M. Then we said, "Let's go out and watch the sun come up. Let's make it a real party." So, we drove out of town to a hillside somewhere and watched the sun come up. That meant I was taking Eleanor home at about 7 A.M. Just as I pulled up to her house, her father was leaving for work.

But that was not really a problem. Eleanor's folks trusted us. They were second parents to me, kinder and lovelier than any son-in-law could have ever hoped for. Even while Eleanor and I were only courting, they began to fill some of the void in my life that was created when my mother died. They were generous and encouraging to me. I was a frequent guest in their home for dinner, and, of course, we shared church activities. I also had come to know and like Eleanor's sister, Edith, and brother, Arvid. We enjoyed going to symphony concerts, visiting art museums, and simply being together.

After we had been dating for nearly two years, our relationship had developed from companionship to friendship to a love that meant everything to us. When I graduated from the university, Eleanor and I were ready to talk about marriage. I set about making our financial future more secure.

The depression was deepening in the summer and fall of 1931. Times were tough for the Sheldon Company. I knew that it was hard for Sheldon to justify the salary and expense account I was getting. I told the officers at Sheldon that I would like to take on another line to sell, and that I would turn over the commissions to them to deposit toward my account.

I had heard of a company called Tyler Sales Fixture Company of Niles, Michigan. They had developed a new fixture for grocery stores, a produce counter that had a pipe and a baffle plate where a stream of water was thrown and converted into mist and then sprayed over vegetables, to keep them dewy fresh. I thought, that ought to sell. I arranged to sell those produce counters as a sideline. I was thrilled when the Red Owl grocery chain, which was opening one new store per month, entered an agreement to put one of the Tyler produce counters into every store. I had an order from them every month. Soon, I was turning over more commissions to Sheldon than they were paying me in salary. Sheldon's sales manager wrote me a note that said, "Elmer, this is ridiculous. We're going to give these commissions back to you. If you think you can look after our interests while also doing this for Tyler Sales Fixture, more power to you." That made me feel more secure. At the nadir of the depression, I had two jobs.

Early in 1932, Eleanor and I decided that the time had come to announce our engagement. We carefully arranged a time for me to talk to her father when she could simultaneously break the news to her mother. We wanted them to hear from us at the same time that we were in love and wanted to set a wedding date. When I reached Gust Johnson Lumber Company, I was so pepped up that I just about exploded. Grandpa sensed I had something major to say. He said, "Let's go into the office where it will be a little quieter." He heard me out with a smile. Then he said, "We like you, Elmer, and we think it would probably be all right." Eleanor's mother was similarly encouraging.

We set a wedding date of September 1, 1932, almost three years from the day we had met. We were only twenty-three and twenty-one when we married, yet I think we were ready. We were sure of our feelings for each other and as secure as two young people could be in the midst of terrible economic times.

Eleanor decided to leave the university when we got married, and postpone the completion of her degree. That was quite a concession on her part.

I thought, now she has really decided that this is OK. We had better get married quickly, before she changes her mind!

As our big date approached, I called my sales manager at Sheldon, Ed Sheridan, and asked for permission to take a week's vacation the first week in September. I told him I was getting married. He was incredulous. "You're getting married?" he asked. "Yes," I replied. I allowed as how it was about time, that my bride was a lovely lady whom I had dated for three years. He said, "Elmer, we can't guarantee you a job, let alone the income you're now making. This is no time to be taking on extra responsibilities. For goodness sake! You should give up any idea of getting married right now." I remember smiling as I replied, "Ed, I didn't ask you for marriage counseling. All I asked you for was a week off after September 1. We're getting married. The depression is going to have to look after itself. We'll look after ourselves. We're getting married."

Of course, we were married at Grace Church. It is a lovely little red brick church, nestled with the university campus on one side and, in those days, an attractive residential area on the other. The houses nearby were large and, in those years, very desirable. That neighborhood has lost a lot of its charm now, I am sad to say, partly because of the encroachment of the freeway and the university.

Years later, the growth of the university threatened Grace Church's survival, but by then I was in a position to intervene. I was on the Board of Regents when the development of the health sciences complex was being planned, almost in Grace Church's backyard. I knew that the university had an understanding with the church that it would not be taken for the project. Still, whenever I would see new blueprints, I would look for Grace Church, just to be sure it was still there. One time I noticed that the church was missing. I quickly called the university architect, Hugh Peacock. "What's happened to Grace Church?" I asked. "Oh, Elmer, we're going to have to take that property," he said. "We've got so much going on in that area. We just can't have that little void." "You can't do that," I said. "You just can't do that. In the first place, you have an understanding with those people. They're trusting you. The university can't be in a position of going back on an understanding with a church congregation. And furthermore, I was married in that church." He paused for a long moment. "OK," he finally said. "We'll put it back." Now Grace Church is on the National Register of Historic Places. That should protect it.

Grace Church had a diverse membership. It included students and professors from the university and professionals in the community—doctors, dentists, lawyers. One active family was the Bjornsons, including the long-time Minnesota state treasurer Val Bjornson. Val was a true orator, with a deep voice, a wonderful vocabulary, and a rolling Scandinavian accent. I always thought he was underemployed as state treasurer—he would have made a fine U.S. senator. His father and another Grace Church member, C. J. Swendsen, were two of the so-called Big Three administrative chiefs who ran welfare and other social services for state government in the first part of the twentieth century.

Eleanor and I had a wonderful time planning our wedding with Pastor Wendell. We had become close friends. He and I liked to have lunch together and then go to Crist's Book Shop in St. Paul. He shared my love for books and book collecting. Our private euphemism for buying books in those days, when our budgets were tight, was "sinning." He would sometimes whisper to me as he greeted me on Sunday morning, "I've been sinning this week, Elmer." I used to wonder what other parishioners thought, if they overheard us!

I would always want to treat Pastor Wendell to lunch, but in my student days and the years soon thereafter, he would never let me pick up the tab. Years later, I tried a new device on him. I took him to the St. Paul Athletic Club, where I had become a member. We had a nice luncheon. Then I said, "There's one thing that's unusual about this place. They don't take any money. You can't pay. The fellow that runs this place is an autograph collector. All he wants is for me to sign this check. That's the only compensation he'll take." Of course, Pastor Wendell caught on. "OK, Elmer. You win," he laughed.

We had such good times, talking together at long length about theology, church history, leaders of the church, and current events too. He met with Eleanor and me before the wedding—more for purposes of planning the ceremony than to do any marriage counseling. I am sure he considered us a good match.

It was a lovely wedding, with beautiful music. My sister, Caroline, and my brother Arnold were in the wedding party. Eleanor was a radiant bride, in a gorgeous dress of ivory satin. I was in a tuxedo.

I was in a trance throughout the ceremony. Before it began, I sat waiting all alone in the vestibule near the front of the church. I kept thinking, "In a few minutes, they're going to come for me, and I'm going to walk out to the altar, and I'm going to be married to Eleanor!" I wanted to impress the moment on my mind. I was ecstatic about having won her consent to marry. I was deeply in love with her. It makes me shiver just to think of it.

After a reception at the Johnsons' home, we went to our new home, a pleasant house on Hendon Avenue in the St. Anthony Park neighborhood in St. Paul. We always called it the Hendon House. It was a house Eleanor's folks had built, subject to a small mortgage, which we assumed. We had taken some care not to be the victims of any kind of shivaree. The wedding of one of Eleanor's friends was marred by hijinks that I thought were disrespectful. I went so far as to talk to Grandpa Johnson about asking a plainclothes policeman to be in attendance at the reception to keep things orderly, just in case. But I trusted my brother Arnold. I told him of our plans to spend our first night at the Hendon House and then leave the next day for our honeymoon. We had reserved a room at the Basin Harbor Lodge in Vergennes, Vermont, on Lake Champlain. Our bags were already packed before the ceremony.

I trusted Arnold too well. Somehow, he got into the house before us and put a large amount of rice in our suitcases. On our entire trip, every time we opened one of our bags, rice spilled out. It was a dead giveaway that we were newlyweds.

Newlyweds

T HE DAY AFTER OUR WEDDING, Eleanor and I drove to Milwaukee and took a boat to Muskegon. The next day we drove to Detroit, got on another boat to Buffalo, then drove to Basin Harbor Lodge in Vergennes, Vermont, where we stayed for one week.

I had never been to that part of the country before. But we had read about it in advertisements and had chosen it well in advance. When I travel, I always like to make my arrangements ahead of time, so I know where I am going. I do not like to spend time planning a trip while traveling. I think that detracts from the enjoyment of what I am seeing and doing.

Something happened during that week in Vermont that I have never told Eleanor (though when she reads this, the cat will be out of the bag). There I was, a solid, responsible married man, on my honeymoon with my beautiful bride. But I was also a twenty-three-year-old on vacation, and I had a streak of daring in me. One afternoon when Eleanor was resting, I ventured out on Lake Champlain in a sailboat. I knew nothing about sailing, though I had read about how to tack. There was a brisk wind, and Lake Champlain is a big lake.

I was soon in trouble. I could not turn the sailboat around. The more I pressed on the rudder, the faster it went, because it was tending to heel over. I was scared that I was going to have a tragedy. But after a few desperate maneuvers, I finally got it around and returned to shore, somewhat shaken. I decided that I had better learn more about sailing before going out in a sailboat on Lake Champlain again.

We came home to the Hendon House—a brand new house with very little furniture. Neither of us brought much to our marriage in the way of furniture. But from the start, the Hendon House had a piano—a parlor grand Mason-Hamlin, one of the finest pianos ever made.

My insistence got us that piano, before we bought any other furniture. It goes to show that I am not very practical sometimes. But I still think it was a good idea to buy it. Eleanor is a talented musician, and she deserved a fine instrument to play. And at the bottom of the depression, grand pianos were a drug on the market. I think we paid just $700 or $800 for it—a lot of money for us at that time but a wonderful investment.

In 1985, when we built the house we live in today, the first new piece of furniture we bought for it was a new grand piano. We had given the Mason-Hamlin to our daughter, Emily. By then, I had learned to play a little, too. There were a couple of pieces I could play quite well. One was "The World Is Waiting for the Sunrise." A friend who heard me play it once said, "Elmer, I have never heard a person play so well with such a limited repertoire."

Eleanor and I both loved music and loved to have it in our home. One of our favorite radio programs early in our married life was *The Ford Sunday Evening Hour.* It was classical music accompanied by some brief program notes. I looked forward to that broadcast each week.

Years later, Bill Kling from Minnesota Public Radio called me and said, "Elmer, we've just arranged to broadcast the Minnesota Orchestra, and it occurred to me that you and your company might like to sponsor those broadcasts." I happily agreed. H. B. Fuller Company has been a sponsor of the Friday night broadcasts of Minnesota Orchestra concerts since they began almost three decades ago.

As soon as we were married, Eleanor and I developed a budget. I was making $135 a month. We decided that we should save 10 percent of that income, not in order to buy something, but for capital and long-term investment. Further, we decided, as our income increased, we ought to save a larger percentage. Every incremental increase in income should lead to a larger share of savings. We were careful financial planners. Eleanor was the family bookkeeper. She kept track of what we spent on everything. I made a chart of what I thought a nice increase in income over time might be. I remember thinking, if I could ever make $500 a month, I would have it made. All that care with money and attention to savings became crucial to us nine years later, when we had a chance to buy controlling interest in Fuller.

Nothing like that was on our minds in the fall of 1932. We were intent then on getting settled in our first home. We also had politics on our minds—at least a little, anyway. It was a presidential election year, one made all the more crucial by the worsening economic crisis. Eleanor and I both would be casting our first presidential ballots. It was a matter of some concern to me whether I was to continue the Andersen family tradition of voting Republican, or become a Democrat. Like many others, I was dissatisfied with the economic performance of the Republican president, Herbert Hoover, and was interested in a change.

That summer, the Democratic governor of Maryland, Albert Ritchie, captured my imagination. I thought he had provided marvelous leadership in Maryland. I decided that if the Democrats nominated him for president, I would vote Democratic in November. I had my radio tuned to the Democratic National Convention and listened with great interest. It was quite a contest, until William Macadoo swung California to Franklin Roosevelt in the expectation of becoming secretary of state, and John Garner did the same in Texas, expecting to become vice president. I thought all that deal making was shameful—neophyte that I was. The Democrats went on to nominate Roosevelt; I voted for Hoover and have been a Republican ever since—though not without some misgivings along the way.

After settling in, our next goal was to get Eleanor back to the university. She was one year short of completing her degree requirements when we married. We had decided that we did not want too many years to elapse before she finished. She resumed her studies part-time in the fall of 1933.

We needed to cut expenses and make home life simpler to accommodate Eleanor's student status. That is why after less than a year in the Hendon House, we turned it over to tenants and moved into a little upstairs apartment at 3505 Eighteenth Avenue South in Minneapolis. Among its virtues was that it was close to a streetcar that would take Eleanor to campus.

The move into that little place was an adventure itself. Our apartment had an outside stairway. We moved on a hot summer day. One of the items we were not about to leave behind was our grand piano. But when the movers got to the place and saw the stairway and the doorway into the apartment, they thought differently. "There's no way that we can get that piano into that apartment. No way," they said. I was stumped for a minute, but I thought the task was not impossible. Then I said, "I'll tell you what. If you'll just pick up the piano and carry it in, we'll go down to the corner and have a beer." One big guy looked at the other big guy and said, "Let's try it." In no time, the piano was in, and we were enjoying a cold one at the corner pub.

In our new apartment, a little closet off the dining room was going to be converted to my library. I furnished it with a table from a secondhand store, and book boxes that my brother had arranged for Sheldon to make for me a few years earlier. I wondered what to do about lighting. I do not know why it did not occur to me to run an extension cord and lightbulb in there, but wiring was often less than adequate in those days. It occurred to me that Grace Church used candles every Sunday—and they were new candles, every Sunday, even though the candles from the previous Sunday were never used up. I inquired what happened to the partially consumed candles after Sunday services. "We usually throw them away," was the reply. "Throw them my way. I think I could use them," I said. So my little library was illuminated by church candlelight. Maybe that was what made it so special to me. I have never enjoyed any home library—even the fine big one I have now—as much as I enjoyed that little one in the closet.

I loved married life, but by the summer of 1934, I was growing dissatisfied with life as a traveling salesman. I was usually on the road for a week at a time. I hated being away from Eleanor for so long, and I knew that my absences would become more difficult if we had a child.

I shared this concern with the manager of the Minneapolis School Supply Company, Vic Watson. He passed along word that H. B. Fuller Company in St. Paul, a manufacturer of school paste, was looking for someone to hire in sales promotion. "It's a very small company, Elmer, but it has a good clean reputation, and it might be worth looking at."

Not long afterward, I was driving in St. Paul on what was then called West Third Street (now Kellogg Boulevard), and I noticed a sign on the side of a building: H. B. Fuller Company. I thought, well, it would not hurt to go in and see if that job is still open, and see what the people look like. I was ushered right in to see owner and president Harvey B. Fuller Jr. The job was still open. We began to visit about how I might fit in at Fuller. It certainly was a small company, with annual sales in 1934 of $125,000—less than my own sales at Sheldon had been the previous year. But I liked Mr. Fuller. His style, values, and general outlook on life were appealing to me. And the job he offered did not involve traveling. After a few more visits with Mr. Fuller, I accepted.

Leaving Sheldon tugged at me a little. But Mr. Sheldon, who had been so kind to me and to my brothers, was by then spending long winters in California and was not as involved in the business. Severing my tie with that company meant severing a tie to Muskegon. By the time I left Sheldon, I was truly a Minnesotan.

Sheldon sent me on a last trip through North Dakota and Montana, and way out to the West Coast, to Portland, Oregon. It was a long train ride. The manager at the Northern School Supply Company in Portland said something to me that, in a nutshell, describes the distress of the depression. He said, "You know, Elmer, we thought we had built up this business pretty fast. But it was nothing compared with how rapidly it faded away."

I was so far from home and had been gone for so long that I called Eleanor and asked if she would meet me in Montana, so that we could travel home together. Plucky as she was, she joined me in a little town in Montana. We shared each other's company as I made that final journey home. On October 8, 1934, I entered the employment of H. B. Fuller Company.

By then, we again had new living quarters. We learned of a lower duplex in Prospect Park in Minneapolis, not far from where Pastor Wendell lived. We admired his tidy neighborhood when we visited him. The duplex was at 147 Bedford Street, just three or four doors south of Franklin Avenue. The little street was notable because at its end stood a house designed by famed architect Frank Lloyd Wright, owned and occupied by a university official. The Bedford Street duplex was roomier, more comfortable, and more accessible than our upstairs apartment. We moved there in the summer of 1934.

The owner, Mr. Folwick, lived upstairs. He was a sober person who did not get much enjoyment out of life. And I am afraid I did little to sweeten his disposition.

My interest in nature, cultivated on my boyhood walks at Lake Mona, stayed with me into adulthood. I always enjoyed collecting nature specimens. On one of my rambles, I found a deserted hornets' nest. I brought it home and put it in our storage area in the basement, and promptly forgot about it. One spring day, I heard Mr. Folwick cursing and storming around in the basement. I went down and discovered that my hornets' nest had not been abandoned after all. Its inhabitants had emerged with the spring and were giving Mr. Folwick a fine chase. He let me know he considered collecting a hornets' nest a ridiculous thing to do.

The duplex's old-style water heater was the source of more difficulty with our landlord. It was not an automatic model. It had to be lit to take a bath, and then shut off afterwards. Once we forgot to shut it off. We went to bed and woke up during the night to a thumping noise in the basement. It was the hot water heater, nearly ready to blow up. Mr. Folwick heard it too, and he was already downstairs. When I got down there, he said, "You forgot to shut off the water heater," and then proceeded to scold me so severely, I thought he was going to evict us then and there. I said over and over, "I know it's terrible and I'm terribly sorry and we'll never do it again." Finally he calmed down enough to let us stay.

We remained on Bedford Street until Eleanor graduated from the university in 1937. She graduated with a major in history, and with great admiration for the famous historian who had been her adviser, Harold Deutsch. He served the university for over a half century and is remembered as one of its greatest professors.

Eleanor's progress toward her degree had been slowed by one little interruption. Anthony Lee Andersen was born on December 10, 1935.

Becoming a parent was a tremendous thrill. The very idea that two people, in combining their love, could produce a third human being captivated us. We were very happy to be parents. We got so excited about every phase of Tony's development. When Tony was about to take his first steps, I bought a movie camera—a big, bulky thing in 1936 and an extravagance, but one we felt was justified. We have a movie of Tony's first steps in our little duplex on Bedford Street. Those were wonderful days.

Not too long after Tony's birth, Eleanor went back to the university. We figured that if she were going to complete her degree, she ought to do it then and not wait until there were more babies to care for. After her graduation, we returned to the house on Hendon Avenue where we had been honeymooners.

Eleanor and I developed a way of relating to each other that has suited us well for nearly seventy years: We do not talk about everything. There ought to be a certain mystique about love and marriage. Talking about everything in great detail diminishes the mystery. Not all of life, of art, of music, of anything should be thrown out on the table and torn apart and dismembered. It is too precious. You sense music. You sense art. Some parts of life are better just experienced.

I sensed early on that Eleanor did not want to discuss a lot of intimate things about our relationship. She is a very private person. We developed a way of sensing each other, of being attuned to each other through nonverbal cues, and of modifying our own activities in accord with the signals we observed. I can tell when Eleanor is the least bit upset about something, so I quickly change. Spouses indulge each other, and Eleanor has been very indulgent of me when I have set out to do some wild things. She would not say anything. She would just let it work itself out, let me stew in my juice for awhile, until my wild hair was shown to be either genius or folly.

The secret of a happy marriage lies not in solving differences but in avoiding them. It helps to have separate spheres of influence, so that you do not have to decide everything jointly. There are some parts of the family life that a husband can take care of on his own. A lot of discussion would just delay activity. There are little things about managing the household that are important to Eleanor and maybe less so to me. But the household is her province, so she makes the calls, and I yield to her judgment. If those little things become discussion points, they can get way out of hand.

One of the lessons family life should teach us, because it also applies to the larger society, is that you cannot always have your own way. Sometimes you have to indulge your friend, your club, your party, even your nation. I have thought of that often in connection with the Republican Party. I have been a Republican all my life, and I have often felt the need to indulge the Republican Party as it tears off in a direction that I disapprove.

The Quakers have a wonderful trait. They never vote on anything. When people feel that their point of view is outside the consensus and a consensus is forming, they "stand aside." That is such a lovely expression: to stand aside. Let life go on. Let a person live his or her personal belief, without making an issue of it. It is so important to be gentle with one another, to understand where people are coming from or where they are going, and to simply value people for their human qualities.

Desiderius Erasmus, who is my favorite character, was a great scholar of the Reformation. His portrait hangs on our library wall. He wrote a wonderful little piece called *In Praise of Folly*. Erasmus satirically praises all kinds of folly, including his own. He mentions himself by name and lists his faults. Out of it comes the message that this is life. This is humanity. We have to be tolerant, even as we try to improve. All of us can do better. That is the purpose of life: to try to live better with each other, to try to live better with ourselves, to try to live better with all with whom we come in contact. We must recognize folly because it exists and can point the way toward improvement. You do not fight it. You do not fight life; you enjoy life.

My career change resulted in more time for Eleanor—and, shortly thereafter, for Tony too—just as I had wanted. But it also cost us the car Sheldon had provided for me since I had first come to Minnesota. I took the streetcar to work. That daily trip produced the added bonus of a new friendship, one I treasured through the years. I met Cecil March on the streetcar. Cecil worked in the 3M glue bond lab. We had a mutual interest in politics and were both members of the Liberal Republican Club and active in Republican politics in southeast Minneapolis. Like me, Cec wanted to be at work early. Mr. Fuller was frequently at work before 8 A.M., and I always wanted to be there even earlier than he was. Cecil and I had many nice visits on those dark early mornings.

We got along without a car for a few years. When we finally decided we needed the mobility a car provides, we did not want to spend much money. We came upon a Buick Cabriolet Deluxe model of ancient vintage. I think it was made before cars were invented! It was a four-passenger coupe, a big, cumbersome thing, with two doors; one front seat folded over as you got into the back seat. Then, on part of the back seat, there was a raised storage box with a lid. Tony just loved to sit up on top of that storage box, because then he could see over the heads of those in the front seat. This car so endeared herself to us that we gave her a name: Victoria.

We could not keep Victoria going in the two winters we had her. She spent the cold months up on blocks. One spring, when I wanted to get her going again, I took her to a garage. I said, "As I remember, the lights went out last fall. We've got to have lights. And the brakes are pretty weak. They ought to be tightened up. There may be other stuff you'll see it needs. But do all you can do for $10. That's all I can afford." The mechanic complied. During the depression, a mechanic would rather spend a day on an old car and make $10 than sit idle.

Victoria came to an inglorious end. Eleanor was driving down Como Avenue toward Minneapolis one day when there was a loud clatter and clunk. With a stream of clutter falling behind her, the car gradually rolled to a stop. The metal straps holding the battery in place had rusted through, and the battery had fallen out. Now, I am able to put up with a lot, but I hate to have Eleanor inconvenienced in any way. After she did that to Eleanor, Victoria and I had to part company. Still, no car ever superseded Victoria in our affection—even though she let her battery fall out.

We replaced her with something sensible. Many years passed before I had another car with enough personality to merit a name. That was Gladys, my little 1977 Ford Escort. I drove her hard as I made my rounds to ECM newspaper offices in the early 1980s, delivering my editorials every Monday morning. Gladys was a wonderful car. She was dependable, always ready to go, and economical too.

Only during the governorship did we have a luxury car, and then only briefly. It was traditional for Minnesota's governor to use a Lincoln or a Cadillac. But I thought we ought to have a car made in Minnesota. I asked the Ford plant in St. Paul, which specialized in building trucks, whether they would build a Ford automobile for the governor of Minnesota. They did it. I drove a fine, respectable Ford for the rest of my term. One of the first things my successor, Karl Rolvaag, did after he took office was ask the legislature to provide funds for a Cadillac again. His chief of staff, William Shovell, contended that a Ford was beneath the dignity of the office. When reporters asked me about that, I replied that a governor's dignity depends on his conduct and the wisdom of his decisions, not on the car he rides in.

At Fuller, my first assignment involved direct mail advertising. I kept a list of our customers and potential customers for our products—asbestos dry paste, Lastiko wall sizing, wet paste, and so on. I wrote letters to the firms and institutions on the various lists, soliciting business.

Our products were very low cost, and freight rates were high. That limited our market geographically. A comment by a person at 3M illustrates the limitations of the business I had joined. Minnesota Mining was considering a venture in the adhesives industry then, and they were seeking information. I told him that our biggest volume item was case sealing glue. We sold it in fifty-five-gallon drums, each drum would seal about thirty thousand cases, and we sold it for $27.50. He thanked me and rose to leave. "I think I know all I need to know about the adhesive business," he said. "I don't think Minnesota Mining is interested in anything that sells for $27.50 in a fifty-five-gallon drum that does thirty thousand of anything." Later, 3M became one of our best customers.

I also worked with Fuller's two salesmen, preparing their route lists and providing them with customers' previous purchase records. Mr. Fuller was a meticulous person. He insisted that records be kept on every customer, complete with accurate addresses and correct spelling. He created multiple files with that information, one for advertising, one for bookkeeping, one for sales. He was highly organized for a small business at that early time. In fact, he was so thorough that it limited his productivity. Things would be delayed because he could never quit working on anything until it was done to his satisfaction.

I quickly saw opportunities to assist him, and decided to work closely with him to make his job as easy as possible. One thing I did was to go with him and represent our interests in a new organization, the Adhesive Manufacturers' Association, founded in 1934. It was one of the many trade associations formed at that time at the urging of President Roosevelt to set price guidelines and serve as an antidote to economy-depressing price competition. Mr. Fuller quickly regarded me as his right-hand man in that organization. He trusted me to let him make any important decision and to be loyal to his decision. That meant a great deal to him. Running a glue business was not Mr. Fuller's prime love in life, but it was his living, and he appreciated someone who was willing to help him on his terms.

We hit it off personally. On Saturday mornings, when I would come to the plant on my own time and find him there, we would sometimes go together to the St. Paul Hotel or the Minnesota Club for lunch.

When Tony was four or five, I began to take him along to the plant on Saturday mornings. He loved to join me. He would occupy himself around the plant while I did a little work. Once I tried to explain to him how the company worked. I said, "We make glue. Mr. Ray Burgess, out in the plant, makes it. I'm in charge of selling it, and Mr. N. C. Stork "—he was the treasurer—"takes care of the money." In his young mind, that took care of it. This man made it. This man sold it. This man took care of the money. So he walked over to Mr. Fuller and asked, "Mr. Fuller, what do *you* do here?"

Tony and I often went to Nardi's at noon on Saturdays. Nardi's was a little Italian restaurant at Seven Corners. Nardi was a genial fellow who took an interest in his customers. He never liked to give anybody any change. If you gave him a dollar for a sixty-five-cent lunch, he wondered if you would like a chocolate bar or a pack of cigarettes for that other thirty-five cents. Tony still talks about Nardi as he recalls his childhood.

I always thought of myself as a salesman. On one of our Saturday ventures, I decided to teach little Tony how to sell. I took a broom. I said, "Tony, I'm going to sell this broom to you. Then, I want you to take it and sell it back to me." I held the broom. I said, "Now, this is a very fine product that we're proud to make. This handle is carefully chosen from straight-grain hardwood. These fibers in the broom are carefully grown to be tough and long-lasting, so they don't give up easily." I went through all the details of that broom and hailed it as a marvelous product. Then I gave it to Tony. "Now, Tony, you sell it to me as best as you can." He paused for a minute. "Sir, I think you'd like this broom," he said. "It sweeps clean." I thought, who is teaching whom? I was lost in the technology and not focused on what the broom did. Tony taught me a good sales lesson: get to the heart of the matter.

Soon after I joined Fuller, it moved. When Third Street was widened and renamed Kellogg Boulevard, all the buildings on the south side of the street were demolished. The Fuller plant was among them. Fuller's new home was on Eagle Street, down at the bottom of the hill below Third Street, in the abandoned plant of the Ryan Milk Company. It needed a lot of repair, but it was available quite reasonably. Everybody at Fuller pitched in to clean up the dirt that had accumulated during the years the building had been vacant.

I was enthusiastic about my work at Fuller. I soon determined that if the company would take some initiative and risks, it had a good chance to grow. It was growing gradually despite the depression. In 1937, the fiftieth anniversary of the company's founding, it had its biggest sales year to date: $212,000. I did not see that trouble was just ahead.

Fuller Threatened

A BLOW STRUCK FULLER in December 1937 that would have knocked many other small companies out of business. Elmer Park and Calvert Leggett, the two most experienced of the company's three salesmen, and Frank Altman, Fuller's chief processing man in the plant, banded together to form their own firm. The Park, Leggett, Altman Company was established in Minneapolis before Harvey Fuller heard a word from the three men. In fact, Mr. Fuller got the news from the head of another adhesives company. Park, Leggett, and Altman planned to use all they knew about Fuller's processes and customers to compete with Fuller. They thought they could run Fuller out of business.

A change I had pressed Mr. Fuller to make may have precipitated their move. I had concluded that we could increase sales if we hired a third salesman. Park and Leggett objected. "There's only so much business to be had, and we're dividing it two ways now. If we have a third salesman, we'll be dividing the available business three ways," they said. I disagreed. "Don't you see that a third salesman could have a multiplying effect, not a dividing effect? There could be more business for all of you if a third person was on the job." My argument was persuasive with Mr. Fuller but not with the salesmen. They struck out on their own out of fear that their livelihoods were about to be diminished.

Their departure came at what was already a stressful time for the company. The nation was still in the depression's grip in 1937. Conditions actually worsened that year. And another St. Paul company, Economics Laboratory, introduced a product called Soilax that competed with one of Fuller's products. It made us worry that Economics Laboratory could become a broader competitor, right in our backyard.

Fuller started 1938 in trouble. Right after the departure of Park, Leggett, and Altman, Mr. Fuller summoned Ray Burgess, the plant manager, and me to an urgent meeting at his house. We knew we had to act fast to save the company. I knew what needed to be done and who had to do it. I said,

"You'd better get me a car, because somebody has got to get out to the customers, right quick."

I was a traveling salesman again—doing the very thing I wanted to escape by joining Fuller. But the situation was dire. A company with a long and honorable history was at risk, along with the jobs it provided—including my own.

H. B. Fuller Company was founded in 1887 in Chicago by the first Harvey Benjamin Fuller, my boss's father. In its early days, it moved to St. Paul. Its main product was a wet paste used primarily for hanging wallpaper and attaching labels to packing crates. Old H. B. added to the business by inventing the all-steel adjustable scaffolding. It was a tripod with individually adjustable legs and pegs for paint and paste cans. It became a favorite among painters and wallpaper hangers during America's construction boom after the turn of the century.

His son and my boss, H. B. Fuller Jr., joined the business in 1916. He was called Harvey. Business was not his real love. He preferred art and writing. But he worked hard at making the business thrive. He was instrumental in incorporating the company in 1921, the year his father died. He did one other thing that proved vital: in 1920, he hired a talented chemist named Ray Burgess. Burgess created H. B. Fuller's line of adhesives for the canning industry, a line that gave the Fuller Company new life.

Now, with that life threatened, I traveled intensively, almost desperately. Eleanor was left at home with tiny Tony. I regretted having to be away from them. But I credit Eleanor so much for how she managed. She was a terrific homemaker and mother. She never talked about wanting to do anything else but to raise our children and provide us with a comfortable, orderly home. I always saved Sundays for the family. I still do. And I would read to Tony, and later to his brother and sister, every evening that I could.

One of my calls in 1938 was on B. F. Robertson, manager of the paint division of Farwell Ozmun Kirk, a leading wholesale hardware house and a neighbor of the Fuller plant in St. Paul. He was sitting at his desk when I walked into his office. He did not look up or say anything, so I just stood, waiting for some sign of recognition. After a moment, without looking up, he said, "What the hell do you want?" I told him that we had had a change at the company and that new people would be calling on him. I wanted to assure him that we would take good care of him, and we wanted to be assured of his business. He said, "You take care of us; we'll take care of you."

Later, I witnessed an incident that made me admire Robertson much more than I did the first time we met. I was calling on their retail store on

Robert Street while Robertson happened to be there. Then a truck driver from his company came in, wearing a suit coat and no overcoat. It was a cold day. Robertson gruffly said, "Why aren't you wearing an overcoat?" The driver answered, "Sir, I don't have an overcoat." Robertson looked at him and took his coat off. He said, "You know, I've hated this darned coat. It doesn't fit me very well. Maybe you could get some use out of it. Here, try it on." He gave him the coat off his back. I thought, what a man! He can be as grumpy as he wants to be with me. He reminded me that a grouchy disposition can be a disguise for a particularly soft heart.

Fuller was not completely out of luck in 1938. We still had Ray Burgess in our laboratory, and he still had the know-how to create new products that customers wanted to buy. Canners were some of Fuller's most important customers. Their labeling machines would roll a can down an incline. It would go over some rollers and pick up some adhesive, take one revolution to pick up the end of a label, and then take another revolution to wrap the label around itself. Just before the end, a little bar would spread adhesive on the other end of the label to make it stick. A pick-up adhesive and a lap-end paste were both needed in the canning operation. Pick-up adhesive came in two forms, hot or cold, for two different labeling processes, though hot pick-up was more commonly used. The problem with hot pick-up adhesive was that cans varied in temperature through the day. That in turn affected the reaction of the can with the paste and the label. If the can was too hot, the pick-up adhesive would be too liquid and would not set fast enough to pick up the label. The trick was to make an adhesive that would work as well on hot cans as on cold cans.

Another problem was that canners wanted adhesive that was light in color, so it would not stain through the label. Yet, the traditional products, up to that time, were dark. They were made of rosin and petrolatum.

Our main competitor in the canner adhesive field was a Milwaukee firm, F. G. Findley Company. Findley came out with a light-colored, wide-range hot pick-up that was a good product. It began to be a strong competitor just when we were having competitive trouble in Minneapolis.

We had to do something. Ray Burgess and his young assistant, a recent Macalester College graduate named Richard E. Smith, began work on an adhesive made with an oil with a high melting point. They found their oil with the aid of one of the most forthright sales presentations I had ever heard. I overheard the young salesman's pitch: "Mr. Burgess, this is the first time I've ever called on an adhesive company, so I don't have any idea what you use. The fact is I'm pretty new at my own company, and I don't know our own line very well. Here's a list of everything we make, and it seems to me there ought to be something in here you could use."

That salesman was, eventually, getting carload orders for this material. We insisted that it be shipped in blank bags. That is how worried we were about our competition. In any conversation that might be overheard, we called the new oil "dope." One day, Burgess called me to his laboratory to show me a new adhesive he had brewed. He had poured some into the lid of a gallon can to get a thinner film, to show off its light color. He was emphasizing with the lid as he said, "I really think this is the best gol' darn hot pick-up we ever made." As he struck the lid, the film of glue shattered. It broke into lumps. I said, "Ray, you may have discovered something more than you realize." In cold weather, canners had to chisel rock-hard adhesive out of a five-gallon pail. In the summer, the same glue was half melted and pulled out like taffy. Either way, adding adhesive to labeling machines was a miserable job. Burgess's discovery with the can lid that day started Ray and Dick experimenting with an adhesive that would remain in lump form until it was added to a labeling machine. They came up with a formula that did not fuse and that resisted high temperature.

I told them, "Just give me a few five-pound boxes of that and turn me loose. If this isn't a salesman's dream, I've never heard of one." I had a standard procedure for selling Fuller's new lump adhesive. I would walk into a canning plant, get into the warehouse where the labeling crews were working, and set down the five-pound box of hot pick-up. I would have it open so the light-colored lump was visible. Pretty soon, the machine operator would ask, "What's that?" I would say, "That's lump hot pick-up. You just take a lump out of a box and put it in the pot." "Oh, the hell you say?" he'd say. He was suddenly very interested, because he was the guy who struggled with the old product. The operator's curiosity about the new adhesive lumps was such that, invariably, he would shut off the machine, clean out its adhesive pot, put our product in, get the machine going—and discover that it worked. It was the most wonderful selling experience I ever had.

We put out the word that our only concern with our new product was that it might fuse in summer temperatures—something that we knew was not a concern at all. We knew that cautionary note would get back to the competition and deter them from trying to imitate us. That is how badly we wanted to cool our competitors' zeal.

Soon after I started selling our new lump hot pick-up adhesive, I told Mr. Fuller that I thought it could be the company's salvation—if we could just take it to more of the nation's canners. "I know there's a limit on how much canner adhesive we can sell around here. But there are a lot of canners in the country. If we go to where they are, they'll buy our product." Mr. Fuller replied by lecturing me on the dangers of "remote control." He was not a believer in doing business far from the main office. He wanted things right under his nose and at his attention. But our situation demanded that we take a few chances. He was willing to let me try. He said, "You explore it, Elmer, and we'll talk about it."

The first area I explored was the Rio Grande valley of Texas, an area rife with canners. I wrote letters, quoted our prices, and sent some samples. I learned that one of our competitors had a warehouse there but was charging high prices. Our normal price, plus freight and warehouse charges, was much less. One canner wrote, "I think you have something to offer us, and if you'll come down and talk about it, I'd be glad to help you get in business here."

I went to Harlingen, Texas, and met with the canner. He recommended someone who could represent us locally, a colorful old salesman named J. R. Welch. He became our sales representative and, when we opened a warehouse there, our warehouse manager. Before long, Welch achieved the distinction of being the first Fuller salesman to sell a full carload of adhesive to one customer. Welch claimed he made a customer of every canner in the valley.

That success heightened my desire to explore other markets. Next on my list was Florida. Lenfestey Supply Company of Tampa serviced the canning industry of Florida with practically everything but adhesives. They had a wonderful salesman, Charlie Weihrs, who ingratiated himself with the trade. He became our man in Florida, and that business soon flourished.

Next, I went to Ogden, Utah, and contracted with another cannery supplier, George W. Goddard, to be our sales agent. Thus, by early 1939, we had three agents in fertile parts of the country bringing in additional business to offset some of the losses we suffered to local competition. Mr. Fuller was pleased with what I had done.

But there was one arrangement that he negated, involving the salmon industry. In those days, salmon was packed aboard fishing boats equipped with canning facilities. Those boats would come back after two or three months at sea with a full load of canned salmon. The ships' principal supplier in Seattle was the Jack Horner Company. Horner got adhesives from National Starch—then called National Adhesives—the biggest company in the business. I entered into correspondence with Jack Horner, and totally through an exchange of letters and samples, he became interested in our lump adhesive. Horner agreed to try it on one ship, over a period of some time.

That news caught the attention of National Starch and its president, Frank Greenwall. I later came to know and admire Frank very much. He told me that his last name was originally Greenwald, but he had felt compelled to change it to Greenwall to better disguise the fact that he was Jewish. He enlightened me about the persecution under which Jewish people labored in American business in those years.

Greenwall wrote Mr. Fuller a letter: "Dear Harvey: I understand that your fellow, Elmer Andersen, has been negotiating with the Jack Horner Company, a prized customer of ours. I have to tell you, Harvey, that if he persists in doing that, we'll establish a plant in Minneapolis and compete with you head-on."

That threat jarred Mr. Fuller. We were having enough trouble with local competition. He said, "Elmer, I think we have to give it up." I argued with him. "We're doing well. We're doing well in Texas, in Utah, and in Florida. We're entitled to that business. We have better products than National. We're giving better service. We're giving them a fairer deal. National won't put a plant in Minneapolis. They don't do anything for spite. They do things for money. The only way they'd put a plant in Minneapolis is if they could make it a success. They'll study the situation here. They'll know it's no market for them. They're out for big stuff. Don't let them intimidate you." He said, "Let me think about it." But he didn't think long. He came back and said, "Elmer, I can't stand it. I have to write and tell Frank Greenwall that we'll give up the relationship with Jack Horner. I just ask you to terminate the arrangement as best you can."

I did as he asked. I always supported Mr. Fuller, even when he made decisions that I would not have made if I had been in his position. I never told a soul—other than Eleanor—that I disagreed with him and was only doing something because he made me. I was loyal to him when he made the final decision. Before his mind was set, I would attempt to persuade him as much as I dared. When I knew what he wanted, that became my position.

Once when I outlined Mr. Fuller's plan for the coming year to one of our salesmen, he looked me straight in the eye. "You know damned well, Elmer, that if you were deciding this, you wouldn't do it this way," he said. "That's not the point," I said. "Harvey and I have talked it over. He's listened to me. I've given him my ideas. He's made the decision, and that becomes my decision. Let's do it."

After our longtime salesmen Park and Leggett left in 1938, I persuaded

Mr. Fuller to try compensating our new salesmen on a commission plan. I wanted the salesmen to do better, and thought this was the incentive they needed. That was not how I sold it to Mr. Fuller. I told him it would save money. My proposal was that if the salesmen sold no more in the new year than in the previous year, they would be paid less. Only if they increased their sales would they make more than in the previous year.

Then, I took it up with the salesmen. It took them only a minute to figure out that they were going to make less money if they did no better in the coming year than in the previous one. But I persuaded them that the opportunity to make more money was worth that downside risk. They agreed to try it for a year. They all did well, and sales increased 25 percent in that test year. At the end of the year, I called them together and said, "You've done quite a job. But I've talked it over with Mr. Fuller, and he thinks it was a good trial, but we ought to go back to the old plan of just a salary and expense account for the salesmen." They looked aghast. "What do you mean, Elmer?" they said. I began to grin. "I was just testing. I knew you could do it, and you've done it. The new compensation plan is going to stay. Just go to it. The more you make, the better we like it." That developed a tremendous steam in them that was evident in the rest of our meeting. Afterwards, Ben Fuller, Harvey's son, spoke up: "Elmer, if our competition had sat in on this meeting, they'd be scared to death."

We worked hard in 1938 and 1939 to stay ahead of the competition. It was not at all clear that we would survive. I remember feeling gloomy on my thirtieth birthday, in 1939. Friends in the industry were telling me, "Elmer, you're not going to be able to survive that competition in Minneapolis. You know Mr. Fuller." Some well-meaning friends began to suggest that I look for another job.

Then, in the fall of 1939, Mr. Fuller had a stroke, and things became all the more difficult. He never worked a full day after that. I became Fuller's de facto general manager. Mr. Fuller's stroke was a shock. He was only in his early fifties, and he appeared to have taken good care of his health.

Things were so bad that I even talked to my brother Arnold about the possibility of going back to Muskegon. He had bought Lake Shore Corporation, an industrial supply house, and was building that business. He asked me to help, but he wanted me to come back as an employee, not a partner. I did not want to do that. I thought brothers should not have a relationship as employer and employee. I stayed with Fuller.

Eventually, Park, Leggett, and Altman came to disagreement among themselves. They sold out to a Chicago concern, which folded the business after a few years. Their experience taught me a lesson: salesmen are wrong to think they own their customers, and that if they move, they can take their customers with them. Customers are loyal to themselves. They judge for themselves whether a new deal is going to be better for them than the old deal. And there is a strong sense of loyalty to a brand they trust.

Late in 1940, before we knew that we had bested our crosstown competition, there was another development. I was at an Adhesive Manufacturers' Association meeting in Chicago when a couple of men from a leading company in Chicago, Paisley Products, a division of a company called Morningstar Nicol, asked me if I thought Fuller could be purchased. I said, "I wouldn't think so." I explained that it was already a second-generation family company, and that H. B. Fuller III, known as Ben, had recently joined the business. "I've always assumed that Ben would succeed his father," I said. "We aren't so sure," they said. "Why don't you talk to Mr. Fuller to see if he'd be interested? We'd like to have you stay on as manager if we did buy the company."

When I got back to St. Paul, I told Mr. Fuller of my conversation with the Paisley representatives. "They want to know if you would consider selling. If you would, they want you and they want me, too, to come to Chicago so they can talk to us." Mr. Fuller did not brush aside the suggestion, as I had expected. I could see right away that he was considering it.

Not long afterward, on a Sunday morning, Harvey Fuller called and said that he and Emma, his wife, wanted to meet with us. They came to our house on Hendon Avenue wearing serious expressions. "We've been thinking about it," they said, "and we've decided that we would be willing to sell." Mr. Fuller's health was a big factor in their decision. I said, "We'd better go to Chicago." But my mind was racing ahead, not to selling the H. B. Fuller Company, but to buying it myself.

Part II

TAKING CHARGE

A Risky Venture

E ARLY IN 1941, Mr. Fuller and I went to Chicago at the invitation of Joe Morningstar and Murray Stempel of Paisley Products to hear their proposal for acquiring H. B. Fuller Company. Officially, I was Fuller's sales manager, the number-two man in the company. But since Mr. Fuller's stroke in 1939, I had been functioning as general manager. Nevertheless, at the meeting with Paisley, I kept quiet.

The Paisley proposal was cut and dried. For $50,000, they proposed to take over all of the assets and the name, and to have a completely free hand in what they did with the company thereafter. It was a brief and straight-forward meeting.

On the slow train ride home, I sat quietly for a long time, as did Mr. Fuller. I am sure he was mulling over the offer. Finally, after a few hours, he said, "Elmer, what did you think of it?" "I didn't think much of it," I said. "I think it's a small price to pay for a two-generation company that has a good name, has had honest dealings, is in a good market, and has a good future. Times are difficult now, and a war may be coming. But Fuller is a good company."

Then I said what was really on my mind: "Actually, Harvey, if you want to be relieved of the leadership and the majority concern, we could work out a deal within the company. We could give you whatever you want, and keep the company going under the same name and with the same people. I think there's a way to just about go along as we are, except that you'd be re-lieved of whatever you want to be relieved of." He said, "If you think that's possible, Elmer, why don't you work it out, and we'll talk again." That is the way we left it.

I started scrambling to put together a reasonable proposal: I would pay Mr. Fuller $25,000 for half of the stock, the same price Paisley was prepared to pay. In addition, I would provide a pension income for Mr. Fuller of $400 a month for five years, $300 a month for the next five, $200 a month for the next five, and $100 a month for the next five. Those seem like very small figures now, but coming out of the depression, they were respectable amounts. He would keep half of the stock and keep his hand in the company to whatever extent he pleased.

The proposal was tailored to my notion of what would please Mr. Fuller. He wanted to be relieved of management responsibilities, but he wanted Fuller to remain the same company with the same name. He wanted to retain an interest in it. He wanted to watch it grow.

The down payment I proposed on the stock purchase was $10,000. Eleanor and I had been saving money since the beginning of our marriage. Scraping together what we could, we came up with $5,000. I did not know how we could raise any more. I had a little Fuller stock, on which I tried to borrow money. No bank would take it as security. I could not get a loan from a bank. I asked Mr. Fuller about reducing the down payment to $5,000. He said, "Elmer, I really think in a deal this big, it ought to be $10,000. See what you can do."

I had no parents to turn to, but I had Eleanor's parents. Gustaf and Elizabeth Johnson came up with the additional $5,000 we needed. Those dear people made it possible. They were supportive of what we were trying to do. Grandpa Johnson said, "I think you can do it, Elmer. I think it's an opportunity. It's a good little company. We'll help you make it go."

Eleanor, too, was encouraging. When I talked with friends, they were discouraging. They said, "Elmer, this is a terrible time to enter into a business of your own. There's a war going on in Europe, and we're bound to get into it. When we do, there will be no place for any domestic manufacturing. All manufacturing will be for the war effort. You'll just be put out of business. The smart thing to do is to wait and see what happens. Wait until the war is over."

Many people think there is wisdom in waiting until everything is right. I have always wanted to do whatever I can right away, when I have the chance. If you act, then at least you are in motion when you meet whatever comes along. That is what life is—meeting challenges. If you wait too long, you lose out.

When my down payment was in hand, Mr. Fuller said, "I think you've worked out a fine plan. Let's get George Morgan." George Morgan was the venerable head of the Briggs and Morgan law firm. He was a marvelous lawyer, a great human being, and a friend of Harvey Fuller.

When the three of us met, Mr. Morgan turned to me and said, "Who is going to represent you, Elmer?" I said, "Mr. Morgan, I thought you could represent both of us. We don't have any differences. It's just a matter of drawing the papers the way Mr. Fuller wants them. That's agreeable with me." He said, "I can't represent both of you. That's contrary to legal ethics. I'm Harvey Fuller's lawyer. I look out for his best interests. You should have a lawyer to represent yours." "I don't need a lawyer," I insisted. "All I want to do is what we've laid out here that Mr. Fuller would like to have done. We don't have any differences. I'll be my own lawyer. Let's get it done." He drew up the contract, which was perfectly agreeable to me, and we signed it.

On July 1, 1941, shortly after my thirty-second birthday, I became president of H. B. Fuller Company. As soon as I was in charge, many things began to happen. I had stored up many ideas, things I wanted to try if I ever had the final word. For example, I wanted to improve working conditions in the plant on Eagle Street—a two-story building with a basement containing the boiler plant. It was a good-sized plant, maybe a quarter of a city block in size.

The floor of the plant was at ground level. Trucks that came to be loaded with shipments were at a higher level. So, a ramp would be put on the back of each truck, and drums would be rolled up the ramp. That was difficult and dangerous work, requiring a couple of men, because each drum weighed as much as six hundred pounds. One of the first things I did was install a lift at the loading door so that trucks could be loaded and unloaded safely. The fellows in the plant surely appreciated that.

Another problem at the plant needed quick attention. Eagle Street is near the Mississippi River. When the river flooded, the sewer could not handle the flow of water. It would back up into some of the basements at the lower end of the system, including ours. Every time there was a big storm, our fellows knew there would be a stinking, dirty mess to clean up in the basement. It bothered me terribly to ask them to do that work. So, we put in a check valve—a great big valve on the outlet line from the plant to the sewer. At night, the men would screw it shut so nothing could back up into our basement.

Taking steps like these gave me good relations with our plant workers. We were such a small company that we got to know each other quite well. There were only fifteen people in the company at that time: three salesmen, two in the dry paste department, three in the wet paste department, an engineer, three women in the office, Mr. Stork, Ray Burgess, and me. Mr. Fuller made it sixteen. Mr. Stork was a Dickensian bookkeeper with a green eyeshade and a stand-up desk. He added to our image as an old-fashioned but dependable little company. We were a close-knit group, often visiting in each other's homes and sharing in each other's activities.

One of the first hiring decisions I made turned out to be one of the best. Not long after taking control of the company, I hired Donna W. Petersen, a young lady from Hudson, Wisconsin, as my secretary. Donna stayed with me for forty years, through every turn in my career, and she was a marvelous secretary. She became an extension of me, multiplying my efforts by her own. She was accurate in dictation and letter writing, so I could dictate a letter and not have to see it again, not even to sign it. She kept my schedule in perfect order, so I always knew where I was supposed to be. Planning trips, arranging appointments, communicating with anyone I needed to contact—those things and more she performed gracefully and pleasantly. Everybody who knew me came to know Donna and to appreciate her gracious, patient, approachable manner.

Donna never married. Her work for me was her life. Eleanor liked Donna, and we stayed in touch with her after she retired. One day when she was our guest for lunch, she said, "Elmer, I don't enjoy anything I am doing now as much as I did my work for you. I think you need some help." So, she began to come to our home from Hudson to do secretarial work. She did that for several years, before the ailments of age made that impossible, and now she is getting along quite well in retirement.

Another change I made soon after taking charge turned out to be more important than I first realized. Mr. Fuller had bought supplies in small quantities and paid premium prices. I thought we could cut our costs substantially by buying in larger quantities. One of the products we bought was glucose. A truck would come and deliver glucose into a twenty-gallon tank. Delivered that way, in such small quantities, it was a high-priced item. I changed the order to a carload of glucose in barrels, many times what we usually bought. A few days later, the corn processors who supplied us called. "Elmer, we're concerned," they said. "This is an awfully big order for your company." I said, "I know. We've just got to buy better, so we can sell better and do more."

Soon we were buying other materials by the carload instead of the truckload. I began to negotiate for better prices. It was a big step when I negotiated for a year's supply of rosin.

With a much bigger inventory, we needed more storage. Our building had high ceilings, so we began to build balconies. Andrew Danielson, a builder who was a dear friend of Grandpa Johnson, would add a balcony whenever we needed more space. We crammed that little building full of raw materials, containers, everything.

We changed our buying habits in the nick of time. On Sunday,

December 7, 1941, Eleanor, Tony, and I were sitting down to a family dinner after church. Eleanor was about five months pregnant. We were listening to a musical broadcast as we ate dinner when suddenly the music was interrupted with the news that Japan had bombed the U.S. fleet at Pearl Harbor. I looked at Eleanor, fully aware of her pregnancy, and at little Tony, and thought, Oh my! This could hit us hard.

Immediately, there was a clampdown on all buying of materials. Manufacturers were permitted to obtain only a percentage of what they had purchased during the last six months of 1941. Because that was when we had been doing so much buying, we were able to buy more than we needed.

Soon that word got around. We had been trying to sell adhesive to National Biscuit Company's plant in Minneapolis, but Nabisco did not want to deal with an adhesive company that could service only one plant. Now the Nabisco manager in Minneapolis was calling me. He said, "Andersen, we're just desperate for glucose for our cookies and crackers. I'd be willing to pay quite a premium for it." I said, "I'll tell you what we'll do. We do have more than we need, and I'll sell you some. But I'll sell it at what it cost us. I don't want to be in the position of doing any black market trading." I didn't say anything about any return favors. I thought, if he is a decent guy, he will help us someday. Sure enough, he said, "Elmer, I'll do my darnedest to get some business for you out of National Biscuit." He did not deliver right away, but he did later, when we were in a position to supply more plants.

After Pearl Harbor, everybody was looking for a way to help the war effort. I heard about one difficulty for American troops in the South Pacific that resulted from landing on islands that lacked docks, piers, or other facilities for ships. The Marines and Navy sailors had to throw material into the water and float it ashore. Their shipping cases were not watertight, and fell apart. The military needed water-resistant adhesives to package war material. In 1941, no such thing existed.

Dick Smith, our young lab man, and I made the rounds of chemical companies, looking for a clue that would lead us to the formula for a water-resistant adhesive. Somewhere—I have forgotten exactly where—somebody said, "Varnish is water-resistant. If you could figure out a way to emulsify varnish, you might be able to do it. If you've got a casein solution, it might be that you could emulsify hot varnish into a casein solution and have a water-resistant adhesive. You ought to try it."

When we got home, I went to see B. F. Robertson, the manager I had met at our neighboring St. Paul paint factory in 1938. He was immediately interested, because he wanted his products designated as essential for the war effort, to aid his own acquisition of materials. So, we began to experiment with a casein solution. Casein is a milk derivative. Meanwhile, Robertson made varnish. Then we would send a truck to his plant to get drums of hot varnish, pour them into the mixer with the casein solution, and whip it until we had an emulsified, hot-varnish casein product.

It worked. We began to sell casein-varnish adhesive to the military. It immediately gave us priority for obtaining materials. The adhesive was successful, except for one problem. Milk is short-lived, and so are casein solutions. Spoiled milk smells awful. We began to have difficulty with it spoiling. We developed a timetable by which the customer had to use it. We told them, "Don't order any more than you can use in three days. We'll keep you in fresh adhesive." Then we went to the chemical companies to find a preservative for a casein-emulsified solution. The Dow Chemical Company came up with Dowicide A & G.

That was a tremendously important time for Fuller, and a tremendously absorbing time for me. I was traveling, the men at the plant were working on our new product, and we were all desperately hurried. We needed a product that would get us declared an essential industry so we could continue full operation during the war.

As I worked so hard, I wondered if I was doing what I ought to be doing. I was too old to be drafted, but I wondered if I should volunteer for military service. Although I dreaded the idea, I thought it was my duty to consider it. I went to the recruitment office and talked to an officer. He said, "What do you do?" I told him I was at the Fuller Company. "What are you making?" he asked. I told him. "Are you making anything essential to the war effort?" I told him about our water-resistant adhesive, and that we were selling it to the military for use in shipping crates. "Stay there and run that company. It'll do more good than anything you'd do in the army," he said.

With another baby on the way, I was relieved. Our second son, Julian Lee, was born on Easter Sunday, April 5, 1942.

Run the company I did. I got involved up to my elbows. During the war years, I occasionally worked in the plant, filling and labeling drums. Everybody had to pitch in to get the job done. I found working side by side with the plant men interesting, and it strengthened their loyalty to me and to Fuller. They saw that I was not above coming to the plant floor when they needed help, digging my hands in the glue, filling up five-gallon pails, and helping them complete the job. We were all working fifty and sixty hours a week. We all had the same goal: to produce a good product for the war effort and still have some time left over for our families.

One day, I found a *New Yorker* cartoon on my desk. I never knew who laid it there. It showed the pay window in an industrial company, and all the workmen lined up to get their weekly paycheck. One person stood out from all the others because he was dressed in a suit and had a walrus mustache. He was saying to the person behind him, "I used to be president of this outfit, until I found out what was going on." I just loved getting that cartoon, and the positive message it seemed to convey from whoever left it for me.

The war was still on when I got a call from Harvey Fuller. He and his wife had decided to move to Santa Fe, New Mexico, permanently. Their two daughters would move with them; their son Ben would continue to work for the Fuller Company. Would I be interested in buying the remainder of his Fuller stock? Indeed I was, though I had to stretch again financially. I gained full control of the company in 1944.

The move to a warmer climate may have helped Fuller's health somewhat. Still, he was only fifty-nine when he died. It is a shame that he did not live to see more of what became of the company that his father founded, and that bore his name.

During the war, Fuller's purchases were all made on the basis of their priority in the war effort. There were volumes of regulations that determined what was a priority purchase and what was not. A little company like Fuller could not possibly keep track of all the regulations. But I had a sense of what was marginal.

We used cast iron nozzles for sandblasting monuments. I wanted to order more from a foundry in Winona, Minnesota. I remember thinking, how essential is a monument? I could argue that you have to keep track of your dead people, but I knew I had a weak case. I thought, I had better not hide anything. I wrote a full statement of what we were getting, what priority we were applying, and why we thought it was justified. Then I signed it and had it notarized to authenticate the date it was written, and I put it in the file. I did that for two or three acquisitions. We were fighting for existence, but we did not want to get in trouble with the U.S. government when it was at war. And the penalties for violations were severe.

Sure enough, an inspector called on us some years after we ordered the nozzles. He said, "We know it's not a big item, but you've been getting some nozzles from a foundry in Winona that's largely engaged in the war effort. What's your justification for doing that?" I went to my file. I said, "It was a marginal decision. We're a little company. We can't keep up with everything, but here's what I wrote at the time." He read it and then said, "Since you were at least willing to be out in the open about what you were doing and why you were doing it, I'm not going to make any report against you." But, he added, "You were close to the edge."

I got a good taste in those years of government regulation of business. It seemed like a terrible nuisance at the time. All the controls and reports and rules to monitor became tedious for a little company, especially one that wanted to grow. But reflecting on it later, I saw some value in the war regulations. They forced us to know what we were doing, and to make plans, set budgets, and get organized. The discipline was good for a little company that wanted to become a lot bigger.

Fuller Matures

I WAS SERIOUS ABOUT MAKING H. B. Fuller the leading adhesives manufacturer in the country. I believed that more plants, strategically placed across the country, would make that dream come true. The only question in 1943 was where the first new plant should be.

We quickly narrowed our location options to two: Kansas City and Houston. Ray Burgess, our senior engineer, and I visited both cities to make the choice. Houston was growing rapidly. Yet it struck us as primarily a single-industry town. It did not have much diversity in manufacturing and food packing—industries that use adhesives. Kansas City had a much more mixed economy, including small adhesives customers. On that basis, we chose Kansas City.

I decided to discuss the matter with Mr. Fuller before we proceeded. After all, he was the major minority stockholder. I could have predicted his response: "Elmer, if I had to do it, I wouldn't do it at all. I just hate this remote control effort. I don't think you can run things from a distance." But he was fair about it. He said, "I'll tell you, if you think you can do it, do it. I won't stand in your way."

Some of our people in the plant felt the same way. One wonderful woman, Hazel Strese, was a bookkeeping assistant at that time. I confided in her. She said, "I don't think we should do it, Elmer. It will just take business away from St. Paul. Why can't we just do more business from here?" She didn't recognize that high freight rates made that strategy unworkable.

Only a few people were encouraging. Most people tend to think in terms of negatives—an interesting psychological phenomenon. People like to tell you why you should not do things. My response is, "Don't think in those terms. If you dwell on the negative, it will come to pass. Think instead in terms of what you want to do, and what you have to do to accomplish what you want to do."

Negative advice did not deter me in the slightest. I was sure of what we were doing. I have sometimes said, not entirely facetiously, that confidence is a great substitute for knowledge. Sometimes, you can know too much and discourage yourself from action. In the 1940s and 1950s, advantage went to those who acted. Those who waited often got buried.

I went to Kansas City to find a plant we could rent cheaply. I found one for $125 a month in a beat-up old warehouse district, where most of the buildings had been vacated during the depression. It was a four- or five-story building. We needed high-pressure steam, and this plant had a very old boiler. I had an insurance company check the boiler. Their inspector said, "Andersen, you can't run this at any more than eight or ten pounds per square inch of pressure. This is really a low-pressure boiler." I was not going to take that for an answer. I said, "Would you do this: Would you let us go ahead if we promise that once a year, you can come back and check our boiler's safety?"

On that basis, we rented the building, old boiler and all. It occurred to me that we might want to buy the building someday. The realtor insisted that I meet with the building's owner to discuss that possibility. The owner was an amenable fellow, but he did not seem very shrewd in handling his affairs. He proposed an option to buy at a fixed price during the term of the lease. Then he turned to me and said, "What do you think the price ought to be?" "Usually, a rule of thumb is that a month's rent is 1 percent of the value of the building. So, at $125 a month rent, the normal rule of thumb would be that that building is worth $12,500," I said. He said, "Okay, that's all right with me."

So we got the building for $125 a month and an option to buy at $12,500. We moved in. It was a narrow, tall building, not ideal, but we made it go. Two of our St. Paul people transferred to Kansas City. One was Robert E. Foley, who became the Kansas City manager. The other was John T. Spaniol, who was to run the plant. Bob Foley had been a salesman. John Spaniol had been a process man under Burgess. They were to hire the rest of the help they needed there.

Our plan was to reach a break-even point financially in Kansas City as soon as possible and then to organize that plant as a separate corporation and give Foley and Spaniol the option to acquire equity, up to 25 percent for Bob Foley and 15 percent for John Spaniol. Majority control would remain with the parent company. That became our pattern with later expansions. I thought an opportunity for an equity share was important to recruiting and retaining good people. It would give them a sense of participation in the growth of the company.

Our engineer in St. Paul, Fred Greenham, went to Kansas City to help install equipment. He performed so well that we gave him $500 in stock when the Kansas City plant incorporated. When he came back from one trip there, he told me about an incident on the train: "You know how the men on the train get together in the smoker room in the morning to shave and get ready, and everybody is talking. They talk about where they're going and what they're doing. Somebody asked me what I was up to. I said I was getting a plant going in Kansas City. One of the fellows said, 'Are you one of the owners of the company?' I was just about to say, 'Oh, no, of course not,' but I stopped and thought for a moment. I said, 'Yes, I am one of the owners of the company.' Elmer, I felt so good about that." That story confirmed for me that our equity policy was having its intended effect.

After Mr. Fuller sold his remaining shares to me in 1944. N. C. Stork, the treasurer, and Ray Burgess offered me their few shares too. I bought them. For a short time, I owned 100 percent of H. B. Fuller Company, but in 1945, equity sharing became the rule at H. B. Fuller. I came to feel strongly that if things in a business are going to be good for anybody, they have got to be good for everybody. Otherwise, the business is not secure.

That applies to the nation as well as to business. We are in a dangerous position in our country when poverty is on the increase, and the gap between those who have and those who have not grows wider.

Foley performed well in Kansas City. He came from a fine Irish family in Aitkin, Minnesota. He made friends, including a banker who became interested in some young fellows from Minnesota who were trying to get something going.

When we had sales meetings in Kansas City, we would make a contest of cold calls on potential customers. Whoever sold the least had to pay for the dinner that night. All of us would spend the whole day calling on potential customers. Calling on existing customers was not allowed. During one such call, I tried to convince someone to try our case-sealing adhesive in place of silicate of soda, a cheaper and less effective product. The man finally said he was willing to try a five-gallon pail at the barrel price.

I said, "I'd really like to send you a fifty-five-gallon drum, on approval. If you use five gallons of it and you don't like it, you can send it back. You're going to like it. It's going to work. A fifty-five-gallon drum is the lot that you ought to be ordering." "Listen, young man," he said. "You come in here brand new. You've got a new company. We're willing to help you, and I'm willing to give you a five-gallon pail order to try out your product, and you aren't satisfied. What's the matter with you?" I grinned and said, "I'll tell you. I'm in a contest. I've got some buddies out here selling, too. I need

a fifty-five-gallon drum order, or I'm going to be stuck for dinner tonight."
He was a good sport. "Okay," he said. "I'll take a fifty-five-gallon drum
on trial."

We used to play tricks on each other. One Friday night, we seemed to
have a hard time getting our business done. John Spaniol repeatedly raised
questions that kept our meeting going. Our rule was that we had to finish
our business before we went to dinner. We would start a meeting at 5 P.M.
and be through at 7 or 8 or 9, but even if it ran quite late, we would not eat
until we finished. That night, it was about 11:45 when we got done. Then, it
suddenly dawned on me: "John, you old son-of-a-gun. You didn't want to
go to dinner on Friday. You wanted to go to dinner on Saturday." He was a
Catholic, and he couldn't have meat on Friday. He grinned. "I was just
dreaming about that big steak," he said.

Our team—all young men, all trying to build their careers along with
our business—had such harmony and confidence in each other. We just
blossomed.

But getting established in Kansas City was not easy. Adhesives are tricky,
and they are an important part of a manufacturing or food processing operation. If a customer was getting along well with the product he was using,
he did not want to change. Most adhesives users in Kansas City were buying products from Chicago. Finally, an incident there opened things up for
us. A truck strike erupted in Chicago. Shipments to Kansas City stopped.
Suddenly, our phone began to ring. The voice on the line would say, "Do
you remember that sample you sent? That worked pretty well. I think we'd
like to try a little more of it."

Materials restrictions during World War II also presented a challenge for
us in Kansas City. To get the materials to start a plant, a business needed to
have been assigned a high priority by the federal government, and to apply
for permission to proceed. That took a lot of time—and just as we never
had much money in those days, neither did we have much time. I was sure
we were going to be approved, because we were producing a product that
was useful to the military. So, I began to apply the priority we had been assigned in St. Paul when ordering material for Kansas City, before it had
been approved for our new location. On the day before we were going to
open the Kansas City plant, approval of the priority level we had been seeking came through. Our sins were wiped away.

Meanwhile, we acquired a big wartime customer in Indianapolis. Ben
Fuller, the grandson of the company's founder and son of my former boss,
was interested in relocating. I asked him to go to Indiana and explore the

possibility of basing his sales work there, rather than in St. Paul. He went to Indianapolis and announced that he would stay.

But he was soon in Cincinnati, the site we had chosen for our third plant. It was a broadly diversified city, full of adhesives customers. In 1944, we rented a six-story building with a rare water-powered elevator. Ben Fuller became general manager of that new Fuller operation, and Fred Greenham again engineered the building's rehabilitation into an adhesives factory. We bought the building in 1945 with $3,300 down and a $7,500 loan. Just over a year later, the Cincinnati operation was in the black and became a separate corporate entity.

Then, in one twelve-month period in 1947 and 1948, we started two plants, Atlanta and San Francisco. We were moving fast, we were stretching our human capital thin, and we were short of money. Ray Burgess, our senior plant man, and Hazel Strese, from our front office, moved to Atlanta to start the plant there. Ray was a dour Scotsman from New England, as straight and true and honest as could be. He wrote a letter I saved through the years. It read: "Elmer, I can't go on the way we're going. I can't be ordering material and not know whether I'm going to be able to pay for it. Our funds are so short. I just can't function that way. If we can't keep all these places going that we're starting, let's close them so that we're solid in what we're doing."

I wrote back: "Dear Ray. You certainly shouldn't be under the stress that you are. It's unnecessary. We're enclosing a check to increase your balance at the bank. You know, Ray, the way we work is that we order raw material; we hurry up and convert it to adhesive; we hurry up and sell it; then we hurry up and collect, so we can pay for what we bought. That's what business is all about. Sometimes, there's a little lag of time in the operation. We're going to pay our bills. I have to tell you that at the time you were writing about your bank account, you had more in your account in Atlanta than we did here in St. Paul."

Meanwhile, in California, a man who had been with National Starch and Chemical applied to join us, and we hired him. His name was Dougald Barthelmess. He was as daring as Ray Burgess was cautious. He was always pressing me to spend more. I had to call him and tell him, "Doug, we're so pressed for money that we can't put any more into California. If you can't make it go with what you've got now, we'll just have to close it up and re-open it at some later time. We're spread too thin, and it's now getting dangerous." "Okay. I'll try and make it go with what we have," he said—and somehow, he did. But I always believed—though he never told me and I never asked him—that he put in some of his own money to keep the San Francisco plant going.

He had more difficulty in 1951, when the San Francisco plant was destroyed by fire. But Barthelmess hired a contractor who knew how to hustle. Sixteen days after the fire, the still roofless plant began producing glue again.

About a year later, Barthelmess started agitating for the establishment of a plant in Portland. "Elmer," he would say, "the freight rate from San Francisco to Portland is terrible. We're competing with Seattle. We've got to get a plant going in Portland." "Dougald, we can't think about that now," I said. I told him to wait six months. Two months later, he was on the phone again, begging to begin operations in Portland. That went on every month until six months had passed. When I finally gave him the OK, I heard him breathe a sigh of relief over his phone. He said, "Boy, am I glad! We're making the first batch tomorrow." That was the spirit of the enterprise.

H. B. Fuller Company was doing a lot of hiring in those years. I gave the plant managers great latitude in hiring the personnel they needed. In fact, I gave them a free hand in most things. I told them: "If you want to know what I think about anything, call and ask me. If you know what you want to do or what you ought to do, go ahead and do it. Don't bother to ask me. If you decide you want to ask me, and what I tell you is contrary to your own judgment, use your judgment. I won't hold it against you if it goes wrong. I don't want to be looking over your shoulder telling you what to do. You're the manager. You decide."

I did not want the local managers burdened by a lot of policies set in St. Paul. My instructions were never to answer a customer's question, or refuse their request, by saying "That's company policy." I told managers to explain their reasons for doing things a certain way. If they found their standard practices made no sense for a particular customer, they should change their practices.

I always wanted to hire people who I believed had the potential to be a manager in some part of the operation. I wanted people who could grow and develop along with the business. I liked to get college graduates, but the main thing I looked for was character. I wanted somebody who was honest, trusting, decent, and caring toward other people.

I would hire a college graduate and try to convince him to work for a time in the plant. I said, "If you're going to have a future in this company, you've got to know the business. The way to know the business is to get your hands in the glue out in the plant, help pack five-gallon pails, and

Arne and Jennie Johnson Andersen, about 1898.

Elmer Lee Andersen in his baptismal gown, 1909.

Arnold, Elmer, and Marvin Andersen at Lake Michigan Park in Muskegon, about 1916.

Elmer and his family gather on his confirmation day, in May 1924, on the lawn of a friend's home near Our Savior's Lutheran Church in Muskegon. *From left:* Arnold, Caroline, Jennie, Elmer, and Marvin Andersen.

Elmer's high school graduation portrait, 1926.

Eleanor Anne Johnson, age six.

Gustav Johnson, Eleanor's father.

Elizabeth Johnson, Eleanor's mother.

Elmer upon graduation from the University of Minnesota, 1931.

Elmer and Eleanor on their wedding day, September 1, 1932.

Grace Lutheran Church, as it looked when Elmer and Eleanor were members.

Elmer Andersen and Harvey Fuller Jr. outside the H.B. Fuller Company's new plant on Eagle Street in St. Paul, 1937.

H. B. Fuller employees gather at a party at the Andersens' Deer Lake Cottage in July 1937. *Standing from left:* Betsy Fuller, Ben Fuller, Cynthia Burgess, Elmer holding Tony, Eleanor; *seated on bench:* Ray Burgess, Harvey Fuller, Emma Fuller, Bess Burgess; *seated on grass,* Barbara Fuller.

Boy Scout Tony Andersen, about 1946.

Seventeen-year-old Julian Andersen as Bob Cratchit in a production of
A Christmas Carol at St. Anthony Park Lutheran Church.

Young equestrian Emily Andersen.

The Andersen family in 1954: Elmer and Eleanor with Tony, nineteen; Julian, twelve; and Emily, almost nine.

State Sen. Elmer L. Andersen, 1957.

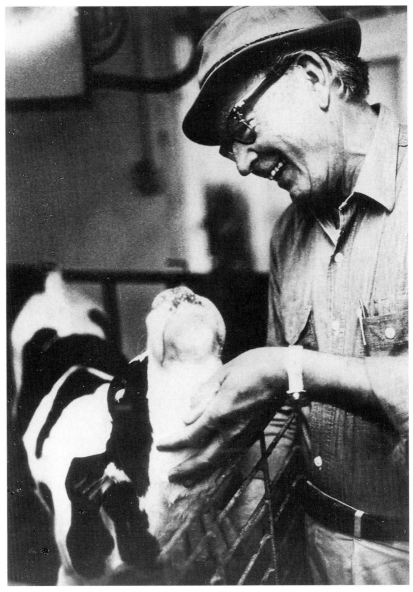

After Elmer established the Deer Lake dairy farm in 1953, his weekends were consumed with the chores and pleasures of a dairyman.

learn how our products are made and why they are made that way." Many of them would not do it, but those who did, did well.

I also regarded sales work as basic training for managers. Maybe it was because I had been a salesman myself, but I always thought selling was the most important aspect of the business. I agreed with the founder and publisher of *Parade* magazine, Red Motley, when he said, "Nothing happens until somebody sells something." Learn to sell, and you can learn everything else.

I never liked to let anyone go. At first, when someone I hired was not working out, I thought it was a failure on my part—that I had made a poor decision in hiring or had failed to adequately train or nurture him or her. Finally I came to understand that it did people no favor to keep them on when they were not going to advance with us. It was kinder to them to release them and help them relocate in something more promising for them.

One such case involved a young man whom I liked very much personally. I told him, "Allen, I've liked you as much as anybody we ever hired, but it isn't working out. This isn't your place. What I'd like to do is give you six months of time with pay to do whatever you need to do to discover what you want for yourself. You're a wonderful guy. You ought to be doing something important. Go find out what it is."

He came back about three months later. He said, "Elmer, you were nudging me in a way that you didn't realize. I have felt a call for the ministry for a long time. I finally decided I had better go into it, so I'm going into the ministry." About four or five years later, when he had finished his studies and had a pastorate and a wife and family, he came to see me again to report that things were going well. I was so pleased to help someone like him find himself and mature and develop.

Every potential manager I hired was a man—even during the war years, when industrial doors were opening for women. At that time, we simply did not think of women in management or factory positions. We employed women in office positions, where they had substantial responsibilities. At that time, few women prepared to have other careers, because opportunities were not available to them. Now, fifty years later, the rigid gender roles that were taken for granted then seem discriminatory. That is one indication of how much American society changed in the second half of the twentieth century. Eleanor has helped me convert my thinking about women's roles and has taught me a great deal of gender sensitivity.

When I considered hiring a married man at Fuller, I always would seek an opportunity to meet his wife. I continue the practice today at ECM, though now the job candidates are often women, and I am asking to meet husbands as well as wives. A supportive spouse is terribly important to a person's business success.

Our expansion plan after World War II was to start a new plant as soon as the last one we started was breaking even. Propelled by a strong post-war economy, we were moving fast—and we were working our money over-time. After Atlanta and San Francisco came Dallas, Memphis, Buffalo, Newark, and Waltham, Massachusetts. By 1960, H. B. Fuller had fourteen adhesives plants—two of them outside the United States—three specialty plants, and eight warehouses.

We had also dramatically expanded our line of products, thanks to the top-notch lab work that was occurring not only in St. Paul but at nearly every Fuller plant around the country. By the mid-1950s, the Fuller line in-cluded casein glues for wood products, polyvinyl acetate glues for furniture and cabinet manufacturing, and urea formaldehyde resins—all of which sold well in the building boom of the 1950s. We developed an epoxy resin adhesive sold under the name Resiweld that was extremely strong, and was used in industries from aircraft manufacturing to electronics. Other Fuller adhesives went into products as diverse as cigarettes, frozen juice cans, paper bags, and ice cream containers.

By our lights, Fuller was flourishing, but then we were more interested in sales and growth than we were in profit. Fuller was never the darling of the analysts, who thought we should pay more attention to the bottom line. Our goal was to double our sales every five years. That worked out to 14.4 percent sales growth per year. I made a chart projecting growth at that pace, plotted against our actual growth as it occurred. The lines nearly matched. That pleased me more than fat profits could have.

It seemed we were always short of ready cash, but we compensated with creative financing. The option we had to buy our first expansion building in Kansas City became important in one such ploy, when we needed cash for expansion in the mid-1950s. The option in Kansas City was fixed at $12,500. I thought, if we would buy the building, then sell it to somebody and rent it back, we could generate a little cash. I exercised our option, then went to an insurance company in Kansas City to try to sell the plant. They looked it over, then asked us how much we wanted for it. I said, "$50,000." That amount did not seem to surprise the insurance company officials. They were thinking about the building's revenue-generating potential. Soon I had sold for $50,000 a building I had purchased not long before for $12,500. With the $37,500 difference, H. B. Fuller moved in 1955 from an outdated plant in Newark to our first brand-new one in Linden, New Jersey. It was a modern, single-story structure designed by Bob Foley, our first manager in Kansas City. That same design went into a 28,000-square-foot building in St. Paul's Midway area that became H .B. Fuller's corporate headquarters in 1959.

When N. C. Stork retired in 1951, we needed a new finance officer. I called our auditing firm, Broeker and Hendrickson, and asked if they would be terribly offended if I approached their associate Dave Croonquist, who had done our audit the previous three years. With their permission, I called Dave. "I'd love to join your company," he said. That was the beginning of an important association for Fuller, and a dear friendship for me. One of Dave's important accomplishments was establishing a tie with the Mutual Life Insurance Company of New York as our lenders. Dave was a hawk on monitoring our adherence to loan covenants. If it looked like we were heading into difficulty, he would go to New York to discuss the matter with Mutual Life.

Our expansion strategy kept the competition baffled. But we encouraged their confusion by intentionally spreading misleading signals about our affairs. They thought we were struggling mightily to keep all the new plants afloat, when I knew we had a lead-pipe cinch.

The previous leaders in the adhesives industry operated in New York, Chicago, and San Francisco. They had huge plants and big established investments. They could not start a new plant. What would they do with their big old plant? By comparison, we were popping around the country and setting up small plants in lively little markets. We kept our real estate costs down. We did not have large freight charges to pass on to the customer. National Adhesives, the biggest company in the industry, was very focused on making money. They maintained their prices at a high level, even when their share of the market dropped, in order to make more money. That was a blessing for little companies like Fuller.

Frank Greenwall, the president of National Adhesives, was a great one for keeping tabs on other glue companies. Fuller irritated him because he could not figure us out. At one Adhesives Manufacturers' Association meeting, he asked, "Elmer, does your company have any policies at all? Is there anything that you stand for as a company?" "There sure is!" I said. "We stand for a lot of things." "We find such a difference in your operation from one place to another. We don't know what to make of your company." I said, "One policy is that the manager of the local plant is responsible to serve the customers of his area, and do what is necessary to do so. If the manager in Atlanta does something different than is being done in Kansas City, it is because Atlanta is different from Kansas City. We don't serve a rule of law set in the general headquarters"—as I knew National did. They had firm companywide policies. As companies get bigger, they tend to want to standardize. They have rules that everybody is supposed to follow. I have always rebelled against rules. "Our policy," I told Frank Greenwall, "is that we serve customers."

I had to explain that to National Biscuit Company once, after Fuller had become a big supplier of their adhesives. They had a laboratory that took samples from all their plants. When I visited the lab, I was asked why Fuller products with the same name were so different in different plants. "We get the same number product, 228 Paste, and it's different from the samples that come in," the lab technician said. "Don't you have any standards as to how you make it?" I said, "Our standard is to meet the local condition. Weather can affect how adhesives work. Humidity can affect paper stock and how well it takes adhesives. Our managers locally are authorized to make such minor adjustments in the product, to make it work well. We work with the machine operators in the plants. We could have a standard product that you might think is wonderful, but it might be miserable for the people in your plant in some other part of the country. We keep your plants running. We don't sell products. We sell service."

The competition was stuck, and we knew it. They could match neither our service nor our price. We were a long way from it in the 1940s, but we already knew then that we would someday be the industry's leader.

Business Priorities

ANY BUSINESS OUGHT TO HAVE three things clearly understood by all those it touches. It needs a philosophy, a guiding sense of its role in society, its values and its purpose. It needs a mission, a clear statement of its goals. And it needs a strategy specifying how it intends to accomplish its mission. Many businesses focus on strategy without giving any thought to philosophy or much attention to mission. Those businesses might enjoy some success, but I think it is bound to be short-lived. A solid grounding in philosophy and mission are what see a business through the years. Those ideas are what give even a far-flung business a personality and an integrity all its own.

I began to think about what constitutes sound business philosophy well before I went to work for H. B. Fuller Company. I thought a good deal about Fuller's mission and strategy when I was an employee there. But once I took charge of Fuller and saw its potential for growth, those ideas became more than abstractions. I saw plainly that if Fuller remained one little glue plant in St. Paul, it soon would wither and blow away. The cost of freight for our adhesives was so high that even selling in Chicago was prohibitive. As the depression ended and the economy began to grow again, national trading was becoming the standard. We had to become a national company. We could not do it by shipping. We had to do it with branch plants.

Fuller's mission, I determined, was to become the number one adhesives company, first in the nation, then beyond. Our strategy would be to locate branch plants within three hundred miles of any customer in the United States. That was an ambitious strategy, but one I believed was necessary and achievable. I pored over and over this in my mind, until by 1943 I was so ready to start expanding that I could hardly stand it.

We would do it, I decided, with a corporate philosophy centered on service. From the start of our period of rapid growth, I wanted to be able to articulate our philosophy clearly and impart it to the many new people we would be hiring. Knowing our philosophy, and believing in it, was essential to our success. A strong and appealing philosophy is what would energize and motivate our people, and give the name H. B. Fuller a reputation for a certain quality of performance, no matter where we located.

Our corporate philosophy was built around four priorities in a definite order. Our highest priority, we determined, should be service to the customer. Anything the customer wanted should be seen as an opportunity for us to provide it. We used to get calls on Friday nights from a customer saying, "Gee, the boss decided we have to run through the weekend, and we don't have enough glue to last us. Could you get us a barrel over here?" Mueller Can and Tube, a big customer, would make those Friday night calls with some frequency. We never refused them. We would get a shift of workers to come down on Friday night, or Saturday, or Sunday, to meet their needs.

I would say to our people, "Think of it as an opportunity and be happy about it, happy that somebody had an emergency that gives us an opportunity to show that we'll do anything to serve a customer." I tried to instill the idea that what we were selling was not a product; we were selling a service. We were selling trouble-free adhesive operation. Our customers should have the assurance that their adhesives were worry-free products. If they had trouble and called us, we would do whatever was necessary to get them out of trouble. Our philosophy was to make customer service number one.

Number two was that the company should exist deliberately for the benefit of the people associated in it. I never liked the word *employee*. It intimated a difference in class within a plant. We always used the word *associate*. We wanted to be associated. We were all in the same group. We took an interest in each other's families. We were going to help our people and their families get an education. We were going to help them fulfill their lives. We really cared about them, and we were going to seek ways to show it.

When we opened our plant in Kansas City in 1943, we looked for a way to convey the feeling of caring for each other that we had in St. Paul. How could we let our new workers know we really cared about them? We struck on the notion of making each employee's birthday a personal holiday. I wrote to the Kansas City employees—and told the St. Paul employees, for we did it for them too—saying, "Washington was important to us, and so was Lincoln; but so are you. We want *you* to have a holiday. It's your holiday to think about yourself and your family and how you're doing and how you're doing with us. If you get any ideas of how we can better fit into your life and contribute to it, let us know."

Fuller may have been the first in the nation to give employees a birthday holiday. When we announced the new policy, Ben Fuller was already on hand in Cincinnati, where Fuller opened a plant in 1944. He gave the story to the *Cincinnati Inquirer.* The *Wall Street Journal* picked it up and ran the story with a box on the front page, "New Holiday Invented." It was the first time Fuller was recognized for innovative employee benefits—but not the last.

We provided health care coverage beginning in 1942, with the total cost borne by the company. I reasoned this way: If we have health care and the employees pay for it, they have to make money. They have to pay for it out of their paycheck. Before they get their paycheck, they have to pay taxes. If we pay it, it is a pre-tax expense to us. When the employee pays, it costs him more than it does us.

Not long after providing health coverage, I extended the benefit to our retirees. The usual employee health insurance plan ended coverage when a worker retired. I thought that was ridiculous. It was wrong for people to spend their whole careers working for a company, only for the company to shut off their health care when they need it most. I went to our provider, and I said, "We want to increase our coverage to cover retirees." The insurance man said, "You can't do that. It will raise your costs tremendously." This was two decades before Medicare was established. Employer-provided health coverage for retirees was almost unheard of. "Look, we're going to do it," I said. "If you don't do it, somebody else is going to do it. Let's talk about it, and see if there isn't some basis on which we can try it out. Maybe it isn't going to be as bad as you think it is." Finally, they agreed, provided that retirees were not more than a small percentage of our group. We were hiring young people at such a pace that our retirees were always within the requisite small percentage of our total group enrollment.

It would warm my heart at Christmas parties when somebody would come up and tearfully say, "Elmer, I can't tell you what that health coverage has meant for us. Dad was sick this year and was in the hospital. You know how the bill can mount up. It was $5,000. The part we paid was $32.40." Of all the employee benefits we provided, I thought that was one of the finest.

I was equally proud in the 1980s when Tony, then Fuller's CEO, extended health insurance benefits to retirees' spouses. That was an exceptional and generous provision, one that again set Fuller apart.

We wanted to do something special about vacations. Vacations are often taken for granted. You serve so many years with one week's paid vacation. Stay longer, and you get two, and then maybe three weeks. We decided to go one step farther. We devised what we called the "bonus vacation." If a person served for ten years, they were given a bonus vacation in that tenth year, and another every fifth year thereafter. The bonus was an extra two weeks of time off, plus $500, free of deductions.

We used to bring all the employees in a plant together a few times a year to share what was going on, and what we were thinking of doing. Beginning in about 1970, I also videotaped a briefing to employees, so the same message would reach all our plants. It was at one of those sessions with employees that I unveiled the bonus vacation. I could see some eyes widen and then roll when I said, "There are a couple of catches to this." Sure, their expressions seemed to say, he says he is going to give us two weeks extra vacation and $500, and now is he going to take it away. "There are two provisions that we expect you to adhere to," I said. "One is that you can't take the extra time to stay home and paint the house. Two, you can't take the extra money to catch up on car payments or other bills. You've got to take the time and the money and go have fun." We really meant it. That is what our people needed. I wanted to start them dreaming about the possibilities. I said, "Do something. We permit accruing vacation time, so when you know that your bonus vacation is coming, add a few weeks to it. Go to Europe. Go do what you never dreamed you'd be able to do. You're an important person. You're as much entitled to go to Europe as anybody else."

The bonus vacation became very popular. It had an especially strong effect on Dick Koch, a foreman in the St. Paul plant. Dick was a wonderful man who decided with his wife early in their married life that they were going to devote themselves to their family and have as many children as came to them. They had fourteen children. After the bonus vacation was announced, Dick came to me and said, "Do you know what you've done to me, Elmer?" I said, "Dick, what in the world have I done to you?" He assumed a brusque manner. "Our kids have been reading *News and Views*"— our company publication—"and they found out about this bonus vacation plan. They've decided that Mother and I, who have never gone away on a vacation, have to go on vacation. They're determined that we've got to go to Hawaii. We've had to give in. The oldest ones say they are big enough to look after the family. They say that after all these years of caring for them, it's high time we got off and had a vacation on our own. So, we're going to Hawaii. That's what you've done to me."

We never had a more devoted fellow than Dick Koch. I associate him and his family with another benefit Fuller offered—college scholarships for employees' family members. A number of the Koch children went to college through the Fuller Scholarship.

Every Fuller associate was asked to write a letter from time to time, reporting how he or she was doing personally. We asked, do you like your work? What job would you rather have? I was surprised when a couple of plant men wrote that they dreamed of being salesmen. They were the most unlikely prospects to be salesmen that I could imagine. But I was not one to squelch ambition. "If you think you can do it, you're sure going to have the opportunity," I told them. One of the two did not like selling, with its long hours and paperwork, as much as he expected. He went back to the plant. The other fellow, Jim Kadidlo, did so well that he was Fuller's first salesman to accomplish a million dollars in sales on his own effort. You never know where talent hides.

To aid our salesmen, we provided them with company cars, complete with air conditioning. Air conditioning was new and expensive in the 1940s, but I thought it would be a good investment, so that our salesmen could reach a date fresh and cool, instead of hot and wrinkled. Our first company cars were for salesmen; I did not have one until much later.

I always tried to favor the working men. For example, when we started our pension plan, it was for incomes up to $30,000. It did not cover the full incomes of those who made more. We thought they were capable of putting some money away for their own retirement, while the lower-income people would have more difficulty saving. I was conscious of wanting to treat all Fuller workers equitably, and to do as well as we could for people with lower wages.

We took great pride in offering our people a generous, enlightened package of benefits. Those benefits paid off. No company ever had such fiercely enthusiastic and loyal people as Fuller did. They were people the company could depend on in times of trouble to make whatever sacrifice was needed to keep the company strong.

One year soon after the war, the business was not going so well. I was a little worried about giving a pay increase when I thought the company was not going to have a good year. I called all the people together around the first of the year. I said, "I know it's been customary for years now to have a pay adjustment the first of the year. There's not going to be one this year. I'm really concerned. We've done pretty well, but we have to be careful. Things can turn against us, and we have quite a bit at stake. I don't feel comfortable adding to the company's expense right now. I hope you'll go along with that. But let me tell you this: if at the end of the first quarter, I'm proven wrong and things are going better than I expected, we'll have pay increases retroactive to the first of the year."

I cannot say my news was enthusiastically received, but it was accepted. Our people understood the need to redouble their efforts in sales and cost efficiency. I think they appreciated being told forthrightly and directly what our circumstances were. As a result, at the end of the first quarter, we did do better than I had planned. I was good as my word. Fuller issued pay raises retroactive to the beginning of the year.

In 1968, we were on the verge of becoming a public company. Underwriters interviewed us to gather information for potential investors. They asked about our employee benefits. When I got halfway through my recitation, one of them spoke up: "That's enough! You have so many benefits, people won't want to buy your stock. They'll want a job!"

Fuller's third priority was to make money. To survive, you have to make money. To grow, you need money. To conduct research and develop new products, you must have money. The need for money can be desperate at times. But corporations must put the quest for money in its proper place. Excessive pressure for profit is what causes too many businesses to err in their treatment of customers and workers.

Too much focus on money also distorts good judgment, I have found. Students make a terrible mistake if they decide not to press on in higher education because of its cost. Business executives err when they decide to pass up a promising opportunity because of lack of ready capital. When a goal is worthwhile, there is almost always a way to pursue it, even when money is scarce. Decisions should not be governed by monetary concerns. I have often advised people, "Don't think about how much something costs. Think about what you want to do. If you want to go to Harvard University, decide you're going to go, and go. Do whatever is necessary to get there." I recognize that what I am saying may sound impractical. But I have found so often that poor choices are based on a shortage of money, when in fact it is a shortage of resolve that is the real issue. The decision—making a decision—is crucial to success.

I often told shareholders at Fuller's annual meeting what our priorities were. I would say, "If your main purpose for being here is making money, you could maybe make more elsewhere." Some would blink at my candor. But if they stayed long enough, I could usually make believers out of them.

Our philosophy did not leave out service to the larger community. We put it in fourth place, behind service to customers, our associates, and the bottom line. Community service cannot be paramount to a business, but it ought not to be omitted, as it too often is. Business must concern itself with the larger society—for reasons of self-interest, if nothing else. The quality of life in a company's hometown is important to that business's welfare and future. I think every businessperson has a responsibility to contribute something to the community, through government service, involvement with schools, or charitable volunteer efforts.

That four-point philosophy was the foundation of our efforts, first at Fuller and later at ECM Publishing. I also carried this philosophy to the other corporate boards on which I served. At various times through the years, I was a member of the boards of the Hormel Company in Austin, First Trust Company of St. Paul, Minnesota Mutual Life Insurance Company of St. Paul, and the National Association of Manufacturers. The latter organization was not known for enlightened or liberal thinking, on any issue. I was surprised to be invited to join its governing board. But I was told that its leaders wanted me to provide the board with some diversity of opinion.

I am well aware that my corporate philosophy is at odds with the thinking of many, if not most, American businesspeople. Many businesspeople maintain that a company is in business, first and foremost, to make money. I find that thinking shortsighted—as much so today as it was fifty years ago. This nation cannot become stronger, in either economic or human terms, unless its businesses put their customers and workers first. Businesses are key to building the nation's human resources. If America's people are forced to live and work in an environment of poverty, poor housing, inadequate training, and limited opportunity, the whole nation will suffer. If they live and work in an environment that encourages them to be at their best, the whole nation will benefit.

Family Man

H. B. FULLER WAS NOT ALL that was expanding in 1946. On December 7, Emily Elizabeth Andersen was born. She is our only daughter, and the only one of our three children not to have the middle name Lee, which is my middle name. Emily was named for her grandmother Elizabeth Johnson.

The name Lee recurs in our family tree quite often. We have grandchildren named Nathan Lee and Benjamin Lee. But nobody wanted to name a baby Elmer! I have noticed that my first name does not make any top-ten popularity lists.

I once asked Minnesota's other Gov. Elmer Anderson, the late C. Elmer Anderson of Brainerd, what in the world the *C* stood for that he would rather be called Elmer. I supposed that I was one of the few people who could ask him that question without giving offense. He told me his first name was Clyde, the same as his father's, and that when he was born, it was decided he would be called C. Elmer instead of Clyde Junior. He is survived by a son, Clyde Elmer Anderson III, who is known as Clyde.

Our family and our business grew simultaneously. That meant that there were times when I had to sacrifice one for the sake of the other, or to spend time on one at the expense of the other. But Eleanor and I worked hard to provide a strong, loving home for the children. Travel became a permanent part of business for me, but I made an effort to join in family activities when I was home.

In 1934, Eleanor's parents bought a farm on Deer Lake in Polk County, Wisconsin, that became a focal point for family fun. The Johnsons built three cottages on the property with the intention that one would be available for each of their three children and the children's families. There were summers when Eleanor and the children were there all week long, and I would make the fifty-mile commute from there to St. Paul, driving to the city on Monday mornings and back again on Friday nights. We could not afford expensive entertainment when the children were small, but we had the outdoors. The children had the fun of hiking, fishing, boating, and swimming. They all came to love nature, as Eleanor and I do.

Even as a small boy, Tony loved to fish. He became a fly fisherman and learned to tie his own flies—a skill I never possessed. When we were driving back and forth to Deer Lake, if we saw a dead skunk or muskrat on the highway, we would have to stop and clip off some of the animal's hairs for him to use in fly tying. He caught a nice big bass once on a fly that he had tied himself, and we were so impressed that we had it mounted. He still has that fish.

Tony was an outdoor athlete, always eager to learn new skills. He was quite small when I tried to teach him to ski in the backyard of the Hendon House, where there was a rather steep little hill. I had never skied myself, but I thought I knew how it was done. I told him to hold his weight forward, so his weight could pull him downhill, but not so far forward that he would lose his balance. He said, "You know, Dad, I think I'd understand it better if you did it." There was nothing for me to do but to put on his short, child-sized skis and give it a go. Of course, the skis shot out from under me, and I landed on my back. I thought for more than a second that I had broken something. Tony got a big kick out of my antics. Somehow, he did learn how to ski—in fact, he excelled in both skiing and ski jumping. One of his joys at Deer Lake was water skiing. As he grew older, he taught his siblings and cousins how to ski. Now he is teaching his grandchildren.

Our second son, Julian, was six when our neighbor Tom Barnard suggested a new family activity: "Elmer, it's about time you and your boys had a trip in the canoe country." I confessed that I had never been to Minnesota's Boundary Waters Canoe Area—in fact, I had never paddled a canoe. But Tom persisted. He said, "I've made a lifetime career of canoeing. I'd like to take you and the boys on a trip." Tony was twelve and a seasoned outdoorsman. I knew he would love such a venture. I was not as sure about little Julian. But Tom was reassuring. "I know the canoe country and I know Julian, and I say, 'He's ready.'"

We accepted Tom's invitation to join him and a military friend he had also invited. We had two canoes to transport three men and two boys. Julian was the cabin passenger. He sat in the middle of the canoe. He did not paddle, but he carried his own Duluth backpack, hiked over the portages, and had a wonderful time. From age six until his graduation from Carleton College, he visited Minnesota's canoe country every year. Later, he was joined on some of those trips by his sister, Emily. Though she was more than three years younger than Julian, she was an athletic girl who could carry a canoe at a young age.

Even when he was young, Julian showed good sense in traveling. In the wilderness canoe country, he was careful. He had a good memory for portage points. He would come to a lake that we had visited before, and know right where the portage was, even when I could spot no sign or landmark to point the way. He was a natural outdoorsman.

He spent several happy summers at the YMCA's Camp Widjiwagon near Ely, Minnesota. The camp gave Julian a wonderful experience when he was in high school. The camp set out to reenact a portion of Sir Alexander Mackenzie's 1789 exploration of Canada that ended at the Arctic Ocean. A team of three boys, all experienced, and a leader went out in two canoes. Julian was chosen for a segment of the voyage, Fort McMurray, Alberta, to La Ronge, Saskatchewan, a thirty-day journey. It was wild country. In one far-northern remote settlement, Lake Isle-a-la-Crosse, he came to a little trapper-hunter outpost and met a Catholic priest, Father Moreau. The boys helped the priest split wood and make other preparations for winter. Julian was drawn to Father Moreau.

Three years later, he announced that he and a friend, John Wilke, wanted to visit Father Moreau again. So, on their own this time, they paddled a canoe to a point near his village. They had corresponded with the priest and had agreed on a meeting point. They spent a couple of weeks with him. I think that was one of the most satisfying things Julian ever did as a boy. He much appreciated being permitted the freedom to do it.

When he moved to Seattle, Julian became a mountain climber, not only of Mount Rainier and the mountains nearby but also of the mountains of South America and Mexico. He climbed Mount Aconcagua, a famous peak between Argentina and Chile. He made it to the last stop before the summit, but stormy weather kept him from going for the top.

I never really worried about Julian, at any age. I knew he would never take a risk that he could not handle. Tony was more daring. Maybe that is why Tony experienced more injuries as a child. The only childhood emergency Julian ever had was the time he pulled a springform cake pan over his head and got it stuck. Eleanor called a neighbor, Lyle Haff, who solved the problem. I was out of town. I was also gone the time Tony fell against the radiator and needed stitches in his head. Eleanor remembers my absences when she recalls those moments.

As a father, I believed in letting my children take risks, follow their hearts, and become unique people. But I was also strict—at times, maybe too strict. I wanted them to behave and to obey. I wanted them to be on time. I wanted them to do their homework. I wanted them to be prudent and careful with money.

One day, a neighbor called. He said, "Elmer, do you know what Julian is doing at school?" I said, "Apparently, from the way you say it, I don't." "Ask him if he loans money to anybody. He's running a small loan business. Check on his interest rates," my tipster said. I talked to Julian that night. "Jul, do you ever loan money to any of your classmates?" "Yes," he said. "How does that come about?" "Oh, they want a dime for a candy bar, or a nickel or a quarter to get something. I usually have a little money, so I loan it to them." I asked, "Do you charge them interest?" "Yes, I charge them a little bit. If somebody wants to borrow a dime, I charge them a penny a day; so if they pay me back the next day, it only costs them a penny." "What if they don't pay you back the next day, do you remind them that their interest is counting up?" "No," he said. "I figure they should keep track of that."

I pointed out that on an annual basis, the interest he was charging on a ten-cent loan was 3,650 percent. "I really don't think you ought to charge your friends interest," I said. "If your buddies need a loan, loan them a little money, and don't charge them any interest. You'll have other opportunities to make money."

Julian had money to loan because he did not spend his money. He was prudent, as I had encouraged him to be. I once noticed a lot of change in his coin purse. I said, "Jul, isn't that quite a bit of money for you to be carrying around?" "Yes," he said. "It's been kind of piling up lately."

Julian was a more placid child than Tony was, and had a quick mind that absorbed a lot of what he heard and saw. When he was in kindergarten in 1947, his teacher asked him for his address. She was preparing the children to know that information, should they ever become lost. Julian replied, "I live in the Twelfth Precinct of the Tenth Ward." It was apparent what kind of household he came from!

When he moved from kindergarten to first grade, he was assigned a teacher named Miss Schneider, whom we came to highly respect. We asked Julian how he liked his new teacher. "Oh," he said, "she's wonderful. She even loves the naughty ones." How observant, I thought—and what a tribute to a teacher.

I enjoyed following the children's lessons and supplementing them with educational projects of my own invention. When Emily was grade-school age, I once told her that the world was full of useful and interesting information for her and that it was hers for the asking. To prove the point, I asked her to close her eyes, spin the globe, and let her finger come to rest on it. She did as I asked, and opened her eyes to find her finger pointing to the Falkland Islands, in the South Atlantic. I then told her to write a letter addressed to Postmaster, Falkland Islands, asking for information about the islands, their people, and their products.

She did as I suggested, and before long a large envelope full of brochures and fact sheets arrived from the British ministry in the Falklands, then a British possession. The bundle was accompanied by a polite letter suggesting that while the enclosed information was gladly supplied, further exchange of letters was not advisable! The official who complied with her request apparently was not interested in acquiring a young pen pal in St. Paul, Minnesota.

Our activities as a family included trips to the Minneapolis Institute of Art, visits with Eleanor's family, and church events. When the children were still small, we left our dear Grace University Lutheran Church and joined St. Anthony Park Lutheran, closer to home.

St. Anthony Park Lutheran Church did not sponsor a Boy Scout troop, but St. Anthony Park Congregational Church did. I had been a Boy Scout in Muskegon and thought it was a good program. So when Tony went into Boy Scouts, I went with him. I became scoutmaster of Troop 17 of St. Anthony Park Congregational Church.

Scouting gave Tony and me a terrific experience in the summer of 1952, when he was sixteen. We went to the Boy Scouts' first-ever National Jamboree, at Valley Forge, Pennsylvania. Five boys from our troop, a camping and canoeing group, attended the National Jamboree that year with me. Those five scouts still canoe together to this day—though now they call themselves "The Geezers." Their most recent trip was in 1999.

The Jamboree gathered fifty thousand scouts into more than six thousand campsites of eight scouts each. Each group of eight boys cooked its own food. I was on the sanitation committee for one district of this huge place. Our committee had a difficult task. We needed to make sure only fresh, untainted food was served, to avoid any dysentery or food poisoning. Convincing scouts to throw away what appeared to be unspoiled food was difficult. We told them, "Under ordinary conditions, this would be wasteful, but, here, there's a great hazard of infection and pollution." We had to doctor the drinking water with chlorine. If someone assigned to treat the water failed to do so, we were authorized to put a double-dose of chlorine in their water, to give them a good taste of the stuff. Hog farmers picked up the garbage early each morning. We had to be up around 4:30 or 5 A.M., to see that the garbage was picked up and to make sure it did not contain tin cans or bottles.

I was concerned about the condition of the campsite assigned to our boys at Valley Forge. When we examined it before pitching our tents, it was all poison ivy. We had to apply an anti–poison ivy spray before we could use the site. Some boys at the Jamboree were stung by poison ivy, but we managed to keep our patrol free of it.

Dwight Eisenhower spoke to the fifty thousand boys on the last night of the Jamboree. He was president of Columbia University and soon to become the Republican candidate for president of the United States. We thought of him not as a politician but as the great hero of the European victory in World War II. After he spoke, there were fireworks. It was a tremendously inspiring evening, and my first exposure to Eisenhower, whom I would come to know better in a few years.

Scouting was an important activity for Tony and me. I enjoyed much about it—the creed, the system of badges and awards, the exposure to nature, the inspiration to lead a life of service. I was part of the Indian Head Council leadership group for many years and received the Silver Beaver and Silver Antelope Awards for leadership.

When Julian was a small boy, he was part of a Cub Scout pack that met in our home on Hendon Avenue. But as he grew older, he chose to participate in the YMCA's youth programs, not the Boy Scouts. When Emily reached scouting age, Eleanor and Emily got involved with Camp Fire Girls. Her troop, too, met in our home.

I spent a lot of time teaching Sunday school and leading scout activities because I like working with younger people. I find them inspiring—and I enjoy trying to inspire them. Paul Ridgeway, Minnesota's extraordinary arranger of special events, helped me plan my ninetieth birthday party. He told me that when he was in sixth grade, his class visited the state capitol. When they came to the governor's office, I came out of my inner office and shook hands with every student. "I never forgot that," Ridgeway said. "That's why I did it," I replied. You do not know what seeds you plant when you reach out to a child.

Recently a high school boy called on us. He said he and fifteen other young people were trying to raise $5,000 for a library fund at a school district some distance from our home. He came because a friend of mine told him, "Elmer Andersen loves books. You ought to see Elmer."

He was a promising young fellow. I told him, "Keep your sights high. If there are sixteen of you raising money, $5,000 isn't a big enough goal. Get a bigger goal. Have you talked to the librarian? Tell her that her job depends on books, and she ought to give to the book fund. Go to everybody. Make lots of calls, and expect lots of money. You'll be disappointed at times, but you'll do better in the end if you raise your sights."

That is the message I tried to give young people, including our own three children: Raise your sights. The potential of every individual is so great. Most people's development does not begin to reach their potential. I think we have only a remote idea of what full human potential is. When people are inspired to greatness, they can do tremendous things.

A *Reader's Digest* article once advised, "Give your hobby its head." If there is something you really love to do, and you are doing something else for a living, make a change. Do what you love to do. I believe I was not an indulgent parent, but I tried to give my children a chance to do what they loved.

So when Emily developed a passion for horses as a young girl, and clung to that passion as she grew, I did not stand in the way of her becoming a horsewoman. Even when she was quite small, she showed indications of possessing both a love and a facility for riding. I used to take her for pony rides at Como Park when she was a toddler. Those rides, around and around, left her unsatisfied. "Well, you've had your horse ride," I said to her after one such excursion, when she could not have been older than three. "Yes, Daddy," she said, "but it wasn't a horse." She already wanted more.

Before long, the whole family was making Sunday excursions to riding stables. A man at one stable once said to me after watching us ride, "I suppose you know who is the natural rider in your family?" "No, I don't," I said—knowing only that it was not me. "Who is it?" "It's that little girl of yours. She rides like she grew out of a horse."

By her teenage years, Emily had became an accomplished rider. She was not interested in just riding through the countryside. She wanted to learn to ride competitively as an English horsewoman. That involves riding around the ring, going over jumps, measuring your gait, and watching your own posture and how your knees hug the horse. It is a challenging, disciplined way of riding.

Emily's hobby became an activity that involved Eleanor and the whole family. We would accompany her to horse shows. In the season, there are horse shows nearly every week, involving riders who are constantly trying to improve their performances. We came to know families who were well known in riding circles. And we were thrilled when Emily was able to outscore them in competitions, including the Minnesota State Fair. She succeeded because she has her mother's trait of persistence.

My one regret about Emily's riding career was that I did not buy one particular horse that she wanted. It was a $3,500 horse, for sale at the State Fair, and I thought that was too much money, even for a special animal. Not long afterward, she had an accident with the horse she already owned, and suffered a concussion. She came out all right, but I felt guilty. I thought, I should have bought that expensive horse. Maybe, if I had, this never would have happened. I never let money dictate family decisions after that. I thought, doggone it! If there is something we need, let's get it, and worry about the money some other time.

Each of our children found early interests that ran deep, and that they pursued into adulthood. For Tony, there was camping, skiing, canoeing, and one thing more—the H. B. Fuller Company. The little boy who loved to visit the Fuller plant with me on Saturday mornings stayed attached to the company as he grew. He was a natural businessman. He worked sporadically in the plant while he was a student at Macalester College, and then took an official job when he graduated in 1957.

We were emerging as a successful company then and were getting offers from would-be buyers. I would not so much as talk to anyone about selling Fuller. I did not want any rumors to start that would upset our people. But not long after Tony joined us full-time, the Corn Products Refining Company did what I had once advised them. They came to us, unsolicited, handed me an envelope, and said, "Call us if you're interested." The envelope contained a substantial offer for the company.

I called Tony. "We had better look at this," I said. "Tony, here's your opportunity. If we sold out, you could go into about any kind of business you wanted. You could have your own business, and do it in your own way." "No," he said. "Dad, all I want to do is stay with Fuller and keep going just as we are going. We're doing great. I just want to keep at it." He was faithful to his word.

Time for Politics

SOMEHOW, I ALWAYS FOUND TIME for politics. In between work and family, I would squeeze in Liberal Republican Club meetings, precinct caucus meetings, county conventions, and Republican state conventions. I liked serving on platform committees. I was in favor of an energetic program and wanted the party to dedicate itself to doing important things.

Watching the New Deal unfold convinced me that I had been right not to switch to the Democratic Party in 1932. President Roosevelt disappointed me by asking Congress to pass bills that he knew were unconstitutional. He was reckless in his disregard for the Constitution. When the Supreme Court would not uphold his legislation, he tried to pack the court in 1937. It was an outrageous thing to even attempt to do. None of the legislation Roosevelt pushed so hard for—the National Recovery Act, the Reconstruction Finance Corporation, the Agricultural Adjustment Act—had much of a beneficial effect on the economy. The New Deal did not end the depression. The war in Europe did, beginning in 1939. It created a sudden demand for material from the United States.

But in two respects, FDR gained my profound respect. One was that he lifted the spirit of the American people at a time when that may have been the most important thing a president could do. The nation was desperately discouraged in 1933. People needed to hear his message of freedom from fear and freedom from want.

The other admirable thing about Roosevelt was his determination to overcome his paralysis—and to keep it hidden from the public. I recently read *FDR's Splendid Deception* by Hugh Gregory Gallagher. It described Roosevelt's fear that the public would not accept a cripple as a leader. He went to extraordinary steps to hide his disability. He would assume a jaunty air, with a perky cigarette holder and a big smile, get people on both arms, and swing his legs as if he were walking to a rostrum. He gave an appearance of great buoyancy and confidence and went through great pain and effort to do so. I came to admire him, but in four elections, I never voted for him.

In 1938, I was active enough in Republican affairs to come to know Harold Stassen, the young Dakota County attorney. He was only thirty-one years old—two years older than I—but he was a natural leader with a big voice and bold ideas that captivated people. He captivated me. I became one of the people identified with the Stassen group.

Stassen sought the Republican nomination for governor in 1938. His opponent was Martin Nelson, a lawyer from Albert Lea, who had run without success against two Farmer-Laborites, Gov. Floyd Olson in 1934 and, after Olson's untimely death, Gov. Elmer Benson in 1936. By 1938, Benson was vulnerable. His policies were farther to the left than Olson's, and some of the people in his administration were less than honest. Nelson prevailed upon the Republican state convention to endorse him for a third try at the governorship. Stassen decided not to take the convention's rebuff as the final word. He filed against Nelson in the Republican primary.

A riding club in South St. Paul, Stassen's home territory, became a core unit in Stassen's campaign. Many of the members were young people who worked in the stockyards and moved cattle on horseback. They were excellent riders. Their campaign tactic was to truck horses and riders to the outskirts of a town that Stassen planned to visit. Just in advance of his arrival, they would ride into town in Old West style. Stassen himself would follow in an open car. It just electrified the little towns in Minnesota to have these young people come riding in on their horses to show their support for Stassen.

I was not one of those riders. In 1938, with all that was going on at Fuller, I was in no position to be running around the state in a political campaign. But I was part of the campaign's strategy team. I much approved of the way Stassen and the riders drew attention to his candidacy.

Stassen won both the primary and the general election in 1938 by strong margins. One of his associates, Lester Badger, was assigned to recruit people for his administration. Badger came to me and said that Stassen wanted me to join him in state government. What job appealed to me? I was pleased to be wanted, but Eleanor and I did not take long to decide that we did not want to make a living at politics. We wanted our political activity to be public service, not a career. We wanted the independence of a separate source of income.

When elected officials make governmental service a career, they lose a great deal of freedom and flexibility. They become too dependent on reelection, and they lose the nerve it takes to vote contrary to the crowd. The trend in that direction is not a positive one. There has to be a way to keep public service appealing to people with established professions whose motive is service, not personal gain.

Although I did not take Stassen's offer in 1939, I was tempted sufficiently to recognize how much I wanted to serve in government someday. I was so interested in government that I had even been keeping scrapbooks on the legislature. They were making the laws that governed the people, and I always liked being where the big decisions are made. I like to run things. I vowed that someday, I would run for the legislature.

In late 1939, I decided to share that goal with Mr. Fuller, to sound him out. I told him I had a desire to serve in the legislature. I had no immediate plans to run for office, I said, but I wondered whether he thought doing so someday would be compatible with my work at Fuller. He allowed that he would have no objections, should that day come.

I did not tell him about my two other objectives of long standing. I wanted to own and operate two things—a weekly newspaper and a farm. I knew something about newspapering. One might say it is the industry I cut my teeth in. I never got over my love for that business, and I always wanted to operate a weekly newspaper. I did not have in mind that we would have as many as we do now, but I wanted to have one. My idea was that even one newspaper in one community can do great good. It can lift its readers' aspirations, taste, and knowledge. I believed then, and I still do, that if a newspaper plays that role, its community can blossom.

I had no farming experience whatsoever then. But since 1934, we had spent a portion of every summer at the farm that Grandma and Grandpa Johnson bought on Deer Lake, near St. Croix Falls, Wisconsin. It included a house, three cottages, a barn, and forty tillable acres. Our love for that place fueled my agricultural interest.

One of the three cottages at Deer Lake Farm was rented to the Lipschulz family from St. Paul, a fine Jewish family. In the 1930s, it was not always easy for Jewish families to find rental property. Grandma and Grandpa Johnson had no hesitation whatever about renting to them. I enjoyed watching the patriarch, a venerable old gentleman with a white beard, fishing on the dock. When he wanted a minnow or a worm, he would call to the grandchildren, and they would scamper like rabbits to do his bidding. He was a real authority figure whom they respected—and whom I respected in turn for the values he was teaching his children. We came to know the Lipschulz family very well.

The family contacted me when I was governor, twenty-five years after we had met. Dad Lipschulz was being considered for membership in the St.

Paul Athletic Club. The family had reason to worry that the membership was being delayed or denied because he was Jewish. I said, "We can't let that happen. I'll check into it." I called the Athletic Club. The membership official said, "We're trying to keep a balance in our membership." I recognized that polite-sounding euphemism for discrimination. I said, "You can't do that. This person is a fine man. I've known this family for many years. You couldn't have a finer, more decent, more respectable member than Mr. Lipschulz. You can't, you just cannot do this in this state. You'd better act on his membership application." A call like that from a governor can inspire quick action, especially among people who are aware that a band of news reporters is always close at a governor's hand. Mr. Lipschulz was soon a member of the St. Paul Athletic Club.

I could not act on my ambition to run for the legislature anytime soon after my conversation with Mr. Fuller. Events at Fuller, at home, and in the world simply would not let me. I took a step back from politics for a time.

But in 1944, Dick Golling, part of the Stassen team, came to see me. He said, "Elmer, you've got to get back into politics. We want to send Warren Burger to the national convention from the Fourth District. His opponent lives in your precinct. His name is Tom McGill. We want to defeat him in his home precinct, and you've got to do it."

Things were going well enough at Fuller for me to agree to make the effort. We organized the two precincts of St. Anthony Park and defeated Tom McGill in his backyard. That got me back into the flow of precinct, district, and county politics again.

In 1948, my Stassen associates called again. "Elmer, we want to send you to the national convention this year," they said. I happily accepted. I was at the convention in Philadelphia and was able to participate in Stassen's nearest miss for the presidential nomination.

Eleanor, twelve-year-old Tony, and I traveled to the convention by train. When we got off the train and got into a cab, the driver asked, "Are you coming to convention?" I said we were. "Are you a delegate?" he asked. "Yes, I am," I said. "I've got to tell you, it's all settled. They all got together out at the Pew Farm over the weekend. It's going to be [Thomas] Dewey on the third ballot." And it was.

Tony and Eleanor sat in the balcony of the convention hall. I could watch Tony as he kept tabs on the vote count for Stassen. When the count was in Stassen's favor, he would hit his fist down. He had a great time.

Dewey was not popular in Minnesota. But having been a national convention delegate, I worked hard for Dewey in the 1948 campaign. Late in the campaign, Dewey scheduled a stop in Minnesota. I was among the local people who met with his advance men about a week before his visit. We pleaded with them to ask Dewey for a stirring talk on farm policies. "The farm vote is hanging in the balance, and we don't hear any farm comments from Dewey. Now, he's coming to St. Paul. He's *got* to give a farm speech," we said. Their answer: "He doesn't want to get into farm issues." He gave a talk on foreign relations in Minnesota, and a bland one at that. I was most disappointed that night.

The following Saturday, President Harry Truman came to Iowa, stomped through the cornfields, made a big publicity hit, and then came to St. Paul. His speech was broadcast on the radio. I sat in my driveway, having just arrived home from a meeting, and listened to every word. It was a rip-snorting agricultural speech. He was going to do something for the farmers. That was the speech we wanted Dewey to make. Dewey thought he already had won the election when he came to St. Paul. He was just going through the motions. After the election, *Life* magazine showed two pictures: one of Dewey going down to vote, smiling and confident as anybody could be, and the second, of him sitting by his radio on election night, incredulous at what he was hearing. I was not as surprised as Dewey was.

Harry Truman was an easy man to underestimate. He was known to some of our Fuller people in Kansas City. He came from an ordinary background and had been a dry goods merchant. What we knew about him in Minnesota was that he was a nonentity from Boss Pendergast's political machine in Kansas City who had been plugged in as vice president—and now, because of Roosevelt's death, he was president. One of our Kansas City people said, "Elmer, can you imagine that fool as president?"

In retrospect, I admire Truman a great deal. He is testimony to the faith America should have in its ordinary people. He was not brilliant. He was not highly educated. But he had solid convictions, and he stood by them. He believed in the country. He believed in saying things the way everybody would understand them. He did well in Korea. I think he will be remembered as one of our country's worthwhile, sturdy presidents.

In 1952, it was Warren Burger's turn to go to the national convention again—and it is good that he did. Burger had worked his way into the party's establishment and was on the Credentials Committee. He supported seating the rump delegation rather than the regular delegation from Texas. The rump delegation supported Dwight D. Eisenhower; the regulars backed Ohio Sen. Robert Taft. Seating the rump delegation made the difference in

Eisenhower's nomination. Stassen was a candidate again that year too, but in the end even the Minnesota delegation went for Eisenhower.

Stassen's career was a rather unfulfilled one. After being elected governor three times, he joined the navy in 1943. In 1944, he could have been elected to the U.S. Senate when Edward J. Thye was elected, but he deferred to Thye. He was serving as administrative officer for Adm. William "Bull" Halsey in the Pacific and participating in the drafting of the United Nations Charter. In 1948, he might have been elected to the Senate, but he had his heart set on the presidency. Even though he would have had to push aside Sen. Joseph Ball, an incumbent Republican, he should have gone for the Senate.

I have always had tremendous respect for Harold Stassen. In sheer intellectual capacity, he is the ablest person I have known. I think he was by far the ablest Minnesota governor, the one who had the greatest accomplishment in total. He was the one who brought fiscal discipline into state government, imposing the requirement that the budget had to be balanced. If revenues fell short, spending had to be cut. Since Stassen's day, Minnesota has never engaged in deficit financing.

As governor, Stassen was orderly, organized, thorough, detailed, and tough. He understood that in government, it takes a lot of doing to get things done. He exerted power—something I never did quite as easily or as well. I do not go at things quite as hard as Stassen did. He could use people, if need be, in pursuit of his goal. I think that is quite often true of generals and people who have great responsibility. They simply cannot be sidetracked by concern for personal relationships. Stassen was a tough political manager, but he was an able one, and he was always focused on a public purpose. I never saw him do one single thing for personal profit or gain.

I was part of Stassen's campaign committee in 1948, when he made the best of his drives for the presidency. My state was North Dakota. I never felt I registered strongly with Stassen. If I had, I would have been assigned a larger state. Yet I campaigned in North Dakota like I was running for sheriff, and I wrote reports on my activities. I remember how pleased I was when I got reports back from Stassen with the little note, "This is an excellent report." I carried North Dakota for Stassen. It was the only state, other than Minnesota, that gave its full vote to Stassen on all three ballots of the 1948 convention. It was tough holding them in tow. I took pride in doing a good job for him.

On a sunny afternoon before the convention, Stassen called a campaign committee meeting in his backyard. He arranged the chairs so the people attending had their backs to the sun, and he faced the sun. I thought, what a considerate thing to do. He was not wearing sunglasses, and the sun was just piercing. But with great facility, he called on the committee member assigned to every state, heard the reports, and told what he knew. He was the general, in charge and impressive.

Our relationship while he was governor and active in national affairs was sporadic and not really close. We became closer in later years. He seemed pleased in 1952, when he was president of the University of Pennsylvania, and I visited him during our trip to the Boy Scout National Jamboree at Valley Forge.

A more recent exchange offers an insight into the man today. In 1992, the last time he ran for president, I sent him a contribution of $2,000, the same amount I had sent another friend, Gene McCarthy, who was also making a quixotic presidential bid that year. I thought, I have to send Harold as much as I gave my Democratic friend. Later, I got a letter from Harold: "I didn't get very far this time, and I didn't use very much money. So, I'm enclosing a check for the unused portion of your contribution." He sent back something like $1,200, a huge part of it. Harold and his wife, Esther, live at Friendship Village in Bloomington now, where, despite health problems, he keeps a hand in politics.

The summons I received in 1944 to Burger's aid quickened my desire for political involvement once more. My chance came soon. In early 1946, I received a call from my streetcar-riding friend of ten years earlier, Cecil March. He had become a 3M manager. Cec said, "Elmer, we've got to do something about Congress in the Fourth District. Frank Starkey (the DFL incumbent) has a drinking problem, and labor doesn't want him to stay in. Yet he's insisting on running again. Labor is going to have to replace him. If we come up with a good candidate, we can elect a Republican for the first time in many years. I've got just the candidate. I want to have lunch so you can meet him."

Not long afterward, at the St. Paul Athletic Club, March introduced me to Edward J. Devitt and his wife. I liked Ed right away. He came from East Grand Forks, Minnesota, where his father had been a railroad man. That meant he had labor connections. He was an Irish Catholic. An Irish Catholic friend of labor makes a good Republican candidate in St. Paul. I became secretary of the campaign committee. The chairman was an older, respected St. Paul lawyer, Carl Cummins, the grandfather of Carl "Buzz" Cummins, the lobbyist and leader in the Citizens League in recent years. Karl Klein was the treasurer—and not always a graceful one. I made a call with him once to solicit a contribution to the Devitt campaign. He went to pull out a pledge card, but instead he pulled out a lot of cash and spilled it all over the desk. Our would-be donor said, "I don't think you need any contribution from me."

One thing that was different about campaigns fifty years ago is that the candidate had nothing to do with fundraising. Devitt never asked anybody for money, and neither did I when I ran. That was the job of a campaign finance chairman and finance committee. The candidate knew who contributed but not how much. That approach is vastly superior to the way campaigns are run today.

My early fundraising calls for the Devitt campaign included a stop at the office of Homer Clark, one of St. Paul's business titans. He headed West Publishing Company and was also a principal in Waldorf Paper Products. Nothing happened in St. Paul that did not somehow involve Clark. The Devitt campaign needed his support from the outset. I told him, "We've worked out a very careful budget. We're going to need $30,000." "Elmer, $30,000?" he asked. "We've never spent that much on a congressional race." "We haven't been winning either," I replied. "You can always lose cheap. We have a real chance to win, but if we're going to win, we have to put on a strong campaign. We've gotten bids on material and checked ad prices in the paper and radio spots. We need $30,000. We aren't going to win if we don't get it." "OK, I'll support you," he said. His contribution was crucial to our effort.

Another episode involving Devitt says much about the kind of man Clark was. After Devitt was in Congress, Clark found himself in need of an updated passport in a hurry. He sent a wire to Devitt, asking him to please check with the State Department and get his passport ready, so he could pick it up in Washington on his way to Europe. Devitt complied and then sent Clark a wire advising him that the passport would be waiting for Clark in Devitt's congressional office. When Clark arrived, he proceeded to hand Devitt seventy-two cents for the wire that Devitt had sent to him. Devitt said, "Mr. Clark, you don't need to pay me seventy-two cents. The government, in its great generosity, provides me with funds to write letters and send telegrams."

Later during that campaign, I went to Corpus Christi Catholic Church, on Cleveland Avenue in St. Anthony Park. (The congregation has since moved to Falcon Heights.) The parish priest was Father Guiney, an earthy, warm, hard-working man who was very close to his parishioners. I can still see the bowl of candy on his desk. He spoke favorably about Devitt when we first met. The second time I called on him, I said, "Father Guiney, we have some literature that we'd like to pass out. We'd like to put one on every car around your church on Sunday morning, if you think that would be appropriate." He smiled a little. "Andersen, if you'll give me the circulars, I think I can use them pretty effectively," he said. I suspect they may have been handed out at the door the next Sunday.

Father Guiney had given me an insight into the workings of the Catholic Church. It can be a strong political organization—one with an excellent sense of timing. I was told after the election that in one of his sermons, Father Guiney said there was a moral issue in the congressional race, and that it was important that people in public office should be moral, straight people. He did not malign Starkey by name, but he got the message across.

Labor handled the situation the same way. Our campaign never made mention of any problem Starkey might have. No news article reported it. But labor spread the word, and that did it. Devitt was elected to Congress in 1946.

I visited Devitt in Washington more than once. He was part of a new Republican majority and was a popular member of the freshman class. He was a handsome fellow, considerate and gentle in his mannerisms. I came away with a sense that it is a tremendous challenge to have any influence as one member of a legislative body of 435.

That new Republican Congress went too far too fast. Labor had had its own way in Congress for a number of years, and some reforms were needed to rein it in. But Congress overreached with the Taft-Hartley Act, a package of antilabor measures that became a rallying cry for labor and the Democrats in the 1948 election. Labor's hostility to Taft-Hartley was a major factor in Devitt's defeat in 1948 by a rising young professor from the College of St. Thomas, Eugene McCarthy.

I was so disappointed by McCarthy's victory. Yet just two years later, when my own name was on the ballot, my campaign path and McCarthy's frequently crossed. We became acquainted and were soon friends. He is so incisive and true in his judgments of right and wrong. We remain in touch still. Our relationship shows how friendships in politics can cross party lines.

After his 1948 defeat, Devitt was appointed probate judge by Gov. Luther Youngdahl. In 1952, I was manager of the campaign for the entire state Republican slate. With Dwight Eisenhower at the top of the ticket, the Republican Party carried more offices that year than it has since, in any election. Ed Thye was reelected U.S. senator. The day after the election, I went to see Thye. I said, "Ed, there's nothing that I want. I'm not interested in going to Washington. I've got a business to get back to. But, there's an underemployed person that I think you know over in the county court-house. Ed Devitt is probate judge; he ought to be a federal district judge. Would you be willing to name him at your first opportunity?" He said, "There's only one person I would give priority to for that appointment, and I have to check with that person to see if he's interested. I have a feeling he may not be." I understood. I knew he meant Warren Burger. I also knew that Burger was already set up with Eisenhower's choice for U.S. attorney general, Herbert Brownell, to join his team. Later, Eisenhower appointed Burger a circuit court judge, and President Richard Nixon appointed him chief justice of the U.S. Supreme Court.

When I saw Thye again, he confided, "The person I had in mind isn't interested. I'll give you my word and at the first opportunity, it will be Ed Devitt. I think there will be a chance not too long ahead." Devitt became a federal district judge in December 1953 and had a long and distinguished career.

After the 1948 election and the defeats of both Dewey and Devitt, my enthusiasm for politics was at a low ebb. I went back to Fuller and told my staff, "I've had it now. Gee whiz! I've been a delegate to the national con-vention. I've managed a congressman's election, and I was involved in a na-tional campaign. I'm satisfied to come back and pay attention to Fuller."

They said, "That's great, Elmer. But we don't believe you."

State Senator

I LIVE IN WHAT WAS ONE of the most populous state senate districts in Minnesota in the 1940s, District 42. It extended from the Anoka County line on the north to the Dakota County line on the south, and consisted of all of northern Ramsey County west of Rice Street, and roughly all of St. Paul west of Hamline Avenue. It was one of six senate districts in Ramsey County, but it encompassed one-third of the county's population. That imbalance occurred because in the first half of the twentieth century, Minnesota did not regularly redraw its legislative district boundaries to adjust for demographic change. District 42 had grown to become the third largest district in population in the state, behind only the district that encompassed all of Hennepin County outside of Minneapolis, and the district that took in all of south Minneapolis.

If the District 42 of the 1940s had not been reapportioned, today it would include several hundred thousand people. Then, although the district's population was large and growing, it was still sparse enough to be called "rural Ramsey," and for the schools to be part of a county district, not city districts. Many of the present suburbs did not yet exist. Much of the land was farmland, occupied mainly by hog farmers, who fed their pigs raw garbage from the Twin Cities. It was not a pleasant business, but it was productive for people who like pork.

District 42 was not only notable for its size. It also was home to two of the legislature's leading members. The district's senator was Charles N. Orr, the leader of the senate's Conservative majority. At that time, legislators did not run with party designation. They divided themselves into caucuses known as Conservative and Liberal. The Conservative group in the senate included some Democrats—or people who had been Democrats before the merger that created the Democratic-Farmer-Labor Party in 1944. For example, Sen. Gerald Mullin of Minneapolis, a progressive person and a Democrat, caucused Conservative. At the same time, the man widely considered the most conservative member of the senate, B. G. Novak, a liquor dealer from St. Paul, was a member of the Liberal caucus. He was a capable legisla-tor—skillful enough to sell the idea that stopping price competition among liquor retailers would induce less drinking!

One of the two house members from District 42 was Claude Allen, an-other Conservative, who in prominence and power was second only to the house speaker. He was chairman of the Appropriations Committee and the watchdog of the treasury. I did not agree with his way of handling state spending. He always wanted to postpone expenditures, even essential ones. He would wait until the situation was critical, and by then, costs were high-er than they would have been had he acted earlier. He thought he was sav-ing the state money; I thought he was mistaken. Allen eventually succeeded me in the state senate, when I chose not to run for reelection.

Today, District 42 leans toward the DFL Party. In recent years, it has sent several notable DFLers to the legislature, including Ann Wynia, now the president of North Hennepin Community College. But in the 1940s, the district had a high percentage of Republicans, many of them active in party affairs. I was one of them.

I meant it when I told my Fuller colleagues after the disappointing 1948 election that I was through with politics for awhile, but I had not aban-doned my goal of someday running for the legislature. I still loved the human interplay of politics, the competitive struggle for power, the premi-um put on ingenuity and resourcefulness. But I was not interested in run-ning against either Orr or Allen. In January 1949, at the start of a new leg-islative session, it did not appear that either of those two legislative titans would step aside anytime soon.

Then, on January 10, Orr had a heart attack while driving to work, and died. A special election was called for February 8, just a month later. The primary would be in two weeks. Gov. Luther Youngdahl imposed a tight schedule because the legislature was in session.

Immediately, I began to think about filing. A number of my fellow Republican Party workers urged me to run. One who called on me was Warren Lundgren, an agent for Northwestern Mutual Life Insurance Com-pany of Milwaukee. "You can make it," he assured me. "It will be quite a contest, because it's a big district and there will be a lot of candidates, but you ought to run."

Eleanor and I talked it over. She said, "You've had this on your mind for so long, you'd better do it." That sealed it. I decided to run.

So did nineteen other people! Lundgren was right when he predicted a large field of candidates in the special election primary. Distinguishing myself in that long list was a major challenge. Yet because of my activities in the community in the late 1940s, it was a challenge I could meet more readily than most other candidates.

I had become involved with Family Service of St. Paul and was a member of its board. Through the board's Case Work Committee, I came to know social workers and to better understand the trouble families can fall into. I learned that family problems are often associated with either poverty or alcohol. I also became more aware of the problems faced by handicapped people. That was one of the reasons why, as a legislator, I wanted to do something about special education, and why I became active in the Child Welfare League of America. The league is a network of more than one thousand state and local agencies involved in work including adoption, residential care, and foster care. It serves as an information clearinghouse, a training center, and a voice for its members in Congress. I was a member of the league's board from 1958 to 1971, and its president from 1965 to 1967.

In 1941, after I took control of H. B. Fuller Company, Harvey Fuller talked to me about the Rotary Club. He said, "Elmer, I think you'd like it. It's a group of good fellows, and they stand for what you believe in. I wish you'd let me propose you for the Rotary Club." I agreed and soon found myself reveling in the Rotary. I just marveled at the good work it did in the community and for its members.

In 1948, Walter Spriggs, a plumbing and heating retail dealer and an active Rotarian, called on me. He said, "Elmer, the past presidents of the Rotary Club have a get-together to decide who they think ought to be nominated for leadership. Anybody can be nominated from the floor, but we want to be sure there are nominees who know they're going to be nominated and are willing to take on the responsibility. The custom is to nominate someone for vice president, and then he automatically becomes president a year later. We want to nominate you." I replied, "Walter, I would love to be president of the St. Paul Rotary, but I've only been a member for seven years, and, at that, I'm one of the younger members of the club. I would think I'm not ready." "That's not for you to judge," he said. "We judge that. All you have to determine is whether you're willing to serve."

I was delighted to serve. I became president of the St. Paul Rotary Club for the year beginning on July 1, 1948. We had a large club, about three hundred members, and an old club, only the tenth organized anywhere. (Interestingly, Minneapolis was the ninth. They were organized a day apart—Minneapolis on February 9 and St. Paul on February 10, 1910.) I came to know all the lore. I made it my business to become acquainted with every member. I would pore over our membership books so that I would know and recognize each member. I organized a rotational seating system at meetings so people did not become clannish but interacted with other members.

Another of my activities in the late 1940s was Community Chest, now called the United Way of St. Paul. What a great concept Community Chest embodies, to have everybody in town solicited at one time, in one large drive, to support so many worthwhile agencies. In those years, I was in the ranks of the organization, going door-to-door, soliciting contributions.

Not many years later, in the mid-1950s, I became chairman of the drive for greater St. Paul, as they used to call the portion of Ramsey County outside the St. Paul city limits. My chairmanship came about because the Community Chest had not reached its fundraising goal for two or three years. I was on the board of directors. At a postmortem meeting after one of those disappointing campaigns, I said, "Do you know why you didn't make it? You didn't ask for enough." They said, "Elmer, we didn't make the goal. What do you mean we didn't ask for enough?" "You didn't give incentive enough to the people who benefit from the drive," I said. "Here's what you did. All of the agencies submitted requests for what they felt they had to have. I don't think they pad their requests. They know that money comes with difficulty. When their requests were added, you thought it was too much money, so you cut it back. That meant that even if the goal was reached, the agencies were still not going to get what they felt they needed. They had no incentive to get out and help us raise the money. If they knew they would get what they need, they'd work much harder."

The following year, I was asked to be chairman. I said, "OK, I'll be chairman on one condition: that you make the goal the total of what the agencies say they need. But, please, tell them to be strictly fair about it. Tell them we are going to raise what they need. That way, we'll make the goal." My strategy worked. The campaign produced an enormous effort and reached its goal.

I was a bold chairman of the Community Chest—so much so that I did something I doubt any recent United Way chairman has done. When one of the St. Paul department stores, the Emporium, reported the results of their employee solicitation, I called their chief executive. "I'm sorry," I told him, "but this is not good enough. If we are going to have any chance of reaching our goal, you must do better." I convinced the Emporium to go back to their employees and ask them to increase their pledges. When the results from the Emporium came back the second time, they were three times larger than they were after the first solicitation.

My other community connections in 1949 were membership in St. Anthony Park Lutheran Church and involvement with the Boy Scouts, including service on the Indian Head District Council.

It probably is not accurate to say that I was a prominent person when I ran for the legislature the first time, but I certainly was active. Someone on my campaign committee once remarked, "Elmer, for all the activities you've been in, you're sure unknown!" That comment expresses the challenge every nonincumbent faces. Nearly everybody has to know you for you to succeed. With less than a month to campaign in a large district, I could not meet enough people to be effective. I had to depend on others to spread the word about me.

As usual, I relied on Eleanor, and she had a great idea. She got a campaign chain letter going. She made kits containing ten letters, while we recruited campaign volunteers to receive the kits. Each person recruited would sign the letters in the kit and prepare envelopes to mail to ten people. The letters asked the recipient to sign and prepare envelopes for ten more identical letters, to be sent to people of their choosing in District 42. Those people, too, were asked to prepare ten letters to their friends. We told the first person, "You've got to ride herd on the people to whom you mail your letters, to see that they all do their thing." Instead of depending on people to mail the letters themselves, we asked that the letters be turned in to headquarters, so we could stage the mailings appropriately. The real reason for that request was to make sure the people we recruited got the job done. Our tactic worked. We went through three mailing cycles, so that, in theory, each original kit reached a thousand people. The letters multiply rapidly, which was crucial in such a short campaign.

We made use of another mail campaign among well-known people in churches, clubs, and organizations. We asked them to send a postcard of recommendation to the members of their group who knew them but might not know me. The postcard was to the effect, "I know Elmer L. Andersen." It would describe some of my activities and wind up, "I give you my personal recommendation, and I urge you to vote for him." Soon postcards like that were in the hands of many of the district's churches, clubs, and veterans' organizations. I was not a veteran, but veterans' groups would quickly check me out and pass the word that I had not done anything to avoid service, and that my company had contributed to the war effort. Those groups gave me plenty of support.

Still, running in a field of twenty candidates is a daunting experience. At one League of Women Voters' candidates' forum, I looked up and down the line of candidates on the stage and marveled at the diverse assemblage. There seemed to be a little bit of everything there. One contender was a good friend of mine, William Randall. He later became county attorney for Ramsey County and held that post for several decades.

From that field of twenty, Bill Randall and I were the two candidates who survived the primary. It was a joy to see the primary election returns from my home precinct in St. Anthony Park. I got 386 votes; the other nineteen candidates combined got 80.

Bill and I had a friendly rivalry. Once during the two-week campaign that followed, we ran into each other at radio station WMIN, where we were on the air, one after the other. We teased each other about people who were supporting both of us. I told Bill, "You know, you think you've got Mrs. So-and-So rooting for you. Do you know that she's working for me a good deal?" "Oh, is she really? That So-and-So," he said. "Well, did you know Mr. XYZ is on my committee?"

On February 8, I was the victor, by a fairly comfortable margin. St. Anthony Park had the biggest turnout of any region in the district, and its vote went more than 70 percent for me. That meant the most to me on election night, knowing that my neighborhood turned out strongly in support of me.

Bill Randall called to congratulate me. He said, "I want to tell you, Elmer, I won't run against you as long as you're in the senate. If you ever decide you don't want to run again, please let me know. I might want to run again then." I said, "I sure will do that, Bill." It was a promise I kept eight years later.

The very next day, I took my seat in the chamber of the Minnesota Senate. With the session in progress, there was no orientation period for me. I had to plunge right in. That first day, I learned one of the most important lessons any legislator can learn. The first intense debate I witnessed on the senate floor was between Al Sletvold of Detroit Lakes and Gerald Mullin of Minneapolis. I do not remember the issue, but I certainly recall the vigor with which they debated. They were not calling each other names, but they were stressing their points with great fervor. I thought, My gosh! Those guys must hate each other. At the close of the day's session, I watched as Sletvold went around the chamber and came down the center aisle to where Mullin sat. He picked him up, put his arm around his shoulder, and continued on down the aisle, past my seat at the front of the chamber, just right of the center. I heard them speaking as they passed. Sletvold was saying, "I'm sure you know, Gerry, there's nothing personal in anything I said." Mullin said, "Oh, of course, I know that, Al. Let's go out and have a cup of coffee."

I learned right away: always stay on good terms with people whose ideas differ from yours so that you can work with them tomorrow even if you differ today. Hot topics are unavoidable in the legislature. Success often depends on learning to disagree with civility and keeping on good terms with the other members. Respect their differences. Differ vigorously. Oppose actively. Maintain your own position. But respect their right to their position, and let the procedures, rules, and customs of the senate decide who wins. That was an important lesson.

The second day, I learned another good lesson. On the floor, the senate took up the calendar, that day's list of bills slated for final action. I turned to my copies of the bills on the calendar, and I tried to study them. I wanted to figure out what they meant and how I should vote on them. I was having a hard time catching up. Some of the bills were not easy calls for me after just one reading. I thought, I just will not vote on them. I am only going to vote on the ones that I can understand, on which I know what I want to do. I will skip the others. So, I did. Adolph Johnson, who was the Associated Press capitol reporter at that time—and one of my constituents—came over and said, "Elmer, I noticed you didn't vote on some of those bills in the calendar." I said, "Adolph, I'm trying my best to catch up. I studied them, and I wasn't quite sure what the net effect was or how I should vote. So I decided to not vote on them." He said, "Elmer, you'd better learn right now that you're not expected to know everything about these bills, but you are expected to vote." That was excellent advice.

Johnson was my first friend in the capitol press corps. Eleanor and I had known Adolph and his wife, Mary Eva, in other connections in St. Anthony Park. Soon after I arrived at the senate, I met Jack Mackay, Adolph's colleague at the Associated Press and the father of businessman and author Harvey Mackay. I understood and liked journalism, so I responded positively to the reporters at the capitol. I made it my policy from my first days there that I would always return reporters' calls promptly. Reporters always have looming deadlines. I thought, the least I can do when they call me is to get back to them as soon as I can. My other rule in dealing with reporters was to answer their questions forthrightly and not beat around the bush. If they ask an embarrassing question, so be it. Answer it, and tell the truth. With those practices, I got along fine with the media.

That is not to say I was satisfied with the treatment of every story. For example, I would call a press conference to announce a five-point program that I thought was going to do a lot of good. I would describe it in detail. Then, the reporters would begin to ask questions about other things. When the paper came out the next day, my five-point program would be about two inches on page 12. On page 1, there would be something I said in response to a question about some hot issue of the day. I decided I had to accept that treatment, though I tried my best to devise ways to get good play for the story I wanted told. I decided I had to meet capitol reporters on their own terms.

Some reporters became good friends. One of them was Jack Weinberg of the *Minneapolis Tribune*. He came to me one day and said, "Elmer, I just have a yen to send you an invitation to my daughter's wedding. Maybe you'd like to come to the Jewish temple and see a Jewish wedding." I said, "I'd love to. I've never attended a Jewish wedding. We'll come." One part of the ceremony at that wedding impressed me very much and revealed something about the Jewish community. The mother and father of both the bride and groom escorted each to the bower where the bride and groom were to be married. That moment conveyed the idea that this was more than an event involving two people. The wedding was the joining of two families. It was beautiful.

I developed an appreciative feeling about the Jewish community of Minnesota. I used to go to B'nai B'rith meetings, contribute to Jewish schools and organizations, and support bond drives for Israel. Rabbi Bernard Raskas of Temple of Aaron in St. Paul once invited me to speak at that synagogue. I thought that was a high honor. When he introduced me, he said, "His name is Andersen, but we think of him as," and he spoke Hebrew words that mean "our friend" and sound a little bit like Andersen. Rabbi Raskas and I still keep in touch.

Gunther Plaut, another St. Paul rabbi, became a friend. When I was governor, Rabbi Plaut was called to a new position at the Holy Blossom Temple in Toronto, Ontario. He said, "Elmer, it would mean a good deal to me and get me off to a good start if the governor of my state would come to my inauguration."

I agreed to come. The installation was on a Saturday afternoon; I planned to fly to Toronto on Saturday morning. But a storm prevented the plane from landing in Toronto. It landed in Philadelphia. I chartered a small plane, knowing that sometimes, small planes can safely navigate through storms that larger aircraft cannot. The charter pilot said that it might be a rough ride, but he assured me he would make it. He was as good as his word; he got me to the service just as it was starting.

I was asked to speak a few words. I said, "The Jewish community has come through three phases. One phase was horrible persecution and rejection.

The second phase, a lot of it in the United States and Canada, was hard work and segregation. Now is the time for the third phase. You have proved your talents, proved your abilities, proved your worth. Come into the open, and take your rightful place in the full community."

It is a terrible thing for a people to feel so close to persecution all the time. What a weight our Jewish neighbors have carried, knowing that at almost any time—as happened in the twentieth century in Germany, as has happened so many times throughout history—people can be cruel to them. I have wanted to do what I can to lighten their burden. The highest award I ever received was when somebody made a plaque for me bearing the word for a useful citizen in Hebrew, a *mensch*. That is what I have always wanted to be, an honorable, useful citizen.

I quickly learned the mechanics of the Minnesota Senate and became very active. An issue that captured my attention early was mental health. The topic was sweeping the whole country at the time, in part because of the advances in the treatment of mental illness being achieved at the Menninger Clinic in Topeka, Kansas. The Menninger brothers were great communicators as well as medical pioneers. Among the people who took interest in their message was Luther Youngdahl, Minnesota's progressive Republican governor.

Youngdahl made an issue of the terrible conditions in the state's mental hospitals. His budget called for doubling state spending on state hospital care for the mentally ill. The per capita expenditure for food in our mental hospitals, at that time, was sixty-five cents a day—a pittance even in those pre-inflation days. The Mental Health Association joined with the governor in seeking more humane provisions for the state's mental illness victims. Within weeks of my first election, the association invited me to visit a mental hospital. I had never visited one, and I was curious. I readily agreed.

We went to the hospital in St. Peter. I was shocked by the condition of the people, poorly dressed, poorly fed, poorly cared for, and huddled up in corners of a bare room. I had never seen human beings in such desperate conditions. It took me two weeks to sleep well again after the shock of seeing people in those circumstances. I was also stunned when we walked into a room where an autopsy was being performed. I nearly keeled over.

I left St. Peter convinced that we had to do better for the mentally ill. Like-minded Minnesotans were beginning to speak out. I received a letter describing one family's struggle to provide treatment of a relative with mental illness. The family had exhausted its resources and had to commit their loved one to a state institution. They went to visit the state hospital where their family member would be committed and were appalled by the poor conditions they saw. The letter begged, "For God's sake, vote for that mental health appropriation."

Letters like that, written with deep feeling, can have profound influence at the legislature. I tell people who want to contact their legislator: "Write a letter. Don't write a letter somebody gives you, but write a letter from your own experience, something you know about, however personal it may be. One letter can make a difference." More than forty years after leaving the senate, I can recall in detail particular letters I received from constituents.

Minnesota could still do more for the mentally ill. I think it was a great mistake when the state began closing mental hospitals. The theory in the 1970s was that drug technology had progressed to such a degree that long, tedious psychotherapy was not needed anymore. Drugs were thought sufficient to control patients' attitudes and conduct. Community clinics became the thing. But the obvious weakness in that program is that sick people cannot be expected to take their medicine as prescribed. Minnesota traded a bad situation for a worse one, one in which a large number of mentally ill people are moving freely within the population. Their conduct is unpredictable. They can be paranoid, self-destructive, or violent. Eliminating the option of an institutional stay for people who truly need that kind of care was wrong.

The worst mistake of all was closing the state hospital in Rochester in the early 1980s. It was the surgical center for all patients living in state institutions. Mayo Clinic used that as a clinic base for teaching doctors, and charged little, if anything, to the state. That asset was wiped out for largely political reasons.

When I was a new senator, some people in the business community thought I might be a dependable voice for their interests. My instincts were to be just the opposite. I was on the board, at that time, of a savings and loan association. The officials there indicated to me that they expected me to handle their legislation. "No," I said, "I couldn't possibly. Not only will I not handle the legislation, I don't think it would be appropriate for me to even vote on it." I was true to my word. When bills pertaining to savings banks came up for consideration, I would ask to be excused from voting because I was on the board of a savings and loan association. It was novel in those days to be that careful about conflict of interest, but I did not want senate service to bring me any personal advantage. I did not advertise that I was in the adhesive business. I never mentioned Fuller. Most of my senate colleagues thought I was a lawyer, and I did not disabuse them of the notion. Having a clean record was important to me.

I discovered that a new senator's seat location on the senate floor might determine what bills he sponsored. Seated right behind me was Sen. Ansgar L. Almen, from Lyon County in southwestern Minnesota. He was an educator and a genteel, scholarly man. He tapped me on the shoulder one day to tell me about a bill and ask for my support. He was a master at the soft sell: "I have a bill that I'd like to tell you about, senator. I don't want to get you in trouble in your first session, so I have to tell you this is controversial. But I think it might appeal to you because I know you've been interested in education. This is known as the Teacher Tenure Act. All it provides is that if a teacher is being fired, she has a chance for a hearing and an opportunity to know why, and to present her side of the story. That way, a teacher can't be dismissed without cause, without explanation."

It sounded reasonable to me. It was not uncommon then for teachers—especially young women—to be treated less than respectfully by their school boards and superintendents. I agreed that more professional courtesy was in order. I became a sponsor with Senator Almen of the Teacher Tenure Act, and it became a law.

I worked particularly hard on two bills in my freshman session. One resulted from a visit I had from a delegation from a state archaeology organization. They told me that Minnesota was the worst-mapped state in the country. It had been mapped in nineteenth-century fashion, but the maps needed for twentieth-century precision work were those made by the U.S. Geological Survey. The survey would come to Minnesota and even provide federal matching funds for the work, if the state would agree to pay a share of the costs. The lobbyists said, "Do you know that during the war, industries wanted to come to Minnesota and couldn't, because there was inadequate mapping of the topography so they couldn't know where it was feasible to build? They didn't know about water levels or topographic levels. They didn't know anything about the state from a mapping standpoint."

Getting topographical maps made for Minnesota became one of my first senate projects. The legislature passed the topographic mapping bill in 1949 and kept funding it in later years, until Minnesota became the best-mapped state in the country.

My other freshman project was to correct a defect in the governance of St. Paul schools. Before 1949, St. Paul schools were not governed by an independent school district. The school district was a department of city government. One of the city council members was Commissioner of Education and operated like a boss of the school system. The other city council members had areas of dominion. Schools had no governing body to look after their interests and to levy taxes sufficient for their needs. The schools were infused with local politics. The system became even more complicated by reason of the mayor's power to appoint council members to their various departmental portfolios. These appointments were political in nature, and not based on experience or competency.

This arrangement was so bad that it contributed to some of the first teacher strikes in state history. Not long before my election to the legislature, I was shocked when the teachers of the St. Anthony Park school our children attended were picketing in front of the school yard. I told some of them how dismayed we were to see teachers we respected on a picket line rather than in a classroom. They said, "Elmer, you have no idea how bad we feel. We hate to be on strike. But something has to be done to call attention to conditions in St. Paul. Direction of the schools by city council members is impossible. It has to be changed."

Those words were on my mind when I got to the legislature. I quickly was in touch with some of the key advocates for an independent school district, including a dynamo named Mrs. Henry Kramer, Alan Ruvelson, and Edna Paul, who went on to become a member of the first St. Paul school board. I introduced a bill to provide an independent school district for St. Paul.

I told the education people, "We've got to get business behind this. We've got to get labor behind it. We can't make election to the school board a partisan, political thing. We must find some kind of mechanism to bring people together." The mechanism we developed was the St. Paul School Committee, involving representatives of the Chamber of Commerce and organized labor as well as leaders of the education community. Its purpose was to recruit noncontroversial, well-qualified candidates for the new school board my bill would create.

I wanted organized labor at the table on this and other issues too. I wanted to count labor among my political friends—even though we did not have a union at Fuller. I was told about this conversation between some labor lobbyists: "Where did this Andersen come from?" "He's got a little paste company down on Eagle Street in St. Paul." "Who organizes it?" "It isn't organized." "It isn't organized? Let's go down and organize it." The other fellow said, "You go down and organize it. Those guys are in heaven down there."

Fuller was never organized. Some unions made overtures to our workers, but the workers would not even attend a union meeting. I appreciated the fact that our people did not feel the need for a union, but I respected what unions had meant and had done for working people elsewhere. And union support was helpful to a senator from a big urban district.

One of the six senators from St. Paul, Milton Lightner, was a very conservative man who opposed government regulations of all kind and taxes of every nature. He was genteel, upright, well mannered, groomed, and polished—but also difficult. He fought the school district bill. Finally, I said, "Milton, there's got to be a basis on which you'll compromise on this. I'm willing to compromise. But there's going to be an independent school district in St. Paul. What do you want? If you study this at all, you've got to agree that we need an independent school district." He said, "I'll tell you, Elmer. If you put that bill of yours up to a plebiscite vote of the people, and they approve it, then I guess I'll have to admit they better have it." "I agree to that right now." I said, "We'll pass the bill contingent upon a public vote at an independent election." That provision in the bill meant that Mrs. Kramer, Alan Ruvelson, Edna Paul, and a host of other school advocates had to mount a public campaign. They worked tirelessly to build support among every constituency in the city. I helped, too.

In October 1950, St. Paul voters approved the change from a commissioner form of school governance to an independent school district, with an elected school board. Full fiscal independence did not come until 1964, but school reform in St. Paul was well begun.

Mr. Chairman

I HAD TO WIN MY SENATE SEAT all over again in November 1950. After my hard-fought victory in the special election in February 1949, the campaign twenty months later was an anticlimax. I faced only token opposition. Much to my gratification, St. Anthony Park turned out strongly for me again.

My opposition was even weaker in 1954, the third and final time I ran for the senate. I had hopes of running without opposition that year. But in the last hour of the last day on which candidates could file for office, a man named Fred Blum wandered into the Ramsey County filing office and said, "Who is running for county commissioner in my district?" There were three or four. "Oh," he said, "that's not for me. Who is running in the house district?" There were two or three running there. Blum said, "Who is running against Senator Andersen? He's my senator." "Nobody has filed against him." "That's for me."

I decided to teach Blum a little lesson. I decided to organize heavily in his home precinct, the area around Macalester College. I announced to Macalester College students that I could provide them with an internship experience in political campaigning. About fifteen students volunteered. I said, "You're going to have as your project just one precinct, but you're going to organize it like no precinct was ever organized before. After this experience, if you ever run for elective office, you'll know how it's done." I taught them how to get polling lists, call on everyone who voted, find out who was going to vote for me, give them a reminder call just before the election, arrange transportation to the polls—in short, to do all of the things a good political organization does. We overwhelmed that precinct. My opponent learned not to be so casual about seeking public office.

The ease of my 1950 election helped wear off the novelty of senate service. Actually, at the start of the 1951 session, I felt like a veteran and was eager to get to work on weighty issues. I was counted as a second-term senator even though I had served less than two years of the four-year term that

Charlie Orr began in 1947. Second-term rank brought with it a coveted seat on the senate's Finance Committee, which along with the Tax Committee is where real power resides in the Minnesota Senate. Practically every activity of the state comes before the Finance Committee. University presidents, business executives, and leaders of every activity in need of state funds come to the committee to plead their case.

I took my new committee assignment gladly, but I soon learned that in the Finance Committee, seniority was everything. In those years, senators even sat at the meeting table according to seniority. The chair was at the head of the table, and all the seats were assigned. The newly appointed committee members were at the table's tail end and were expected to keep quiet.

We new members of the Finance Committee soon formed a rump sub-caucus that we called "The Tail Enders." We badly wanted to participate in the committee's work and felt left out by the old-timers at the head of the table. They would mumble among themselves, grunt out a motion, and decide questions almost privately. We were supposed to just go along. One day I suggested, "Why don't we vote 'No' real loud on one of these things, to get their attention?"

The group agreed and picked the issue on which we would make our protest. The older senators droned along in their usual way. When they came to a vote, a loud "No!" came from our end of the table. The chair was Henry Sullivan from St. Cloud, a staid, orderly person. He looked over his glasses down the table at us and soberly inquired what the trouble was. "You're not paying enough attention to us," we said. "We can't hear what you're saying up there. We thought we'd call your attention to the fact that we're here." Sullivan did not seem amused.

Gradually, however, we got the recognition we sought. I came to love my work on the Finance Committee. It afforded me a fine education in government, politics, and human affairs.

Richard Griggs from Duluth showed me how great the impact of one person can be. Griggs, a regent for the University of Minnesota, was a leader in getting the Duluth State Teachers' College converted to a branch of the university. He wanted the school to give up its stuffy old building and build a lovely new campus on a hill overlooking the city and Lake Superior. He was among the first to have a vision for what the University of Minnesota-Duluth could become. He engineered a strategy for financing: he would get the county to put up one-third of the money, the state would appropriate one-third, and private donors—meaning Griggs himself—would be tapped for the remaining third. He came before the Finance Committee with this proposal, and with few friends to speak in its favor. The university was not enthusiastic about having a branch campus in Duluth, and few Minnesotans outside northeastern Minnesota had much interest in the idea. Griggs made an impassioned plea before the committee. Then there was dead silence. So, I spoke up—as I was always willing to do. I said, "When a community will put in one-third of the money for a worthwhile project, and raise one-third of the money privately, and asks the state for just one-third participation, we ought to do it, Mr. Chairman. I move approval and a recommendation of the bill to pass." I thought Griggs would crawl over the table and hug me. The bill passed, and the University of Minnesota-Duluth got its hillside campus.

That led to a friendship with Dick Griggs, the Duluth dynamo. He was a big-game hunter who loved to roam the world, even as a very old man. I remember calling on him when he was in his nineties. He said, "Elmer, I used to think I was pretty well off and could do things, but I'm living too long. I'm starting to wonder whether I'm going to come out even." Dick was an example of pioneering Americans who have a vision and are willing to pitch in and make it come true.

Another illustration of the power of one determined citizen came from a woman whose husband was a patient in a state tuberculosis sanatorium. She called on me in the 1953 session to complain that smoking was allowed in her husband's ward. She was sure the secondhand smoke was bad for him— a view that would be scientifically confirmed decades later. She asked, could there be a law that would place patients who did not smoke in nonsmoking wards? It seemed reasonable to me. I offered to check a few facts and get back to her in a week.

I called Gov. C. Elmer Anderson's commissioner of welfare, Jarle Leirfallom. I said, "Jarle, do we allow smoking in our TB sanatoriums?" He said we did. "Is it possible that a person who doesn't smoke would be subjected to the smoke of others in the ward where he was cared for?" Yes, he said again. I said, "Is that such a good idea?" "No," he said, "it's not a good idea. But there's a limit to how many things we can attack at one time. When we're working on TB, we can't really undertake to get people to quit smoking." "Could you live with a law that provided that anybody who did not smoke would be housed in a ward where nonsmoking prevailed?" He said, "We could live with it. I think it would be a pretty good law."

When the patient's wife called on me again, I told her I would introduce a bill for no-smoking wards in the state sanatorium. But, I said, "I have so many bills that I'm working on that I can't give this much attention. You'll have to do the lobbying work." "Oh, I'll do that," she said, with a note of determination in her voice that pleased me very much. She became a one-person blitzkrieg at the legislature. Working night and day, she contacted every legislator about smoking in TB sanatoriums. Not long afterward, I was busy in another meeting when I was summoned to appear before the senate's Welfare Committee by its chair, Sen. Harry Wahlstrand of Willmar. He wanted me to bring the sanatorium bill before the committee immediately. "That woman is here again," he said. She made a nuisance of herself but for a good cause. The bill passed and became law because one person was dedicated to getting it done.

Being on the Finance Committee led to knowing Sen. Gerald Mullin, who was selflessly devoted to the University of Minnesota. He was *the* university legislator. He represented a northeast Minneapolis district and was a lawyer by profession. He once asked whether I knew about a bill regulating garbage. "I sure do," I said. "It's causing me trouble, but we have to pass it." I had pig producers in my district who fed their animals raw garbage. The garbage bill would require that it be cooked before it could be fed. That could put all those hog producers out of business. One senator, Jim Keller from Winona, was in the garbage-hauling business, and he detested the bill. He was quietly trading his vote on other bills with anyone he could get to vote against it. Mullin said, "Elmer, I made a terrible mistake. I made a deal with Jim Keller to vote against the garbage bill, in return for his vote on the university budget. You know how hard I have to work on that budget." I knew. "The proponents of the garbage bill have taken a count, and it's just about a tie. You've got to get busy and pass that garbage bill, or I'm going to be in the dog house for the rest of my life." He feared the wrath of the university health researchers who were proponents of the bill.

As a favor to Mullin, I got busy on that garbage bill. It passed by only one vote. Mullin voted against it—he had to. That demonstrated how far he would go to help the university. He was instrumental in securing the gains the University of Minnesota made in national stature during the 1950s, though his contribution was not widely known outside the legislature.

Mullin was a fine man whose interests reflected his love for learning. All senators seemed to have pet topics they would trot out during floor debate at times when they wanted to stall a vote until absent members arrived. For example, one senator always wanted to speak in favor of a constitutional amendment allowing trial de novo, or new trials, when cases were decided on technical grounds. Mullin's great theme was the early Greek city-states.

He admired their form of government. He would launch into an oration on how the Greeks did things, how great their leaders were, what marvelous ideas they produced, and how we should all study them.

The senate was full of interesting people, many of them great talkers. It was typical for someone to stand and say, "I really hadn't intended to speak on this issue," and then drone on for a half-hour.

I made the warm friendship of Sen. Tom Vukelich of Gilbert, on the Iron Range. He was a typical son of the Range—born of immigrant parents, fiercely loyal to his region, and dedicated to making government serve people. His background was modest but bolstered by willingness to work and an appreciation of education. The Iron Range was home to a number of junior colleges, which grew into the community colleges of today. At that time, junior colleges were the financial responsibility of local school districts. Even though the region was flush with tax money paid by the mining companies, Range legislators wanted more from the state for their junior colleges. Their appeal came before the Finance Committee. Vukelich thought I was a great guy because I was the first member of the senate to support state aid for junior colleges without having one in his own district. Of course, it was not Vukelich who convinced me. My own experience at Muskegon Junior College made me see the value of those institutions, especially to young people without much means.

The Finance Committee was not my only assignment. Perhaps because of my involvement with Family Service in St. Paul, I became a member of the Welfare Committee. Before long, I had visited every one of the state's mental hospitals and correctional facilities. In 1953, I initiated a committee study on the problems of alcoholism, to be done during the interim between legislative sessions. Up to that time, the state did not recognize or address alcoholism in any way, except at the Willmar State Hospital, where an able man named Nelson Bradley managed a program that housed totally destitute alcoholics who had been declared wards of the state. But even there, the policy was to do little more than sober up the patients and send them home. State policy was not to treat alcoholism as an illness.

The interim study done at my instigation led to a change in that policy. The legislature established a program to treat alcoholism within the state Department of Public Health and also urged the state's employers to treat chronic alcohol abuse as an illness, not as employee misconduct. We wanted a new response to the chemically dependent worker—not dismissal, but diagnosis and treatment, the same response as to an employee fallen victim to heart disease. I believe the legislators of the 1950s helped bring about a more constructive and compassionate attitude toward alcoholism in Minnesota.

I sponsored a bill to require that the counselors for alcoholics employed in state facilities must themselves be recovering alcoholics. My idea became law and gradually caught on in other states too. But it was not an easy idea to sell. Take the response of Claude Baughman, a crusty senator who seemed to like to take me on. He rose on the senate floor with the observation that "the good senator from Ramsey [County] has brought us many unusual ideas before. But I never thought I'd see the day when anyone would say that a person had to be a drunk in order to qualify for state employment!"

My work at Family Service gave me an interest in adoption. In the 1950s, it was illegal for adoptive parents to be charged or to pay anything for obtaining a child through an adoption agency. Charles E. Dow was head of the Children's Home Society of Minnesota, the state's leading adoption agency. It was located in my district, so I knew of its fine reputation. Dow told me that the no-charge policy was not serving Minnesotans well. "We cannot afford to develop our services to the full," he explained. "As a result, adoption is becoming an activity of lawyers, who can charge, and they charge plenty. They make no real effort to match the children and their backgrounds with those of the families they are going to be in. Children are commodities to them. It would really improve child placement if we had some income, so we could perform more services and do a better job than these attorneys are doing." I knew his organization could be trusted to be reasonable in its charges. Dow pointed out that "people have expenses when they have a child naturally. It seems unreasonable that they can't pay anything to offset the cost involved in adopting a child."

He convinced me. I introduced a bill to permit paying fees for services by adoption agencies. It quickly became controversial. A lobbyist for the Catholic archdiocese named Father Meagher opposed my bill in no uncertain terms. Father Meagher was a strong, able advocate for whatever he believed in, and a vigorous enemy of whatever he opposed. I was never sure why the Catholic Church was so hostile to my bill. But their opposition kept me from succeeding. I passed the idea on to young Al Quie, a freshman senator from Dennison who went on to be a congressman and governor. He eventually succeeded with the bill. That started what has become the standard for adoptions all over the country. Professional agencies replaced private attorneys as the main source of adoption services. I am convinced that children were the beneficiaries of that change.

My experience with the adoption bill only strengthened my belief that you never lose when you are working for good in the public arena. Everything you do contributes something, if only something that others can pick up in the future and carry a little farther. Ultimately, good ideas prevail, and until they do, you can take satisfaction in knowing that you did what you could for a worthy cause.

I also served on the Conservation Committee, the panel that had oversight of environmental matters. I gravitated to environmental and state park issues. My partner on one of them was Sen. Grover George from Red Wing, a modest, soft-spoken, faithful man. He came to me with an idea: "Elmer, the people of my district would like to have a state park at Frontenac. I don't know how to go about it. I wonder if you'd help me."

I wanted to see the place, so we drove southeast of St. Paul to Red Wing, then several miles farther to a dramatic river bluff. We needed to cut through brush to climb to the top of it. When we reached the top, a gorgeous view of the wide Mississippi River was before us. I wondered how such a spectacular river area could have escaped development for so long. I told George that I would be delighted to help preserve that spot as a state park.

Senator George became the chief sponsor of the bill to establish Frontenac State Park, and I was an especially active cosponsor. My efforts attracted the notice of Judge Hella—who was not a judge but the head of the Parks Division of the Department of Conservation (the Department of Natural Resources today). Hella began to seek me out and talk about his vision for state parks. Soon, we were planning other parks. Fort Snelling State Park, Bear Head Lake State Park, and Voyageurs National Park were already on our minds in those years.

A Conservation Committee hearing gave me the privilege of witnessing the clash of two of Minnesota's larger-than-life characters, Sen. Gordon Rosenmeier and environmentalist Sigurd Olson. In the early 1950s, President Harry Truman had imposed a ban on airplane flights over the Boundary Waters Canoe Area, to protect the region's wild character. Rosenmeier, a Little Falls attorney and the powerful chair of the senate's Judiciary Committee, introduced a resolution to memorialize Congress to repeal that ban. He argued that the ban was an intrusion on Minnesota's sovereignty.

Sigurd Olson came to the capitol from his home in Ely to oppose Rosenmeier's resolution. He was already northeastern Minnesota's leading voice for natural preservation. I met him for the first time at that committee meeting. I was most impressed with his sincerity and eloquence and his apparent immunity to snide remarks. The point was made that he was a canoe outfitter to wilderness campers, and so had a personal stake in the airplane ban. I could see him bristle, but he would say nothing. He was a gentle man. He convinced me that we should keep the airplane ban. I knew the area well enough to know that those who opposed the ban had matters other than the region's long-term good at heart. I helped defeat that resolution. President Truman's ban remains in effect to this day.

Olson and I eventually became friends. I had a wonderful experience with him when I was on the Board of Regents of the University of Minnesota in the 1970s. He was slated to receive an honorary degree from the University of Minnesota-Duluth, and I was asked to present it to him. It gave me a chance to pay tribute to a man with whom I had worked on many environmental projects. I was delighted to place the hood over his head.

One of my great disappointments relates to Olson. He once suggested, "Elmer, you and I should have a canoe trip together. I'd like that, and I think we'd have a good time paddling and visiting. Sometime, when you see a few days open, give me a ring and I'll try to get my schedule in order." To my regret, I never did.

I also came to admire Gordon Rosenmeier—even though I differed with him often. He was an able person, a shrewd debater, and a masterful legislative manipulator. I am sure he was an effective trial lawyer. He had a knack for finding something that related to his Judiciary Committee's responsibility in every major bill that came along. He managed to get his hands on any bill he wanted to shape or kill—and his reach was long.

With Rosenmeier, one always had to be on the lookout for some undisclosed agenda or consequence. Take his bill on mineral rights. In northern Minnesota around the turn of the century, land was valued for its trees, nothing more. The area's rich mineral deposits had not been discovered. When the land was cleared, its owners considered it worthless and would let it revert to the state for unpaid taxes. But some smart lawyer devised a way for people to reserve the ownership of the mineral rights below the land's surface, even while losing title to the surface. These mineral rights reservations were not registered at that time, and taxes were never paid on them. The surface was sold to people who built homes and other buildings. Rosenmeier sponsored a bill that, as he presented it, was aimed at "protecting the owner of the surface." If the mineral rights owner wanted to mine the minerals, he would be required to reimburse the people who owned the surface land. I pointed out to the senate that there was more to Rosenmeier's bill than protecting the homeowners' rights. "Don't you see what this really does? This gives the owner of mineral rights, who never pays any taxes, never even discloses whether he owns them or not, the right of eminent domain, to take over the surface whether the owners wish to sell or not. Of course, he should reimburse them, but he shouldn't have the right to move them against their will." I managed to kill the bill, but it passed after I left the legislature. Keeping Rosenmeier in check required vigilance.

Rosenmeier represented power and people who operated from positions of power. He hated public housing, which was a new concept in the 1950s. I supported it. I would argue, "There are some things that are essential to people's welfare, and housing is one of them. Unless you want to put people in an environment that gives them miserable lives, you ought to help with housing." I helped create the first housing authority in Minnesota; Rosenmeier fought it.

We fought vigorously but well—that is, with no personal animosity or anger. In fact, we became good friends. We drew closer after we were both out of the legislature. I was even asked to speak at his funeral. He makes me mindful of a fellow board member on the University Foundation to whom I once said, "I never liked anyone so much with whom I disagreed so often." I loved him because he was so able.

My years in the senate coincided with the service of Archie Miller of rural Hennepin County as majority leader. He had succeeded my District 42 predecessor, Charlie Orr, as leader of the Conservative Caucus. As I advanced in the organization, I began to think about who might succeed Miller. I knew Gordon Rosenmeier wanted to be the senate's leader, partly because his father, Christian Rosenmeier, had held that position in the 1920s. Miller decided to leave the senate the same year I did, in 1958. He was not succeeded as leader by Rosenmeier but by another splendid man with clear strength of character, John Zwach of Walnut Grove. I like to think that while I was on my way out of office, I had something to do with Zwach's climb into leadership.

When Zwach had served in the house, he had been something of a maverick, a moderate-to-liberal thinker in the Conservative Caucus. In other words, he had been like me. But in the senate, Zwach was more in tune with the Conservative majority. We sat together on the Finance Committee. He had a distinctive, high-pitched voice and a tendency to elongate certain syllables. For example, when I would propose to spend what he thought was too much, he would say, "Senator, don't you think you're going a little *strooong* on that item?"

Zwach moved from the house to the senate in the 1948 election. But the senate's rules provided that the clock started running on seniority not when a senator took office but when the majority caucus admitted him to its ranks. Zwach's maverick status in the house made him suspect in Conservative eyes. Even though he was elected in November and I not until the following February, I was admitted to the majority caucus first. I had more seniority than Zwach did.

That came to be important. I was on the senate's Organizing Committee, which gave me some influence over the committee assignments of other senators. In 1955, Zwach and I were both eligible for major chairs. Two committees were up for assignment, Education and Welfare. I knew Zwach wanted to be chair of the Education Committee, which carried more status. I also thought I knew more about welfare than the technicalities of education. My additional seniority gave me first choice. So, I conferred with Zwach. I said, "John, I have great confidence in you. I know you're Catholic. If you'll tell me you won't show a bias in favor of parochial schools in running the Education Committee, I'll step aside. I'll take Welfare and you'll get Education." That is how he became chair of the Education Committee and I took the helm of the Welfare Committee at the start of the 1955 session.

When I decided not to seek reelection in 1958, I talked to Zwach again about his senate role. I told him, "Gordon Rosenmeier wants to be majority leader. He really shouldn't be. He doesn't always represent the caucus or the public interest. I admire and respect him, but he shouldn't be our leader. I'm leaving the senate, but I thought this: if you're willing to consider being majority leader, I'll spend a lot of time working to elect people who will support you." He assured me that he was willing to serve. I got busy and did as I vowed. In 1959, Zwach defeated Rosenmeier in a close contest and became senate majority leader. He left the senate a few years later to run for Congress, where he served with distinction for eight years. We remained good friends until he died. His daughter Barbara Sykora is a member of the Minnesota House today.

Being a member of the Organizing Committee had several advantages. Not only could I help decide committee chairs, but I could also choose my own seatmate on the floor. My seatmate in the early 1950s was Ray Julkowski, a lawyer from Minneapolis. When he was defeated, I was to have a new seatmate. I went to Harry Wahlstrand from Willmar, who as chair of the Organizing Committee could place senators where he thought they might serve best. I said, "I want a farmer this time, a real dirt farmer, so I can hear earthy opinions. I want him sitting right next to me."

So I was assigned to sit next to Joe Josefson from Lyon County. He was a successor to my friend from my first days in the senate, Sen. Ansgar Almen. Josefson was just what I was seeking, a down-to-earth farmer. We had a great time together. We disagreed on many things, mostly because of the genuine differences between city and country districts.

The farm bloc controlled the legislature in the 1950s. The state had not had a proper redistricting in many years, so district lines had not kept up with the changes in the state's population distribution. City legislators were greatly outnumbered. Anytime there was any issue of city versus country, the farm bloc would come together and decide the matter in the country's favor. Yet I had a slight advantage—or so I thought—because I was counted as part of the so-called farm bloc, a caucus of senators with rural interests. I inherited that status from my predecessor, Charlie Orr. In his day, western Ramsey County was dotted with farms. I still represented a dwindling number of hog farmers.

Early on, I learned that the advantage of membership in the farm bloc had its limit. Somebody had the idea that it was unfair that Ramsey County was charged gasoline tax on fuel that county vehicles consumed while servicing the capitol buildings. It was a pretty thin argument over a small amount of money, but I was willing to try almost anything. I managed to get to the floor a bill to exempt Ramsey County vehicles from a portion of their gas tax bill. When it came up for a vote, to my surprise, it was overwhelmingly defeated. My farm bloc friends had all opposed it. Senator Almen, who sat behind me, tapped me on the shoulder and said, "Senator, I hope you didn't take your membership in the farm bloc too seriously."

A number of outstate senators became my good friends. I was especially fond of Oscar Swenson of Nicollet, a great leader in the farm bloc and an old-timer when I arrived. He could tell wonderful stories about the days of Gov. Floyd B. Olson and senate legends such as A. J. Rockne from Zumbrota. While in St. Paul, he stayed at the Angus Hotel on Lowry Hill. I used to drive him there after evening sessions. I would drive slowly and pepper him with questions, so I could learn as much senate history as I could. He seemed to me to be typical of Scandinavian pioneers, independent, clearheaded, and forthright.

Even though I had achieved the title "Mr. Chairman," the 1955 session was a discouraging one. The work of the Welfare Committee was not popular. In the 1950s, there was little sympathy for people who were impaired or experiencing difficulty. In fact, the public's attitudes then are much like they have been in the 1990s. Then and now, people say of those receiving government assistance, "We're going to get them off their duffs and get them working." That is an attitude of punishment rather than aid. The difference is that people have more information now and ought to know better. Then, people were unaware of how many human problems are beyond one individual's ability to control. Data were lacking and often inaccurate. Industry did not take responsibility for its people. A lot was not known.

Much of the abuse of welfare is by vendors, not by recipients. I came to resent the behavior of the nursing home industry. Minnesota provided medical care, including nursing home care, for any indigent older person. All that was required was a doctor's signature attesting that nursing home care was required. The nursing home industry was quick to exploit that situation. Now the single biggest item in the state human services budget is nursing home care, and a legal specialty has grown up around counseling people how to divest themselves of their assets so that they become eligible for government support in a nursing home.

It is the hardest thing in the world to help where help is needed, without exposing yourself to abuse. I was liberal on welfare needs. But I really bristled when I thought state assistance was being abused. I would become annoyed when I heard about blind people seeking all kinds of things that were way beyond reason for the state to provide. I wanted state money to be used to rehabilitate people, to give them the help they needed to help themselves. But then, I wanted the state to step aside and let them make their way.

Welfare issues were not easy. But in the 1955 session, it seemed that nothing was. I ran into trouble with my plan for combating drinking while driving. Even one of my dearest friends in the legislature, Rep. Peter Popovich of St. Paul, opposed me. My proposal was that when a person's driver's license was revoked because of a conviction for driving under the influence of alcohol, a special license plate should be put on his or her car. It would identify the car as the property of someone whose license to drive had been revoked. Then, if an officer spotted the car on the road, he could stop it and ask to see the driver's license. It would be a way to catch offenders who were driving without a license. I thought that was a reasonable thing, but lawyers in particular opposed it. Under my scheme, people caught driving without a license would automatically face further punishment. I think lawyers like more wiggle room in driving laws than my idea afforded.

I also believed that the most severe traffic violations should lead to the confiscation of the offender's vehicle. Some drivers simply should not be on the road. It seemed to me that confiscating the vehicle was much more effective than revoking a driver's license. Sure, maybe an offender will find another car somehow, but if he or she violates again, the state could confiscate that car too. I thought it perverse that the state confiscated weapons that were used illegally to threaten a deer but did not confiscate a vehicle that threatened human life. But few other legislators saw the issue that way.

The one bright spot in the 1955 session was the enactment of Minnesota's first modern-era civil rights bill, the Fair Employment Practices Act. It outlawed discrimination in employment on the basis of race, color, creed, religion, or national origin. It also created a Fair Employment Practices Commission to investigate complaints and take corrective action when warranted. I was its chief sponsor in the senate. Passage of that bill was a marvelous moment, both in Minnesota history and my own. Minnesota was only the fifth state in the nation to enact such legislation.

I had long believed that the ill treatment of people because of characteristics such as race or religion was shameful, and that society ought to use every tool at its disposal—including government—to end such hateful practices. But I was also proud to sponsor the Fair Employment Practices Act because I had become well acquainted with several leading members of Minnesota's black community.

One special friend was Ed Hall. I had known him before I was elected, because his daughter Ermine had been a classmate of Eleanor's at Minnesota College, a Lutheran high school. He and his brother ran a barbershop on Grand Avenue in St. Paul that was the political center of the neighborhood. All the politicians went there to pick up and distribute bits of news. For the price of a haircut, patrons at Ed Hall's shop could meet candidates, legislators, even occasionally a governor. It was a remarkable spot.

Ed became secretary of the barbers' union. He kept in touch with all the barbers through his union work and proved to be a good politician in his own right. Not long after I arrived in the senate, I approached Ed with a question: "How would you like to be up at the Capitol?" "I think I'd like that," he said. "I think I can get you in as a sergeant at arms in the senate." Not every freshman can make such a promise, but I had inherited some of Charlie Orr's patronage as well as his seat. It quickly became apparent to some of the senate's old-timers that quite a few people in the visitor's gallery were watching me. That was because Ed would point me out to people who came to the gallery and tell them what a fine young new senator I was. Ed was a wise man and a genuine friend, one to whom I could turn for counsel. We became so close that Eleanor and I would occasionally worship with him at his church, Pilgrim Baptist in St. Paul.

The idea of making racial discrimination illegal was a new one in 1955, and even in a progressive state like Minnesota, it was controversial. Many in the business community deeply resented the idea of outlawing discrimination in employment. They claimed that government should not be permitted to interfere with their ability to hire and fire employees at their own discretion. It was difficult for them to accept the idea that the state could impose on them an obligation to be ethical in their personnel practices. They felt that they were doing all that government should ask of them, simply by providing jobs.

The business attitude infected many members of the senate's Conservative majority. I had to win support for the bill in both caucuses for it to pass. Fortunately, the senate included many people who put the principles of fairness and justice ahead of loyalty to particular interests.

Debate on the night the senate passed the bill was long and strenuous. But for me, that night's most memorable moment came after the vote to pass the bill, when the senate had recessed for the night. As I prepared to leave the chamber, I could see a black sergeant at arms edging toward me, wanting to say something. I paused. He said, "Senator, tonight you made me feel like a real man for the first time in my life."

With the exception of the Fair Employment Practices Act, few of the things I set out to do in 1955 had been accomplished. I ended the year discouraged. My old friend Adolph Johnson of the Associated Press sensed how I was feeling, and came to me with wise words: "You've got to realize that the legislative process was never intended to be easy." I reflected often on that comment during the years ahead. Adolph was right: enormous persistence is required to see a public project through from concept to completion. One or two setbacks are no justification for giving up.

But now and then comes a legislative year when everything seems to fall into place—a year like 1957.

An Outstanding Session

W HEN PEOPLE ASK WHAT I CONSIDER my most important project
in a long life of public service, my mind turns to the 1957 legislative
session and special education. The 1957 legislature produced a number of
landmark achievements. Among them was a group of bills providing programs of special education for children whose exceptional needs were not
well met in the normal school situation.

The work on those measures started in 1955. In the years when the legislature met only in odd-numbered years, it was customary between sessions
for interim commissions to study particular projects and prepare major bills
for the forthcoming session. The interim commission on special-needs children came about as a result of my visits with Dr. Maynard Reynolds of the
University of Minnesota. The education of exceptional children was his
specialty. I became excited when I learned how much had been developed
in that field, and that no state was doing a comprehensive job implement-
ing the newly acquired understanding of those children's learning potential.
There was a need, I thought, that Minnesota could meet.

The commission appointed to examine the matter included me as chairman and Senators Al Quie of Dennison (a future congressman and governor), Stanley W. Holmquist of Grove City (my brother-in-law and a future
senate majority leader), and Joe Vadheim of Tyler. On the house side were
Wayne Bassett of Worthington, Sam Franz of Mountain Lake, Joyce Lund
of Wabasha, and L. B. Erdahl of Frost. Franz was the commission's vice chairman, and Quie was its secretary. Two devoted staff members, Abner Johnsen
and Esther Bauer, also contributed much to the commission's success.

Maynard Reynolds was our guide. He alerted others in his field to our
study and called our attention to them and their work. We learned that we
should use the word "exceptional" rather than "handicapped" to describe
the population of children we were examining. Gifted children were among
those not well served by the typical school situation, and needing special
facilities and curriculum. Furthermore, the gifted were receiving the least

attention of any category of exceptional children—a problem that persists to this day. Talented youngsters can easily become bored if they are not adequately challenged, possibly leading to behavior problems that can distort their entire lives.

The commission reviewed all the legislation and programs already in place in Minnesota dealing with educating exceptional children. The conditions examined included blindness and visual impairment, deafness and hearing disability, speech defects, physical disability or disease, emotional instability and psychotic conditions, gifted attributes, and mental retardation in both moderate and severe forms. Next, we set out to determine what other states were doing. These were big undertakings, but we became a dedicated group, willing to work long hours, as we perceived the great opportunity that we had to improve young lives.

Our feelings were stirred by what we learned. Many children once thought incapable of intellectual development and consigned to a lifetime of custodial care could learn and function in society. Research had revealed that even the severely mentally retarded could learn to do simple tasks, and the mildly retarded could become self-supporting. Children with Down's syndrome could eventually be employed and live independently, with the right care and consideration. In other words, talents remained undeveloped, lives were diminished, and potentials were left unfulfilled. We vowed to change that situation.

The commission held hearings around the state, and individually and collectively made many visits to facilities serving exceptional children. We learned a good deal. On one occasion, we visited a group of children afflicted with muscular dystrophy who were struggling to walk. We were warned before entering the classroom that the children might fall. Even if we felt impelled to help them get back to their feet, we were asked not to do so. It was up to the child to regain an upright posture on his or her own. As we watched the children going down the double-bar equipment, one of them did fall. Sure enough, we felt that we should rush to help the youngster. But we obeyed orders and watched as the little girl pulled herself over to an upright bar, then drew herself back to her feet. Her smile of accomplishment and satisfaction was unforgettable. I learned that day not to help so much that we deny people the satisfaction of hard-earned accomplishment.

On another occasion, we visited the home of a little blind girl. She seemed to skip around the house as freely as any child. We wondered how that was possible. We were told that everything was carefully placed and never relocated, so after the child had learned the location of the furniture through touch, she could move around confidently.

We asked the parents if the child's disability had in any way impaired the opportunities of the family's other children. The mother replied, "No, quite the contrary, she has taught the other children the value of the sense of touch, and how it can be used. Their lives have been enhanced by her blindness, not limited." Experiences like that encouraged us to think that much could be done in local schools to adapt people with disabilities to a regular life experience, rather than set them aside in residential learning centers.

Our study indicated that Minnesota and other states had done a few good things for some children, but not a single state had a coordinated, complete program to serve all those needing special assistance. For example, Minnesota had a splendid school for the blind and another for the deaf, both residential centers of high quality. For other special-needs children, Minnesota offered virtually nothing. One major decision we confronted was whether to opt for more residential learning centers, or to keep the child at home and bring new programs to him or her. We determined that while nothing should be done to injure the residential centers Minnesota already had in operation, much more could be done by allowing children to stay in their homes and providing special assistance to them in concert with the regular school curriculum.

We proposed authorizing any Minnesota parent who felt a special-needs child was not receiving adequate educational opportunity to call on the state commissioner of education and ask for an investigation of the child's situation. If the commissioner determined that the child was not receiving adequate learning opportunities, he had the responsibility to find services for the child somewhere and send the bill to the local school district. This proposal got the attention of local school districts and gave them incentive to do more locally for special-needs children. To ease the schools' burden, we suggested that state aid for exceptional children be distributed on a per teacher basis, not a per pupil basis, to avoid overburdening districts with unusually small numbers of exceptional children.

More teachers of special education were needed. We recommended that St. Cloud State College (now St. Cloud State University) and Mankato State College (now Minnesota State University-Mankato) offer the state's first programs for training teachers in special education. To encourage young people to enter the field, a scholarship program was devised.

Children with emotional disturbance or psychotic conditions posed special problems that we felt had to be met in some way other than a normal classroom. We proposed the building of a center for emotionally disturbed and psychotic children at Lino Lakes, to be staffed by specially trained professionals. We met with experts at the Menninger Clinic at Topeka, Kansas, a leader in the study and treatment of emotional and psychotic disorders, to help formulate our plans.

We brought a challenging set of recommendations to the 1957 legislature. Yet the full package was enacted into law. For the first time in anyone's memory, all the recommendations of a legislative study commission were enacted in the first legislative session following the study. We succeeded because the need was compelling, the opportunity attractive, the legislature responsive, and the profession cooperative and united. We impressed on the professional community that if they went to the legislature divided, with some insisting that the best way to meet children's needs was in residential schools and others supporting our recommendations for integrating exceptional children into the regular school program, nothing would get done. The professionals agreed to present a united front, which helped a great deal in passing the legislation.

An organization called Friends of the Mentally Retarded was also most helpful. They educated families about the potential of their mentally retarded children and removed the stigma many families of retarded people felt. In those years, some families actually hid mentally retarded children, out of fear that others would think that the retarded child's siblings would someday give birth to mentally retarded children too. Attitudes like that were in play when we inquired why Otter Tail County had no classes for the mentally retarded. The reply was that no mentally retarded children lived in Otter Tail County! It took years before people understood that in most cases of mental retardation, the hereditary influence is slight. Any family could produce a retarded child. I like to think that the interim commission contributed to the eradication of misinformation about exceptional children, as well as to the creation of opportunity.

We benefited from the cooperation of Sen. Robert Dunlap of Plainview, who sponsored a bill in 1957 to match federal funds that were newly available for library service expansion. It permitted counties in rural areas with limited library service to join forces in establishing bookmobiles and other book services. We approached Bob with an offer: Since we were interested in libraries, and certainly he was interested in special education, why not pool our resources of legislative support and enact both programs? He agreed. Minnesota not only became a special education pioneer but also became the first state to fully match the new federal money for rural libraries.

So many other people were helpful that I cannot begin to name them all. But I must single out my friend John Zwach, the chairman of the senate's Education Committee. He was responsive to the commission's recommendations.

The bills we passed in 1957 put Minnesota in the forefront in special education. As a result, local school districts were obliged to provide a suitable education for all the children in their jurisdiction. Parents had recourse when they believed their children were not adequately served. Funds were provided for special education personnel in local schools, for training of special education teachers, and for scholarships to encourage young people to enter the growing field. Also authorized was a new facility for emotionally disturbed and psychotic children at Lino Lakes—though the legislature did not stay with our original concept. The cost of professional help at the new center proved to be about $25,000 a year per child—an enormous amount of money at that time. The legislature balked at costs that high, and the Lino Lakes institution eventually became a center for juvenile offenders, rather than a treatment center.

Years passed before Congress followed Minnesota's lead and enacted a national program of special education. The courts also weighed in with new requirements, and the program became more complicated and legalistic. But Minnesotans can take pride in knowing their state was among the first to assure every child the opportunity to learn.

I had several other major bills on my docket in 1957. One was the creation of the Metropolitan Planning Commission, the body that was the precursor of the Metropolitan Council in the Twin Cities. The planning commission was the Twin Cities area's first attempt at regional coordination of decisions involving land use, infrastructure development, and population growth.

In the 1950s there were already upwards of three hundred units of government in the metropolitan area—cities, counties, school districts, townships, and special jurisdictions all counted—and there was no coordination or relationship among them. One community was perfectly free to install a landfill right next to where an adjacent community planned to build a school. It seemed obvious to me that some entity to do common planning for the metropolitan area would make a positive contribution to the ungainly status quo. I could not imagine that there would be any opposition when I first proposed the creation of the commission in 1953.

I was wrong. There was opposition almost everywhere, at least at the outset. I found an ally in the Municipal League—now known as the League of Minnesota Cities—and a few of the area's planning professionals spoke in support of the idea. But almost all of the units of government in the Twin Cities area were opposed. The central cities were afraid it would lead to suburban areas seeking services at the expense of the city taxpayers. The suburbs and counties were afraid of domination by the central cities. Every jurisdiction had its turf and wanted to protect it.

I saw that if any joint planning were to occur, we would have to start modestly. We emphasized that the commission we proposed would not have any authority to stop development. In its final form, my bill provided that if a local government jurisdiction was planning to make any major physical change, it had to give the planning commission sixty days' notice. The planning commission would then have sixty days to consider it and express an opinion. That opinion would not be binding on the governing bodies of the jurisdictions in question. The planning commission would have no authority except the weight of its professional expertise.

Then, there was the matter of how it would be funded. I felt that any agency of that kind had to have an established source of revenue. I favored a levy on all property in the metropolitan area, but the jurisdictions involved preferred to make an annual appropriation to the commission. That would, in essence, make the funding of the commission voluntary and would guarantee its failure, in my view. That argument over the commission's funding prevented its enactment in 1953 and 1955.

Supporters of the planning commission proposal worked hard to rally support between sessions. By 1957, their work was paying off, but there were still a few holdouts. A major one was Anoka County. The Anoka County Board told a sorry tale of being overburdened by public property that paid no taxes. They had a mental hospital, and they had distressed school districts, and they simply could not afford a planning commission or its burdensome opinions. I decided that some higher-order salesmanship was in order. I invited the whole Anoka County Board to dinner at the Minnesota Club. After a convivial meal, I made my plea.

I said, "A planning commission isn't going to require you to do anything. You can use your own judgment, and if you dislike the recommendations, you can disregard them. Doesn't it make a little sense that if there are three hundred units of government whose actions affect each other in a concentrated area, that something ought to be done to coordinate them, and get a little cooperative planning into the process?" By the end of the evening, they dropped their opposition.

The dispute over financing the commission with a fixed levy that stymied the bill in 1953 and 1955 eased somewhat as the composition of the legislature changed with each election. The bill passed in 1957, creating a planning commission that was assured of the revenue from a metrowide levy of a small fraction of a mill. It was among the first commissions of its kind in the nation.

The commission worked so well that, before long, a further need became evident. It was not enough to tell people what they ought to do. Some enforcement authority to block certain actions was warranted. It also became clear that some services should be provided on a metropolitan basis, rather than individually by each jurisdiction, however coordinated they were. Sewage disposal was a case in point. A sanitary sewer system that served the whole region was clearly superior to multiple systems, all patched together. By 1967, the legislature decided that something more than the Metropolitan Planning Commission was needed. That is how today's Metropolitan Council was born.

I am convinced that the Met Council would never have been created if a Metropolitan Planning Commission had not first introduced the idea of cooperation to the region's governments. Cooperation is a hard thing to come by in any human relationship and is especially elusive in government. Achieving cooperation in the Metropolitan Council was well worth the years of struggle and compromise that preceded it.

Another big bill in 1957 made Minnesota one of the growing number of states that moved clocks ahead one hour in the spring and back one hour in the fall. "Daylight saving time" was a fighting phrase to a lot of Minnesotans that year—and I was in the middle of the fray.

The night before the daylight saving time bill was scheduled to come to the senate floor, I did what you are not supposed to do: campaign in the chamber while the senate is in session, conducting business. I had to creep around, hoping that the lieutenant governor or whoever was presiding would not gavel me out of order—even though he knew full well what I was up to. Senators then and now find that if they are quiet enough, they can get by with a little lobbying on the floor. I went up and down the whole senate chamber, talking to every senator. I thought I had the votes I needed, and that debate could only hurt my cause. So my message to every senator was simple: "I think we ought to get rid of the daylight saving time bill quickly. Tomorrow, when it comes up, if you can vote for it, please vote for it. If you have to vote against it, vote against it. But could we have *no* debate, no discussion? Let's just vote it up or down, and be done with it."

I had counted carefully, so I thought I had a slim but solid majority. But when I got to Sen. George O'Brien of Grand Rapids, he made me doubt my count. "Just pause for a minute, Andersen," he said. "Up in my area, there are about six of us who can go either way on daylight saving. We're from resort country. Resort-goers come up and play golf. They like that extra hour in the day. So, we have reason to please our resort owners and vote for it. But, we're also in agricultural country. You know the real reason the farmers oppose it." I said, "Yes, they have a valid reason." The reason was that dew covers the fields in the morning. If daylight comes an hour later in the morning, there will be dew an hour longer, and an hour of potentially productive time in the field is lost. That was the only valid reason. Daylight saving opponents used to talk about a lot of other things—about "God's time" and disruption to livestock—but those arguments were spurious by comparison to the loss of field time on dewy mornings.

O'Brien said, "There's one issue on which there is no debate in my district." He referred to a bill I sponsored that was intended to compel every county to make a minimum levy for welfare costs. Some counties were not doing their share, even though they had large populations of needy people and received sizable amounts of federal and state aid. Several counties in O'Brien's area were in that category. I had worked hard to get the minimum levy bill out of my Welfare Committee and onto the full senate's docket for floor action.

O'Brien said, "Andersen, our people hate that. All of us up there are pretty poor. Your bill is going to have only one result: it's going to cut the amount of welfare aid we get. If we could get rid of that bill, we could all vote for daylight saving very readily. If that welfare bill stays on general orders, we're going to vote against daylight saving. We've done a little counting, too, and we think we've got the balance that you need." I did some quick mental computation and realized that he was right. "George, I have never done this before," I said. "But, so help me, I'll move the welfare bill back to committee if that will suit you. I'll do it on motions and resolutions tomorrow morning before we vote on daylight saving." He said, "Elmer, that will be OK."

The next day, when I stood up and moved that my welfare bill be referred back to committee, my allies on the bill looked at each other in disbelief. They knew the bill advanced sound policy. They knew I had fought my heart out to get the bill to the floor. Here I was, turning it back. Then up came the daylight saving bill. The press table was full of correspondents. They were expecting a long, hot debate. As the bill's sponsor, I rose to initiate the discussion. I said, "I'm sure everyone is acquainted with the provisions of this bill. We've debated it long and thoroughly. I move that it be recommended to pass," and I sat down.

The senate's presiding officer looked around for others seeking recognition to speak. Not a soul stood up. The reporters asked each other, "What in the world is going on?" After a poignant pause, the presiding officer called for a vote. The bill passed by a fairly good margin. That was how daylight saving time came to Minnesota in 1957. And that explains why the law to this day requires a minimal local effort for education but not for welfare.

Only one measure that year brought me more mail than daylight saving time. That was a bill to do away with trading stamps. The retail merchants came to the legislature and pleaded with us to pass some kind of a bill that would outlaw the distribution of trading stamps at their stores. They wanted to end the practice themselves, but they just did not have the discipline or the courage to unilaterally quit giving away trading stamps. Curt Carlson, the founder of Gold Bond Stamps, had correspondence stations set up in all of his stamp redemption stores where people could write letters in protest of this legislation. Carlson employees would address the customers' letters, stamp them, and get them on their way. We had a blizzard of mail on trading stamps. The bill did not pass. Retail merchants ultimately found the courage to stop giving away trading stamps on their own.

I was in the thick of all the major battles in 1957, which was one of the most productive legislative sessions of the twentieth century. Yet I felt myself moving into an awkward position. I had become quite prominent in the conservative group of the senate, yet I was not always comfortable with their positions on issues. I was in a powerful spot. I was the only senator, other than the majority leader, who was on the Rules Committee, the Organizing Committee, and the Committee on Committees—the three panels that essentially ran the senate, right down to determining where senators would sit and what their committee schedules would be.

But I was well aware that I was also increasingly identified as the most liberal member of the Conservative Caucus. I felt restive being regarded as a leading member of the majority group while disagreeing with them so often.

It was decent of the Conservative Caucus to support a maverick like me as much as they did. I had good friends in the Liberal Caucus. One of them was a freshman senator named Don Fraser—the future congressman and Minneapolis mayor. His father, Everett Fraser, had been dean of the Law School and one of my professors at the University of Minnesota. The Conservative majority brought out of committee a bill on workers' compensation that I thought was awful. The bill's sponsors said, "This isn't where we're going to settle. We just want a good bargaining position when we go to conference committee with the house." "That isn't the way it ought to be," I argued. "We ought to pass a bill that we believe in and then fight for it. We shouldn't do something that's an embarrassment and then think we're going to come up somewhere better later."

I talked to Don Fraser. I said, "Don, that's a terrible bill they're coming out with. I'll tell you what I'll do. I'll try to drum up some Republican opposition to the committee report, if you'll organize your Liberal Caucus members. Let me know." He came back a day or two later. "Boy, Elmer, our people think it's a terrible bill. They'll go whole hog with you and all the others you can get." So, we upset the majority report of the conservative group that dominated the senate.

When I would do things like that, others in the majority would be less than pleased. They assured me they held no personal animosity toward me, and they respected the effort I put forth, but they were saying aloud that they wished I could be more in tune with them. Sometimes the caucus would attempt to present a united front on a particular issue. They would ask caucus members to agree to vote together as a group. I never would agree to a caucus vote. I made that clear when I came into the caucus. I said, "I cannot sublet my vote. I'm going to vote my conviction no matter what the caucus decides. I'll go to the caucus meeting, hear the arguments, and give the caucus position every consideration, but don't count on me." Quite often, I would not vote with the caucus.

Though I had been quite effective up to that point, my ability to continue to play the role I had known was increasingly in doubt. When the 1957 session ended, I thought, I have done about as much in the senate as I can do.

By the end of that busy session, I was also beginning to feel that I had been away from my business long enough. I could not give Fuller the attention it needed when I was in the legislature. I used to say to Fuller employees, "There's only about so much of me you can stand. If I were here all the time, I'd drive you crazy." I was only half joking. I expected a great deal of those around me. I thought it was good for Fuller people that I had other activities, so that I did not wear them out. But by the close of the 1957 session, I was hearing inklings of some difficulties in the company that only I could resolve. There were some decisions needed that others could not make. Among them were issues associated with the move of our corporate headquarters from downtown St. Paul to a new building in the Midway area.

I was a strong believer, then and now, that political service should be an avocation, not a career. I think elected officials need connections outside of government to give them a more balanced perspective on the issues they confront. An elected official can easily get caught up in a political whirl that is unrealistic or unrepresentative of the lives of average people. I can remember as governor, I used to try to mentally reach beyond the swirl of capitol affairs and ascertain where the people were. I understood fully why Gov. Rudy Perpich would sometimes leave the capitol for a time, with no announcement, and visit coffee shops around the state. He was trying to find where reality was.

I have advised many a would-be politician not to rely on politics for a livelihood. Not only is that an uncertain and weak position to be in, but it also is a position that can influence one's judgment, for the worse. You can do unnatural things if you believe that you simply have to win the next election.

Not long after the session ended, I called Bill Randall, whom I had defeated in the special election in 1949. He had become Ramsey County attorney. I said, "Bill, eight years ago, you asked me a favor, and I agreed to do it. It was to tell you if ever I decided to leave the senate. I'm telling you very early, and, please, keep it confidential because I'd like to make the announcement in my own way, at my own time. I've decided I'm not going to be running again. I wanted to give you the first word, so you would have a year or more to prepare if you would like to run." He said, "Elmer, I don't think I'm going to do it." He enjoyed his work as county attorney and made a fine contribution in that role. But he would have been a good senator from District 42.

I was at peace with the decision to leave the senate. I had accomplished much of what I had set out to do. It felt like the closing of a chapter. It had been a rewarding experience, but it was over. It was time to go back to work at Fuller.

Another campaign was not far ahead. But as I left the senate in 1958, I did not see it coming.

Dairyman

THE PROPERTY ON DEER LAKE near St. Croix Falls, Wisconsin, that Grandma and Grandpa Johnson bought in 1934 was beloved territory for Eleanor, the children, and me. Originally, it included a farmhouse and barn and forty acres of land. The Johnsons contracted with their builder friend Andrew Danielson to construct three cottages on the lakeshore, one of which was reserved for our family's use. We spent as much time as we could at Deer Lake each summer. During several summers, Eleanor and the children remained there for weeks at a time, while I drove the fifty miles to St. Paul on Monday mornings, and then back again on Friday evenings.

The Johnsons originally intended to move to Deer Lake year-round when they retired. But in 1953, they told us their plans had changed. Their children and grandchildren were in the Twin Cities, and they did not want to spend their last years so far from the people they loved. They decided to give one cottage to each of their three children and then sell the farm.

But selling the farm was unthinkable to Eleanor and her brother and sister. They wanted the farm to stay in the family. We were willing to undertake the responsibility. The Johnsons approved too, and offered to sell it to us at the same modest price they had paid nineteen years before.

One of my fellow Rotarians was both a practicing dentist in the Twin Cities and a farmer. I sought him out for counsel. "What about owning a farm?" I asked. "Is it a worthwhile venture?" He responded by raving about the joys of farming. It would add years to my life, he said. While on the farm, I would forget all my troubles. The children would love it. They would learn about life in a wonderful way. "Elmer, it's the nicest way to lose money you could imagine," he said.

We decided to see for ourselves whether he was right. We had thought about owning a farm for years. I had not thought of owning one in Wisconsin—certainly not while I was a legislator in Minnesota. But we could not let Deer Lake Farm slip away. We took it over, and that was the start of thirty-five years in the dairy business.

Like Grandma and Grandpa Johnson, we were only in residence at Deer Lake in the summers. But we saw the farm's potential to be more than a vacation site. We set out to make it a full-scale dairy farm.

I embarked on a serious study of dairying to find out what size herd was the most cost-efficient economic unit. We learned from experts at the St. Paul campus of the University of Minnesota that an eighty-cow milking herd was the ideal size for an economically efficient, family-sized operation. That meant a total herd of about two-hundred head. That became our plan.

Next, we decided we wanted a registered herd. We decided on the Holstein breed and joined the Holstein-Friesian Dairy Association of Brattleboro, Vermont. I learned to brag about the advantages of Holsteins and tease about the other breeds, just as if I had been a farmer all my life. Once at a farm meeting, I expressed sympathy for a Jersey breeder who lost a cow to a deer hunter. "I can understand a Jersey being mistaken for a deer," I said. "I just can't understand her being mistaken for a dairy cow."

One of our neighbors in St. Anthony Park was a retired dairy farmer named W. S. Moscrip. He was an extraordinary dairyman. His farm at Lake Elmo produced one of the finest herds in the country. He was a leader in the National Dairy Association and became one of the agriculture lobbyists known as the "Four Horsemen" at the legislature. They were Bill Moscrip, the dairyman; Jay Seneca Jones, the head of the Farm Bureau; Norris Carnes, president of the Central Livestock Exchange in South St. Paul; and John Brandt, the chief executive of Land O'Lakes, Inc. They and their constituents could block anything having to do with agriculture.

For example, when it was proposed to enrich bread with vitamins, they balked. They insisted that adding vitamins was not necessary if milk was added instead. As a result of their lobbying efforts, Minnesota consumers did not see vitamin-enriched bread on their grocery shelves until it was commonplace in many other states.

One of the things Moscrip fought was the sale of yellow-colored oleomargarine, the butter substitute we take for granted today. That was a big battle. As far as Moscrip was concerned, margarine was a phony product because it came from vegetables, not cows, and it certainly was not going to be colored yellow to look like butter. Finally, when consumers put pressure on legislators to allow the sale of the same yellow margarine they could buy in South Dakota or Iowa, the law allowed the sale of a bead of food coloring in white margarine. The consumer would have to open a little capsule of coloring and knead it into the margarine to make it yellow. That silly situation lasted for years. It was a testimony to the political power of Bill Moscrip and the dairy industry.

Moscrip used to get up each morning at about 4:30 A.M., and he thought everybody else did, or should. By the time he had eaten breakfast and read the newspaper, it was 5:30 or 6:00. That is when his business day started. He thought nothing of calling me at 5:30 or 6:00 A.M. to talk about legislation. I never adopted his dairyman's schedule, but after I bought Deer Lake Farm, I became more appreciative of his calls. He was willing to give me advice about the farm as well as pending legislation.

Farming became much more than a hobby for us. The whole family was involved. Tony was a teenager when we bought the farm, and he lent a hand, particularly with haying. At that time, haying involved raking the hay onto a hay wagon and laying a rope sling across the hay at intervals of about three feet. At the entrance to the hayloft, those slings full of hay would be gathered up, and the hay would be pulled to the hayloft door. A team of horses was needed to do the pulling. Tony learned to drive that team. He thought it was great sport to see the big sling of hay go up, then hit the pulley, and go into the barn. He would pull a cord to loosen the sling so the hay would drop. He then had to lead the team back to its original position to pull the next sling.

At first, I helped with haying too. But I decided not to ride atop a loaded hay wagon after once sliding around on slippery new-mown hay and nearly falling off. I decided that falling off a hay wagon and breaking my neck would be a ridiculous way to go!

We had a big barn for hay that was a joy for the children—our own, their cousins, visiting friends from St. Paul, and neighboring children from around Deer Lake. They messed up the hay, but since the cows did not mind, neither did we. The children loved to watch the cows and thought it was fun to climb to the top of a hay mow and then slide down. There were always a lot of cats around the barn, and kittens available for adoption. That fun was just what I had thought having a farm would be. It was a family experience that taught lasting lessons about life: how creatures are born, how they grow up, how they need care, and how some do well and others do not. The children learned much.

Eleanor thought that as part of the learning experience, we ought to drink milk from our own farm, particularly while we were there in the summertime. But she was not about to drink raw milk. Any milk she gave our children had to meet her standards of sanitation. So, we bought a home pasteurizer. We took raw milk to our cottage and pasteurized it ourselves, and then chilled it. I became so aware of the importance of pasteurization that I helped sponsor a bill in the legislature that outlawed the sale of unpasteurized milk off the farm. Consumers could still go to a farm and buy unpasteurized milk, but any milk sold off the farm had to be pasteurized.

In farming as in any other venture, I was interested in expansion. I decided that we should move the barn and the cattle away from the lake. The old barn was close enough to the shore that seepage could occur. I worried about the cattle standing in water. We bought a parcel across the road and quite a distance from the lake to avoid contamination problems. There, our modern barn was built. It was a free-stall barn—no stanchions to confine the movement of each cow. I wanted happy cows. The floor was slatted, and an enormous pit was dug underneath the slatted floor to gather the manure. It could be pumped out easily and distributed to the fields. Sadly, that fine barn was one of several buildings we lost in a fire in August 1972. We had to rebuild, and quickly, to give our herd quarters.

We began to add land in the late 1950s. I collected maps and information about the soil in the area, looking for more land to purchase. The area around Deer Lake traditionally had been dotted with small farms, 40 to 120 acres. A two-hundred-animal herd needed a lot of feed. We made about ten different real estate transactions in our first few years and built up to a base of about 1,200 acres of noncontiguous land.

At one time, there were four houses on the properties we acquired—and we needed them, because we had several employees running the farm. The workload was heavy. Milking eighty cows twice a day is a big chore in itself, not to mention feeding and looking after the herd, moving the calves around, and getting the heifers bred. At planting and harvest seasons, the crop work was demanding too.

We added to the workload in the early years by undertaking some environmental restoration projects. One of the fields we acquired from the Johnsons had been cleared down to the lakeshore. We thought the shoreline should be wooded again, as it was before settlers arrived. We made an arrangement with Tony and his friends, all then in their late teens, that when they came to Deer Lake for a weekend, they would plant trees on Saturday mornings. Then they could have the rest of the weekend for fun. We borrowed a tree planter from the county agricultural agent, ordered seedlings from the state nursery, and planted a fringe along the shore. Those trees now provide lush shade for homes that have since been built along the lake.

We wanted to encourage birds and other wildlife to use Deer Lake Farm. That idea led to the establishment of Deer Lake Farm Nursery. We bought seedlings, shrubs, and other plants from wholesale growers in large quantities and planted them in the areas where they could provide feed and cover for birds and other wildlife.

The property included two ponds, or remains of ponds, that we excavated and restored. One we called Elizabeth Pond, after Eleanor's mother, and the other, Jennie Pond, after my mother. We were so pleased when we saw wood ducks in the ponds the spring after they had been restored, knowing that they would nest there. Then we seined the lake to get minnows and other small aquatic life to put in the ponds. We thought we had really succeeded when we saw great blue herons feeding on frogs in the ponds we had created. It is amazing that if you provide the environment for wildlife, wildlife suddenly appear. A rare spruce grouse showed up in a spruce tree one day, to our surprise. Another year, an indigo bunting took up residence. It had a beautiful iridescent blue color, and a distinctive whistle that would sound from the late afternoon until sunset. My encounters with those birds were unforgettable.

We had help from some interesting people. Usually we had one hired person work around the garden, mow the grass, and help with planting. Tom Barnard had that job for a number of years. He was the retired manager of Interstate Park on the St. Croix River. Another talented gardener was Mike Cotch, who took particular pride in the flower garden. Bob Stadt built paths through the woods and around the ponds for us, using a team of horses with great skill. The team would respond perfectly to his voice commands. They would go or stop or turn without him ever having to touch the reins. I marveled at his relationship with his animals.

We planted hundreds of trees every year. Gradually, as we added agricultural land, we converted all of the land on the original lakeside farm to natural plantings. Today a visitor would never guess it had been farmland. The old farm became a great place for hiking, studying birds, collecting leaves and butterflies, and appreciating nature. Deer loved the tall grass that was allowed to grow. They could hunch down in the grass during the day and roam at night without danger from hunters. We posted signs on the farm prohibiting hunting. Some hunters were not too appreciative, but we thought the deer and other wildlife needed a haven.

By the late 1950s, Deer Lake Farm had been transformed from a summertime retreat for our family to both a nature preserve and a modern dairy farm. It took us about six years to convert our milking herd entirely to registered Holsteins. The last unregistered cow we sold was named Sunrise. I hated to sell her. She was a wonderful cow, but her offspring were not part of our future, so she was not part of our future. We sold her to another dairyman, who had a grade cow herd.

One of our goals was to breed superior offspring. The bull is important in that process. Usually, bulls were graded by how their female offspring performed compared to their mother. At that time, if the offspring did better than the mother, the improvement was credited to the bull. Later, it was determined that cows too could pass on to their offspring a better milk-producing capacity than they had themselves. In other words, it takes two good parents to produce a good cow.

We developed our own formula for evaluating a bull. We used records about bull performance published by the federal government and then used our own system for choosing the best of the better bulls. We used artificial insemination. There was a tank for semen, and our farm managers did the inseminating. We did not use a bull naturally, except on rare occasions when we were proving a young bull. Proving a bull means to establish the value or the worth of the bull as a sire. It is a protracted process. You breed a bull and a cow to get a calf. That takes nine months. If you are lucky, the calf is female. If the calf is male, you must start over. The young heifer needs to be fifteen months old to be bred. A calf will be born nine months later. Then the heifer begins to milk, and establishes a record to compare with her mother. The sire is evaluated on that basis.

Every farm has its own prefix incorporated into the name of the registered animals it produces. Our prefix was Deer Lake. To use the farm's prefix in the animal's name, the animal has to be conceived at the farm, not just born there. If we bought a pregnant cow, her calf would carry a name prefix from the farm where conception occurred. The names can become quite complicated. We tried to establish a family line. One of the great bulls of Wisconsin, raised at Green Bay on the state reformatory dairy farm, was called Wisconsin Admiral Burke Lad. The reformatory's prefix was Wisconsin. Wisconsin Admiral Burke Lad was a great bull. That was one line of breeding to follow. Another bull we liked very much was named Pabst Sir Roburke Rag Apple. Every name meant something. The Pabst brewing family owned the farm that originated his line. Rag Apple was a breeding family that went way back. Burke always meant Wisconsin Admiral Burke Lad. When the name Burke appeared in any animal's name, it always went back to the great Wisconsin bull.

I became interested in naming the cattle and registering the calves. I used to love the late nights I would spend charting calves, keeping records, and preparing the papers to register each one. I sketched the calves too. A sketch or a photograph of the calf was required so that it could be described and identified.

Our animals began to be classified. The national Holstein organization sent an expert around to grade the cows, comparing them with standards for the breed. The classes they used were poor, fair, good, good plus, very good, and excellent. Ninety points or higher was an excellent cow. One calf born at Deer Lake became an excellent cow. When the classifier came, he was drawn to this big, wonderful cow. He said, "Turn her out. I want to have a better look at her." When we took her into the barnyard, he said, "There's an excellent cow if I ever saw one." We were thrilled, because only about one cow out of every hundred is classified as excellent. It was an achievement for a businessman-politician who took it into his head to try to produce a better animal.

We arranged for production testing of the cows by the Dairy Herd Improvement Association, an agency of the U.S. Department of Agriculture. Once a month, their inspectors would come to the farm and measure the milk given by each cow at each milking session. On the basis of that information, they could project with a fair amount of accuracy what the cow would produce during a lactation cycle. A freshening cow gives her maximum amount of milk the first few months, then begins to taper off quite predictably. The data the association provided for us allowed us to keep detailed production records on all of our animals for years.

My objective was to be recognized as a Progressive Breeder, which meant accomplishing three things. First, more than 90 percent of the milking herd had to be home bred. That takes a great deal of time, considering that half of the calves born each year are bulls. Second, the herd classification average had to be a certain amount above the national average. That is a moving target. Every dairy operation tries to surpass the national average, so the average keeps rising. Third, the herd's milk production had to be 30 percent higher than the state's herd production average. It had to be your herd, it had to be a quality herd, and it had to be a high-producing herd. All that was accomplished at Deer Lake Farm in 1984. We received the Progressive Breeder Award that year. The recognition was more than a point of pride. Animals out of a Progressive Breeder herd brought more money at auction, since they were considered a product of an excellent operation.

The award came with a large, heavy bronze plaque that I cherish for all the years of work it represents. It reads: "In recognition of achievement through an improved breeding program based on production testing, type classification and herd health for the advancement of Holstein-Friesian cattle."

We showed animals at district shows in Wisconsin and won our share of cups, ribbons, and awards. We also took some animals to the Minnesota State Fair but did not do as well there. Our best animals did not stack up well against the tremendous cows that came to the fair from all over Minnesota. Minnesota produced terrific dairy herds and great dairymen. The key to their success, always, was that they made dairying their life.

Much as I enjoyed the business, I could never give it my all. While I was busy at the legislature, I had little time for the farm. While I was governor, I could pay it no attention whatsoever. Nonresidential management of a dairy farm is not ideal. My advice to someone interested in owning a dairy farm today would be to make a job of it. Live there, be there all the time, establish standards, and see that they are followed, and a dairy farm can be a good business. But it is a demanding, 24-hour-a-day job. There is so much to attend to—calving, illness, accidents, a fence down, and animals on the loose, milking two or three times a day, 365 days a year. I gained great respect for a wholesome quart of milk.

Even for full-time farmers, dairying has been a tough business in which to make a profit for a generation or more. Overproduction is the reason. The federal government instituted programs to consume more milk and reduce dairy outputs, but those programs could not counter the improvement in cows that has occurred. Not long ago, a cow that produced ten thousand pounds of milk during a lactation cycle was an average animal. Then, it went to twenty thousand, then thirty thousand. With a gallon weighing eight pounds, thirty thousand pounds of milk is a lot to produce in ten months.

I loved dairy farming. But eventually I concluded that we had been at it long enough. I gave our farm manager an opportunity to take over the business in 1985. We offered him an attractive sale price for the herd and the equipment, and had a rental arrangement for the land and buildings. It went pretty well for two years. Then came a 30-percent drop in the price of milk. That killed our project with our former manager.

We had a dispersal sale of the animals and the equipment, and went out of the dairy business in 1988, thirty-five years after we started. We did not put the farm up for sale because dairying was disastrously unprofitable. Most of the land was rented to other farmers; a small portion was sold.

A fortunate arrangement developed in recent years. We sold the home place to a young couple who have worked with us in town faithfully for a number of years, Randy and Tawny Christenson. We met Randy when he was an undergraduate student at Northwestern College and worked at our home part-time. This arrangement continued while he went on to get a bachelor of science degree in mechanical engineering from the University of Minnesota. Since launching his career, he has arranged to be with us two days a week. Tawny, a former 3M employee who now works at home to care for their two young children, also transcribes our correspondence dictation. The Christensons have been enormously helpful as we have adjusted to the realities of advancing age. They jumped at the chance to own the farm. We put a special price on the buildings and land. We are pleased that they have built a new home on the place.

In 1996, we placed Elizabeth Pond and eighty acres of surrounding land into a land preserve to honor the memories of Gustav and Elizabeth Johnson. The parcel includes what we called the Trillium Woods, for the spectacular show of trillium it gives every spring. We secured a large granite rock, installed on it a bronze memorial plaque bearing the Johnsons' names, and conducted a little family ceremony to mark the dedication. It was a fitting climax to our adventure in farm life.

The other day I asked Eleanor, "How much is a pound of butter these days?" She said, "The last one was $4.39." I said, "$4!" There were times when we were farming that milk was getting $3 a hundred weight—one hundred pounds of milk for $3, or about 6 cents per quart. When I think about what we went through to produce clean, pure milk at that price— what a bargain we provided!

Partner

ELEANOR JOHNSON ANDERSEN is a remarkable woman. She is deliberate and thoughtful in her decisions. Once she makes a commitment, it is deep and abiding.

A number of major decisions confronted our family in the 1940s and 1950s, as my involvement in business, politics, and the community deepened. Though Eleanor often let me take the lead, we always made big decisions together. Eleanor was not as quick to decide a question as I was. She would generally raise more questions, to be sure I was thinking through all the alternatives and possible consequences. She would caution me against entering into things too hastily, and urge me to gather all the salient facts. Her standard comment was, "We don't have to decide that right now, do we?" But when she saw that I really wanted to do something and convinced herself that I was not going to get into trouble, she would assent. Then she became energetic in her assistance.

We never disagreed on fundamental matters. We shared the same values. We both grew up in Scandinavian Lutheran homes where honesty, caring, generosity, learning, and culture were prized. We both wanted the same things for our family.

Eleanor's purview has been our home, where she has raised homemaking and motherhood of children, grandchildren, and great-grandchildren to a high art. She pays attention to the little details that make a home pleasant. She frequently rearranges art, plants, furniture, and other household items. Pictures will be on the wall for awhile, then they disappear and something new shows up in their place. She sets an attractive table for every meal. She takes great care in the preparation of food, making sure our fare is low in fat, modest in salt, and strong on vegetables and fruit. I am sure that one reason for our longevity is that she has given us a balanced diet that has not encouraged debilitating disease. We serve liquor only when there are guests to accommodate. Our personal tastes favor light consumption of alcoholic beverages. Eleanor never smoked. I did for a time but quit when the first health warnings about smoking were issued in the mid-1950s.

Eleanor has had a busy life right from the start of our marriage. In the first years, she had to cope with my rigorous schedule as a traveling salesman. Just as I started a new career that allowed me to be home, she became a mother—and then a university student once more, completing her degree. Fortunately, her mother was on hand to help with child care. Eleanor graduated in 1937. Just a year later, I was on the road again, trying to keep H. B. Fuller Company alive. Those were not easy days for either of us.

In 1938, while I was in the Rio Grande valley of Texas on Fuller's behalf, I had a yen to visit Mexico. I went on a Lions' Club weekend excursion from the Rio Grande valley to Monterrey, Mexico, and got a sample of a place I wanted to know better. So when my next business trip to the Rio Grande was scheduled in 1940, I arranged for a two-week vacation for Eleanor and me in Mexico immediately afterward. I thought the two of us were due for a special trip. Little Tony remained behind with his grandparents, Elizabeth and Gustaf Johnson.

We took a train from Brownsville, Texas, to Mexico City. The first leg of the journey was through a heavily wooded area that had recently flooded. The railroad track was under water, and the train just crawled along. We looked out the window and could see nothing but water all around us. Then, occasionally, the train would flush out huge flocks of flamingos. That gorgeous sight—huge, lovely birds taking flight from a watery wilderness— was our introduction to Mexico.

We finally got to Mexico City and had a glorious time. Our plan was to make the trip educational as well as fun. We were eager to learn about native art and the history of Mexico, particularly the pre-Columbian period, which we knew little about. We did not want to stay at a tourist hotel and have a cloistered experience. A real Mexican hotel had more appeal. We found the Hotel Isabel near the Zocalo, the central plaza adjoining the cathedral. The first morning, to order breakfast, we began to speak English. The waiter said, "This morning, English. Tomorrow morning, no English. Breakfast Mexicano." I quickly learned that toast was *pan tostado* and eggs were *huevos*. Our waiter was such a good teacher that I was able to order breakfast in Spanish wherever we went.

We spent our days strolling through little shops and factories, absorbing art, history, and culture as we went. We were fascinated to watch glassblowers make tiny figurines at one shop. At a Mexican market, we learned that the natives came great distances for market day to sell their fruit. In Puebla, we bought a large, beautiful pot, a fine example of Puebla art.

The highlight of the trip came when we visited the home of Diego Rivera, the famous artist and muralist. It was a little two-section home, one part blue, the other pink. He lived and worked in one portion, and his wife lived in the other. A small hallway connected the two parts of the house. We thought it would be wonderful to bring back an example of his art, so we went to a gallery that had available several pieces of a series he had done on Mexican life. There were two baby portraits, a little girl and a little boy. We wanted to bring the little girl home.

But we had also visited the shop of a silversmith named Spratling. It offered sterling silver tea services, with trays and pots of indigenous design. The one we found especially beautiful was called Aztec Rose. But, we thought, we can not afford both that and the Rivera. For a couple of days, we were back and forth between the art store and the silver shop trying to decide which we should choose.

A French lady who was the clerk at the art gallery took an interest in our dilemma. "Don't make it so hard for yourself," she counseled. "Don't use your travelers' checks or your cash to buy this. You should have it. It's clear that you love it. Just give me a check on your bank back home. It will be a long time before that check ever clears."

We took her up on her offer and brought home both the Aztec Rose silver service and the Rivera original. We have accumulated many other examples of Mexican art through the years, but those two pieces remain favorites. Decades later, the Mexico City Palace of Fine Arts staged a retrospective exhibit of Rivera's work. The baby portrait we have is atypical of his work and valued because it is rare. The Palace wrote us to ask if we would loan our Rivera to the exhibit, which we did. We sent it back to Mexico. They insured it and took good care of it, and finally sent it back. Being without it for a time made it all the more special to us.

We fell in love with Mexico on that special trip in 1940. We were amazed at the sophistication of pre-Columbian art, not only the Aztec, Toltec, and Mayan, but also the art and artifacts of the Incas of Central America and South America. One law the Incas imposed on the tribes they subjugated fascinated me. If anyone stole from the ruling Incas, the penalty was death. But if people stole food because they did not have enough work to earn a living and feed their families, the punishment fell on the mayor of the community, not the thief. Providing everyone with the opportunity to work was considered a community responsibility. I thought that was a progressive idea, perhaps more advanced than some of our ideas about work today.

Our return trip featured a voyage on a freighter of the Standard Fruit and Steamship Company, operating between Veracruz, Mexico, and New Orleans. At the appointed time, we took a train from Mexico City to Veracruz. It was a scenic ride as we descended into the lush, tropical border country. At every stop, there were not only the usual food vendors but also people selling hollowed-out bamboo segments filled with beautiful white gardenias. The prices would be high when the train pulled into the station, but as it began to leave, prices plummeted. It was at one such hasty moment that we yielded and bought a lovely bouquet of the fragrant flowers.

Perhaps the need to collect and carry our flowers made us late getting out of the train in Veracruz. When we went to the baggage area, our bags were gone. In their place were two bags belonging to someone else. We guessed that somebody going on the same ship we were had taken our bags by mistake. So we took a chance, grabbed the two remaining bags and hailed a taxi to take us to the boat dock. Our taxi driver knew little English, and our Spanish did not include the technicalities of boats and wharves. But he seemed to know why we had come to Veracruz and where we were going. The one bit of English that he knew, he said repeatedly: "I am your friend." However, as he drove on and on into the darkness, we wondered if we had fallen into the hands of a bandit who was taking us to a remote place for nefarious purposes.

Finally, a dock appeared, and there, alongside it, was the ship we were to take. As we unloaded, voices up on the deck called down to ask if we were the Andersens. We said, "Yes, we are." They called back, "We have your bags up here." We called back, "We have yours down here." Everybody was greatly relieved.

Our passage to New Orleans was pleasant. Freighters were equipped to handle a limited number of passengers. Ours was a party of eight. With two attentive stewards to look after us, we had a delightful time. The stewards were constantly bringing tea or coffee between meals, and the meals were generous and well prepared. Stationed around the ship were bunches of bananas that we could sample at will. The ship lumbered through the Gulf of Mexico, trying to keep up with the porpoises. It was a restful windup to a strenuous, unforgettable Mexican holiday.

Not long after that wonderful vacation we were confronted with the opportunity to buy controlling interest in H. B. Fuller Company. Eleanor was much involved in that decision, as were her parents. She became acquainted and friendly with many of the people at Fuller, but she was not directly involved in Fuller operations.

One might say that she was in the background, as far as the public was concerned. She was very much in the foreground so far as I was concerned. I appreciated her judgment, because she is good at evaluating people and situations. She kept me from many a misstep in business by saying, "I think you ought to wait," or "I think you ought not do that."

But once a thing was decided, she had staying power. She is not easily discouraged. Sometimes, when things were not working as planned and I would wonder whether our effort was worthwhile, she would be the one to say, "Maybe you need a good night's rest. Things will look better in the morning."

She knew me well enough to know that, for me, sleep was a great cure for almost any problem. I think that is true of most people—so much so that when I am asked for advice about a problem, my advice usually includes, "Go to bed. Sleep on it. Things will look different in the morning." People who are worn down physically are also worn down mentally and do not function very well. During the years when I was a legislator and governor, I did not sleep much. Four or five hours per night were usually all I could manage. I thought that much sleep was sufficient, and that I had boundless energy. But Eleanor was perceptive about my need for more rest, and she would encourage me to get it.

When my political career began in earnest in 1949, Eleanor was more directly involved than she had been at Fuller. She did precinct organizing, telephoning, and campaigning for me. When I was elected to the legislature, she attended meetings of a group of legislative wives—a large group in those days, since during my five sessions all but a couple of the 201 legislators were men. She followed my legislative work closely. I was never involved in anything that we did not talk over at home. I would come home bursting with ideas for bills and reactions to legislation or events of the day. She would greet me, ready to listen and respond. During the sessions, I prepared and distributed a newsletter to my constituents that she helped write and edit. She was a listening post. Wherever she went, she paid attention to what people were saying about the legislature or particular bills, and passed what she heard on to me.

She helped me overcome what I believe is the most characteristic trait of elected officials—paranoia. During a campaign or a legislative session, you work so hard. You get keyed up. You feel good, but you are more drained physically and emotionally than you realize. You are less able to put events into a healthy perspective than you should be. Little slights become major in your mind. You are quick to think that someone is trying to take advantage of you. You lose your sense of proportion and your cool head.

I became upset over a completely trivial thing connected with the Governor's Fishing Opener in 1962, when I was running for reelection as governor. I caught a nice walleye and put it on my stringer. When I held it up for a photographer, one of the links of the stringer's chain hung over the fish's eye in such a way that it appeared sunken in the photo. The DFL state chairman, George Farr, accused me of displaying a fish that had been caught long before—and, he intimated, not by me. I was angry—as any true Minnesota angler would be. I wanted to do something in response. Fortunately, Eleanor and other people around me calmed me down and convinced me to keep silent. They were right. I did not need to reply—the journalists in my boat that day and several of the state's editorial writers took care of Farr and defended my honor as an honest angler.

During the early years of my political involvement, we had small children at home. Emily had just turned three when I was elected to the state senate. Caring for the children always came first for Eleanor. She never strayed far from home in the years when they were there. She did everything that could be done for our children. At that time, cod liver oil was the recommended nutritional supplement for children. She saw to it that all three children got cod liver oil, every day—but she would go to the trouble of lining the spoon with orange juice to make the nasty potion more palatable. I think they never fully appreciated her efforts in that regard.

When our children were infants, doctors recommended strict adherence to a four-hour feeding schedule. You did not let babies sleep until they woke up and were hungry. Neither did you feed them early, no matter how they howled. They were on a four-hour schedule. That is a tough routine for a mother to maintain—especially one whose husband was frequently away on business trips. But it was considered the right way then, and Eleanor stuck with it.

She developed a hobby that she could pursue at times when the children did not need her immediate attention. She became a weaver. She had an eight-harness loom. I used to help her with the warping. She did beautiful weaving of place mats, runners, and decorative items, using a variety of patterns. She joined the Weavers' Guild and became quite knowledgeable about the craft and acquainted with others who practiced it. Anna Schmits, an artisan whose weaving we admired very much, became a particular friend.

Eleanor had her hands full in 1950, when we moved into a new house.

We loved our dear house on Hendon Avenue, where we had been newly-weds and our children had been babies. But not long after Emily was born, we began to wish for a larger house with more bedrooms. We decided to build a home. We found a lot at the corner of Hoyt Avenue and Grantham Street, across the street from University Grove in the St. Anthony Park section of St. Paul. Architects Milton Bergstedt and Jim Hirsch designed a modern-style house for us, and contractor Ed Fridholm built it.

Gradually, as the children grew, Eleanor felt she could pursue a few interests outside the home. She became a member of the board of the Children's Home Society, the child adoptive agency, and has served in that capacity for more than twenty-five years. She has been involved in numerous committees and projects for the society and was invited to become an officer of the board, but she declined.

She is also a longtime board member of the Schubert Club of St. Paul, a wonderful organization devoted to seeking out promising musicians early in their careers and bringing them to the concert stage. It is one of the oldest fine arts organizations in the country. The board organizes concert programs, and administers scholarships that have enabled many talented young people to get more education. The Schubert Club does a superb job, filling the Ordway auditorium with concert after concert. I marvel at them.

We used to host a recital by Schubert scholarship recipients in our home each year. The audience would be the young performers' parents and friends. It was inspiring to see how dedicated, talented, and disciplined the musicians were. Those traits were especially evident in several Asian-American young people whose parents were relatively recent immigrants. They performed well, and their parents were so proud. It was a joy to see young people emerging from foreign cultures, taking on the United States, and doing well.

Eleanor is a gifted musician herself. Her minor at the University of Minnesota was music. But she confined her performances to the piano at home. We used to play some simple duets, and she accompanied Tony and me when we both took clarinet lessons. That was the kind of home-based, family-centered activity that she loved.

Eleanor undoubtedly looked forward to more time for family activities like that when I finished my last legislative session, in 1957. Neither of us knew then that we would soon be busier than ever before. A great adventure was just ahead.

Part III

GOVERNOR

Candidate for Governor

WHEN I LEFT THE LEGISLATURE in 1958, I truly thought I was done with elective office. Fuller needed me, and with the family, community activities, and the farm, I had enough to keep me occupied.

Of course, I also stayed attuned to public affairs. One could not serve for five sessions of the Minnesota Legislature and do otherwise. I monitored news developments daily. I had always been an avid reader of newspapers and magazines, and a consumer of broadcast news. I regularly read the *Manchester Guardian,* the *London Economist,* and a number of domestic papers, including those published in both Minneapolis and St. Paul.

In 1959, a strike broke out in Albert Lea at the Wilson meatpacking plant. Tensions ran high on the picket line. The company brought in strike-breaking workers—scabs, as they were called by the striking union members—and the union people were bitter and angry. Gov. Orville Freeman called out the National Guard, which closed the plant. That action was seen as supportive of the union's efforts to enforce the strike. It was the wrong thing to do.

The Wilson Company took Freeman to court. A federal judge ruled that the governor had violated his constitutional powers and ordered him to withdraw the Guard, which he did. But soon thereafter, in a highly publicized speech, Freeman said, "I did what the court ordered me to do. But if I had it to do over again, I'd do exactly what I did."

Those words bothered me deeply. It was wrong for a governor to be told by a federal court that he had violated his oath of office, and then to say that he would violate it again if he could. That was too much for me.

My feelings were not rooted in any prior conflict between Freeman and me. In fact, our relationship was excellent while he was governor and I was an active state senator. A good legislator informs the governor of what he is trying to do, knowing that he will need the governor's approval for his bills to become law. He asks the governor if he has any ideas about the measure, so they can be incorporated, if possible. I had frequent meetings with

Governor Freeman. I respected him as a hardworking, honest, dependable person. He was sound, and I liked him.

I had a fine working relationship with his welfare commissioner, Morris Hursh. We worked together on my bill for an Equalization Aid Review Committee for welfare in 1957. That was the bill to require counties to levy a minimum amount to cover welfare costs, in the same way the state requires school districts to levy a minimum amount for local school support. The welfare bill died as part of the compromise struck to pass the daylight saving bill. But while it was still under active consideration, I won Hursh's support for it. Then we went to see the governor. I told Governor Freeman, "I'm willing to go out on a limb and fight to get this done, but we need to have your understanding that you won't make it a political issue in the next campaign. It's the kind of thing that could be honed into a political argument." He agreed that he would not make it a political issue in any way. Our relationship was such that I knew I could trust him.

Nevertheless, in 1959 I thought he made a profound mistake in his handling of the Wilson strike, and that his comments afterward revealed poor judgment. I thought, "If somebody who can defeat him doesn't run against him in 1960, I'm going to run."

By 1960, Freeman had been governor for three terms. He was first elected in 1954 and was reelected in 1956 and 1958. The only Republican who wanted to challenge him in 1960 was P. Kenneth Peterson. Peterson had been mayor of Minneapolis and had been chairman of the state Republican Party. He was a good fellow, and we were friends, but I did not believe he could defeat Freeman. He was quite conservative, perhaps too much so to win statewide office. And I thought he did not have the drive that it takes to unseat a sitting governor.

Other people began to encourage me to run. I talked to some of my oldest political allies in St. Anthony Park. In fact, they may have been the ones to approach me. Ever since my election to the state senate, those friends had harbored high ambitions for me. I used to temper their eagerness by saying, "I've got a family. I've got a business. Take it easy." One of those supporters was Warren Lundgren, the general agent in St. Paul for the Northwestern Mutual Life Insurance Company of Milwaukee. He had encouraged me to run for the senate in 1949, and he was back again ten years later, urging a run for the governorship.

Because of my legislative service, I also had acquired supporters around the state. One was John Egan, the sales manager for what was then called Wood Conversion Company at Cloquet, a division of Weyerhaeuser. He was a dynamo. We connected in part because both of us were salespeople and respected the traits in each other that made us good businessmen.

Then there was Tom Swain. I met Tom in 1956 when he was named executive director of the commission to celebrate Minnesota's statehood centennial. He became a close friend right away and has remained one for more than forty years.

Tom impressed me from the start. He has the best-organized mind I have ever encountered. With him, everything is in place, on time, tidy, and well planned. He is a prudent person. He grew up in a family of modest means. It was a big treat for him to have one cream soda per week. He is also a candid person. He is thoughtful, but he does not hesitate to speak his mind. He does not pander in any way. When Tom spoke on an issue, I knew he was not holding back. He has a tremendous capacity for work, and he enjoyed work, just as I did.

It is in both of our natures to take life seriously. Life is not an entertainment vehicle. Life is an accomplishment vehicle. Real living is working, doing something and making a difference. It is hard for Tom, as it is hard for me, to stand by when a problem presents itself. We want to pitch in and do something about it. I trusted Tom, he believed in me, and so our lives were linked. Since we met, he has been involved in nearly everything I have done in the public arena. And he has provided volunteer leadership for a score or more public service organizations.

At first gradually, then more speedily, influences built in favor of a run for governor. I must confess that I was receptive. Eleanor was involved in the exploration process, and she, too, looked positively on the idea. There was no great moment of decision for the two of us. That I would be a candidate just emerged in our thinking. One might say that natural forces took over. I announced my candidacy officially on January 5, 1960.

Soon I was meeting other influential people in Minnesota—people of good standing and good judgment who were willing to help elect a new governor. For example, Tom arranged a luncheon for me with Otto Silha, the vice president and business manager of the *Star* and *Tribune,* the jointly owned newspapers in Minneapolis. Silha would soon become publisher of the newspapers, and we quickly became friends.

Another key person was David Lilly. David Lilly's grandfather had been a principal in the founding of First National Bank in St. Paul. His father had been president of the bank. Dave founded the Toro Manufacturing Company, known around the world for making top-quality lawn mowers. I asked Dave to be the chairman of my campaign's finance committee. He is good at raising money—not just for political campaigns but for many worthy causes. For example, he was a vigorous fundraiser for the University of Minnesota, and instrumental in making positive changes in the functioning of the University of Minnesota Foundation. He has great ability.

Cecil March, my old friend from our streetcar-commuting days in the mid-1930s, was on hand too. Cecil was a group vice president at 3M and worked closely with Archie Bush, the executive vice president who had long been the right-hand man of 3M chief executive William McKnight. Cecil was a strong supporter of my candidacy. When he told Bush about my intentions, Bush was enthusiastic too. He told Cecil, "Cec, I don't know how much this is going to cost but don't let it fail for lack of money." How much he contributed to my campaign, I do not know. I did not know how much anyone contributed to the campaign. But I know Bush gave quite a bit, because Cec used to go to him when the campaign needed to issue a circular or book some advertising. Cec never shared the details with me other than to say, "Elmer, just believe Archie Bush is a good friend of yours."

That is the way honorable campaigns were run forty years ago. There was a wall between the candidate and the fundraising operation of a campaign. There was no legal limit on individual contributions then, but the candidate was often not aware of how much money a particular individual had given. And the candidate never was involved in soliciting gifts. I suppose that when I saw Archie, as I did from time to time, I thanked him in general terms for his support. But I never said anything about specific contributions, and I certainly never asked him for any.

I had a fairly large group of supporters who had worked with me on various projects, in the legislature and elsewhere, and had become friends. We called the group the ELA Volunteer Committee. Its chair was Constance Dillingham, who later became Constance Otis, wife, and later the widow, of Justice James C. Otis. She played an important role in the campaign. So did Minneapolis attorney John Mooty, who already then was a wise, deliberate, careful worker, both as a lawyer and a political operator. One of my regrets as I left the governor's office was that I was not able to offer him a place on the state supreme court. He would have been an excellent justice.

Don Padilla was our publicist. He was the founder of a large public relations firm in Minneapolis, which was called Padilla and Sarjeant originally and is Padilla Speer Beardsley today. He said, "Elmer, the first thing we've got to get is a good picture of you." He did not think the photos I had were suitable. He brought me to a photographer he trusted, who took a campaign picture of me. Before long, Don took charge of my schedule, making sure I did what was needed to get people's attention and win their votes. As the campaign developed, Don frequently traveled with me to help me get my message out.

Young Lyall Schwarzkopf was a campaign worker, assigned to seek the support of people with a political following. He went on to be a legislator, then city clerk and administrator of Minneapolis, then, briefly, chief of staff for Gov. Arne Carlson. Lyall was the ablest political operative I have ever known.

Relationships that I developed early in business and politics seemed to continue and multiply over time. I loved the people who rallied to my side early, and I had absolute confidence in them. We came to know, trust, and rely on each other. All of those in my campaign circle did well later in life. Watching them flourish through the years has been a source of much satisfaction.

In those days, mounting a statewide campaign meant recruiting good people for the main tasks—finance, publicity, volunteer coordination—and then turning them loose to do what was needed. There were no high-priced consultants, no pollsters, and no political action committees or national party bosses telling us what to do. Campaigns were simpler then, and more fun.

My core campaign committee met one morning each week for breakfast at a little Midway restaurant. Those sessions charted the campaign. Don Padilla, Connie Dillingham, and Dave Lilly were always there. Others came when we needed them. At those sessions, I came to an early understanding with Dave: "Let's run as good a campaign as we can. But let's not have any debt at the end." Further, I told him, I intended to put very little of my own money into the campaign. I lacked the means to do so in those years, and I thought the campaign would be stronger if it was financed with the donations of others.

One of my oldest friends in Minnesota politics was state treasurer Val Bjornson, whose whole family I had come to know in Sunday school at Grace University Lutheran Church. Val told me one of his campaign secrets. He would always go to the local newspaper office when he visited a small town. He would ask to use a typewriter and then sit down and bang out a news story on his visit to the town. The editors loved it, because they never had enough reporters to cover every visiting politician. Coverage of the visit of State Treasurer Val Bjornson by State Treasurer Val Bjornson would show up in the next edition.

I liked the idea. I told Don Padilla, "We ought to go to every radio station in every town we visit, and just talk. And we have to go to every newspaper office. You ask to use a typewriter, and you write a story while you're there, so it gets in. We shouldn't depend on a local reporter writing the story. You write it." Don thought it was worth a try.

Off we went around the state, in a vehicle that became something of a symbol for our campaign. It was a makeshift pickup truck with a body on the back, and a little step up to climb into it. We could sit in the back and invite one or two people in for a chat or a cup of coffee. We could have a snack there. If the need had ever arisen, we could have slept there.

I liked to make campaigning fun. I believe participation in politics should be enjoyable. I liked to have music at rallies, and I would try to arrange for a high school group or a local band to perform. A theme song that developed was the old Glenn Miller hit "Elmer's Tune." The band would play that when I was introduced.

I liked to inject a little humor in my speeches. I told one joke again and again that year. It is a story that makes people a little uneasy about its outcome. When it ends innocently, they enjoy it very much. It is about a typical little Minnesota town that had a Lutheran church and a Catholic church. The priest had become quite friendly with some Lutheran businessmen. Once when they were having coffee together, as they frequently did, he said, "I wish some of you fellows would come over to my church sometime. We won't try to convert you, but you'd see what my life is like, just as I enjoy seeing and sharing some of your experiences." So one Sunday, three of the businessmen marched off to the Catholic church. They arrived a little late, and the mass was already in progress. When the priest turned and saw his three Lutheran friends standing in the back of the sanctuary, he whispered to the altar boy, "Get three chairs for the Lutherans." The altar boy did not understand what the priest said, so he did not respond. The priest faced the altar again. When he turned back to the congregation, his three friends were still standing in the back. So, a little severely, he hissed to the altar boy, "Get three chairs for the Lutherans!" The altar boy knew he had to do something. So, he turned to the congregation and announced, "This sounds as strange to me as it will to you, but Father says to give three cheers for the Lutherans."

John MacDonald, a reporter for the *Minneapolis Tribune,* traveled with me often in 1960. Once he was standing next to our daughter, Emily, as I told that story. He said to her, "He never changes a word, does he?" After the campaign I promised Eleanor that I would not tell that joke ever again. I have just broken my vow.

Our first task was to defeat P. Kenneth Peterson for the Republican endorsement for governor at the party's state convention. I determined that I needed party endorsement. Without it, I doubt I would have continued my campaign.

Then, as now, the Minnesota Republican Party was split between liberals and conservatives. But the liberal faction was larger then. My campaign had something to do with building that faction, by getting our people elected as delegates at the county and district conventions. The rift between liberals and conservatives was such that the party decided to have two keynote speakers at the state convention, to satisfy both sides. Arizona Sen. Barry Goldwater, who became the party's presidential candidate in 1964, was the conservative keynoter; Chuck Percy, a radio manufacturer in Chicago who went on to represent Illinois in the U.S. Senate, was the liberal speaker. He was there at my instigation. Percy became a friend as I counseled him on the transition from a career in business to one in politics.

The Republican State Convention of 1960 was a spirited affair. It was at the Leamington Hotel in Minneapolis and ran on for three days, with business including endorsements for governor and U.S. senator, and the election of national convention delegates. The long agenda tried the patience of a couple of my supporters who were not used to the methodical ways of political conventions. Dave Lilly was one of them. He turned to me late one night while the proceedings were droning on, and said, "Elmer, right now, I think I know more about politics than I want to know."

But when the moment came to endorse a candidate for governor, the suspense was already over. Peterson had been persuaded to yield to me, and run for the U.S. Senate instead—a noble gesture, since his DFL opponent would be the formidable incumbent, Hubert Humphrey. The convention endorsed me by acclamation, and the party came together nicely behind my candidacy. Peterson supported me without hesitation. Former Gov. C. Elmer Anderson headed a group he called "Andersons for Andersen." No other serious Republican candidate surfaced in the primary. I had the good fortune to be able to concentrate on the fall campaign against Orville Freeman from June on.

I spent much of the summer stumping the state. I was in every one of Minnesota's eighty-seven counties in 1960. I came to know all the Republican county officials and their families too. I stay in touch to this day with the Republican Seventh District chairman in 1960, Arnold Anderson of Montevideo. Anderson, a mortician, took a real interest in my campaign and even traveled with me.

Another fine worker was Rudy Rice of Roseau County, near the Canadian border. His daughter Janice was an accomplished singer who eventually joined the Minnesota Opera Company. Many years after the campaign, when her last name was Hardy, I met her and surprised her by asking, "Aren't you Rudy Rice's daughter?" I could then relate to her how important her father was to my campaign. He carried Roseau County for me, even though he thought I was not as conservative as I ought to be. That is the kind of party loyalty that existed in those days.

My reputation as a liberal legislator made it hard for some Republicans to accept me. I would tell them, "You know, I'm really not all that liberal. If you'd let me write the law, I'd write something that's pretty close to the middle ground. But in the legislature, I had to start out in left field in order to wind up in the middle. I had to anticipate compromising at the end."

I see government as the people's partner, a useful tool in getting the people's work done. I hate the impression that some politicians convey today that government dominates people and that we have to minimize government. Government is the way people have of getting together and cooperating to get things done. Of course, government is complicated. This is a big country. Of course, government reflects human weaknesses and frailties and difficulties. People run it. And they need it.

It was said of me in 1960 that I was more liberal than the DFL governor was. It was true, if one defines being liberal as being unpopular with the business community. I had sponsored the Fair Employment Practices Act in the legislature over business opposition. I was never in favor of cutting taxes. Even though I was a businessman myself, I paid the price.

A decade later, the business leaders of the Twin Cities put on a big affair for one of my successors, DFL Gov. Wendell Anderson, in the Crystal Court of the IDS Tower in downtown Minneapolis. I was present too. Anderson was an artful practitioner of middle-ground politics. A fellow approached me who I knew was a staunchly conservative Republican. He said, "Elmer, this shows you what the business community can do for a guy who really works with them."

They never sponsored a bash for me. I did not mind, because I did not expect it. My opinion then was that businesses did not do enough to lift the lives of the people they touched. It is still true today. Though businesses have become more socially conscious and more involved in their communities, they do not do enough, because they could do so much. Businesses are good at doing what makes them feel good. They will not be meeting their full obligation to society until they give until it hurts.

I told campaign audiences, "I'm convinced that if there's going to be a good life for me, there has to be a good life for everyone. If there isn't a good life for everyone, my own life is in jeopardy." I would say the same thing today.

Running for statewide office is much different from the campaigning I had known as a legislator. Legislative campaigns can be personal. A candidate can meet voters individually, door-to-door, one at a time. That does not work for a candidate for governor. I might meet 1,000 people in a full day of campaigning. If I did that every day for a year, I could come in contact with 365,000 people, some of whom might remember me on Election Day. That would take heroic effort, yet it would have put me in touch with only 10 percent of the people of Minnesota in 1960—and a smaller percentage today. Those numbers drove home to me the impossibility of basing a statewide campaign on personal appearances. A good organization—a human network of supporters—is what wins statewide elections. An organization can multiply whatever a candidate says or does many times over. In a good campaign, there is not just one candidate. Every friend of the campaign in the organization represents the candidate to the people he or she meets. I learned to depend on that kind of support.

The lesson was essentially the same one I had given the branch managers at Fuller. I would always tell them, "No matter how smart you are and how hard you work, there's a limit to how much you can accomplish by yourself. That isn't going to be the measure of your success. You're going to succeed if you recruit good people, motivate them, inspire them, draw out their potential, and build an organization that is an expression of yourself." The same principle applies to every group endeavor. When one person tries to do it all, the goal of the organization will not be met. Success depends on group effort.

We concentrated not so much on what I did personally but on how many people I could reach via the media. As long as we had good news coverage, I did not care how many people were at a meeting. I cultivated the media. I was cooperative with reporters any time they wanted anything, because I understood that they were my vehicles for reaching the voters.

Radio and newspapers were still the most important media in 1960, but television news coverage was taking hold, as was paid TV advertising. I filmed my own commercials for television. At first, my staff prepared scripts that they wanted me to read or recite into a camera. That approach did not work well. It seemed unnatural to me. One of the film crew said after one of the many takes, "Let's face it. He can't read. Let's just let him talk." I liked that idea. So I asked my staff to ask me a question off camera. They would roll the film, and I would answer the question with whatever came to mind.

I said what I felt and believed for the state. Those ads seemed to work. I think I gained voters' confidence because they had a feeling that I was genuine, and not staging anything.

The media gave my campaign intermittent coverage during the months that led up to the September 13 primary. But coverage became intense a week later, when Republican presidential candidate Richard Nixon came to Minnesota and campaigned through the state by train. I rode the train with him from Fargo to Minneapolis, where a big evening rally took place at the Minneapolis Armory. Crowds turned out to meet the vice president at whistle-stop campaign appearances along the way. Nixon was kind in introducing me at every stop.

One little incident aboard that train made a lasting impression on me, because I thought it revealed a great deal about the character of the man who eventually became our only president to resign in disgrace. We were having lunch in the club car. Some local Republican Party officials and contributors had joined us for that leg of the trip. Nixon's wife, Pat, was with him, and I was sitting next to him. At one point, I could sense that he wanted to address the group. He paused. The group quickly became quiet— everybody except Pat. She was speaking to one of the people who had just joined us, and she had not caught his signal. Rather sharply, he said, "Pat!" The way he called her to attention bothered me. I thought, that fellow is not respectful of his wife. It was a little more of an order than it needed to be, and it certainly was not polite. I thought, I am not going to like this man—and I never did. I did not want anything more to do with Nixon. I had caught a whisper of a flaw in his character, and it was all I needed. For a time I tried to talk myself out of my negative judgment. I told myself it was unfair to judge him on one momentary exchange. Then my better self would say, "Yes, but it *was* a critical moment. He could have been polite to his wife. She was going through a lot for him, and she deserved better."

I also met John F. Kennedy that year. One day in late winter, I got a call from Otto Silha at the *Star* and *Tribune*. He said, "Elmer, there's a Gridiron Dinner coming up in Washington. You ought to go to one. I think you'd find it interesting. Mr. Cowles and others have suggested that we invite you as a guest of the *Tribune* to sit at our table." John Cowles Sr. owned the Minneapolis newspapers and was becoming a supporter of mine.

So I went to the Gridiron Dinner—the Washington press corps's annual no-holds-barred night of fun with the president and Congress. It happened that the Massachusetts group was sitting right next to Minnesota's—and sitting right next to me was John Kennedy. It was during the Wisconsin pri-

A campaign billboard atop the headquarters of Applebaum's stores, 2225 University Avenue, in August 1960.

Former Republican Gov. C. Elmer Anderson went public with his support for Elmer's campaign for governor shortly before the 1960 Republican state convention.

The Andersen campaign truck offered refreshments for the candidate and supporters.

Emily and Eleanor Andersen traveled with Elmer during the final days of the 1960 campaign.

The Andersens gathered in their living room the morning after the 1960 election, when a photographer called to take a picture of Minnesota's new first family. The result was Elmer's favorite family portrait. *From left:* Tony, Emily, Tony's wife, Alice, Elmer, Eleanor, Julian.

Inauguration Day, 1961.
Elmer and Eleanor on
their way to the ball.

The portrait taken of the new
governor by the Minnesota
National Guard in
January 1961.

Striking a blow for Minnesota tourism, Governor Andersen and his top aide, Tom Swain, stepped outside the capitol for an ice cream break during a mild spell in February 1961. "We wanted to counteract the conspiracy of misinformation about Minnesota's cold winters," Andersen said.

Governor Andersen hosted a gathering of Minnesota's living governors in 1961. *Back row:* C. Elmer Anderson, Edward J. Thye, Hjalmar Petersen, Elmer Benson; *front row:* Elmer L. Andersen, J. A. O. Preus, Harold Stassen, Luther Youngdahl.

Elmer met with E. A. "Al" Vigard after he became interim president of H. B. Fuller Company in 1961.

Governor Andersen signs the Fair Housing Bill into law, April 1961. *From left:* Samuel L. Scheiner, Curtis C. Chivers, Mrs. Harold L. Feder, Monroe Schlactus, Josie Johnson, the Rev. Denzil A. Carty, Ernest C. Cooper, the Rev. Alton M. Motter, James K. Luger, Matthew Little, Timothy Howard, Alan D. Bennett, the Rev. Terrence Murphy.

To celebrate the arrival of the Minnesota Twins in Minnesota, Governor Andersen invited twins from Minneapolis and St. Paul schools to a reception in the capitol rotunda on April 19, 1961. More than three hundred pairs of twins turned out. The man behind and to the right of the governor is Twins owner Calvin Griffith.

Governor Andersen made highway safety a theme of his administration.

As part of a *Today Show* salute to Minnesota, Governor Andersen was interviewed by NBC anchor John Chancellor in November 1961.

At the urging of civil defense officials, the Andersens converted a basement room of their home into a fallout shelter. When it was ready, the governor gave reporters a personal tour.

Emily and Eleanor Andersen together in the kitchen at 2230 West Hoyt Avenue, St. Paul, 1961.

Governor Andersen visited reservations and attended ceremonial events to draw attention to the needs of Minnesota's Native American residents. In the summer of 1962, Elmer and Eleanor attended a Sioux centennial observance at Prairie Island.

Governor Andersen and California Gov. Edmund "Pat" Brown listen to a briefing by New York Gov. Nelson Rockefeller, head of the National Governors' Association Civil Defense Committee, in Washington. The date was October 27, 1962, the day that Soviet ships heading for Cuba suddenly turned around, and the Cuban missile crisis ended.

Former President Dwight Eisenhower made a brief campaign appearance with Governor Andersen in the final days of the 1962 campaign.

mary campaign, when Kennedy was going head-to-head with Hubert Humphrey. When he learned that I was active in Minnesota politics, I had his full attention. All during dinner, he pumped me for information about the kind of campaign Humphrey would be running.

The rap on Kennedy was that he was too boyish to be a presidential candidate. He cultivated a little cowlick in his hair, and that added to his youthful image. People belittled his ability and stature. I concluded that night that the critics were wrong. When I got home, I told a number of people: "Let me assure you: Jack Kennedy is fully mature. He hasn't grown up in the Kennedy family and Massachusetts politics for nothing. He's a sharp, educated, talented, tough guy. Toughness is the emphasis. He's no pushover." The Humphrey crowd in Minnesota soon learned that I was right.

In 1960, the economy was stagnant, both in Minnesota and the nation. Duluth and the Iron Range were experiencing real distress, and farm income was discouragingly low. Freeman claimed that Minnesota had led the Midwest in job growth during his years as governor. The claim sounded nice, but said little. I pointed out that census reports showed that the state had actually lost production workers between 1954 and 1958. And our population growth had lagged the rest of the nation's so much that the state was slated to lose a congressional district in the post-census redistricting, and go from nine members of the U.S. House of Representatives to eight.

I favored taxation based on ability to pay. That is why I opposed proposals to institute a sales tax, unless low-income Minnesotans, senior citizens, and people raising large families could somehow be spared its burden. Many other Republicans preferred a sales tax to the income tax. Freeman spent a lot of campaign time and energy trying to link me to that position. But he could not make his charge stick. My opposition was one of the reasons Minnesota had no sales tax until 1967.

I wanted lower property taxes for farmers, homeowners, and small business owners. I wanted to eliminate the highly unpopular personal property tax. I wanted complete tax reform that would bring to the fore some incentives for business growth. I believed that if businesses grew, Minnesota could meet its needs without a tax increase. But if the economy remained flat, a tax increase in 1961 would be hard to avoid—and I told Minnesotans so, in just those words.

Jobs, economy, concern for people—those were the things I stressed. Once when I addressed a union audience, I said, "I know most of you are Democrats, and you're encouraged to vote the party line. But let me tell you, I've handled some pro-worker legislation that the Democrats wouldn't handle." I told them about my efforts to equalize the pay of heavy equipment operators doing road construction for counties throughout Minnesota. I succeeded in abolishing a pay structure that set a lower wage for workers in nonmetro counties. If we want to have a strong rural economy and keep young people living there, we have to pay them well. Paying more for work performed in the metro area only serves to attract qualified workers to the city. The change I sought was controversial. Outstate county boards liked getting more highway for their construction dollar. But I succeeded. I regret that after I left office, the county boards again pressed for lower wages in rural counties, and got their way.

I used my campaign speeches to attempt to generate public interest in my ideas on a number of topics. I proposed to exempt from the property tax the first $7,500 of value of a homestead owned by a senior citizen. I called for an end to mandatory retirement at age sixty-five. I wanted more public housing, including some reserved exclusively for the elderly.

I wanted more funding for agricultural research at the University of Minnesota, with an eye toward developing a stronger food processing industry in rural communities. My goals were twofold: one, to offer farmers premium-price local markets for their commodities; and two, to provide more jobs paying decent wages to attract young people and stabilize the rural population. Such a strategy would still be good for outstate Minnesota.

Then, as now, northeastern Minnesota was a DFL bastion. But mindful of the weakness in the mining industry, I campaigned there many times and put forward a series of proposals for stimulating the region's economy. I wanted to assure the mining companies that they would be taxed equitably as they developed the taconite industry. I suggested a job-training program for youth and a retraining program for older workers, coupled with incentives to attract new businesses to the area. One industry I wanted to see flourish was tourism. I proposed the establishment of a nonprofit organization that could draw on federal, state, and private resources to improve and promote recreational opportunities, and I urged more attention to conservation of natural resources. Before long, the *Minneapolis Star* reported that a "guerilla war" was being waged on my behalf among disenchanted DFLers on the Iron Range.

I was especially interested in taking steps to encourage growth in one of Minnesota's oldest industries, timber. I proposed to accelerate reforestation efforts and intensify research into forest management, so that more trees could be harvested without putting the state's forests at risk. I also wanted research to discover new uses for the state's abundance of low-grade timber.

I was always vitally interested in the University of Minnesota. But in 1960, the state colleges also needed a governor's attention. I wanted a new state college established in the western part of the state. I wanted the state colleges governed by an independent board, much the same way the University of Minnesota was.

In those days before the construction of the interstate highway system, the annual traffic fatality rate was appallingly high. I issued a twelve-point highway safety proposal that included drivers' education in all Minnesota high schools, compulsory chemical testing of drivers suspected of intoxication, and required installation of safety belts in new vehicles.

From a strategic standpoint, there were three main events or turning points in the campaign. First, I needed to make contact with my opponent. I had to get into the ring with him, figuratively speaking. I realized that he, as the incumbent, could ignore me and get by with it indefinitely. I kept challenging him to debates, and he kept shrugging off my requests.

Then I began to criticize his administration of the state mental hospital system. I had learned a great deal about those facilities as chairman of the senate's Welfare Committee. I knew what improvements had been made, and what was still needed. I called a news conference on September 9 in Marshall to charge that Freeman had not done as much as he could have for mentally ill Minnesotans. I advocated a serious program to upgrade the professional training of mental health workers and bring more mental health services to parts of the state that were poorly served. *Minneapolis Star* reporter Wallace Mitchell was traveling with me. He made my mental health press conference page-one news. Freeman had to respond to what I had said. That next day, I told our campaign's executive committee, "Now, we're in business. We've got the guy in the ring, and we can go after him." That was turning point number one.

Evidence that I was gaining ground came in the form of the vote totals in the September 13 election. I was unopposed in the Republican primary for governor, while Freeman had a token opponent in the DFL primary. Nevertheless, I polled more votes than the incumbent governor did, a fact that led one prescient newspaper editor to comment that I "could well defeat the governor" in November.

Not long after the primary, Freeman finally agreed to a debate sponsored by the Junior Chamber of Commerce and the University of Minnesota. It was staged on October 9 in Northrop Auditorium, the cavernous hall at the

University of Minnesota, because interest was running high. I was an old debater. I learned one thing in debate: if you decide the issue on which the debate revolves, you win. I went into that debate determined that I was going to pound home my issue and toss aside quickly or humorously any points that he made. I was going to force Freeman to face up to his decision to send the National Guard to the Wilson strike to side with the strikers.

I was relentless on that point. I would say good things about the governor, but then I would always add, "He made a mistake. It's an inexcusable mistake. He betrayed his oath of office, and that cannot be condoned. He should have known better. He had been governor long enough to know what a governor's obligation is. He made a profound mistake that justifies his discontinuing in the office." My strategy assured that the Wilson issue would be the one the reporters would pick up in their stories. Freeman had to answer me, and he answered lamely. The next day, reporter Jim Klobuchar's report for the Associated Press began with my charge that Freeman had led "a highly political, dictatorial, arbitrary and angry administration." My strategy had worked. The debate was the second decisive point in the campaign.

A third and most telling event occurred at Fosston, a little town in northwestern Minnesota, on September 29. I was campaigning in that region of the state, and so was Freeman. Reporter Wally Mitchell was with me again. That morning, he said, "Elmer, do you know where Freeman is today?" I did not. "He's at Fosston. He's speaking at a Rotary Club. Aren't you a Rotarian?" "Sure, I am a Rotarian," I said. Mitchell said, "Why don't you go and make up attendance at the Fosston Rotary Club, and hear what your opponent has to say? It would be a good story for me." He talked me into it. By lunchtime, we were seated at the Rotary Club of Fosston. That little club was thrilled to have the governor as their featured speaker that day. When Freeman entered the room, people surrounded him. He did not see me. He did not see Mitchell. He went to the head table and stayed occupied with those around him during lunch. He still did not know I was there. Finally, he was introduced to speak. He stood up, looked over the audience, and saw me. He just about collapsed. He became agitated and angry. "I didn't know this was going to be a debate. I didn't know my opponent had been invited here," he sputtered. "I want to have the ground rules explained."

The president of the club tried to soothe him. "There is no debate. Andersen is just here as a visiting Rotarian, making up for missing his meeting in St. Paul. He heard you were going to speak, and he decided to come and hear you. He isn't going to have anything to say." Finally, they gave him enough reassurance that he delivered his speech. I left at the close of his prepared remarks. But press reports afterward informed me that Freeman launched into a tirade after I left, pounding his fist and accusing me of demagoguery and "a breach of good taste." A *Fargo Forum* report said Freeman "spoke so furiously it was difficult at times to catch all his words."

The episode may have appeared trivial to most Minnesotans, but to me, it was significant. Freeman lost control. He demonstrated how thin his composure was, and how nervous he was about my campaign. He was no longer sure of himself in the way a candidate must be to win. He was defeated inside. That incident occurred more than a month before the election, but from that time on, nothing Freeman said fazed me at all. I knew I had won.

As a visiting Rotarian in Fosston, I filled out a makeup attendance card to be sent back to the St. Paul Rotary Club to show that I had met my attendance requirement. When I got back to St. Paul, I asked the club's secretary if I could have that postcard. I framed it and have it still.

My sense that the campaign's tide had turned in my favor was confirmed by an October 23 Minnesota Poll, conducted by the *Minneapolis Tribune*. It was the first statewide poll to put me ahead of Freeman, 50 percent to 45 percent. By then, Freeman was attacking me viciously, calling me "deceitful," accusing me of "betraying the farmer and the worker," and referring to me repeatedly as a "wealthy corporation president." All his angry rhetoric seemed to yield for him was a scolding from the state's editorial writers. In the final poll published before Election Day, I was still ahead but by a razor-slim margin, 51 percent to 49 percent.

Our election night headquarters was the Leamington Hotel in downtown Minneapolis, a place that saw many election celebrations through the years. Vote counts dribbled in slowly because paper ballots were still the norm in outstate Minnesota. But Ramsey County voted by machine, and its totals came in first. Ramsey County was DFL territory, but it was also my home base. My analysts did not expect me to carry the county, but I needed to do better than other Republicans had done there in the past in order to win.

As we expected, Freeman carried Ramsey County. But my analysts were upbeat. They came to me and said, "Elmer, you're going to win. He didn't get the vote he needed out of Ramsey County. You've got more than enough out of Ramsey County to win."

I trusted my people to have the numbers right. So from that moment, I relaxed and enjoyed the evening as it unfolded. It was a long night—and not just for me. The outcome of the presidential race between John F. Kennedy and Richard Nixon was uncertain until the next morning. When the returns were all in, Kennedy had carried Minnesota by 22,018 votes. Senator Humphrey had won reelection by about 200,000 votes. But I outpolled Freeman by 22,879 votes. Kennedy carried only thirty-six of Minnesota's eighty-seven counties. I was the winner in fifty-four counties.

The next several days were an incredible blur of activity and emotion. One moment stands out for me. The morning after the election, after a short night, the family dressed and assembled in our living room. Tony had married his college sweetheart, Alice Wallien of Montevideo, Minnesota, in 1957; both Tony and Alice were present that day. Emily was so proud and excited. She was fourteen and loved to campaign with me. We were all so happy—happy that the campaign was over, that we had won, and that a great adventure was starting. A photographer came to take a portrait of Minnesota's new first family. I have always liked that photo.

I may have been tempted to give all the credit for the victory to my Republican team and me. But I knew I had been helped by a number of DFLers who thought Freeman had been governor long enough. He was seeking an unprecedented fourth two-year term in 1960. That bothered some people, even those who liked him. Minnesota was used to frequent turnover in the governor's office. Two-year gubernatorial terms had been the law since statehood was granted, and single-term governors were not uncommon in state history. Some DFLers told me privately that they considered Freeman and his people a bottleneck to the ambitions of younger Democrats. They wanted him to move on.

One who told me as much was Kent Youngdahl, a nephew of former Gov. Luther Youngdahl and an active young DFLer. He was a Hennepin County commissioner and a friend of mine. Not long before the election, he told me, "Elmer, you're going to be elected. You're going to get a lot of Democratic votes. We've got to get Freeman out of there so we can open things up a little. But we're going to knock the tar out of you two years later."

I had been put on notice.

Governor-Elect

T HE DAY AFTER THE ELECTION, I called my first press conference as governor-elect, at the Leamington Hotel in downtown Minneapolis. I had an announcement: I would not wait until inauguration day to begin to work on the economic problems on the Iron Range. I would go to northeastern Minnesota as soon as meetings could be arranged with local leaders. I wanted quick action to alleviate the distress I had witnessed in that region during the campaign.

In the fall of 1960, unemployment was at 12 percent in northeastern Minnesota, an unacceptable level. Dirt swirled in the doorways of empty storefronts along Duluth's Superior Street. Throughout Range cities, residents were leaving in droves, and housing values were plummeting. The supply of merchantable iron ore—ore that could be dug out of the earth and shipped directly to the steel mills in the East—was nearly exhausted on the Range.

E. W. Davis at the University of Minnesota had devised a method of extracting ore from taconite rock, which was in plentiful supply on the Iron Range. But competition from other nations and a concern about Minnesota's tax policies led the steel companies elsewhere. Large deposits of merchantable ore had been discovered in Brazil and Australia. There was taconite in Canada. Duluth was witness to the baleful sight of ships in its harbor, loading equipment from Minnesota mines to be shipped to Canada for use there.

The steel companies maintained that the Minnesota Legislature had targeted them for unfair taxation for many years. Whenever state revenues were short, it seemed, taxes on iron ore extraction were raised to make up the difference. Further, the companies believed that Iron Range communities did not appreciate them. The companies saw the lavish public expenditures their taxes bought, and they felt exploited. For example, at the time it was built, Hibbing High School cost $5 million, making it the most expensive high school building in the country. It had a pipe organ and upholstered opera seating in its auditorium.

Feelings between the mining companies and their workers tended to be mutually mistrustful. I once asked Jeno Paulucci, the food-processing entrepreneur in Duluth, "Jeno, why do you hate the mining companies so much?" He said, "Elmer, I grew up on the Iron Range. We kids used to play in the streets, dirt streets, and these mining guys would come by in their big limousines and kick up the dust. We ate their dust. We hated their guts!" It was as simple and illogical as that.

Just days after the 1960 election, a ruling by state Tax Commissioner Joseph Robertson further alienated the mining industry. A petition signed by forty-three firms had requested that Minnesota tax iron ore in the same manner that it taxed other commercial and industrial property. Robertson flatly rejected the petition. He claimed that local governments on the Iron Range could bring about any needed equalization by adjusting the assessed valuation of the ore. He correctly noted that the total assessed value of ore on the Range had been dropping—but that was more due to the declining economy than any change of attitude by local governments.

The processing of taconite could bring another generation or more of prosperity to the Iron Range. But it would be only a pipe dream if the tax problem could not be resolved. Processing taconite ore was a capital-intensive operation. Huge crushers were needed to reduce the hard taconite rock to a consistency of talcum powder. Then, a magnetic device extracted the iron ore from the powder and molded it into pellets. That was the finished product. The process created a huge quantity of taconite "tailings," a waste product that had to be stored or disposed somewhere.

Yet, despite the expense associated with producing them, taconite pellets were a desirable commodity for the steel industry. They had the advantage of air space between them so that processing them into steel was faster, more efficient, and cheaper than using even the best merchantable ore. That meant that taconite could compete with merchantable ore from anywhere in the world. For Minnesota, taconite was highly desirable too. Processing taconite was not as worker intensive as mining ore, but it would employ a sizable share of the Iron Range workforce.

During the campaign, I had come to know the mayors of the Range communities. We had discussed their deep concern about their cities' future. Together, we came up with the idea of an amendment to the state constitution that would recognize taconite processing as a manufacturing operation, not an extractive operation, and tax it uniformly with other processing industries. The mining companies would be assured that they would no longer be singled out for special taxation. We thought that if the mining companies had that assurance in the form of a constitutional amendment, they would make the investment in Minnesota taconite. Our proposal became known as "the taconite amendment."

The idea was stirring during my campaign, but it did not really take shape until I visited with Iron Range leaders in a series of meetings on December 3–5. I met with dozens of people—labor leaders, mining company officials, civic leaders, legislators—in Duluth, Hibbing, Virginia, Ely, Grand Rapids, and Two Harbors. The wonderful mayors of those cities deserve much of the credit for advancing the amendment proposal. It meant a great deal to them politically to turn full face from what had been the standard local attitude toward the mining companies—that they were cheaters who were not to be trusted—and urge that the companies be viewed as partners with Minnesota. The mayors wisely came to the realization that no good can come from allowing animosities to fester for generations.

Those mayors and I hit it off, despite our partisan differences. I told them, "I would like to do something for northeastern Minnesota. You need help. Nobody else is doing anything. Why don't we get together on a bipartisan basis, and advance a real practical solution that I think will work?"

On their behalf, I went to Pittsburgh to meet with officials of the mining companies. I met Roger Blough, the president of U.S. Steel Company, the parent company of the Oliver Iron Mining Company. I found him to be quite an ordinary fellow and not very attuned to Minnesota's concerns.

By then, I was fully committed to helping the Iron Range in every way I could, despite the fact that there was not much political gain for me in doing so. I did not expect decades of DFL voting habits to change. But when I see a problem, I want a solution, and I want to be part of the solution. I cannot stand to be anywhere where there is something obviously needing to be done, and not respond. The thrill of accomplishment is my satisfaction, not what it does in the auxiliary way of money or politics or favor. I was convinced that the amendment I favored was the right solution. It would bring the desired result. When you have that conviction, nothing stands in your way. You do not give up.

Besides, I had become attached to northern Minnesota. I loved the people there. I understood why they were the way they were. Like many of them, I was the son of immigrants. I knew what it was like to work in a factory. I shared their values—family, hard work, education, each succeeding generation getting ahead.

The need for an amendment assuring mining companies that taconite processing would be taxed fairly became a theme of mine for the next four years. The DFL Party initially opposed it, on the grounds that it showed favoritism to the mining companies. The man who had been elected lieutenant governor in 1960, Karl Rolvaag, led the DFL attack—something the press correctly interpreted as his first move toward a campaign against me in 1962. But there was more than politics behind the DFL view. It reflected the deep-seated mistrust mine workers had for their employers. The state AFL-CIO also rejected the idea, on the grounds that if mining company taxes went down, other taxes might rise. Labor was especially resistant to anything that might lead to the institution of a sales tax.

It was not long before the leader of the DFL party, U.S. Sen. Hubert Humphrey, attacked me for the amendment proposal too. His words stung. At a speech in Duluth, Humphrey allowed that whatever it was that the mining companies had done for me, I had surely paid them off handsomely by proposing the amendment. He suggested that I ought to quit and do something else, because the amendment would never become law.

Yet, with desperate times confronting them, the people of northeastern Minnesota soon began to see the common sense of our proposal. Mine workers knew that something had to be done, and here was one plausible possibility. I was amused, some time later, when I was invited to speak in the Range town of Chisholm. I asked somebody, "Why in the world would anybody in Chisholm want to have me as a speaker? I think I lost Chisholm about three to one." "That's why they want you," I was told. "You got more votes than any Republican ever did there. They would like to hear more from you."

Bringing my campaign so deep into DFL territory in 1960 had been almost an exercise in guerilla warfare. When I visited towns in northeastern Minnesota, I would set up my vehicle with its loudspeaker on a street, and just start talking, with no prior announcement and without waiting for a crowd. Few people stopped, but I knew that people could hear behind storefronts and in apartments over the stores. They did not come out, because they did not want to be seen attending a Republican function. On one such occasion, possibly in Chisholm, I noticed a large man across the street eyeing me menacingly. I wondered what he had in mind when he walked across the street toward me. I thought, My goodness! Does this fellow intend to rough me up? I resolved to stand my ground, keep talking, and take whatever came. He bumped past me as if he were picking a fight, but as he went by, he said, "You're doing okay, kid. Keep it up."

The publisher of the Eveleth newspaper, Joe Orehek, invited me to meet some people in the basement of his home. He felt he had to be in the basement, where those in attendance would be unseen from outside the house. That is how strongly the feeling against Republicans ran in that town. I found campaigning in those circumstances exhilarating. I sensed that I was making progress in a severe uphill battle. Those campaign experiences only added to my determination that if elected, I would press hard for measures to aid that spirited but troubled region.

The meetings in December led to the formation of a new group we called the Northeastern Minnesota Development Association. To head it, we recruited Jeno Paulucci, the Duluth entrepreneur whose Chun King Food Company was one of the few bright spots in that city's economy that year. Jeno was a volatile person. He was fabulously successful in business and a man of integrity. For many years, he was the only businessman to have paid back a loan he received from the Iron Range Resources and Rehabilitation Board (IRRRB). But he was a demanding person and easily angered. He was unhappy with me when I refused to let him select the new chairman of the IRRRB. Though we both worked hard for passage of a taconite amendment, we parted company before the 1962 election.

One of the ideas I tossed out was the possibility of a new ownership strategy for state-owned forest lands that might encourage a wood-processing firm to locate one or more new plants in Minnesota. I proposed that designated state timberlands be divided into parcels of between 40 and 160 acres and sold to individuals as stockholders, to create a Minnesota Forest Cooperative. The stockholders would elect a board of directors, which in turn would negotiate a management contract with a timber products firm that would abide by the co-op's standards for long-term management of the timber supply as it harvested trees. I got the idea from the Rio Grande valley, where cooperative orchards grow grapefruit and give average citizens the benefits of owning a piece of an orchard. I thought Minnesotans would like the idea of owning a bit of forest, where they could camp or hunt or enjoy the outdoors, and get the satisfaction of contributing to the development of the wood processing industry in Minnesota. And I knew that the state was not gaining as much from its forests as it might. Minnesota ranked about sixth in the country in forested acres, but it ranked only twelfth in the country in its income from that source. Part of the reason was that great areas of timberland had been cut over, then left for scrub without proper reforestation. My plan would prevent that from happening in the future.

My idea met with strong resistance from the wood processing industry. They wanted no change in their existing arrangement with state-owned timberland, which allowed them to cut trees for a fraction of what they cost to grow. And citizens were not much interested in investing money in something that might not produce tangible gain for many years. The idea went nowhere. But I am convinced that it was sound and could still be done.

I offered another idea during the campaign that I believed would benefit northeastern Minnesota and other regions as well. I wanted better management of the state's parks and natural resources. I had seen in the legislature too many ill-planned, last-minute scrambles for the funds needed to properly conserve, use, and develop the state's natural abundance. I called for development of a long-range plan, to include a commission of legislators that would study and prepare initiatives during the period between legislative sessions. I was borrowing from an idea that Freeman's administration commissioner, Arthur Naftalin, had for a legislative commission to review and recommend building projects. My proposal led to the creation of the Legislative Commission on Minnesota Resources, which continues working and serving a useful purpose today.

Of course, I had other pressing duties immediately after the election besides attending to the problems on the Iron Range. A new governor has little time between the November election and the January inauguration to establish an administration. A budget was needed for the coming two years and had to be ready for the legislature in January. An inaugural message had to be written. Key appointments had to be made. So much comes at a new governor, so fast and furious, that he can scarcely absorb it all. For me, that time was hectic in the extreme.

I immediately turned to Tom Swain for help. The task before us required superlative organizational skills, and he possessed them. I asked Tom to be my executive secretary, as the chief of staff was called in those years. Tom helped me recruit other key people for the office.

Milton Knoll, who had been executive secretary of the Republican Party for Ramsey County and a good friend, became an administrative assistant. I knew him not only from party activities but also from his work as a field scout for the Boy Scouts of America in St. Paul and as a division leader in the St. Paul Community Chest when I was the annual drive's chair.

There was George Manser, a former insurance man who had terrific people skills. He became an administrative aide—a sort of go-between, meeting with all the people who wanted to deal with the governor. He later became the chief executive of a successful insurance company.

Don Padilla wanted to return to his business after the campaign, so he found Tom Roeser to replace him as our public relations officer. Tom was a former *St. Cloud Times* reporter who had worked for U.S. Rep. Al Quie in Washington. Tom was a free spirit. He was like an absent-minded professor—almost as disorganized as Tom Swain was orderly. When his wife had their first child, she said to Tom, "Now, Tom, we've got a baby in the house. You're going to have to start looking after yourself." But Tom was a talented writer who had a feeling for people. He was an excellent public relations man and had a sterling intellect. He went on to earn a doctorate at Harvard and become the director of public relations for Quaker Oats of Chicago.

My longtime secretary at Fuller, Donna Petersen, followed me to the capitol, and I was glad that she did. By the time I was elected, she had already worked for me for nearly twenty years. She had learned to anticipate whatever I needed. She was a master at arranging my travel, organizing my schedule, preparing me for my appointments, and keeping me on time. She was consistently gracious and accommodating to anyone who called on her. She also was the keeper of wonderfully detailed scrapbooks, documenting my public career. She was a super secretary.

They were all tremendous, dedicated workers. I have been fortunate in being surrounded by key people of the finest caliber. Most valuable of all, of course, is Eleanor. She devoted her life to our family and me. Being Minnesota's First Lady was not something she wanted to exploit for her own sake or the sake of her own projects. She cared little for recognition. After the election, she was still a family homemaker and a loving person dedicated to others. I needed her steady support more than ever.

In 1960, Minnesota did not yet have an official residence for its governor. So, fortunately, my election did not burden Eleanor and the family with a need to move. We stayed at home, on Hoyt Avenue in St. Anthony Park. We did some official entertaining at home, and some at hotels and restaurants. Eleanor accompanied me when necessary, but I was often alone at those events. We decided early on that she would not attempt to accompany me to all the public functions that a governor must attend in the evening. She wanted to put the family first, and I agreed. Emily was a teenager and needed a parent in the house at night. Besides, I thought, we did not both need to go into politics.

Though Eleanor did not seek the limelight, she got her share of attention. In those days, newspapers had women's pages that focused on social events and often carried photos of the state's First Lady, appearing at a charity ball or tea party. She was photogenic and gracious, which added to her appeal to the press. But Eleanor was never carried away by press attention. Once she saw an item in the newspaper with the headline, "The Passing

Parade," and she pointed it out to me. She wanted me to recognize that the whirl that surrounded us then was nothing more than a passing parade.

The children were supportive of their dad's new role, but they were involved to differing degrees. Emily was an impressionable fifteen-year-old when I was inaugurated. She was proud of her dad's achievements and loved to accompany me to events when she could. I think fathers are fortunate to have daughters, because daughters tend to be more adoring of their fathers than sons are. Sons want to be more independent. Julian, our second son, wanted his own life. He was a student at Carleton College in Northfield when I was governor, and while he was interested in matters such as civil rights, he did not care much about the state political fray. Tony was more interested, but he was married, living in Cornwall, New York, and pursuing a career at H. B. Fuller Company. He had limited time for Minnesota politics.

One sobering change at home was the installation in December of an ominous-looking box. It contained a bell and a light that would signal me in the event of a nuclear or other attack on our nation. I had a briefing with the state civil defense director, Hubert Schon, about my responsibilities as governor if the signal should ever sound. I would declare a state of civil defense emergency, broadcast a message to the state's citizens advising them to either evacuate or take cover, and if necessary and feasible, head to Mankato State College, where arrangements for an emergency state capitol had been made. Those precautions may seem silly today, but they were deadly serious at the height of the cold war in 1960. I know just the presence of that box in the Hoyt House had an effect on Eleanor as well as on me.

Eleanor and I were invited to represent Minnesota at the inauguration of President John F. Kennedy. I thought it would be interesting to go. Further, I thought, why not invite some Minnesota Democrats to go with me. We had some strato-cruiser aircraft available in Minnesota's Air National Guard fleet, so I lined up a strato-cruiser plane and told legislators that if they wanted to go, I could get them there and back. We had a plane full of people going to the inaugural.

Kennedy gave a marvelous, memorable inaugural address. But I was equally impressed with Robert Frost's contribution to the event. Frost read a poem; then newsmen gathered around him and asked him for a comment. He paused for a minute, then said, "Life goes on." Those three words put all the hype and hoopla into perspective. He had the wisdom of years to see beyond the present moment to the larger significance of things.

At the inaugural ball, Eleanor simply shone. It had snowed in Washington the night before, and the weather was cold, wet, and miserable. Many beautifully gowned women hiked up their dresses, took off their slippers, and walked through slush in their stocking feet for a block or more to get to the ball. It was not a gentle occasion. I do not know just how we managed, but I did not see Eleanor walking around in any slush. She was radiant and dignified throughout.

I was impressed with Kennedy. We had a few moments with him that night, and he remembered our conversation the previous spring at the Gridiron Dinner. I liked Kennedy because he was dynamic. Not long afterward, he made his challenge of going to the moon before the decade was over. I considered that a wonderful challenge to our nation's scientific community. He forced them to step up the pace of invention, to accomplish something in ten years that we did not yet know how to do. The space program Kennedy began was an amazing example of the American spirit.

Kennedy once said that he was the first president to be born in a new generation, in the new century. I was slightly older than he was, but I identified with what he said. The early 1960s felt like a new time, busy and exciting, for the nation and for Minnesota.

I was certainly busy. I not only had to find key people at the capitol but also had to put the management of Fuller into other hands for the duration of my term in office. I had not made a change in Fuller's leadership during the campaign, but I knew from the start that if I were elected, I would have to step aside as Fuller's president, at least temporarily. We had the choice of several good people who could take over as interim president. Ben Fuller, the grandson of the company's founder, was one. He was a strong candidate, but he lived in Cincinnati. The appointment would dislocate his entire family for an indefinite period. So, I picked our vice president and manager of the firm's adhesive division in St. Paul, E. A. "Al" Vigard. We had known each other for more than thirty years, and I trusted him highly. Eleanor and his wife had been classmates. We double-dated during our college years. I was best man at Al's wedding. That is how intimately we knew each other. He had been with me at Fuller since 1943.

Al took over the management of a company that had been meeting its goal of doubling in size every five years. By 1960, Fuller had plants in thirteen U.S. cities and two in Canada. Fuller International was headquartered in Nassau, the Bahamas. We had just embarked on a joint venture with a firm in Buenos Aires, Argentina.

At the capitol, one of my first major appointments was controversial with my fellow Republicans. On November 21, I announced that I would reappoint Morris Hursh as welfare commissioner, the same post he had held for years in Governor Freeman's DFL administration. I had good reasons for the decision, which I thought my party would accept. One was that I felt there was no place for partisan politics in the administration of welfare programs. Hursh was widely regarded as the top professional in his field. He had exceptional educational credentials and extensive experience, going back to his service as executive secretary for Gov. Floyd B. Olson in the 1930s. I knew Hursh, and I trusted him, having worked with him while I was chairman of the senate's Welfare Committee. He was honest and decent. I saw no reason to replace him with someone I did not know as well, purely for partisan reasons.

I thought highly of several other commissioners who had served in the Freeman administration. One was Frank Marzitelli, the commissioner of highways and a fine public servant. I had supported him with a financial contribution a decade earlier, when he ran for the St. Paul City Council. He reminded me of that gift some years later. "You know, that was the first contribution I received," he said. "I didn't know how to go about asking for money. You just knew I needed money, and you gave me some. I never forgot it."

In 1969 he called on me again with some news. "They've made an error in planning the new parking ramp for the civic center," he said. It was running onto Fuller property. Furthermore, he said, "We're out of money. What I've got to do is ask you if you'll *give* Fuller's old plant to the city of St. Paul." I said, "Frank, you have certainly learned how to ask!" We did donate our old Eagle Street plant to the city. By then, we had moved our headquarters to a new building in the Midway area.

I decided to ask Marzitelli to take the deputy commissioner's position in the highway department, and to put a new commissioner in charge. David Lilly recommended a retired Army general he had known in the service and considered an excellent administrator. James C. Marshall became my highway commissioner and fulfilled my expectations as a candid, blunt, decisive leader. He approached the job as a general, not a politician.

Those were the years when the interstate highway system was being constructed. The decisions being made in the highway department in those years would have a major impact on the state for generations. Marshall immediately recognized that a major policy decision was needed. "There is one thing you have to decide," he said to me. "Are you going to put the emphasis in the metropolitan area, where the need is greatest, but where you show the least progress for the money? Or are you going to build freeways first in the country, where you can build lots of miles and show a lot of progress at lower cost?" He recommended building in the Twin Cities area first. I agreed, and we proceeded, despite the higher cost and the fact that my political support in 1960 had been stronger outstate than in the metro area.

Not long after we took office, Marshall came to me with a proposal that he said would add millions of dollars to the highway fund without injuring services. "Every little town in Minnesota has a highway garage with a piece of snow plowing equipment in it," he informed me. "It's all obsolete and unnecessary. Now we have big equipment that goes for many miles very rapidly, but we maintain all these little garages because nobody has had the guts to close them. They're wasteful. You ought to just close them all." He acknowledged that eliminating those garages would eliminate some local employment and would be unpopular. But he convinced me. We closed the local garages.

The closing caused an uproar in some places. One little town near the North Dakota border, Fertile, was so upset that they wrote scores of letters and held meetings in protest. In the 1962 election, Fertile, which in 1960 had given me a three-to-one plurality, defeated me by a three-to-one margin. That difference was enough to change the outcome of the 1962 election. I used to say, "There's only about so much good government the people can stand."

In a number of my key appointments, I opted for professional expertise rather than political reward. For tax commissioner (now called revenue commissioner), I turned to Rolland Hatfield, an able career public servant whom I had first known a decade earlier, when he was state tax research director. He was a Republican, but his professional credentials far outshone his political ones. He went on to be state auditor in the 1970s.

In the Department of Conservation (today's Department of Natural Resources) I installed Clarence Prout as commissioner. He was the first professional conservationist ever to be named commissioner of conservation. His predecessors had all been politicians.

I followed the same principle in selecting a commissioner of agriculture. I had great respect for the county agricultural agents of the University Extension Service, and I wanted someone from their ranks to be my commissioner. An extension agent would be well versed in the problems of average farmers. I asked the agriculture lobbyists at the capitol to supply me with the names of some of the most respected county agents in the state. They found Duane Wilson in Gaylord, Minnesota, the Sibley County agent, a man with a wonderful record and a reputation for integrity. He made a fine commissioner of agriculture.

As I was making appointments and shaping my administration in December 1960, I was not thinking about votes. I was determined to do things the way they really ought to be done. So I made changes along the way that angered some people. For example, I eliminated the grain grading positions in the state department of agriculture. Grain grading was no longer a state function. By 1960, it was purely federal work. Yet the governor could appoint five or six people to the salaried position of grain grader, which was described to me as "a nice way of taking care of some people." I thought, none of that with this governor. We abolished the grain grader positions.

I had the same attitude with the preparation of my first state budget. Within a week of my election, I was meeting with people who had a claim on state money, to hear their pleas for consideration in the budget I would present to the legislature in January. I wanted to craft a balanced budget, one in which revenues were adequate to meet the expenditures I believed were necessary.

State Sen. Don Wright of Minneapolis, the chairman of the senate's Tax Committee, gave me what I am sure he thought was friendly advice. "Don't call for any tax increases," he said. "We've got to have some, but don't you call for any. If it turns out that the budget is out of balance, we'll balance it for you."

I rejected that proposition. If I knew that Minnesota needed more money to balance the budget, I thought the governor should be the one to offer a proposal to raise that money. So, I proposed a new tax—a tax on utility bills. I thought that would be fair, because people who had a low utility bill would pay very little, while people with elaborate homes and big utility bills would pay more. I suggested a uniform tax on both telephone and power bills.

One might fairly conclude that right from the start, I was working pretty hard on losing votes in the next election.

1961 Legislature

THRILLS DO NOT COME much faster in life than they came to me at the start of 1961. On Sunday, January 1, Eleanor and I traveled to Pasadena, California, where the University of Minnesota Golden Gopher football team would play the University of Washington in the Rose Bowl. We rode and waved to the throngs at the Tournament of Roses Parade on January 2, and watched the Gophers lose to the University of Washington. On January 3, the 1961 legislature convened to the news that I would propose a budget that called for $39 million in new revenues, but no income tax increase and no sales tax.

Then, on January 4, I was inaugurated as Minnesota's thirtieth governor. The swearing-in ceremony was witnessed by my entire family: Eleanor, Tony, Julian, and Emily; Tony's wife, Alice; Eleanor's mother, Elizabeth Johnson; my brother Arnold and his wife, Eunice; my sister-in-law Ella Andersen; my sister, Caroline, and her husband, Charles Marston; and Aunt Lillian Johnson. Unfortunately, neither Eleanor's father nor my brother Marvin lived to see my inauguration. Gustaf Johnson died in 1959; Marvin left us in 1960. We were to lose Elizabeth Johnson in 1962.

Also present were a number of Fuller employees from all over the country. Our friend Ermine Hall-Allen, Ed Hall's daughter, sang "The Star Spangled Banner" at the rotunda reception on inaugural evening.

The inauguration involved a swearing-in ceremony, an inaugural address, an informal reception, then dashing home to get dressed for a formal reception in the evening in the capitol rotunda, followed by the inaugural ball at the Prom Center. It was a long, festive day full of activities. The grand march at the inaugural ball was a special tradition. The governor and his lady would make a formal entrance and then lead a march, followed by other couples. In turn, one couple would go left and the other right, and walk around the ballroom until they met as a foursome. Then every foursome would split, one going left, the other right, until they met as a group of eight that would proceed as a unit. It produced a sequence of rotating and churning that was quite a spectacle to watch. We marched and danced until the wee hours of the morning, but I must confess my mind was elsewhere. Dancing was fun, but it was not what I was elected to do.

My inaugural address was delivered to a joint session of the house and senate, in the house chamber. I promised an administration devoid of extreme partisanship and proved the point by backing a measure proposed by DFL Attorney General Walter F. Mondale to require charities to disclose details of their administrative operations. I sketched my ideas for greater emphasis on mental health programs, highway safety, a single sanitary sewer system for the metro area, a new state park at Fort Snelling, and natural resource conservation. And I stressed that in order for the taconite industry to grow, the legislature needed to provide assurance that it would be taxed fairly. The need for a "taconite amendment" to the state constitution found its way into all my speeches.

I told legislators that I was concerned about the state's fiscal health. A number of state funds were either running deficits or inching toward them. I promised that my budget would provide enough revenue to cover state expenses and put all state funds into the black.

I would do it with a new tax on electrical, telephone, natural gas, and fuel oil bills—or so I thought. It seemed such a reasonable way for the state to raise money. It conformed to a number of my ideas about taxation. I believe that everybody should pay something for government. No one should have a completely free ride. Government is important to everybody. Everyone uses it. Everyone should benefit from it. And everyone should support it. Minnesota once required that anyone who filed an income tax return had to pay at least a minimum payment—$7.50. I thought that was reasonable. I probably voted for it. But it was terribly unpopular.

I was not bothered that a poor person would pay a few cents more on their utility bill if my tax proposal became law. That would be a way of giving them a sense of participation in their government. I thought it would contribute to people, not take away from them. If you want to aid people, do things that enable them to grow and get stronger. I thought that paying a little tax would have that effect. Likewise, I thought it was acceptable for the richest among us to pay higher taxes. I believed the tax would be progressive, in that it would fall harder on more affluent people, who are bigger consumers of electrical and telephone services.

A utility tax had other virtues. One was simply that it was not a sales tax, which had been much discussed and was highly unpopular with working people in the state. A utility tax was simple, easy to explain, and inexpensive to collect. The power and telephone companies would do the collecting and send the revenue to the state each month. Nothing could be more efficient.

But it turned out that nothing could have been more unpopular. Legislators opposed it. Consumers opposed it. Lt. Gov. Karl Rolvaag, my soon-to-be opponent for reelection, called it "an incredible giant step toward a general sales tax." Nobody favored it. It got no consideration.

The utility companies led the charge against a utility tax. I had a good relationship with the lobbyist for AT&T, Harold Nicols, and I had always admired AT&T as a responsible public utility. He came to me after I went public with my interest in a utility tax. "Elmer, I hate to oppose you on anything you're doing," he said. "I know we need more money in government. But you're talking to me about my job. I've got to oppose that tax. I've got to oppose it vigorously. I know you'll understand that I've got to do it."

I told him I understood. But I wondered, if not a utility tax, then what mechanism could we find to stop the state's slide into deficit spending? I thought it was my job to find a way to do that. I was not satisfied to balance the budget with gimmickry, such as applying next year's state revenue to this year's budget. If I had thought that I would have more than two years in office, I might not have proposed a tax increase so soon. But with the state's Democratic voting tendency, I was not sure I was going to have more than one two-year term. I proceeded, thinking that at least I am going to have the satisfaction of doing what I think ought to be done.

I now think that proposing something that is dead on arrival at the legislature is a mistake. My utility tax proposal did nothing to solve the state's revenue problems. It just got me into trouble.

In 1961, the legislature was still officially nonpartisan. But the caucus labels Liberal and Conservative were increasingly synonymous with DFL and Republican, respectively—and the senate minority had taken to calling itself the Senate DFL Caucus. The house was controlled by the Liberals that year; the senate, by Conservatives. I used to say that I had one house against me and one house I could not depend on. The house majority wanted to win the governorship back. Even house members with whom I had positive personal relationships would batter me in public at every chance. Then some of them would come around privately and apologize. "Elmer, I know you meant well," they'd say. "But I had to go after you." That pattern became common. I found it tawdry. It does not reflect human relationships at their best.

My former colleagues in the senate were more loyal. I could always count on support from my brother-in-law, Sen. Stanley Holmquist of Grove City.

My old seatmate, Joe Josefson of Lyon County, was far more conservative than I was. He thought I was a little off base some of the time, yet he was a good friend. So was the senate majority leader, John Zwach of Walnut Grove. He was such an ally that he voted with me on daylight saving time in 1957, despite strong opposition in his district. After that vote, he spent a weekend back home. When he returned, he told me, "Elmer, that was the worst vote I ever cast in the state senate. When I got home, people said to me, 'John! What did they do to you down there?'"

With support from those friends and others, we got a few things accomplished in 1961. One major development was the switch from annual payment of income taxes to the withholding of the income tax from employees' paychecks. A case could be made for a withholding system on the basis of its convenience and collection efficiency. It allowed for tax collection from transient, nonresident workers who otherwise seldom paid income taxes in Minnesota. But the main reason Minnesota went to withholding in 1961 was that it provided a onetime boost in state revenues—something the state badly needed.

The switch to withholding caused such a big debate that a six-week special session was required to settle the question. Even though my proposal for raising revenue had been shot down, I was not about to let legislators go home without facing the need for more money. Legislators acknowledged that the need was real, but they did not want to go to the public with a sales tax, excise tax, or other permanent new tax to correct the problem.

The income tax was not new. Minnesota enacted its first income tax in the 1930s, dedicating it to education funding. That was the great contribution of Gov. Floyd B. Olson. During the depression, property taxes were hard to collect. Every state needed a new source of revenue. Most states turned to the sales tax. To the credit of Governor Olson and a progressive Minnesota Legislature, this state went to the income tax. Unlike the sales tax, which hits poorer people harder than more affluent people, the income tax rises with ability to pay.

A switch from annual payments to the withholding system of collecting income taxes suited legislators. They could claim that they were not enacting a new tax. Yet it allowed for the collection of next year's tax this year. In other words, it provided a double collection of income tax revenue in the year in which it was instituted. Prior to withholding, the tax on income made in, say, 1961 was payable on April 15, 1962. No part of the tax was paid in 1961. By comparison, withholding took money out of each 1961 paycheck. Legislators knew the public would object to the change unless some portion of the tax were forgiven in the transition year. So they approved forgiveness of 75 percent of the income tax owed in 1962. But that meant that the state still received a onetime, 25-percent increase in income tax revenue, amounting to $35.5 million. Along with a $10 "head" tax, or surtax, on the income tax, and a 1.5 cent per pack increase in the cigarette tax, the budget was balanced.

State Rep. Don Wozniak, a liberal from St. Paul, was chairman of the house's Tax Committee. He was a staunch DFLer who had gubernatorial ambitions of his own and was determined to make life as difficult for me as possible. He spent a great deal of time attacking my tax plan and delaying action on withholding, where he knew I was willing to settle. His foot-dragging was largely responsible for the legislature not completing its work by the April 17 deadline. I called a special session that began on April 24 and did not end until June 8.

Wozniak and others criticized me for not pushing the legislature harder for a particular tax plan, after my ideas had been defeated. I was accused of being excessively deferential to the legislature. But I respected the legislative process and the division of power. I thought there was a limit to how far a governor should go. There is a real difference in function between the executive and legislative branches of government—a difference that is lost on some governors and candidates for the office. The governor's role is to be the chief administrator, to carry out the will of the legislature. It is not to second-guess the legislature at every turn or cast dozens of vetoes after each session.

I was a fighter as a legislator. As governor, I took a more evenhanded approach to some issues. I had my pet projects—the taconite amendment was one—on which I was more active. I also had strong concern about protection of natural resources. But on other matters, I believed legislators should own up to their responsibility to make decisions. I let them work out their differences.

I sensed—correctly—that the people of Minnesota would accept a withholding system. The public was very resistant to a sales tax. They would see any tax change other than that as the lesser of evils. I was not criticized in the 1962 campaign for signing the withholding bill into law.

But I accepted the withholding system knowing that it was only a temporary solution to a lingering problem. It was borrowing from the future. It bothered me that in 1961, we had not put state finances on a sounder footing for the long run. I also disagreed with those who said that government ought to be doing less, spending less, for the sake of a balanced budget. The state should decide to do things based on their merit. The means of the state are enormous, more than ample to provide for legitimate needs. A governor needs to seek good value in state spending. He should not condone sloth or waste. But I could not accept the notion that Minnesota should not do things that needed to be done simply because somebody had the idea the state could not afford it. The state can afford to do whatever it decides it truly needs to do. That is just as true today as it was when I was governor. Today the needs of Minnesota's low-income people, especially children, are overwhelming. Something should be done to assist them, either through a more beneficent tax policy or direct aid. People should not be hungry in our society. They should be housed and educated and given medical care. Minnesota can afford to do more, so that their lives are not a burden.

Another major achievement in 1961 was the enactment of the Fair Housing Bill, banning discrimination in housing sales and rental on the basis of race and religion. Minnesota was the ninth state in the nation to enact such a ban. I was proud to sign it into law. Civil rights had been a concern of mine throughout my years in public life. I considered the ban on discrimination in housing an important companion to the Fair Employment Practices Act that I shepherded through the senate in 1955. Everybody should have a fair chance at employment, and everybody should have a fair chance to live in decent housing.

I was ready to help one day during the 1961 session when Josie Johnson came into the governor's office. Josie was then a young activist in the black community, working as a lobbyist for civil rights measures. She later became a regent and an administrator at the University of Minnesota.

She told me, "The Fair Housing Bill is in trouble. It's in the senate's Judiciary Committee. They're going to vote on it tomorrow morning, and we don't have the votes to get it out on the floor. We think if we get it on the floor, it will pass. Can you help us?" I said, "Josie, you sit right there while I write some notes." I pulled out some stationery and wrote a personal note to every member of the Judiciary Committee in the senate. The note said, "The Fair Housing Bill is important. It means a lot to people. It ought to have a hearing before the full senate. Regardless of how you feel about it personally, won't you respect the tradition of the senate and vote it out tomorrow, with or without recommendation? Please, give it a chance to get to the floor."

Josie came in the next morning and threw her arms around me and said, "It got out! It passed!" The bill went to the floor, and became law.

Concern for civil rights was stirring throughout the nation in the early 1960s. It was a major theme of the first governor's conference I attended, soon after becoming governor. It was in Hawaii, a place chosen because a number of governors were interested in playing golf. I was interested in crafting policy.

I teamed up with two other moderate Republicans, Nelson Rockefeller of New York and Mark Hatfield of Oregon, to try to pass a civil rights resolution at the governor's conference. The nation's governors had never gone on record in favor of any civil rights measures before that time. I wanted to rectify that omission.

I soon learned that for a number of governors, annual conferences were something less than serious business. They would talk gently about a variety of issues, make no great point, and take no action. One amusing exchange reveals the tenor of the event. During a plenary session, Gov. Ernest F. Hollings of South Carolina, now a U.S. Senator, got up and asked the governor of Arkansas, Orval Faubus, to rise, please. When Faubus did, Hollings said, "I just want to bring you greetings from the people of South Carolina. We love you folks in Arkansas. You keep us from being at the bottom of all these damned surveys."

Rockefeller, Hatfield, and I came to such a session with our civil rights resolution. We certainly stirred things up. Some governors seemed offended by the very suggestion. How dare we upstart liberal Republicans bring such a thing to a function devoted to pleasant diversion? It could interfere with the luncheon. It could interfere with the golf game. They were beside themselves. Rockefeller, Hatfield, and I argued that it was high time that the governors took a stand on one of the most important issues facing the nation. The United States had to assure basic rights and decent treatment for everybody. We prevailed. In 1961, the nation's governors went on record in support of guaranteed equal rights for all Americans.

That meeting sealed a friendship among Rockefeller, Hatfield, and me. I was a loyal volunteer in Rockefeller's campaign for the presidency in 1964. Hatfield said to me after our 1961 meeting, "Elmer, anytime you have any project, I'd be glad to join up with you." We saw most issues the same way. We stayed in touch, and I cheered him on through his years in the U.S. Senate. In March 1996, a proposed amendment to the U.S. Constitution for a balanced budget was down to one vote in the Senate. The day before the vote was cast, Eleanor, Emily, and I were in Washington and had lunch with Hatfield. He told us he was going to vote against the amendment. He said, "I'm going to get a lot of heat, but I'm also considering this as my last session." Indeed it was. He is retired now, living in the fine home he built on the Pacific Palisades in Oregon.

Minnesota's early leadership on civil rights reflected the state's progressive political stance, and one thing more. This state has been willing to pioneer, to reach out, and to try something new. We have taken pride in being the first to try something different in education, civil rights, and health care. We have enjoyed the recognition that comes from beginning a new trend or launching an experiment. I think that spirit has served Minnesota well.

We were among the first to establish a Human Rights Commission to investigate complaints of discrimination. I appointed Gladys Brooks, later the vice president of the Minneapolis City Council, as its first director. As a result, she was given a memorable assignment.

Six young people from Edina—five men and a woman—went to Mississippi to join in civil rights marches in the summer of 1962 and were arrested. Their parents were very concerned about them, given news reports about abuse of civil rights activists in southern jails. The parents called me and asked me to do something to assure their safety. So I called Gov. Ross R. Barnett, one of the nation's most notorious anti–civil rights governors. I had met him, and I knew that he had a pleasant side.

I said, "Some of our young people from Minnesota have been in your state as part of the movement down there. They apparently broke the law, or for some reason were picked up and arrested. Their parents are concerned. If they violated your laws, the parents don't question that they have to face the consequences of your justice system. But the parents are hoping that the young people are not being harmed or mistreated. We'd like to send someone down to just check on that." Barnett said, "You don't need to check on anything." "It will make those parents feel much better," I went on. "They've asked me to send someone. I'd consider it a real favor if you would just accept a visitor from Minnesota to visit these young people in prison, and see how they're getting along, and what the situation is." He finally agreed, and asked, "Who are you going to send?" I said, "I'd like to send the director of our Human Rights Commission." "Your wha-at?" he said. "We have a Human Rights Commission in Minnesota that's designed to protect the human rights of every individual in whatever situation they're in. This director would be the ideal person."

I went on for quite a while before he gave me clearance that the director of the Human Rights Commission could come. He said, "What's the time table?" I said, "She can be . . . " He said, "*She*! Is it a *she*?" I said, "She's a very able woman. She's been a city official. She's a competent person. You'll get along just fine with her. She's a practical, pragmatic person. So, don't be concerned because she happens to be a woman." Quite a few more minutes passed before it was, finally, agreed that Gladys Brooks was going to go to Mississippi and visit. She went for two days and was treated courteously. Barnett sent a young male secretary to show her the city of Jackson. She had to insist on being taken to where the Edina young people were jailed, in Parchmon prison. She had access to the young people and saw their spartan cells. Gladys had been warned that she would find a man guarding the young female prisoner. But a woman was posted at her cell when Gladys arrived. Upon inquiry, Gladys learned that that the female guard had been assigned there for the first time that day.

As was so common in the arrests that accompanied civil rights marches, these young Minnesotans had not done anything wrong. They had just been gathered up as protestors and put in prison on trumped-up charges. They were, at least, being treated civilly. They were not being beaten or abused or starved. Gladys made her visit count, because it was just a few days after she left that they were released and came home. The families all felt that her visit had led to their prompt release.

In addition to civil rights and the withholding of income taxes, highway safety was a major theme of the 1961 legislature. While the state's four-lane interstate highways were being constructed then, most highway travel was on narrow two-lane roads. The fatality rate per mile driven in Minnesota was considerably higher then than it is today. With an eye toward reducing the carnage, the legislature enacted several measures: an implied consent law, to remove legal barriers to alcohol testing of drivers suspected of being under the influence of alcohol; an increase in the number of Highway Patrol officers and provision for some troopers to use unmarked cars; and seizure of certain violators' drivers licenses after repeated offenses.

Apart from legislation, I had an idea of my own to improve highway safety. I wanted to find some little device to remind people to be more careful—something simple, inexpensive, and visible. I came up with "Lights On for Safety." I asked Minnesota drivers to please drive with their lights on during daylight hours, and particularly on holiday weekends. Seeing lights coming their way would remind drivers to slow down, be alert, and obey traffic laws. That promotion carried on for a number of months and received considerable publicity, so I believe it served some purpose—other than to occasionally drain someone's battery when he or she failed to turn the lights off.

The fundamental purpose of many laws is just to remind people to be sensible. I like to think that Lights On for Safety had that effect.

The 1961 legislature is remembered for one more thing. That was the session that made the loon the state bird of Minnesota. And that, in turn, reminds me of my dear friend from Stillwater, Rueben Thoreen. After the legislature enacted the loon bill, Rueben came to see me one day. He said, "Elmer, we've had a stuffed loon up in our attic for a long time that I've tried to get rid of several times. My wife will never let it go. But I think if I were to give it to the state in recognition that it's now the state bird, I could get rid of the darned thing." As a favor to him, I agreed to take it and put it in the governor's reception room. But I had to agree with him that it was a rather mangy specimen. I would have wished for something a little more handsome for the governor's most formal room.

A solution presented itself at the 1961 State Fair. As people were zipping by my booth shaking hands, a young girl stopped and said, "I'm so thrilled at the loon being our state bird. I just love the state loon." "You do?" I said. "Would you like to have a stuffed loon of your own?" "Oh, yes!" she said. "We have one at the Capitol, and if you think it would be OK with your folks that you have it, we'll deliver it to you at your home." She assured me that her parents would be thrilled to have a loon that had resided in the governor's office. So, the next day, a highway patrolman was at her door with Rueben's loon. That was how Rueben got rid of the loon from his attic, and I got rid of it from the governor's reception room.

There was also more serious environmental work done in 1961. The legislature approved my proposal for the establishment of a state park at Fort Snelling, the historic spot at the junction of the Mississippi and Minnesota Rivers that is the cradle of modern Minnesota. Governor Freeman helped make that possible by saving old Fort Snelling from destruction when a new highway was built. He ordered the highway department to build a tunnel instead of cutting through the fort. Freeman deserves high praise for that decision. We finished the job by designating a riverside area below the old fort as a state park. It combined with the creation of the Legislative Commission on Minnesota Resources (LCMR) to give our administration a strong environmental record.

The LCMR has had excellent managers through the years. One of the first was Bob Hansen, with whom I particularly enjoyed working. While I was governor, it was reported that there were lakes in Minnesota that had not yet been named. I told Bob, "If there are some lakes that haven't been named, we ought to name them. How would you like to have a lake named after you?" "Oh," he said, "I'd love it." I said, "I think it would be fun to name one Hansen Lake, because you've done some wonderful service." He had been a national commander of the Veterans of Foreign Wars, and for many years was on the governing board of the state Veterans' Home. I contacted the federal agency in charge of place-names and asked them to designate one of Minnesota's unnamed lakes Hansen Lake. They found one in northern Minnesota.

Then Bob and I went there to pound a stake along the shore that read "Hansen Lake." We had to cut through dense underbrush to find the shore. No one had preceded us—of that we were certain. We chuckled, "It's no wonder this place has never been named. Who in the world would ever go through this mess to get here?" We pounded in the stake, then he stood beside it, and I took his picture. He prized that picture for years afterward. On days like that, being governor was fun.

But there were also days that were discouraging. One of the biggest disappointments for me in 1961 was the legislature's refusal to put a taconite amendment to the state constitution on the 1962 ballot. These were the years before annual legislative sessions, so I had no second chance in 1962. A constitutional pledge to tax taconite processing plants at the same rates imposed on other manufacturers was controversial among legislators. It did not help that the mining companies were not terribly enthusiastic about imposing this policy with a constitutional amendment. They were afraid that if the legislature submitted an amendment to the voters and the voters turned it down, they would be more vulnerable to unfair taxation than ever. Their influential lobbyists were telling legislators that they would be satisfied if the fair taxation pledge took the form of a statute. But I knew that statutes change easily from one legislative session to the next. I tried to tell them, "Minnesotans are not going to turn this down." I insisted there was going to be an amendment or nothing. So we settled for nothing in 1961.

I was able to secure $1.5 million for a modest jobs program for unemployed mine workers, called the Conservation Works Program. It was modeled after depression-era federal programs. There was so much unemployment on the Iron Range, so much suffering, that I thought we had to propose everything we could think of to put people to work. One feature of the program was that it included training for other jobs. Many of the workers in the mines had never done anything else. They did not know anything else. Training them for other work enabled some of them to establish new careers and stay in the state.

I had a pleasant diversion on April 21, during the short interim between the regular and special sessions of the 1961 legislature. After years of effort by many people, major league baseball had come to Minnesota, and I had the happy duty to throw out the first ball at the first home game of the Minnesota Twins. I was thrilled, as were most Minnesotans that day. It was considered a great accomplishment for a state to acquire a major league baseball franchise. It was a status symbol of the first order. That day, there was universal pride and praise for the work that had brought that team to Minnesota. Even Twins owner Calvin Griffith, who was not the easiest person to immortalize, was praised to the skies.

There was some irony in my being chosen to toss out the first ball. Many Minnesotans had put great effort into bringing the Twins to the state. But my sole contribution had been six or seven years earlier, when a group was trying to build a major-league stadium in St. Anthony Park. I killed it.

One of the groups working to bring a baseball team to Minnesota, and thereby benefit financially themselves, was headed by William Moscrip, the dairy lobbyist and retired dairy farmer who was both my neighbor and my occasional adviser about Deer Lake Farm. He and the McNeely family, who were involved in warehousing in St. Paul, had a loosely organized group that wanted to put a baseball stadium on University of Minnesota land at the corner of Cleveland and Como Avenues.

University President James Lewis Morrill dreaded the idea. It would bring all the traffic and commotion of major league baseball to the quiet, tree-lined streets of the university's St. Paul campus. But the land in question was vacant at that time, so it was an easy target. It was immediately west of the State Fairgrounds, so it had the attraction of utilizing State Fair parking and bus lines. Further, the Board of Regents was afraid to appear to be standing in the way of bringing baseball to Minnesota. They were prepared to sell the land for the purpose of a stadium.

When the people of St. Anthony Park got wind of the possibility that a stadium could come to their placid neighborhood, they were furious. They had a mass meeting in the auditorium of Murray High School to express their dismay and to tell their state senator—me—to find a way to stop any stadium from coming to St. Anthony Park.

I went to work on the problem and came up with a neat solution. It happens that the St. Paul campus of the university is not in St. Paul; it is in Falcon Heights. A university faculty member, Andy Hustrulid, was a member of the city council of Falcon Heights. I appealed to him: "Andy, there are two resolutions that you could get through the Falcon Heights City Council that could help stop this stadium. One would provide that no permit to build a baseball stadium will be granted by the Falcon Heights City Council. The second would stipulate that if one were to be built, no license to operate it would be issued. If you get me those two documents, I think I can stop it."

So, when the Board of Regents met to approve the proposed transfer of land, I arranged to speak to the board. They did not know what I had come to say. I had kept it a secret, for fear that some counteraction might be started. "I'm afraid there's been a misunderstanding," I said. "The proponents of this baseball stadium think this land is in St. Paul, and they've been concentrating on winning the approval of St. Paul officialdom. But the fact of the matter is that it's in Falcon Heights. And the Falcon Heights City Council has taken two actions that are specific and definitive. One suggests that if you were to transfer this land, the city council would not grant a permit for the building of a baseball stadium there. Secondly, if a baseball stadium were built, they would not issue a license to operate it. There's no way that there can be a baseball stadium on the site that's being discussed."

Dr. Morrill breathed a big sigh of relief. That killed the Como Avenue stadium. Not long afterward, the regents put married student housing on that land, to preclude any more stadium speculation in the future. My neighbor Moscrip was never very kindly toward me after that.

When the Twins finally came to Metropolitan Stadium in Bloomington, I was genuinely pleased, and delighted to throw out the first ball. The catcher who caught my pitch that day was Earl Battey, a black man. After that day, Battey felt that he knew me a little and was bold enough to call my office the following year, 1962, during spring training. He said, "I think the governor ought to know that in training practice down in Florida, we're in segregated quarters."

Battey was right: I did want to know, and I wanted to change the situation, fast. I telephoned Calvin Griffith. "Calvin," I said, "They tell me that there is segregation of players down in Florida for the spring practice." He said, "There has to be. The blacks have to be in their hotels and the whites in their hotels." "We can't have that in Minnesota," I said. I told him I wanted to check his claim that no integrated housing was available. "We'll look into it a little." My staff made some inquiries, and, sure enough, they found a hotel near the training camp that would accommodate both races. Housing a major league baseball team is, after all, lucrative business.

I called Griffith again and said, "We found a place. It's a nice place, and it's nearby, and they'll accommodate you so there doesn't have to be any segregation." Griffith said, "I'm glad to hear that. We'll consider it next year."

"Calvin, it can't be next year. It's got to be now. It's got to be right now." "I don't think I can do that, but I'll look into it," he said.

About two weeks went by. I was not going to let the matter drop. I called Griffith again and said, "How are you doing?" "We really would like to do it, but it's just impossible to get out of our present commitments." "Calvin! Segregation is a hated word in Minnesota. You've got to change, no matter what it costs. You've got to change hotels, and you've got to change now. I don't want to make a public issue of this. But I have to tell you that if you haven't ended segregation of your players in Florida in two weeks, I'll have to make a public issue of it. Then, you'll find out what this state thinks of segregation."

He moved the team within the two weeks. There was no news story about the change, nor ever any report about my role in it. But I am convinced that Griffith never would have ended segregated housing for his ballplayers if I had not pushed him to do so. He was comfortable with segregation because he had grown up that way. Despite those awful attitudes, I liked Griffith. I thought of him as a well-meaning bumbler who happened also to be a good judge of ballplayers. He was the kind of fellow you enjoyed almost because of his shortcomings.

I waited years before telling anybody what transpired between Griffith and me. Every governor likely has experiences like that, when he quietly does the right thing, without attracting attention or creating a disturbance. I took pride in being able to quietly end segregated housing by the Minnesota Twins.

When the legislature finally went home on June 8, 1961, its work was not quite finished. Legislators had failed to draw the new boundaries for the state's congressional districts. The 1960 census had resulted in Minnesota being allotted eight members of the U.S. House of Representatives, not the nine the state had had since the 1930s. The state had to be divided into eight districts before the 1962 election.

The legislature ducked the job because of the pain associated with its inevitable result: one of Minnesota's sitting congressmen would lose his seat. None of them was making the task easy for the legislature by choosing to retire. The most vulnerable incumbent was Walter Judd, a Republican from Minneapolis. A physician by training, Judd was a kindly, busy fellow in Washington, quietly effective. Clark MacGregor, the Republican in the west-suburban Third District, which was to be enlarged, was vigorous and competitive. MacGregor wanted the Third District drawn in such a way that Republican votes were maximized. Unfortunately, that meant taking

Republican votes away from Walter Judd. My campaign attorney and adviser John Mooty was involved in a citizens' committee that tried to negotiate a solution between MacGregor and Judd, without much success.

I wanted the legislature to come back to St. Paul and do the job. I wanted no replay of what had happened thirty years earlier, when the state went from ten to nine congressmen. When the 1931 legislature would not agree on new districts, all of the congressmen had to run at large. There were eighty-nine candidates on the ballot, and every voter had to vote for nine. It was a horrible mess. August Andresen, the fine congressman from the First District, had been ranking Republican member of the House Agriculture Committee and had devoted his career to becoming chair of the Agriculture Committee. He was defeated in that election because he was not known statewide. He was highly regarded in Washington, and he was a guru in his own district, but in a statewide election, he was defeated. He came back two years later to be reelected, but he lost his seniority and never became House Agriculture chair. It was a terrible outcome.

I vowed that if I ever had anything to do with congressional redistricting, that would not happen again. I told legislators that I wanted to call them back in a special session to finish their job. But I insisted on prior agreement on new district boundaries, and a short session to enact what had been agreed upon. That is what happened. The special session took place on December 18 and 19, 1961.

Just as I expected, Walter Judd lost his seat in the 1962 election. He was hurt and believed that the redistricting bill I signed had cost him his seat. But in fact, he polled fewer votes in the part of his old district that he retained than he had in 1960. Minneapolis was swinging from Republican to DFL allegiance. It is doubtful whether he would have been reelected under any conceivable redistricting plan.

Governing

THERE IS MORE TO BEING Minnesota's governor than balancing the budget and proposing bills to the legislature. Among the most important responsibilities of a governor is the appointment of members of the judiciary, from small municipal courts to the state's supreme court. Those appointments can outlast a governor's term by decades and give a governor influence for a long time.

I gave a great deal of time and consideration to judicial appointments. Even for municipal judgeships, the lowest rung on Minnesota's judicial ladder, I interviewed candidates personally, just as if I was hiring them for a key position at H. B. Fuller Company.

I believe my efforts paid off. Every judge I appointed served Minnesota well. Those I put on the high court made me proud. James C. Otis, a Ramsey County district court judge whose father also had been a jurist, was my first appointment, in March 1961. He had been recommended to me by David Lilly, and for good reason. He was highly intelligent and very able.

Not long after that, Chief Justice Roger Dell paid me a visit. He had been on the high court since 1953 and was thinking of retiring and returning to his home and law practice in Fergus Falls. But that was not all he wanted to tell me. He also wanted a hand in selecting his successor on the court. I said, "We'd hate to see you retire, Justice, but I couldn't let you pick your successor. That's my responsibility, and I can't say in advance who it would be. I'll just have to reserve that appointment to my office when the opportunity arises." "Well, then, I don't think I'll retire," he responded. "That's just fine," I said. "You're a splendid chief justice, and I hope you stay on the job as long as possible."

He held on until the severe winter of 1962 hit Minnesota. When he announced his retirement that January, he said his first aim after leaving the court was to take his wife on a vacation in a warmer location. I was free to make my selection, and chose to elevate Oscar Knutson, who had been on the supreme court since 1948, to chief justice. Knutson was an earthy fellow who had practiced law for years in Warren, in the state's northwestern corner. He was smart and solid.

I had one other interview with Dell, soon after taking office. He came to me with what he said was "a serious thing to plant in your mind. There is a prisoner at Stillwater convicted of murder who was part of what's known as Murder Inc. It's an organized crime group that operates all over the country. They take pride in never having any of their operatives spend time in prison. From the time that person was convicted and sentenced, he's been trying to get out. So far, we have prevented it. They seek a pardon. You'll be amazed at the caliber of people who will come to you on his behalf. I just want to assure you, he was justly convicted. He shouldn't be pardoned. He shouldn't be let out."

Just as he predicted, people began to call on me to plead for this person. His health was poor, they said. Nothing was being served by keeping him in prison. It would be a generous act to pardon him and let him have his remaining years free. Distinguished people were calling on his behalf. It showed me that organized crime can operate at any level. I stood firm, and there was no change in his status during my term of office. Ultimately, however, he was pardoned and released.

Elevating Knutson to the chief's position meant that I still had a vacancy to fill on the supreme court. For that spot, I chose District Judge Walter Rogosheske of Little Falls. He had been a state legislator before Gov. Luther Youngdahl appointed him to the district bench in 1950. He was only thirty-five then, which made him one of the youngest men ever named a district judge in Minnesota. He was highly regarded.

Some months after he became chief justice, Knutson came to see me. "Elmer, you've made some splendid appointments to the supreme court," he said. "We now have one of the strongest courts in the country. But we have one member who really ought to retire. That's Frank Gallagher. The supreme court has been his life. He's been a great jurist, but he's failing. He doesn't want to give up, and he really should. I don't know what you can do about it, but anything you can do . . . I thought I'd at least tell you."

I invited Gallagher to my office a couple of weeks later. I had been thinking a lot about what Knutson had said. Gallagher was seventy-five years old in 1962. Before he joined the high court in 1947, he had practiced law in an Irish Catholic firm in Waseca, where he still maintained his home. Robert Sheran was an attorney I knew and admired from a Mankato law firm headed by Gallagher's brother, Henry Gallagher. Maybe, I thought,

Sheran would appeal to Gallagher as a successor. I was undeterred by the fact that Sheran was a DFLer.

"I just want to tell you something, and I don't want you to react now," I told Gallagher. "I just want you to listen, if you would, and go away and think about it, and then come back when you have some thoughtful comment you want to make. If you have any thought of retiring, I thought I should tell you whom I might put in your place. I've always admired Bob Sheran."

I had known Sheran since 1949, when I was a new state senator and he a young but already much respected member of the Minnesota House. He was so eloquent and thoughtful that people used to make it a point to come into the house chamber when he was going to speak about a bill. His speeches were an event. I felt sorry for Sheran in 1950. Armed with assurances of support from DFL Party leaders, he ran for lieutenant governor in the DFL primary that year. But the hierarchy turned on him and backed his opponent instead. He lost and was deeply hurt. After falling from grace with DFL leaders, I supposed that he would have no chance of ever being appointed to the supreme court by a DFL governor. I believed that if he was going to make it to the high court, it was up to me to put him there.

I told all this to Gallagher and said, "I just wanted you to know that if you decide to retire while I'm governor, Robert Sheran will be appointed to take your place. I don't want you to say anything. Just, please, go away and think about it."

He came back a couple of weeks later. When he walked in, I could see that he was tense and emotionally charged. He said, "That was quite a session we had. I don't know how you came up with the name of Robert Sheran, but there's only one person in this state that I'd give up my seat for, and that's Robert Sheran." Tears came to his eyes. "I came in to tell you that if that's still your intention, I'm prepared to write a letter of resignation." I said, "I know it's a big decision for you. So, take your time. But when you're satisfied you're ready, write the letter you want to write. I promise you that Robert Sheran will be your successor."

Then I had to make good on my promise. I had to recruit Sheran, which was not as easy as I had hoped it would be. Judicial pay was terribly low in those years. The chief justice of the supreme court drew the top judicial salary in the state—just $20,000 a year. Most judges made a good deal less. I had to tell Sheran that I would work hard to increase judges' pay. Only then, in early 1963, would he agree to take the job.

That is how Sheran, the future chief justice and one of the most notable jurists in state history, was appointed to the supreme court. I felt so good about strengthening the court by choosing him.

Then the roof fell in. I began to get phone calls and letters—some pretty strong letters—from active Republicans. The gist of their messages was that they had worked hard to put me in office as governor, and it was not with the idea that I was going to appoint Democrats to the highest court in the state. The messages were bitter, accusing me of betrayal.

I never told my critics the whole story of Sheran's appointment. For years, only a handful of people knew about Gallagher's role. I am telling it publicly now for the first time. I did the best I could to assuage people. Nobody could argue that the Sheran appointment was a poor choice on its merit. The criticism was founded entirely on partisan sentiment. I took the heat, knowing that I had solved a problem for the court and made the court strong.

Sadly, my stay in the governor's office ended before I could win the pay increases for judges that I had promised Sheran. The 1963 legislature agreed to a small raise, but not enough. After seven years, Sheran left the court because of a problem with personal finances. I was appreciative when DFL Gov. Wendell Anderson named Sheran chief justice in 1973, after the legislature had finally improved judicial pay and Sheran's children were through college. As chief justice, Sheran made a lasting mark not only with the quality of his decisions but with his efforts to improve the court system. He was instrumental in establishing commissions to set judicial salaries, review a proposed code of judicial conduct, and recruit top candidates for the bench. I headed the citizens' committee he appointed to examine the code of judicial conduct and recommend its adoption.

A governor has many nonjudicial appointments to make too, of course—from commissioners to chauffeurs. My driver, chosen from the ranks of the State Patrol, was Robert Eickstadt. He was a noble, clean-cut, dedicated person who served me well. Many people think of highway patrolmen as being tough guys. Robert Eickstadt was a gentleman. His nature was to be polite and courteous to all. He was the sort of officer who would approach a person caught in an offense with great politeness and say, "I'm sorry to tell you, you've been speeding." He taught me about defensive driving—about the importance of yielding the right-of-way to another driver, rather than racing with other cars to try for lead position on the road. Bob's advice was, let the other guy have his moment, and you are more likely to arrive safely. Safety was a huge concern of his. He helped me establish the Lights On for Safety program.

Bob had a gracious way about him that I think should characterize all relationships. People should respect one another—and it is particularly important that people in power respect their subordinates. Bob understood that the essence of handling power well is to handle it with humility. He died at a young age, much to my regret. His widow remains a good friend.

Having a good and likable driver was important in 1961 and 1962, because I spent so much time on the go. There were an enormous number of demands on my time. Everybody seemed to want the governor to come to an event. The university was getting a new president in 1961, O. Meredith Wilson. That involved a whirl of ceremonies and receptions. The Republican Party was more active then than now and had a number of local, regional, and state functions that demanded my presence. I even had to make an appearance at the World's Fair in Seattle on June 13, 1962, the day designated as "Minnesota Day" at the internationally acclaimed attraction. A highlight of that day was the opportunity to conduct the Owatonna High School Band, which was also representing the state that day at the fair.

Bob often picked me up at home at 6:30 A.M. to take me to a breakfast meeting. I would put in a long day at the capitol, often with a few outside appearances during the day. Then it was not uncommon, late in the afternoon, to go to an airfield instead of home for dinner, and fly off to an evening of activity somewhere in the state. After the evening meeting, when I was looking forward to home and rest, somebody would say, "Elmer, Pete Jones has got a little party going over at his house. Gee, he was a good contributor to your campaign, and a great booster. It would mean a lot to him if you'd go over there for a few minutes." So it would be close to midnight by the time I got on the plane. Then some nice friend would say, "Governor, you ought to try to take it a little easier. You're looking kind of tired."

I kept an incredible pace. I was fifty-one years old in 1960. That made me one of the older governors ever elected. The pace of the office took a toll on me. I did not fall ill, but exhaustion was hard to avoid. I think I compensated in part by sleeping soundly. And often, something I was doing would trigger a rush of adrenaline, and I would get a second wind and persevere. That indicated to me that the potential of human endurance is much greater than we know. The power of the mind over the body is enormous and is seldom tapped to anywhere near its limit.

Knowing that I might have only two years in office, I tried to accomplish a great deal. I set out to visit all of the state's Indian reservations and to inspect unspoiled natural sites that the state might seek to preserve. I flew with state conservation officials in little planes. Once, when flying on a monitoring mission, a loud buzz sounded as the plane rose abruptly. The pilot said, "Don't mind that. That's just the anti-stall warning." I was not reassured.

Another time, we had serviced the plane in Brainerd and were heading home. We had not been long in the air, when whoosh! A great flood of oil covered the windshield. We quickly turned around, and the pilot managed to see just well enough to get back to the Brainerd field. It was discovered that the cap had been left off the oil feed.

I was truly frightened only once in those little planes. It was on a night trip, back from one of my evening escapades. The pilot said, "There's a storm moving in, Governor, but I think we can get ahead of it and land ahead of it, if that's all right with you." "I think if you think that's okay, fine," I said. I wanted to get home to bed.

The pilot had been too optimistic. We did not beat the storm. We were tossed around violently in our light plane, and I was scared. But the pilot managed to get us through it and land safely.

One of the planes that we used was a C47. In March 1962, the governor of Montana was killed in the crash of the same model plane. The stated cause of the crash was metal fatigue. The next time we used our C47, I asked, "How old is this plane we're flying? How tired is it?" It was checked, and sure enough, the bolts that held the wings to the fuselage were found to be cracked. The plane had to be sent to Arizona for repair.

But even after the accident in Montana, I did not think very much about my personal safety. Risk goes with the territory for a governor. He is in public view so much that he is constantly at some risk. You begin to take it for granted. You get hate letters and funny phone calls that you just chalk up to unhappy, unfortunate people. You cannot let yourself dwell on the danger.

In 1962, some farmers and farm organizations became militant in their drive to stabilize farm prices. They advocated keeping livestock and commodities off the market. One day in September, they went one step farther and blocked the roads leading to the livestock market at South St. Paul to keep shippers from delivering cattle and hogs. In addition, all the livestock receiving chutes were jammed.

Soon someone was on the phone to me. "Governor, there's a bad situation in South St. Paul and you've got to do something about it," I was told. I did not hesitate. I got in the car and drove to the blockade point in South St. Paul.

I walked over to the protesters and challenged them directly: "Look, fellows, this isn't the way to go about it," I said. "You just can't do this. As governor of the state, I have to keep this market open. If I have to, I'll call out the National Guard, and nothing good will come out of that. You're not going to win any friends or votes this way. You've made your statement. You've received publicity. Why don't you now just pull your rigs away, and let these farmers who are needing some money get their stock in to market?"

After a brief hesitation, the protesters agreed. I was asked later if I had feared for my safety in those moments of confrontation. Worry of that sort did not enter my mind. I went to South St. Paul that day because I thought it was part of my job, and I had to do it. I wanted to avoid the use of force, and I went in the belief that if I could talk to those fellows myself, no show of force would be necessary to get the market open again.

The farm economy was so weak in the early 1960s that protests popped up in a number of places in the Midwest. We had our share in Minnesota. At about the same time as the incident in South St. Paul, I had a call at home at 2:00 A.M. from a trucker in southwestern Minnesota, on his way to deliver livestock to market in Sioux Falls, South Dakota. While I was governor, I kept my home phone number publicly listed. I wanted people to feel they could call me with a problem anytime, day or night—and they did.

The trucker said, "Governor, I've had my tires shot out from under me." I said, "How many? How bad?" "I've got enough spares to fix them, but they'll shoot them again," he said. "Things are getting pretty rough." I found out where he was. I said, "I'll get some patrol cars there. You start fixing your truck. The patrol will get there before you're done, and they'll help you. They'll go with you all the way to the South Dakota border. We'll be sure you get there." "Thanks, Governor," he said. With his escort, the rest of his journey was uneventful.

A governor has great capacity to help individuals in trouble. Another late-night phone call presented me with an unusual opportunity to help one family. A man's voice told the tale of his granddaughter, a teenager who had been in trouble and had been sent to the girls' training school at Sauk Centre. Now she was being sent to another facility in Rochester, where more sophisticated medical care was available. The man said, "I don't know what they're going to do to her, but I'm afraid they're going to give her shock treatments. She doesn't need that. She's a good girl." I said, "The first thing you need to do is quiet down, or you'll have a heart attack. Let me find out about your granddaughter. Give me your phone number. I'll call you back in a half an hour."

I quickly found out that his granddaughter indeed had been moved from Sauk Centre to Rochester, but it was because she was doing so well that she had been assigned to a halfway house there in preparation for her release. I further learned that her grandfather tended to aggravate the situation by calling officials often and complaining about her care.

I called him back and said, "Your granddaughter is doing fine. She'll do a little better if you don't get so excited about it all the time. Leave her alone. She made a mistake. She went to Sauk Centre. She's in correction. She's doing well. She's going to Rochester now by way of getting released. Don't get so excited about it. Leave her alone. She'll find her way." He seemed much relieved. "Thanks very much, Governor. I'll do that," he said.

Another young girl's problems were the cause of another call I received at home. A man said, "I'm afraid my daughter is running away with the driver of her school bus. I don't know what to do. I don't know how to cope with it. I've been tipped off that they're running off to get married. She's a young girl, just fifteen, and he's a grown man." I said, "There are certain things you need to do. First, take your daughter to your hospital or clinic, and have her checked to see if she's pregnant. I'll get the police after the bus driver. After you have your daughter checked by a doctor, take her to your priest." The man had told me they were Catholic. "Have the priest put the fear of God into her. I'll put the fear of the law into the bus driver, and I think we'll correct the situation."

I had the driver visited by the police and warned, "Look, you're dealing with a minor. You're in serious trouble if you go running off with that girl. You had better find yourself another bus driving job, and stay away from that young woman."

It all worked out well. Some months later, the father called again and said, "I just want you to know, Governor, that the bus driver disappeared. My daughter wasn't pregnant. She realizes that she had a close call to getting into trouble and making a big mistake. Everything is fine. Thanks, Governor."

I did not think of calls such as these as interruptions. I welcomed them. The opportunity to make life a little better for individuals was as important a part of being governor to me as signing major bills or charting new policy. Serving as governor was a very personal thing, a chance to make personal connections with people needing help and to do what I could to assist them. Being governor allowed me to meet more people and tackle a wider range of problems with more resources than I ever had at my disposal before. I wanted to be able to reflect on my years as governor with a feeling that I had made a real difference for some people in Minnesota.

I made it a rule in my office that anytime a group of schoolchildren toured the capitol and came to the governor's reception room, I was to be interrupted, so I could speak to them. It did not matter to them who the governor was, I thought, but it did matter that when they were there, they met the governor. That encounter would give them a sense that they were important to their state. It might inspire them to be interested in government and to want to have a share in it someday. I considered talking to schoolchildren an important part of my job.

One thing I often told schoolchildren was that there was no other person in the world just like them. I said, "The matter of birth is so miraculous. Every person is made up at least a bit differently. There are things that you can do in your life that no one else can do exactly the same way. If you don't do them, they won't get done." I tried to convey the idea that each person has a mission. Each is special, with special talents to be used. I suspect I belabored the point. But since those years, many times, people have told me, "Elmer, when you were governor, I was in sixth grade. We came to the capitol, and you spoke. You know, I always remembered what you said."

I felt a lot of satisfaction in my work. But the main feeling I had as governor was of being overwhelmed with activity. Everything comes at a governor so fast. The daily rush of appointments, phone calls, correspondence, and appearances is so great, it can be disorienting. It is hard to get the rest or the exercise one needs. It is hard to give any single aspect of the job the time one would like to give it. A good governor must have a hand in an incredible number of issues and topics.

One large area of concern is the state's relationship with the federal government. Minnesota and the federal government work together on many things—law enforcement, welfare, highways, housing, and more. During my term, an exchange of state and federal lands was at issue. I had long felt that the checkerboard ownership of land in a vast part of northern Minnesota was not in the state's best interest. Small loggers liked it that way because they could contract with the state to cut timber on a forty-acre stretch and help themselves to some adjacent federal timberland as well. The state could not police them effectively. I thought the resource would be better managed if state and federal ownership were concentrated in larger parcels. I spent a good deal of time negotiating land exchanges with the federal government, with a fair amount of success. More than two hundred thousand acres were exchanged in 1962.

Another particular concern of mine involved the pardon board, which consisted of the governor, the attorney general, and the chief justice of the

Minnesota Supreme Court. My philosophy about corrections is to emphasize rehabilitation, not punishment. I wanted the board to grant more pardons extraordinaire, which not only commute an offender's sentence but, after a time, expunge it from his record. I thought that was important for young offenders who mend their ways and become productive citizens, yet must otherwise carry a criminal record with them all through life. I tried to utilize that type of pardon whenever it was justified. The state ought to forgive people who make mistakes, pay the penalty, and abide by the law thereafter.

I inherited one controversy within the corrections system from the Freeman administration. Late in 1960, the warden at the state penitentiary in Stillwater, Douglas Rigg, was accused of appropriating food from prison storehouses for his personal use. I asked a commission to investigate. When the commission confirmed his shortcomings, I demanded his resignation. I was particularly offended by his taking the best cuts of meat for himself and giving what was left to the prisoners. He would serve the best food to his guests and make them think he was doing such a wonderful job, all at the expense of inmates. That showed a great lack of respect for prisoners, I thought. Wrongdoers cannot learn to do right if they are not treated decently.

Helping to attract new businesses to the state is another gubernatorial responsibility. The unique circumstances surrounding the iron mining industry in the early 1960s made finding new businesses for the Iron Range a top priority. But I was also concerned about the stagnant economy in Minnesota's agricultural region. I believed bringing new industry and more jobs into that area would stop the exodus of young people from the country into the cities. I wondered why Wisconsin's rural area was dotted with cheese factories, and Minnesota's was not.

I went to Kraft, Inc., and asked, "Why don't you have a plant in Minnesota?" "Don't you know, Governor, what's wrong with Minnesota?" the Kraft executives replied. "No, I don't." They said, "You've got a whole bunch of little creameries scattered all over the state, and they're very competitive. Instead of paying the fair price for milk that we'd have to pay, they pay higher prices. But to make up for it, they cheat on the fat content of the milk they receive. We've got to operate honestly. We can't come into Minnesota and engage in that monkey business. If you want to get us into Minnesota, you've got to correct that."

I asked Duane Wilson, my commissioner of agriculture, to determine whether what the Kraft officials had said was true. He found evidence that indeed that sort of dishonest dealing was commonplace in some creameries. I said, "It's got to change. See if you can't quietly go around to those creameries and say, 'Look, this is not the way to operate in Minnesota. We must correct this. We don't want to have a scandal. We don't want to have bad publicity. But we want to be able to attract any fine company in the country to come to Minnesota to be in the dairy business. If this is a problem, just be assured, it's going to change, and you had better change it quick.'"

Wilson visited the creameries he suspected of shady dealing and passed that word. It worked. The creameries began to pay an honest price for milk. The price of milk went down a little, but checks to the farmers went up a little. Best of all, Kraft put a plant in New Ulm, Minnesota. I was glad to solve that problem personally and quietly.

I took an interest in the National Guard. Early in my term, I had the opportunity to appoint the state's top Guard officer, the adjutant general. As always, I wanted to study the situation before making an appointment. The Freeman administration had someone in line for the job, but I wanted to gather some information. I was not content to take the person next in line according to rank. I went down the line, interviewed several people, and came to know a colonel named Chester Moeglein. He was a bright, eager, service-oriented man who had served in North Africa and Italy during World War II, and in the Korean War as well. I reached past several people of higher rank to make him adjutant general. General Moeglein served long and well and was acclaimed by many as one of the state's best adjutant generals.

I thought Minnesota's Native American population had been neglected. So, along with the new state director of the federal Bureau of Indian Affairs, James Hawkins, I toured every Indian reservation in the state. My goal was to see what could be done to lift the standard of living on the reservations. I was surprised to learn that I was the first governor to visit every reservation in the state. The visits yielded two things: a maple syrup production project for the Grand Portage band of Chippewa, which unfortunately was short-lived; and a youth guide program for the Red Lake reservation that worked quite well. The idea was to train young Indians to serve as guides for tourists. They were schooled in tribal history, the region's natural history, and the reservation's current affairs, ostensibly so that they could relay the information to tourists, but also so they would learn it themselves. A secondary benefit came when the guides' parents wanted their children to be proud to show off their homes, so they began to clean up their property. I knew we had succeeded when an administrator of the youth guide program told me, "Those young people are walking a lot taller this fall."

Another result of my trips to reservations was the press attention that came with it. I wanted the public at large to better appreciate our Indian citizens. I was inducted into the White Earth tribe. I still have the paper bearing my Indian name, given to me by the aged chairman of the band. I prize it because they were accepting me as one of their own, and I think those of us of European descent need to accept Indians as our own. I am convinced that the arm's-length relationship we have now between the native and non-native populations in Minnesota must change. Our societies must be integrated.

I also thought part of my job was to increase public awareness of Minnesota's history. I became something of a student of Jonathan Carver's grant and gave a number of speeches around the state about it. Carver was a British soldier who was assigned to explore this area in the mid-1760s. He was an intelligent, honorable man, who made friends with the Indians. There was a cave below what is now Mounds View Park in St. Paul, where Indians would gather. At a meeting there with Carver, the Indians allegedly deeded a big tract of land to him. It extended from St. Paul eastward to near Menomonie, Wisconsin. The story goes that Carver knew that as a British soldier, he was forbidden to accept land in his own name. But he believed that if he returned to Britain with a deed, his grateful nation would award it to him. That is what happened. But on his way back to North America to redeem his property, he died. The deed fell into other hands and was lost. For many years thereafter, anyone with any connection to Carver tried to assert a claim on the land. Meanwhile, the land was developed, sold, and resold. Congress finally appointed a committee to resolve the disputes over Carver's grant, and declared all claims on that basis null and void.

The lore surrounding Carver's grant captured a lot of imaginations in Minnesota. Many people came to me with stories about a connection to Carver, or inquiries about additional evidence concerning the grant. I think St. Paul would have a popular historic attraction if a shaft were sunk from Mounds View Park to Carver's cave. When the railroad was built, the cave's entrance was closed, so it has not been opened for many years, though once a small excavation was done to reveal the top of the mouth of the cave.

A critical piece of the governor's job is to be an advocate for the University of Minnesota. That was not difficult for me. I was always a great believer in education, and I felt a strong personal tie to the university. I tried to safeguard the university from budget-cutters in the legislature. Yet my budget for 1963 did not recommend all that the university wanted. I provided for an increase but not one as large as President O. Meredith Wilson sought. Wilson told the press that my budget was so tight, it would be ruinous to the university if that was all they received. His criticism bothered me so much that I can still feel it a little. I worried that perhaps I had missed something particularly worthwhile in the request. I am subject to self-criticism. But I began to think, too, that he was taking a swat at me when I was politically vulnerable, purely as a lobbying tactic.

I like to think that I was good for the university in one respect. Both in 1961 and 1962, the Golden Gopher football team played in the Rose Bowl in Pasadena, California. The team lost to the University of Washington in 1961, but it defeated UCLA in 1962. I was there officially representing Minnesota both times. The University of Minnesota has not sent a team to the Rose Bowl since. I have often wondered why people have not figured out what made the difference in those years. To me, it is obvious—I was governor.

1962 Campaign

I ANNOUNCED ON JUNE 8, 1962, just days before the Republican state convention, that I would seek a second term. No one was surprised—least of all the state's active Republicans. But a few of them may have been disappointed.

Two years in office had not endeared me to the Republican Party's conservative wing, nor to those who place party loyalty above all other considerations in governing. With them, I had a shaky relationship. I had a habit of appointing people to key positions based on their professional qualifications, not their party connections. I not only gave one or two choice assignments to known DFLers, but I also bypassed party workers in favor of political unknowns with superior preparation for the work at hand. All other things being equal, I preferred to appoint Republicans, but I thought it was up to the Republican Party to serve up the best people.

I was in favor of civil rights legislation and higher spending on education and welfare—none of which appealed to the party's hard-line conservatives. They respected me for being honest and true to my convictions. But they wished my convictions would be a little bit more partisan and not so generous to opposing viewpoints.

But among those in the Republican Party's liberal wing, I was a hero. I was doing everything just the way they wanted it done. I was promoting education, building the state's infrastructure, backing taxation based on ability to pay, and advancing civil rights.

I did not spend much time or effort working at building a stronger connection to the party or at bringing more people who supported me into party ranks. I consider that a failing on my part. I concentrated so much on getting things done as governor that I did not give enough attention to the party. I came to believe later that a governor must assume responsibility for his party, or both will suffer. In 1962, the Republican Party was divided. It was my job to encourage harmony, find areas of agreement, and attract people who agreed with me into party ranks. I did too little of those things.

My political views were much shaped by the progressive movement within the Republican Party in the early 1900s. I was inspired by the ideas of U.S. Sen. Albert J. Beveridge of Indiana, whom I came to know through the book *Beveridge and the Progressive Era* by Claude G. Bowers. Beveridge was a scholar as well as a politician, who along with Wisconsin's Robert M. La Follette advocated a platform of government activism in pursuit of a higher standard of living for all people. The Progressive Era's principles had been imbedded in me. I was sympathetic to making government work for everybody.

Despite the misgivings some Republicans had about me, no one surfaced within the party to run against me. Some people approached U.S. Rep. Ancher Nelsen of Hutchinson and asked him to consider challenging me. But he and I had been friends in the state senate when we served together in 1949 and 1950. He was not interested.

Just as my candidacy for a second term was a given in 1962, the DFL Party's choice of a challenger was plain from the start: Karl Rolvaag, who had been lieutenant governor for eight years, would run against me. A feeble effort to recruit the young DFL attorney general, Walter F. Mondale, as a gubernatorial candidate foundered early. Rolvaag had been leading the party's attack on me almost since the day I was elected in 1960. He had only token opposition within the DFL.

I had known Karl since my state senate days, and had always appreciated him as a thoughtful, decent, well-meaning human being. He was the son of Ole Rølvaag, a famous author and professor at St. Olaf College in Northfield, whose books were on my shelves. I admired Karl still more when, years later, he went through treatment for alcoholism and spoke publicly about the disease he battled for so long.

We were vying for Minnesota's first four-year gubernatorial term. Two-year terms had been the rule since statehood began, but voters in 1958 approved a constitutional amendment for four-year terms for the state's executive officers. It applied for the first time to the governor, lieutenant governor, and other officials elected in 1962. That made the prize all the more desirable to both parties.

I welcomed the change in term length. The governorship is a challenging position, one that nothing can prepare one for. It takes time to learn to do the job well. Two years is only the beginning. In 1962, I had to stand before the voters with my governorship still a work in progress. I sometimes think of Gov. Arne Carlson, whose eight years in office ended in 1998. He had a rough time his first two years. He had trouble finding the right people for his staff. He made mistakes vetoing bills. He proposed a tax plan that fell flat. If he had been required to face the voters in 1992 instead of 1994, he might have been a one-term governor. Instead, with the luxury of a four-year term, he was able to serve eight years, and had wide support when he left office.

But even though I felt as if I had just begun, I was proud of my two years as governor. I had dealt with issues head on, even when I knew that some adverse reaction might follow. I had no hesitation about running again. I had plans for the second term. They included development and protection of natural resources, especially timber, new investment in the iron mining industry, more value-added processing for agriculture, better highways, a unified sanitary sewer system for the metropolitan area, more and better parks, a new four-year college in southwestern Minnesota, and better care for the mentally ill.

The development and implementation of public policy fascinated me. I was a governor who could get caught up in the details. Once, for example, I was called by a state hospital administrator to be apprised about a potentially touchy issue arising in the area of mental health treatment. Research on epilepsy had shown that surgical removal of the calcification of the brain that accompanies the disease could ease the frequency and intensity of seizures. In one unusual case at a state hospital, a patient had been having seizures almost constantly. Surgery seemed the only viable treatment for the poor soul, whose life was at risk. When the surgeons started removing the calcification, they kept finding more and more.

"We wound up taking half the brain, Governor," the administrator said. "We were scared to death what the fate of that person was going to be. The epileptic seizures stopped, so life is much easier for the person. The amazing thing is the half brain that is there is already beginning to pick up some of the functions of the brain that is gone. We thought you needed to know, Governor. If it got out that we had taken half of the brain out of a patient in a state hospital, that could be so distorted that it would be just terrible." I appreciated the political sensitivity of my caller, but I was also glad to learn about this amazing case. I followed the patient's progress for some time. His bodily functions continued, the seizures stopped, and he had a much more satisfactory life with a healthy half brain than with a diseased whole. That case was a testimony to the enormous potential of the human brain.

I was so engaged in policy matters that I was faulted for concentrating on governing and not on campaigning in the summer of 1962. I made some speeches around the state and shook hands at the State Fair. But my mind was always on the things demanding my attention in St. Paul. I paid a price for neglecting my political duties. The *Minneapolis Tribune's* Minnesota Poll conducted at the end of August showed me trailing Karl Rolvaag, 52 percent to 43 percent. It was time to get busy.

I did what had worked so well for me in 1960: I challenged my opponent to a series of debates. That was the standard procedure for a challenger but a bit unusual for an incumbent. Conventional wisdom says the incumbent, with a record to defend, has the most to lose. But I was an incumbent who trailed in the polls—and who had been a debater at the University of Minnesota. I welcomed an examination of my record. I knew debates would serve me well.

A clear contrast existed between Rolvaag and me on a number of issues. The taconite amendment was one. I knew that constitutional assurance that taconite plants would be taxed fairly was the only way to attract the investment in taconite mining that Minnesota's Iron Range needed if it was to rebound from its lingering economic slump. Rolvaag disagreed. He considered a constitutional assurance of fair taxation to be an unfair privilege. But he, too, knew that something was needed if mining companies were to invest again in Minnesota. So he promised them that if elected, he would veto any tax increase on taconite processing.

That was wrongheaded, I told the audience at our first televised debate, on WCCO-TV on September 8. "No industry should be promised that they will face no tax increases," I said. If the state's fiscal circumstances require higher taxes on businesses, all industries should bear that burden. All the state should promise is fairness, and that is precisely what the taconite amendment guaranteed.

I was disheartened by the fierce opposition the taconite amendment received from the DFL Party and the leaders of organized labor—even in the face of statewide polls showing strong support, and the favor it had won among Iron Range legislators and rank-and-file mine workers. Minnesota's failure to pass a taconite amendment had cost the Iron Range more than eleven thousand new jobs, by my reckoning. When I laid blame, I named names: United Steelworkers union officials Earl Bester of Duluth and Nick Krmpotich of Coleraine, House Tax Committee chairman Don Wozniak of St. Paul, and Karl Rolvaag.

My personal attacks were more than the state's union leaders had bargained for. They decided to try to punish me by "disinviting" me to the state AFL-CIO convention in Rochester, where I was scheduled to speak on September 24. I served notice that I would show up at the convention anyway and would ask to address the delegates. When union leaders saw that I was serious, they cooled their rhetoric and urged delegates to receive me respectfully, if not warmly. Defending my record for working people in the lion's den of union opposition made statewide headlines. And the next Minnesota Poll showed that I had narrowed the gap with Rolvaag. The poll results were 49 percent Rolvaag, 47 percent Andersen—too close to call.

Rolvaag and I also disagreed on questions of education. In the early 1960s, Minnesota's schools were bulging with baby boomers. I was convinced that the state should invest more in education. My proposal was for the state's share of school costs to rise from about 43 percent to 50 percent, and for teachers' salaries to rise until they became comparable with salaries paid to other professionals with similar academic training. Those measures would cost the state $130 million in the next biennium.

Minnesota could afford that, I contended, because the state's economy was growing again. Despite continuing weakness in agriculture and on the Iron Range, new jobs were popping up through most of the state in 1962. The total number of workers in the state topped one million in August for the first time, besting the previous record, which had been set two years earlier. Minnesota's unemployment rate in August 1962 stood at 3.5 percent, compared with 5.8 percent nationwide. The state's general fund, which was $2.5 million in the red in 1960, had a $4 million surplus in the fall of 1962. An $18.2 million deficit in the income tax school fund had dropped to $11 million. With numbers like these, and with cost-saving measures I instituted saving millions of dollars within state government, I announced in October that, in my view, no increase in state taxes would be needed for the coming two-year budget period.

Rolvaag wanted to cut the property taxes homeowners pay, and seemed willing to keep a lid on education spending to do it. His education platform was a litany of relatively low-cost, low-impact items. For example, he favored creation of a Minnesota Science Hall of Fame, a state Higher Education Commission with its own cabinet-level commissioner, and a Minnesota Research Institute that I thought would duplicate the work of the University of Minnesota.

The other tax tenet in Rolvaag's platform was a pledge to veto any attempt by the legislature to bring a sales tax to Minnesota. All the states surrounding Minnesota had enacted a sales tax by 1962, and many knowledgeable observers—including me—had begun to believe that eventually Minnesota would join them. But I did not like the idea any better than Rolvaag did, and I had shown as much during the 1961 legislative session.

Rolvaag talked a good deal about resisting a sales tax in the campaign, but my similar position made that a nonissue.

I spoke often about natural resources, because I considered them so precious to Minnesota, and because I knew Rolvaag could not come close to matching my record in protecting and developing them. I had appointed a Minnesota Natural Resources Council that made a series of recommendations in September 1962—all of which I quickly endorsed. The council, headed by Henry T. McKnight, president of the Minneapolis realty firm S. T. McKnight Company, asked for a $20 million state bond issue to finance wetlands acquisition, fish stocking on key lakes, a matching program to help counties acquire parkland, and a whopping thirty-six new state parks. The state park system was growing fast in those years. The 1961 legislature had authorized creation of Fort Snelling State Park; in 1962, I dedicated three new parks that had been authorized during the Freeman administration, Crow Wing State Park near Brainerd, Mille Lacs Kathio State Park near Onamia, and Bear Head Lake State Park near Ely.

A bigger issue than any of these, however, was the controversy surrounding the highway department and my commissioner, retired Army Brig. Gen. James Creel Marshall. These were times of unprecedented activity for the department, as the federal funding floodgates swung open to the states for construction of the interstate highway system. A great deal was happening, very quickly, so there was much for political opponents to second-guess.

Marshall himself became an issue. A native of upstate New York who maintained a home there, Marshall was the first non-Minnesotan ever appointed highway commissioner. He may have been the first person from outside the department to get the job. He had been district engineer of the Manhattan atomic bomb project during World War II. That shows how highly the army regarded his administrative ability. He was a tough-minded, no-nonsense stickler for efficiency and order—all of which made him unpopular with some highway department employees, and an easy political target.

Marshall's efficiency measures put Minnesota ahead of most states in the race to build interstate highways. In fact, in the summer of 1962, Minnesota was ranked third among the states, behind only Maine and Colorado, in prompt use of available federal funds to purchase rights-of-way and materials. That summer, an installment of $53 million from the federal government came to Minnesota ahead of schedule, as a reward for our progress.

But the progress was not fast enough to suit my critics, including Rolvaag. Nowhere in the state was the need for a modern freeway greater than in the portion of Minneapolis south of downtown, where traffic congestion on city streets had become intolerable. Naturally, land acquisition there was particularly difficult. A controversy over where to put Interstate Highway 35W slowed construction. The result was a dispute over how much of the $53 million from the federal government to funnel directly to Minneapolis. Rolvaag wanted me to put fully half of it into that short stretch of highway. I was in favor of emphasizing highways in the metropolitan area first—but not to that extreme.

Other critics from outstate Minnesota faulted us for putting so much effort into freeway building while the state's trunk highway system had needs as well. Depending on the audience, Rolvaag could score points against me either by saying that freeway construction was proceeding too slowly, or that it was occurring at the expense of basic maintenance of existing roads. Both of those opinions were shared by plenty of Minnesotans. But Minnesotans are also a fair-minded people who saw how hard we were striving to build a strong total highway system. I crept ahead of Rolvaag in the Minnesota Poll in mid-October, 51 percent to 46 percent among likely voters.

But on October 25, my campaign was interrupted by events far from Minnesota. I received an urgent call from the White House. President Kennedy had summoned the Civil Defense Committee of the National Governor's Association to a meeting that afternoon, to discuss the crisis that had erupted with the discovery that the Soviet Union had installed thirty missiles in Cuba, ninety miles away from the Florida coast. The situation had worsened when Soviet ships were seen steaming toward Cuba, bearing more weapons that would be aimed at the United States. At that moment, the Soviet ships were still advancing toward Cuba, despite Kennedy's warning that if they did not turn around, the United States would stop them.

I was one of the ten members of the Civil Defense Committee, which was chaired by my good friend Nelson Rockefeller, Republican governor of New York. Nelson and I had become something of a team among the governors since my first governors' association meeting. If I was doing something, I wanted Nelson involved. If he was chair of something, he wanted me on the committee. Nelson and I, as part of the Civil Defense Committee, had met with the president months before to urge his support of state civil defense activities, and to ask for $1.4 billion in federal money to pay for them. It is hard today to realize what a big activity civil defense was in those years, and how soberly people approached it. Civil defense centers were in nearly every community and in many homes, equipped with food and water. We had one in our home. We went along with the idea because it was felt that there was a possibility of an air strike from the Soviet Union, and we should set an example of preparedness for others. Looking back on those shelters now, they seem ludicrous. But they seemed more than justified in October 1962. The Cuban missile crisis was a perilous moment, one of the closest calls that this nation has ever faced.

The White House called me in the morning. "How quickly can you be ready to come?" I was asked. "We want to have a meeting this afternoon." I barely packed and rushed to the airport, where a military plane had been arranged to pick me up and get me there. There was a sense of great hurry and urgency, as if something might happen at any time. By afternoon, ten governors were assembled at the Pentagon and were being briefed on the military and diplomatic situation by the chief of the Central Intelligence Agency, two top men in the State Department, and military officials. We saw aerial reconnaissance photos of missiles mounted in Cuba, pointed at the United States. There was no question what the Soviets were doing. They were preparing for war. It was a hair-raising briefing.

The next day, October 26, President Kennedy joined one of our sessions. At one point in our deliberation, Gov. Edmund G. "Pat" Brown of California asked if there could, please, be an executive session. He said, "I want to talk to just the governors and the president." Brown was deeply shaken by all the information we had received. Everybody else left the room. Brown said, "I've got to know right away, what does a governor do when war breaks out?" The rest of us were caught between smiling at the panic in his voice and giving in to the panic that was flickering in our own hearts.

The president responded calmly. "Pat, you just turn the National Guard over to the U.S. military and look out for your people at home. That's what you do." That made Brown—and the rest of us—relax a little.

We were still there a day later, on October 27, when word came that the Soviet ships had turned around and were headed east. President Kennedy called off the blockade he had ordered off Cuba and promised that U.S. troops would not invade Cuba if the Soviet missile bases were dismantled quickly. That is what happened. I think what turned the tide was the courage of President Kennedy in insisting that the Soviet ships must reverse their course. Soviet leaders may have been misled about Kennedy's resolve after his apparent vacillation during the Bay of Pigs invasion, shortly after he had become president, when the United States called off air coverage with an invasion force already on its way. Cuba and the Soviet Union must have concluded that American policy lacked firmness. They thought they could attack and either get by with it or get far enough along that they would have a strategic advantage. But when Kennedy told the Cubans and Soviets that October in no uncertain terms, "If those ships don't turn around, they're going to be stopped," they believed him and withdrew. That was Kennedy's shining moment as president.

I returned to Minnesota to find that the campaign for governor was taking a nasty turn. U.S. Sen. Hubert Humphrey, the DFL Party's undisputed leader, had come home from Washington to stir things up for the DFL. Working with a number of DFL operatives, including U.S. Rep. John Blatnik, Humphrey inflated a highway worker's allegations that there had been faulty construction on Interstate Highway 35 near Hinckley, between the Twin Cities and Duluth. The reason for it, they alleged, was my desire to hasten the road's completion and dedication on the Thursday before the election.

The charge that construction was faulty was false. Very minor irregularities were found in a subsequent investigation by the federal Bureau of Public Roads, all of which were corrected by the contractor at his expense. The corrections cost the contractor $996.24. These were routine deviations, much like those found on other stretches of new highway all over the country. All of the DFL allegations about major construction errors were found to be without merit. The most damning charge—that concrete was poured on frozen ground, contrary to specification, in order to stage a ribbon-cutting ceremony prior to the November 6 election—was completely groundless. Tests showed that the concrete in question was of greater than required strength and that ground temperature was adequate on the day it was poured, even though air temperature may have dipped below the requisite ground temperature of thirty-five degrees Fahrenheit.

The DFL accusations had their root in the observations of a low-level highway technician named Bob O'Donnell. O'Donnell's job was to run tests on the gravel being used to build the highway, to make certain its coarseness met the roadway's specifications. On September 19, he had run a number of tests that had "failed," according to his understanding. He reported the matter to his superiors, who did exactly what they were supposed to do: inform the contractor and ask for better material, inform the state highway inspector, and make a record of the findings in the project's diary. Nothing was covered up. The allegedly faulty material was inspected by engineers and found to be within the allowable tolerance of deviation.

Whether O'Donnell was aware of all that his superiors did with his September 19 report was never clear to me. But what was clear, as the full story of this episode was revealed after the election, is that O'Donnell took what little he knew straight to his younger brother, Mike O'Donnell, a twenty-four-year-old operative in the Rolvaag campaign. O'Donnell shared the report with the campaign's leaders, who took O'Donnell's account at face value and ran with it. They added to his first account his report of October 23 and 24, that concrete had been poured on a day when the temperature was subfreezing, and therefore, he thought, sure to make poor-quality pavement. O'Donnell's account made no mention of the temperature that really mattered to the work, the ground temperature. If the DFL officials who rode the I-35 accusations so hard in the campaign's final days understood that distinction, they never let on.

Blatnik, chairman of the house committee that investigated improprieties in the federal highway program, called a press conference to say the allegations were "serious," and to suggest that in other states people had been indicted on similar charges. Humphrey, on the eve of the third and final televised debate between Rolvaag and me, had his office say that the flow of federal highway funds to Minnesota would be suspended until questions about construction quality on I-35 were answered. It was a lie. Humphrey had no authority to suspend funds, and no additional dollars were expected until the completion of the highway and the usual audit that follows. Nevertheless, that was the story that Rolvaag and Humphrey carried as they stumped the state the weekend before the election.

Later, it came out that Rolvaag and his wife were never comfortable with what was done with the highway issue on their behalf. Rolvaag did not want to be a party to it, but Humphrey overruled him. Humphrey insisted that throwing these accusations at me was the only way to win. Rolvaag participated, but he did not lead the charge. Neither did George Farr, the DFL state chairman who had been nipping at me and at my administration for two years. Even though his attacks were often quite petty, I admired Farr as a professional who was simply doing his job. It was not his nature to be dishonest.

Humphrey's zeal to remove me was not a mere matter of partisan loyalty or friendship with Rolvaag. He had something more personal in mind. He wanted to be on the Democratic national ticket in 1964 as a presidential candidate if Kennedy did not run again or fell out of favor, or as Lyndon Johnson's replacement as vice president, should Kennedy dump Johnson. If he left the Senate at mid-term, the governor would appoint his replacement. Parties do not hand over senatorial appointments to governors of the opposite party. Humphrey felt he could not be on the national ticket if I were governor, because that would be tantamount to giving away a seat in the U.S. Senate.

On a personal level, Humphrey and I were only slightly acquainted. By the time I became a state senator, he was already a U.S. senator serving in Washington. I first met him in about 1943 or 1944, when he was a professor at Macalester College and I was an active new member of the St. Paul Rotary Club. He was our speaker at a noon meeting. I must say that the first impression he created was somewhat negative. Already in those years, he was a spellbinder. Many in the audience that day were captivated by his oratorical powers. I was not. I thought he was expounding on all sides of every subject, in an effort to ingratiate himself with everybody, no matter what their point of view.

My reading of Humphrey is more positive today. I have come to see him in a new light through the eyes of Minnesota author Frederick Manfred, who was associated with Humphrey during his Minneapolis mayoral campaign in 1945. Manfred's interpretation of Humphrey gave me a new appreciation of all he tried to represent and accomplish. He was exceedingly talented, and he meant well. He had a good heart and a love for people. But he did not have quite the solidity of character to see him through. For example, if he had been strong enough to stand up to Lyndon Johnson on the Vietnam War, rather than towing Johnson's line, he might have been elected president in 1968. Humphrey had a terrible lust for personal advancement and power. If you look around Minnesota, there are not many things that you can point to and say, "That wouldn't be there if it hadn't been for Humphrey." He spent most of his political ammunition on personal advancement, not the betterment of his state. He was able. But in politics and in other walks of life, too, there are a lot of able people, but there are not a lot of fine people.

My personal encounters with Humphrey later in our careers were friendly. When it was reported in 1976 that I had purchased the two newspapers in Princeton and was launching a newspaper career, Humphrey sent me a personal letter wishing me well and expressing the opinion that I would bring something of use to the community. Hubert was a fierce competitor, but he never nursed grudges.

I, of course, had reason not to like him very much. He was the architect of my defeat.

The DFL smear campaign on I-35 was launched in earnest just a week before the November 6 election. A Blatnik operative worked in the Bureau of Public Roads, and a member of Minnesota's politically active Foley family was in the Secretary of Commerce office. Between them, they arranged for two functionaries from the Bureau of Public Roads to come to Duluth on the pretext of investigating highway construction. Their very presence was enough for the DFLers to point to as they asserted that deficient materials were being used to build the road to hasten its construction for political reasons. It was enough for Rolvaag to call for a congressional investigation—and for me to call for one too, on the politically motivated activities of the Bureau of Public Roads.

A dedication ceremony for the highway took place at Hinckley on November 1. Blatnik and W. W. Fryhofer, division engineer of the Bureau of Public Roads, were scheduled to appear but did not. They claimed that they could not attend when "bodies with which they were associated" were investigating the road's alleged shortcomings. I was angry, and, to my regret, I let it show. News stories reported that my voice was hoarse and rough with emotion, and my face was flushed, as I addressed the crowd:

> I deeply resent the cheap, dirty politicians who, to get a few votes, have besmirched Minnesota's good name all over the country. . . . The reason Congressman Blatnik is not here is because he knows I would be shaking my finger right in his face, and asking questions he doesn't want to answer.

Hindsight has convinced me that I employed the wrong approach. I was too defensive. I let them get to me. Instead of delivering a tongue-lashing, I should have pulled a magnifying glass out of my pocket and stooped down at the new highway to make a big show of looking for nonexistent defects. I should have made a joke of their charges, to show how laughable they were. Anger never reflects favorably on anybody.

I did one thing right in my defense. I called U.S. Secretary of Commerce Luther Hodges, whom I had known through Rotary International. I surmised from the DFLers' talk about a possible cutoff of federal highway funds for Minnesota that they might approach the secretary of commerce to sign an order delaying a payment or an order for the state. I called him to inform him about the political motives that would be behind any such request. I said, "I know you can't get involved in a political race in Minnesota, surely not for a Republican candidate. But I wanted to ask you to do one thing: please watch what you're asked to sign relating to Minnesota. Be sure that whatever it is, is justified. I think an effort is going to be made to get you to sign something routinely that will have a big impact in Minnesota. All I ask of you is to just pay attention to what you're signing that relates to Minnesota."

He said he would, and he did. After the election, he told me, "Elmer, they did have a paper they wanted me to sign stopping funding, but I didn't sign it." The day after the election, of course, the request for his signature was withdrawn.

Humphrey was an important person. The fact that he was personally accusing me of tolerating deficient construction practices on the new highway added a great deal to the charges' credibility. Nobody would believe that he would cook up such a thing. On one TV show, the state's three top DFLers—Humphrey, Mondale, and Rolvaag—all spoke in mournful tones about how bad it was that poor construction practices were being tolerated on a major freeway, what a blot it was on Minnesota's good name, and on and on. They were convincing.

The final Minnesota Poll had been conducted from October 26 through October 28—before the DFL charges about I-35 were made in earnest. It showed me leading among likely voters, 52 percent to 48 percent. Moreover, I had the endorsement of most of the state's newspapers, one of whom was already calling the highway issue a "smear." Heartening as that was, I knew that the campaign developments in the last week had probably changed things—and not for the better.

I spent my last day of campaigning in northeastern Minnesota, the region where I had focused so much time and energy as governor. My last appearance was in Hibbing. Then I flew home to St. Paul and climbed into bed at 3:00 A.M. I slept for only a few hours. Eleanor and I wanted to get to the polls early, and I needed to go to the capitol for several meetings. I returned home at 4:00 P.M., and then started making the rounds of election-night parties at 8:30. We arrived at our own party at the Leamington Hotel at about 10:00, to settle in and wait out the returns.

Little did we know that our wait would last four and a half months.

Recount

A S RETURNS SLOWLY DRIBBLED in November 6 and 7, the governor's race became a seesaw affair. First I would be ahead by a few thousand votes, then Rolvaag would jump into the lead, then I would surge ahead again. Rolvaag did well in Minneapolis and St. Paul; I did well in the suburban areas and southern Minnesota. The counts reported by the news media varied all through the night, the early morning, and the late morning. Newspaper photos taken that night of Rolvaag and his wife and Eleanor and me show four tired, strained people, struggling to make sense of a confusing situation.

Eleanor and I left the Leamington Hotel at about 4 A.M. and went to bed with the radio on. At about 5:30 we heard a report that I had pulled ahead. We dozed off—only to be awakened by a reporter's phone call an hour later, advising that the outcome was not yet certain. That afternoon, unofficial returns put me in the lead by 737 votes out of 1,267,502 cast. A few more precincts came in that evening and the lead reverted to Rolvaag— by 115 votes. A snowstorm in far northern Minnesota delayed some returns until Friday. When the unofficial reports were finally all in on Friday, I was in the lead—by 35 votes, according to United Press International; or by 51 votes, according to the Associated Press. But then word of tabulating errors began to come in. On Saturday, Rolvaag was reportedly back in the lead, by 139 votes.

By then, it was clear that none of those numbers was going to tell the final tale. The results would not be official until the Canvassing Board certified them later that month. But whichever candidate was declared the loser by the board was certain to ask for a recount. Armed guards were posted wherever ballots were stored. The political parties put their attorneys to work researching the law governing recounts, while old-timers stepped forward with stories about the last statewide recount, in the state auditor's race in 1934. They had an ominous prediction: It would not be done until February, at the earliest.

Meanwhile, I went on being governor. I kept my full run of daily appointments. I attended the Minnesota-Iowa football game on November 10. People commented on my calm demeanor. I simply focused on the tasks before me each day. No matter the outcome, I thought, I was assured of being governor at least until January. I turned the recount over to others. I did not agonize. I just kept functioning.

The race for governor was not the only close contest in 1962. Rochester state Sen. A. M. "Sandy" Keith, the DFL candidate for lieutenant governor, was ahead of the Republican candidate, Edina state Rep. C. Donald Peterson, by only about 4,700 votes. In the Sixth Congressional District, DFLer Alec Olson was ahead of Republican Robert Odegard by 249 votes. Those races conveyed the impression that Minnesotans were virtually evenly divided in their allegiance to the two major parties. Yet in the Minnesota House, the Conservatives regained control by a big eighty to fifty-five margin. DFLers complained that those gains resulted from the officially nonpartisan status of legislative candidates. They amplified their call for party designation of legislators. Unofficially, the senate Liberals had already changed their name to the senate DFL caucus; the house Liberals followed suit in 1963.

I was determined to make the best of the difficult situation Rolvaag and I found ourselves in. One week after the election, I called a press conference to announce that Rolvaag would receive copies of all documents pertaining to the state budget I was preparing for the 1963 legislature. He would be welcome to attend any budget hearings. I pledged to keep him fully informed on major issues. If a transition in the governor's office was coming, it should be a smooth one.

Further, I announced, I would agree to a recount even if the Canvassing Board put me in the lead. The race was too close and confusing to the public to let the first count stand untested. I was proud of the way Minnesotans were accepting the uncertainty about the election's outcome. I did not want to do anything that might give rise to public suspicion.

People were suspicious enough already. Two days after my press conference, the results of Bureau of Public Roads tests on Interstate 35 near Hinckley were announced. Nothing substandard was found. Bob O'Donnell, the highway worker who initiated the DFL charges, was suspended from his job for two weeks for making false statements on an affidavit claiming irregularities in the road. When the two weeks were over, he resigned, claiming that his coworkers and superiors had harassed him.

If he was hearing harsh comments, it was because people were furious.

They felt they had been duped. The state's editorial writers castigated Rolvaag, Humphrey, and the DFL for their fabrication. One memorable editorial cartoon in the *Hibbing Daily Tribune* showed an angry elephant with a blackened eye, smudged with the stain labeled "Hi-way 35," receiving a note that read: "My mistake, the hi-way is O.K. Sorry. Karl." The cartoon was headlined, "The science of retraction." For his part, Rolvaag continued to insist that some future test would vindicate his claims. None ever did.

The state Canvassing Board convened on November 26 amid hopes that they would bring some clarity to the situation, if not resolution. Instead, for a few days, they made matters worse. The five-member board split three ways over which candidate had won the most votes, and how to proceed. The upshot was to send the matter to the Minnesota Supreme Court. There, the justices acted quickly. They ordered the Canvassing Board to accept amended returns from ten counties that had filed affidavits saying their initial reports were in error. When the amended returns were tallied, I was declared the winner, by a 142-vote margin.

With a recount soon to follow, the Canvassing Board ruling was no cause for celebration. But it was reason enough to think that I would still be governor, for a while anyway, after the 1963 legislature began its work. I began to focus on the budget and agenda I would bring to the session. More spending was overdue on education and mental health care. The Twin Cities area badly needed a single sanitary sewer system. But the thing I planned to push the hardest was what I believed Minnesota needed the most: a constitutional amendment guaranteeing the taconite industry fair taxation. The polls told me that by an overwhelming margin, Minnesotans wanted the taconite industry to develop on the Iron Range. They understood the importance of guaranteeing the industry fair taxes. Two taconite plants were operating on the Iron Range in December 1962, but those firms and others had announced that no additional plants would come to Minnesota unless equitable taxation was assured. Getting a taconite amendment on the 1964 general-election ballot was essential to that region's future.

I had some reason to believe that the amendment would prevail in the 1963 session. By then, it had found some important friends in the house, where it had received such a cool reception before. Roy Dunn, a Conservative from Pelican Rapids and a former majority leader, was prepared to push the amendment. So was the Liberal leader Fred Cina of Aurora, whose role reverted from majority to minority leader in 1963. Even though the DFL Party still opposed the amendment during the 1962 campaign, Cina's role was strong and visible enough for amendment backers to claim bipartisan support. Before the 1963 session began, I met with Cina and Dunn. We agreed that we could not let the house defeat the amendment again. I assured them, "You get this amendment through the legislature, and I'll campaign to get it passed by the people in 1964—whether I am governor or not."

Cina played a pivotal role in what followed. He was as responsible as anyone for shaping the amendment's final language and marshaling the votes to get it through the legislature. He arranged for the amendment to include a preamble, or phrase justifying the need for the amendment— something most constitutional questions do not include. He understood that a simply phrased preamble would help identify and sell the amendment to the public, whereas the wording of the amendment itself might seem foreign and confusing. Cina was a wonderful man and a fine public servant, genuine and strong. After he left the legislature, he became a regent of the University of Minnesota. I liked him ever so much.

In other quarters of the DFL Party, opposition to the taconite amendment was softening. Iron Range legislators were all coming around to Cina's way of thinking. In the senate, my friend Tom Vukelich of Gilbert was a stalwart for the amendment. Other DFLers, aware of how much their party depended on solid backing on the Iron Range to win statewide elections, were taking notice. Still, opposition to the amendment seemed potent in the weeks prior to the 1963 session. I spent almost as much time thinking about the future of the Iron Range as I did about my own.

The recount was a slow process. Oscar Knutson, the chief justice of the supreme court, reflected the impatience of many Minnesotans when in early December he decided he wanted to get things moving—and get the matter off his calendar. He and other justices resented the implication in some national media reports that because four of the seven court members had been either appointed or promoted by me, they were sure to rule in my favor in the end. The high court was determined to play the recount perfectly straight. Knutson directed the recount managers for both candidates to agree on the names of three mutually acceptable jurists to formulate a three-judge panel to oversee the recount. The managers were told to go into a room and not come out until they had three names—even if it took all night. It very nearly did. But on December 10, the high court had three names. The appointed judges were Sidney Kaner of Duluth, J. H. Sylvestre of Crookston, and Leonard J. Keyes Jr. of St. Paul. Kaner was a former DFLer appointed to the bench by Gov. Orville Freeman. Sylvestre had been appointed by Republican Gov. Luther Youngdahl. Keyes had a mixed political history. He had been named a municipal judge by Freeman and a district judge by me. Those three judges in turn determined where the recount would take place (the Ramsey County courthouse), authorized the managers for both candidates to recruit and recommend one hundred three-person teams of ballot counters, and wrote instructions to guide their work. The three-person teams consisted of one Rolvaag representative, one Andersen representative, and one neutral person agreeable to both sides.

The actual counting did not begin until December 20—a time of year when Christmas shopping is about all that ever proceeds quickly. The teams agreed to check only the count of paper ballots. Voting machine counts—which amounted to about a third of the votes cast on November 6—were stipulated by both sides to be accurate. Even so, progress was painstakingly slow. Any stray mark on a ballot, any unusual symbol, any scribble that appeared to erase a first choice, or even a write-in name was considered reason to challenge a ballot and set it aside for review by the judges. By January 1, with the count about two-thirds done, more than sixty-five thousand ballots had been set aside as "challenged." Meanwhile, each side still claimed its candidate was in the lead by fewer than one hundred votes.

Rolvaag was personally active in the recount. I did not visit it once. I received a daily briefing and then tried to put it out of my mind as I went about the usual business of being governor. I asked Richard Kyle and J. Neil Morton, lawyers from Briggs and Morgan, the St. Paul firm I had worked with since my first days at H. B. Fuller, to handle the legal side of the recount for me. Of course, my team was headed by Tom Swain.

Minnesota was in unprecedented, uncharted territory. With me a governor-in-doubt, and Rolvaag potentially a governor-in-waiting, it was only natural that the two parties would differ over what was proper gubernatorial conduct, and what was not. Rolvaag needed to move out of the suite of capitol offices reserved for the lieutenant governor, since Sandy Keith would occupy that space after inauguration day. So I arranged for Rolvaag to have some rooms on the first floor of the capitol. I thought I was doing the gracious thing, so he and his advisers would not need to rent space elsewhere. But Rolvaag's chief of staff Jim Rice called the space "a broom closet," and the name stuck with the media. Rice admitted years later that the space, while cramped, was appreciated. It did not seem that it was at the time.

Three state commissioners' terms expired on January 1; about fifteen more reached full term on or before February 1. A governor is responsible for keeping those positions filled. I did not question my right or duty to make those appointments, but DFL state chairman George Farr did. Just as

I was in limbo, he thought it proper that my commissioners remain in limbo too, on the job until the recount was done. I consulted with my advisers and decided I would make the appointments as usual.

The second day of a new legislative session is traditionally inauguration day in Minnesota. In 1963, that day fell on January 9. With the recount still in progress and my term extended until it was done, I thought at first that I would let that day come and go unnoticed. But as the date approached and the newspapers filled with reports about proposals for legislation, I reconsidered. A legislature needs a nudge from a governor to begin its work. Nothing requires it to be a reactive body, but human nature and institutional custom often make it so. Several leading legislators told me they wanted my help in putting the state's needs into focus at the start of the session. I decided to make a formal address to the legislature on January 9 and do the best I could to keep things as orderly and normal as possible.

Instead of drafting an inaugural address, I prepared a speech I called a "Minnesota Progress Report." I recounted the gains Minnesota had made in the previous two years, in increased fiscal health, an improved economy, better care for the poor and mentally ill, numerous conservation initiatives and—yes—new highways. "You need have no concern for the quality of the work," I said pointedly. "Any minor irregularities inevitably incident to big construction jobs will be corrected at the expense of the contractor."

Then I listed my priorities for the 1963 session. Number one was placing the taconite amendment on the ballot. That was the first step in a twelve-point program I outlined to bring new economic vitality to the state's most depressed region, northeastern Minnesota. It was a comprehensive plan that included stimulus to the tourism industry, construction of a mental hospital on the Range, and greatly expanded research at the University of Minnesota to advance mineral technology. I spoke of the desirability of pursuing direct-reduction iron processing on the Range—something the legislature finally provided $20 million for in 1999, thirty-six years later!

I also addressed the need for the state to replenish the fund that keeps Minnesota's unemployment compensation system solvent. Legislative disputes the previous session had prevented action to add to that fund during the economic slump of 1960 and 1961. Better times were upon the state, but the fund's balance had become dangerously low.

I put off comments about a defining issue for any legislature—taxation. The improved economy erased the need for an immediate infusion of new revenues. But I knew that the state's fiscal house was not in order. In 1962, I appointed a commission to study Minnesota's revenue system and recommend improvements. That commission, headed by Dean Paul Grambsch of the University of Minnesota School of Business Administration, was nearly done with its work. I asked legislators to wait for its report before deciding any tax questions that year.

A few weeks later, the tax commission made a brave recommendation: Minnesota should replace a number of outmoded and unpopular taxes with a general sales tax. The commission favored reducing the sales tax's disproportionate burden on low-income people by combining it with a credit administered through the income tax. I thanked the commission for its work and said that its report would be a long-range guide for the state. But privately I was relieved that I did not need to recommend a tax increase that year. I continued to have reservations about the sales tax and knew that it would never be enacted in Minnesota without a fearsome fight.

The two-year budget I recommended to the legislature on January 23 amounted to $673 million, a $101 million increase over the previous two-year budget. Fully 85 percent of the recommended increase would go to education, at all levels. The first of the baby boomers were about to graduate from high school; the last of them were about to be born. The forecast in 1963 was for the population of eighteen-year-olds in the state to increase by 40 percent in just the coming three years. That huge cohort in the population was straining every educational resource. Like every other state, Minnesota had to step up its spending for schools.

The only other big spending increase I proposed would go for welfare, corrections, and institutional care of the mentally ill and disabled. This was an era of innovation in the treatment of people with mental disorders. For decades, they had been merely warehoused, set aside from society. Beginning in the 1950s, residential care gave way to genuine treatment, preferably in local communities rather than large state institutions. That kind of care could redeem lives, but at least initially, it was more expensive to administer.

The same day I delivered my budget to the legislature, the first phase of what reporters were calling "the recount trial" ended. The ballot-by-ballot count was over. Challenged ballots were being screened. The ones remaining in dispute at the end of that process would be examined in judicial hearings that were scheduled to commence in mid-February. At the end of Round One, Rolvaag was in the lead, by either 138 or 130 votes, depending on whose numbers one believed.

I was soon to have better news. A breakthrough in the fight to pass a taconite amendment occurred on February 1. After a management-union conference in Pittsburgh and heavy lobbying by unemployed rank-and-file miners in Minnesota, the United Steelworkers union dropped its opposition to the amendment. Overnight, union members became its fervent supporters. The change of heart was born of simple fear. Rumor had it that several mines that had closed for the winter would not reopen in the spring. The miners were desperate to try anything to keep their jobs.

After the Steelworkers changed their views, it was only a matter of days before the state AFL-CIO, the Minnesota Farmers' Union, and Rolvaag himself fell into line. Rolvaag officially dropped his opposition to the amendment on March 12. He pinned his rationale for reversing his campaign position on a twenty-five-year sunset provision that was being considered for the amendment. That new wrinkle was enough for him to claim that the amendment he had so bitterly opposed now had "several desirable aspects." He was reaching, but at least he was reaching in the right direction.

It was a season of compromise. Another long-lived controversy moved toward resolution that session. For years, Minnesota's strong dairy lobby had prevented the sale of yellow-colored oleomargarine in the state. Only color-free margarine could be sold—and it bore a tax of ten cents per pound. Grocers near the Minnesota border in Iowa and the Dakotas saw the silly spectacle each day of Minnesota housewives buying large quantities of tax-free colored margarine in their stores. I had urged an end to the colored margarine ban for some time with no success. Finally, Rep. Roy Dunn came up with the formula for compromise: allow colored margarine to be sold; remove the tax on color-free margarine; keep it on the yellow stuff.

Several other proposals I originally made in 1961 and 1962 were advancing. Planning money was included in appropriations bills for a new state college in southwestern Minnesota, an area not adequately served by public higher education. That was the birth of Southwest State University in Marshall. The state takeover of junior college funding from local school districts was moving ahead, and so was a program of natural resources conservation and development that sprang from a commission I appointed in 1962.

Those advances were the highlights of what was unfolding as a surprisingly ordinary legislative session, given the extraordinary situation in the governor's office. Liberals continued to criticize me for making routine appointments, and the few commissioners whose appointments came before the senate were confirmed on party-line votes. The legislature made provisions both to pay for the recount and to provide Rolvaag with a modest office stipend until the result was known. But in most respects, the legislature and I carried on smoothly.

But from mid-February on, I was carrying on with an awareness that I likely would not be in office to see the session through to its end. A supreme court ruling had diminished the number of disputed ballots to a rather small quantity. Those were counted with a trial-like procedure, ballot by ballot. Those trials were not tipping enough votes in my favor to change a shortfall into a surplus. I braced myself for an unhappy ending.

It came on March 15. The legal proceeding that settled the final disputed ballots ended with Rolvaag in the lead—619,842 to 619,751. Morton and Kyle, my attorneys, still had a few legal briefs to file and motions to make, but they told me they did not expect to overcome Rolvaag's 91-vote advantage. They were right: On March 20, the three-judge panel denied my motions and declared Rolvaag the winner of the election.

My crestfallen campaign team wanted me to appeal that ruling to the state supreme court. Some of my allies in the legislature wanted me to appeal, simply to stall my departure and give me more time to sign their bills into law. But Kyle and Morton told me that they thought the district judges' decision was correct. No legal basis for appeal existed. They recommended that I accept it and concede the election. Tom Swain also advised against pressing my case. Questions of fact had been determined. There were no errors of law on which to base a supreme court appeal. Kyle, Morton, and Swain thought an appeal would be viewed as spurious.

But the ultimate decision was mine. For me, it could turn only on one thing: my judgment of what was best for Minnesota. The state had already endured four and a half months of uncertainty in state government. I could not ask Minnesotans to wait any longer for the final results. Moreover, it would only contribute to people's lack of confidence in the system if I asked justices whom I had appointed to keep me in office.

Thus it was that two dramas reached their climax in an emotion-filled three-day period, March 21–23, 1963. Late in the day on March 21, the recount's three-judge panel officially ordered that Rolvaag be named governor. That started the clock on a ten-day period in which I was allowed to appeal the panel's decision to the state supreme court.

On March 22, the taconite amendment I had supported since my first day as governor arrived on my desk, after passage by bipartisan majorities in the legislature. My signature was not required to put the amendment on the 1964 ballot for ratification by the state's voters. But legislators and others encouraged me to conduct a ceremonial bill signing anyway, to underscore the importance of the amendment and recognize those who had worked so hard to win its passage. Many of those present were aware that the occasion was something of a last hurrah for me as governor.

"This is a day of great significance for the people of Minnesota," I said as I signed the bill. "For the first time, iron mining labor and management came together shoulder-to-shoulder to support a measure designed to create more jobs. This harmony may outlast and outweigh even this important measure." Many of those present echoed the headline that day in the *Fergus Falls Daily Journal*. They called the event "A Fitting Climax."

On Saturday, March 23, at a 2:30 P.M. press conference, I announced that I had sent a letter to Rolvaag saying it was my intention on Monday to file a waiver of my right to appeal the decision of the recount judges. My waiver would lead to the immediate issuance of an election certificate to him. Rolvaag would become Minnesota's thirty-first governor on Monday.

My remarks that day were transcribed and printed in a pamphlet titled, "After the Most Careful Consideration." Here is some of what I said:

> Today ends one chapter, admittedly a shorter chapter than I had intended, but there are more to be written. I am disappointed but not the least discouraged; I am defeated but not the least disheartened. I am deeply grateful to the people of Minnesota for the privilege that has been mine to serve as governor of this great state which means so much to me, and to the thousands of unselfish workers for better government who have given me their support.
>
> I am thankful to state employees, department heads, legislators, study group members, and all others who have contributed time, thought and energy to provide such substantial gain in so many areas, in so short a time. May I say a special word of thanks to all members of the news media, with whom I have always enjoyed working, for their diligence in presenting news of Minnesota state government. . . .
>
> My main activity will continue to be in the field of community and public service, as it has been for some years. I would particularly like to pursue the long-range New Dimension Natural Resource Program which we have launched. . . .
>
> Our family is united. Our love has deepened and broadened through this experience, we are thankful we have retained good health, and we continue to be humbly grateful for the rich blessings of God that we have so abundantly received.

When I ended my remarks, I looked at my secretary, Donna Petersen, and saw that she was beginning to cry. Bob O'Keefe, a reporter for the *St. Paul*

Dispatch, was a good friend. He had tears in his eyes. As for me—well, I may have had some just then, too. It was a moving moment. But I was also relaxed, able to laugh and voice confidence in the future.

As the news conference ended, somebody asked, "What is your greatest regret?" I thought a moment, then chuckled. "Not staying," I said.

Part IV

CITIZEN ANDERSEN

On the Rebound

Losing a statewide election by ninety-one votes after a four-and-a-half-month "election night" actually might be easier than losing by a crushing landslide. The sudden jolt of a big defeat can be an almost catastrophic blow. My defeat was more gradual. I had weeks in which to prepare myself. I had the consolation of thinking, in the end, that no one will ever know who really got the most votes for governor in 1962.

I also took solace in knowing that the voters had been duped. The lies told by unscrupulous DFL politicians about the Interstate 35 construction constituted fraud. I blamed them, not the voters—and as a result, I did not experience the sense of rejection that some losing politicians feel. I was disappointed. There was much that I still wanted to do. But it was easy for me to think that the people have chosen, so I will do something else. Disappointments are part of life. You just take them and try to turn them to some advantage.

In later years I came to see that leaving office in 1963 was a fortunate thing. Our lives were greatly enhanced by renewed attention just then to the family and business. Returning to private life when I did preserved my health and may have prolonged my life.

It was a good time to get back to H. B. Fuller Company, where the pace of growth was as rapid as ever. Three months after leaving office, I assumed the new position of corporation chairman. E. A. "Al" Vigard, who had been interim president in my absence, took that title permanently.

Only six years later, Al mentioned a pain in his leg. I said, "Al, you need to see a doctor. Pain in the leg can be symptomatic of something else. You need to find out what's causing it." He did not want to do that. He said, "If I go see a doctor, he'll put me in a hospital and I'll never get out." I insisted. "Al, you just have to see a doctor." He complied, and sure enough, he was hospitalized and never emerged. He had advanced cancer, at age 63. In about a month, he was gone. His passing was much felt by the people at Fuller. They loved and trusted him.

Before I dug in at Fuller, I thought of the family and all we had been through since 1960. Political life is hard on family relationships because it takes a priority over everything. I proposed, "Why don't we all go to Europe and have a nice holiday?" The timing seemed right for a number of reasons. Julian was nearing the end of his studies at Carleton College in Northfield, where he was majoring in mathematics. Emily was entering her senior year at Murray High School, just a year away from leaving home to attend Oberlin College in Ohio. She was a charming, outgoing, fine young woman, a delightful traveling companion.

In mid-July, Eleanor, Emily, Julian, and I were off to New York and then to Norway, Sweden, France, Italy, and England for a six-week tour. Tony and Alice, who was expecting our first grandchild, joined us for the Scandinavian portion of the trip. It was my first trip to Europe; Eleanor had been in Sweden before, as a child.

We took some care with the planning. We did not want to go on a pre-packaged group tour. We wanted to do our own thing. But neither did we want to leave anything to chance. I do not like to waste vacation time buying tickets and finding accommodations. I worked hard at doing all that in advance. We tried to find lodging in local hotels, not hotels that cater to American tourists. We hoped we could better experience a country's flavor that way.

Oslo was one of our first stops. I knew of the Holmen Kollen, a famous ski jump. An inn was perched at the top of the jump. I thought, "That's where we want to stay." We booked a lovely room with a balcony that overlooked Oslo. Every night during our stay, we sat on the balcony and watched the beautiful lights of Oslo come on.

We discovered many more relatives in Norway and Sweden than we knew we had. Eleanor had kept in touch with some of her relatives in Sweden. But the size of my father's family, the Kjelsbergs, was a surprise to me. They were still living in Solør, Norway. My cousin Martin Kjelsberg was close to my age. He traveled with us for a short time to show us his homeland.

In Minnesota I had become acquainted with the Norwegian consul general in the Twin Cities, Thorgier Tobias Siqveland. When his Minnesota appointment ended in 1961, Eleanor and I hosted a reception in his honor in our home. He was back in Norway in the summer of 1963, and when he learned that we were there too, he arranged for me to meet the king. I was to go alone. Protocol dictates that whole families do not meet the king. That privilege is reserved for heads of families. Before the appointed hour, I was coached about how to behave. I was not to ask him any questions; he would ask the questions. I was not to introduce any new subject; he introduced new subjects. When I left him, I was not to turn around and walk away from him. I was to back away from him. All this instruction made me nervous as I entered the king's chamber. Yet when I sat down and began to chat with the king, the atmosphere was unexpectedly informal and pleasant. I forgot about all the rules and had a conversation just as if we were sitting in the lounge of the St. Paul Athletic Club. He was relaxed and cordial and spoke excellent English. The atmosphere was so informal that at one point one of his children skipped into the room and skipped out again when she saw that her father was occupied. There was none of the austere formality that people often associate with royalty.

We talked about the economy of Norway in those years before the discovery of oil off the shore. He said, "Norway is a poor country. Our people are poor, but they don't think of themselves that way. They're independent. They get along. They live with what they have to live with. They work very hard. We have a good, strong country." His abundant pride in his country made me feel good about my Norwegian heritage.

We went next to Sweden, where we headed for Grandpa Gustaf Johnson's family home in Dalsjöfors. Grandpa Johnson's family had lived and worked on the same farm for generations, giving it loving, detailed care. In 1963, it was home to four elderly brothers and one sister. Eleanor's father was the only one of his generation who married and had children. That made Eleanor and her brother and sister very special to their aunt and uncles. I remember their strawberry patch. They cared for those strawberries as if every one was precious. When they cut down trees, they took great pains to select which tree to harvest. They did not go slashing through the woods. Life was important to them and was lived carefully.

I admired the slower pace and attention to detail that I observed on the Johnson farm. Those Swedish farmers lived modestly, yet richly. They savored everything they did to the fullest extent. Compared to them, we ricochet through life. The speed of American life and the gulping of experiences can be an unfortunate thing. Young people get accelerated into experiences they are not prepared for and do not fully appreciate. Too much of life is gone before it is really lived. I think that did not happen on the farm in Dalsjöfors.

We also spent time in Göteborg, Sweden, at the home of Elizabeth Johnson's sister and her husband—Eleanor's aunt and uncle. He was a great storyteller but spoke no English. I did not understand Swedish, so I missed a fair amount of what he was telling us. One story was about an avalanche, which he said was *huller buller.* Later, I asked Eleanor, "What was that expression that he used when he was describing that avalanche?" She said, "*Huller buller.*" I asked her to spell it, and she did. "*Huller buller* means just a torrential movement of anything. *Huller buller.*" I said, "Gee, that appeals to me."

Later, in Rome, we learned about Gian Lorenzo Bernini and his contributions to the architecture, fountains, and public plazas in that city. It came to me: Huller Buller and Bernini. That is a fine-sounding name for a firm of some sort, say an importing company. It sounds so dignified. So, when we got home, I registered the name Huller Buller and Bernini with the secretary of state as an importing company. We began to import glassware and furniture from Norway and Sweden, almost as a hobby. The best glassware manufacturer then in Sweden was called Pukeberg, a name with a rather unfortunate English connotation. I always thought that name affected our success. I had a lot of fun dreaming and playing with Huller Buller and Bernini, but nothing much came of it. I was too busy then with other ventures. We still have the name registered. Someday, I might try to revive that business.

While we were in Sweden, word of our trip reached Carl Rowan, who was U.S. ambassador to Finland at the time. Carl had been a leading reporter for the *Minneapolis Tribune* in the 1950s; later, he was a syndicated columnist. When he heard that we were in Sweden, he mentioned our trip to the Finnish president, Urho Kekkonen. Kekkonen invited us to come to Helsinki for lunch.

The invitation was not a total surprise. While I was governor, President Kekkonen had visited Minnesota. His stop was part of a larger American trip, designed to win over those in Congress who thought he was cavorting too much with the Soviet Union. I was not among his critics. In fact, I admired him. He seemed to be successfully treading a difficult line between accommodating the whims of the Soviet Union, his nation's overpowering neighbor, and preserving freedom and democracy in his own country. He avoided a Soviet invasion yet did not give up his nation's independence.

When he came to Minnesota, I happily cleared my schedule and spent several days traveling the state with him. I noticed that he spoke English very well when we were in the car together, but he always used a manuscript in English when he spoke to crowds. He would give his speeches in both Finnish and English if Finnish speakers were in the audience.

"When did you start learning English?" I asked. He said, "About six months ago." "Six months ago! You speak quite fluently. You could speak extemporaneously." "I think I could, but I wouldn't trust myself. When you're in an official position, someone can leap on the slightest error. That's why I use manuscripts." "How did you learn English so well, so quickly?" He explained that he had a tutor with him all day long. Everything he said, the tutor repeated to him in English. Everything he ate, everything he did, everything that went on was coached to him in English while he carried on in Finnish. After six months of that bilingual life, he arrived in the United States prepared to speak English.

We had a good time together. I went out of my way to say good things about Kekkonen and Finland at every stop we made. I wanted to build his stature, which was at a low point among some Americans. I believed his fundamental principles were sound, and I said so.

When the invitation to lunch in Helsinki arrived, we were happy to accept. President Kekkonen hosted us at an elaborate, formal state luncheon. He awarded me the Commander Cross of the Finnish Lion Order, with a ribbon and medals. The family was most impressed, and Carl Rowan got a big kick out of the occasion.

After Scandinavia, we were on to France, then Italy. The guidebook for Florence, Italy, told us about a little place called Fiesole, a suburb above Florence where a convent had been converted to an inn. I thought, that is for us. We arranged for three rooms, for Julian, Emily, and Eleanor and me. One of the three reserved for us was the room of the Mother Superior. It became a big question among the four of us: Who was going to be in the Mother Superior's room? We had to draw straws. Emily won the draw, and she stayed in the room that had belonged to the Mother Superior. She was elevated to some kind of eminence that night, at least in her own mind.

Our stay in Rome included going to the opera *Aïda,* staged in the Baths of Caracalla. The ancient Roman baths included a huge amphitheater with a large stage. In *Aïda,* live camels walked across the stage in one scene. Emily leaned over to me with wide eyes and said, "Dad, those are real camels!" What a glorious performance it was.

When we returned home in September 1963, it was to a nation roiling in change. The civil rights movement was in full swing, and resistance to it was becoming more strident and violent. Martin Luther King Jr. had inspired the nation in August with his "I have a dream" speech on the steps of the Washington Monument. The word Vietnam was beginning to appear regularly in newspaper headlines. The student protests that were to characterize the latter half of the decade had not yet begun, but campuses were already losing some of their innocence and serenity. The nation was two months away from losing a president to an assassin's bullet.

In 1963 Julian came to me with news from the Carleton campus. "Dad," he said, "there's quite a feeling on campus that there shouldn't be compulsory convocation anymore. Really, it's supposed to be a worship service, and we feel it ought to be voluntary. It loses its significance if you're required to go. We think that compulsory convocation ought to be abolished, and we can't get the president and the board of trustees to pay attention to us. We're thinking of starting some kind of an agitation."

I said, "Jul, I hate to have you get mixed up in a protest movement. I'd much rather try to find a peaceful solution, rather than have anything that approaches violence." I abhor violence. I think war or violence of any kind is a human failure. There must be a better way. I said, "What if I were to write a personal letter to the president and every member of the board of trustees outlining your arguments? Would that satisfy you, at least, if not your fellow students, that a real effort has been made?"

He accepted my proposal, so I wrote a letter. I often wondered what the Carleton president and board thought of getting a letter from me about a matter concerning the internal affairs of the college. I did not say that I was writing on behalf of my son. I said, "We have a son at Carleton, and we've come to understand that there's a feeling against compulsory convocation. I think it's valid." I went through the arguments Julian had made. Not long after Carleton discontinued compulsory convocation.

Julian was caught up in the fervor for civil rights. He spent two interesting summers working as a volunteer with the American Friends Service Committee. The first summer, he was sent to South Carolina with a corps of other college students to conduct a voter registration drive. The next summer, his assignment was to tutor black high school graduates whose hopes of going on to college were hampered by an inadequate high school education. He made a splendid effort with both assignments.

The voter registration drive was risky business—more so than we realized at the time. Only a few summers later three young men were murdered in Mississippi for doing the same kind of voter registration work Julian did. The Friends' approach was to meet with black citizens and tell them that voting was their right and encourage them to insist on exercising it. Julian and his colleagues had clear instructions. They were not to get involved in any argument or scuffle. If there was any sign of interference with their work, they were to vanish. If they were conducting a meeting and heard cars roaring by or angry voices outside, they should quickly dismiss the meeting. Those guidelines saw them through, and they got a lot of people registered.

He told us about one exchange that I found significant. He came to know one family so well that he was invited to their home. While there, he dared to raise a sensitive subject. He said, "The inside of your home is so nice, so well-cared for and so pretty. It's a pleasure to be here. But I can't help but wonder about the outside of your home. You don't cut the grass. You don't paint the house. Why is the outside so different from the inside?" They said, "Julian, don't you understand? If we had a neat lawn, we would be considered uppity. The worst thing for black people in the South is to be considered uppity, because somebody is right handy to knock you down."

Julian's account of that conversation brought home to me anew the level of oppression black people faced in those years in the Deep South. One earlier incident gave me a glimmer of the prejudice they endured. When I visited the Fuller plant in Atlanta in the 1950s, I did what I always did—I walked through the plant, shook hands with everyone I met, and exchanged a few personal words with each worker. One of the fellows said to me afterwards, "Elmer, you did those Negroes no favor by shaking hands with them." "Oh," I scoffed, "don't tell me that." "No, really. I am serious. They will catch hell for being uppity." I said, "Times are going to have to change in Atlanta. I'm not going to change."

Our practice at Fuller was to have Christmas parties for all employees and their spouses. As Christmas approached one year, Atlanta manager Bill Mattox called. "Elmer," he said, "I'm afraid we can't have a Christmas party here." "Why not?" "We can't find a place that will permit Negroes." "Come now—is that really the case?" He said, "You have no idea how strict it is down here. We really can't." "I'll tell you what you do then," I said. "Have the party at the plant, and be sure all the Negro workers know that they especially are invited and welcome to attend. Make it an especially fun time. Spend a little extra. Make it a party they won't forget."

With civil rights and politics much on people's minds, I was flattered to discover upon our return from Europe that I was still on the minds of my political friends. They were mentioning my name often as a possible candidate for the U.S. Senate in 1964, when Democrat Eugene McCarthy would stand for reelection. I was seen fairly sympathetically, almost as a governor-in-exile, because of the way my governorship had ended.

But I did not wait long to publicly declare that I would not run against McCarthy. For one thing, I had become quite fond of Gene in the sixteen years since he had defeated my good friend Ed Devitt for Congress. But the prime consideration was that I had little interest in moving to Washington—and Eleanor was emphatically against it. She may not always have been thrilled with my political ambitions, but she had always supported my bids for the legislature and for governor. I could not imagine running for office against her wishes.

Besides, I already had important political work ahead of me in 1964. I had seen the taconite amendment through the legislature. I was determined to see it through the general election and into the state constitution. The voters needed to be sold on the amendment, and I wanted to help do the selling.

I had to be careful. My successor, Gov. Karl Rolvaag, had come out in favor of the amendment only a few weeks before the legislature approved it. Retaining his support was vital to the amendment's success. If my role was too prominent, he might interpret my activities as a run-up to a rematch in 1966, and withdraw his support. So I recruited Dr. Charles W. Mayo, who was just then stepping down as senior surgeon of Rochester's Mayo Clinic, to be chairman of the volunteer committee for the taconite amendment. I would have him call Rolvaag when we wanted something done by the governor, or needed to inform him of our plans. I would sit at Mayo's elbow to counsel him how to handle anything that came up in the conversation. I advised: "Don't let the governor say 'No' to anything. If he's wavering, give him more time. Urge him to think it over. But don't accept 'No' for an answer. Keep any request open." With that strategy, we got things our way. Rolvaag wound up being such a solid supporter of the amendment that *Time* magazine ultimately gave him credit for the taconite amendment's adoption.

I determined that the taconite amendment volunteer committee needed a paid staff person, and I knew just the one—Rita Shemesh. I had known her since my early days in the legislature, when she was employed by the University of Minnesota to mount a public relations and lobbying campaign in opposition to the antivivisectionists that were then attacking the medical research program. As soon as Rita got involved, the antivivisectionists were finished. We worked together in 1951 on a constitutional amendment to give the university, not the legislature, control of the assets it had received from the federal government as part of its land grant charter. I sponsored the bill; she lobbied the legislature and then took the case for the amendment to the voters. I admired Rita's energy, her confident spirit, and her hard work, and tucked her name away in my mind for future reference.

Initially, the taconite amendment committee had no money for a staff person. I hired Rita personally. She took charge of the campaign and put forth an effort much greater than anything she was paid to do. She poured herself into it. She appealed to every conceivable service club and civic organization in the state to pass a resolution in support of the amendment. She wrote the resolution and sent it to the organizations, asking them to sign it and send it back. She would then publicize the backing of those groups. She bombarded the newspapers and radio stations in the state with news of local support for the amendment. In that way, she built a tremendous sense of momentum, a perception that public acceptance was even deeper than the polls indicated. Her efforts were reflected on the state's editorial pages. In the days before the election, nearly every newspaper in the state endorsed the amendment, in what the *Star Tribune*'s Leonard Inskip called the greatest show of unity ever by the state's editorial writers.

When the campaign gathered steam, the mining companies got involved. They wanted the amendment passed. They enlisted a publicist in Duluth who had worked with them on other projects, H. E. "Wes" Westmoreland. He was an honest and able professional who was adept at raising money. His efforts gave us funds to carry on the campaign. On November 3, 1964, an amendment assuring fair taxation of taconite processing plants became part of the Minnesota Constitution. It passed by a smashing margin, 1,135,877 yes votes to 163,280 no votes. Best of all, it had its intended effect. Within a month of the amendment's passage, plans were announced for four large new taconite plants on the Iron Range.

The only leading state official who never came around in support of the taconite amendment was Joe Donovan, the DFL secretary of state from Duluth. He had inherited the old hate that miners' families had for their employers, and he never warmed to the idea of promising fair treatment to those firms. Donovan was a crusty character, tapped in 1954 by the DFL to run for secretary of state in a year when the party did not expect to win the seat. Nobody was more surprised than he was to win, let alone serve in the office for sixteen years. When he was getting older, he said that the first thing he did every morning was to look in the obituary column in the newspaper. If his name was not there, he got up.

Presidential politics also engaged me in 1964. I was a delegate to the Republican national convention in San Francisco that nominated Arizona Sen. Barry Goldwater for president. He was not my choice. I would have preferred New York Gov. Nelson Rockefeller, my compatriot from National Governors' Association meetings in 1961 and 1962. He had been seen as the party's leading presidential contender until 1963, when abruptly—or so it appeared—he divorced his wife of many years and married Margaretta "Happy" Murphy, the recently divorced wife of a doctor. Both families included children. Particularly in those more innocent days, their conduct was considered more than a little bit scandalous. I thought that at least he had done the legitimate thing by marrying Mrs. Murphy.

Not long after his marriage, Nelson invited Eleanor and me to the Rockefeller family's compound in Pocantico Hills, New York. We spent a lovely weekend there and came to know Nelson's brother Laurance, a business executive and conservationist, and his wife, who was the international chair of an organization for girls, and a distinguished lady. That weekend led to my involvement in a youth movement that Rockefeller was interested in, which in turn led to my being interviewed by Walter Cronkite, the longtime CBS television journalist. Nothing came of the Cronkite interview. CBS did not air any portion of it. But I had fun meeting and talking with the era's top TV newsman.

Rockefeller's remarriage was not popular in Minnesota. So, instead of coming out forthrightly for Rockefeller, we Minnesotans who opposed Goldwater's conservatism lined up officially behind former U.S. Rep. Walter Judd of Minneapolis as a favorite son candidate. We knew that Judd had little or no chance to be nominated, but supporting him kept our options open. The Judd supporters dominated the state Republican convention that year and elected its complete slate of delegates to the national convention—even me, the candidate most disliked by the Goldwater faction. My campaign attorney, John Mooty, presided at that state convention. Lyall Schwarzkopf was our floor manager. Sally Pillsbury assisted him and earned a reputation as a political operative who knew how to count. At a convention, that is high praise.

When we got to San Francisco, to our disappointment, Goldwater had the nomination nailed down. When we were trying to amend the platform, I gave one floor speech at about 2:00 A.M. in favor of an amendment restricting control over use of nuclear weapons to the president, not the military. My amendment did not prevail—none favored by Rockefeller did. I was part of the Rockefeller retinue, where I rubbed elbows with some of the country's most able political minds. Henry Kissinger, the future secretary of state, was part of that group. So was Christian Herter, who had been President Dwight Eisenhower's last secretary of state. Rockefeller believed in studying issues thoroughly, and he could employ topnotch talent to school him in any area he wanted to pursue. One could not help but learn by working with him.

I had tried to assist Rockefeller in the important California primary on June 2, 1964, one of the last big dates on the pre-convention political calendar. That is what put me in such low regard with Minnesotans for Goldwater. On May 19, I visited former President Eisenhower at his home in Gettysburg, Pennsylvania, to plead with him to help us stop Goldwater. I had met "Ike" during the 1952 campaign, and he had campaigned for me in 1960, so I had a little basis of access to him. Walter Thayer, the former publisher of the *New York Herald Tribune,* accompanied me. Thayer and I were intent on getting Eisenhower to say something publicly that would be helpful to Rockefeller in California. He refused to endorse Rockefeller explicitly, but he issued a long statement through the *Herald Tribune* on May 24 that decried Goldwater's views on civil rights and foreign relations. The statement was front-page news all over the country and widely interpreted as a blow to Goldwater. Rockefeller gave me public credit for soliciting the statement from Eisenhower—and thereby made me a target for the Goldwater faction when the state convention chose national delegates.

Unfortunately, Ike was susceptible to argument from the Goldwater side, too. His former treasury secretary, George Humphrey, was a strong Goldwater backer. He persuaded the former president to issue a second statement two days before the primary, denying that he was trying to suggest that Goldwater's views made him ineligible for the party's presidential nomination. We pleaded with Ike, "Don't clarify your statement. Just let it stand." But he did not listen to us. On a fairly close vote, Rockefeller lost California and with it, any hope for the nomination.

For those of us who defined ourselves as progressive Republicans, Goldwater's nomination was a dismaying about-face in national party affairs. Goldwater stood for a federal government less committed to civil rights, less involved in improving the lot of the poor, and more belligerent in the cold war. When the Republican Party embraced him, it seemed to have turned its back on Abraham Lincoln, Theodore Roosevelt, and even Dwight Eisenhower. The party also seemed to be at odds with the views of most Americans. We had many amendments to the platform, pleading for positions we believed better matched the thinking of a majority of Americans. They were routinely voted down. Goldwater had the votes. His people even had guards on the convention floor. It was a militaristic convention, tightfisted, rigid, and unresponsive. The American people responded to Goldwater as I predicted they would. They gave Lyndon Johnson and the Democrats a landslide victory. But Goldwater and the 1964 convention wrought a lasting change in the Republican Party. One prescient analysis in the *Minneapolis Star* predicted that I would have a hard time ever again winning my party's endorsement for elective office.

I said when I left the governor's office that I expected public affairs would henceforward dominate my time and attention. But Fuller occupied me in the mid-1960s to a greater degree than I anticipated it would. The company had grown to a point where it needed the status and capital acquisition capacity afforded by public stock ownership. To become public, we had to have three years of combined control of all our subsidiaries around the country. It fell largely to me to negotiate new equity arrangements with the people I had put in charge of our plants in more than a dozen locations so that they would support combining Fuller's nine subsidiaries into a single corporate entity.

We had organized Fuller as a parent company in Minnesota, with subsidiaries in each plant location. Every new plant started as a branch of the home office in St. Paul. But as soon as a new plant was breaking even, it was incorporated as a separate company. That gave equity or stock options to the people who headed each plant. That meant that by 1965, Fuller and its subsidiaries had many shareholders. The challenge in going public was convincing the shareholders of the subsidiaries to trade their shares for parent company shares so all the stock would be in the parent company for a minimum of three years. Only then would the Securities and Exchange Commission allow us to go public.

It was a matter of some delicacy, because all the owners of Fuller subsidiary stock were concerned about what somebody else was getting. They all wanted a fair deal for themselves. That was hard to come by, given the fact that the subsidiaries were not of equal value. Some stockholders truly deserved more for their stock than others did. It took nearly two years to settle all those negotiations harmoniously, but we did it without a single holdout at the end. One of the happiest moments of my life was the luncheon we had to culminate those negotiations and celebrate the new structure we created. H. B. Fuller was again one company, as it had been a quarter century earlier. It was ready to become a public company in 1968.

After receiving numerous inquiries about merger or acquisition by a larger company, we decided we were not interested and never would be. We took steps at the time of the public offering to make us a poor target for hostile takeover. We created weighted voting preferred stock that we have kept in family hands through the years.

The brokerage house Dain-Kalman-Quayle of Minneapolis handled the underwriting when we went public. On April 25, 1968, 150,000 shares of Fuller common stock were sold. The initial price was $20 a share; by the day's end, it was already $23. A week later, it was $26. The public offering did just what I had hoped. It raised capital to finance additional expansion and made satisfied investors out of owners of Fuller stock.

The public offering sealed my relationship with Wheelock Whitney, one of the key people at Dain. I had also known him through Republican political circles and had admired his intellect and unflagging optimism. I sought him as securities commissioner in my administration and was disappointed when he declined. He worked hard as a member of the taconite amendment committee in 1964 before entering the U.S. Senate race that year. After Fuller went public, Wheelock came on the Fuller board and stayed until he made a career change some years later. He has remained a dear friend through the years.

By the 1960s, Fuller was an international company. We opened our first plant outside the U.S. border in Winnipeg, Manitoba. The second international effort was in Argentina. DuPont, a good supplier of ours, had a man in Argentina whom they made available to assist us. We went into that arrangement with a trusting attitude—too trusting, as it turned out. I felt that no company should have a majority of its stock in another country, so we did not seek to have the majority of the Fuller subsidiary's stock. We proposed having a minority and allowing the local people to have the decisive voice. I signed documents written in Spanish that I had not read. I trusted that those documents reflected the understanding I had reached with the people involved in the transaction. I learned the hard way that trust can be misplaced. We came around to thinking that if our ideals and principles were going to prevail in running the company, we had to be in charge. From then on, we sought majority interest, no matter where a Fuller operation was located. Ultimately, at some expense, we gained the majority interest in the Fuller plant in Argentina.

Fuller was party to some big, far-flung ventures in the mid-1960s—not all of them successful. The biggest mistake I made as a Fuller executive occurred in those years, in connection with a deal in Australia. We were involved in a joint-venture with a company there that was dominated by one shareholder who was often critical of the company's management. We had acquired some stock in the company. I was in Hamburg, Germany, headed for Argentina, when I got a phone call from an Australian brokerage house advising me that this major shareholder wanted to sell his stock to us, for $1 million. I was definitely interested, but I felt that before I proceeded, I ought to at least inform the firm's management. That was a mistake. I called the president and asked if he would have any objection if we made this transaction. He said, "We'd be very concerned, Elmer." Immediately, he took measures that prevented us from making the purchase. We lost the opportunity to become the principal stockholder in that company. It took us more time and expense to reassert our position in Australia, separate from that company.

But in 1964, I also took one of the most important trips in the company's history. Along with our vice president for research and development, Dick Smith, I went to Costa Rica to meet a young University of Kansas Ph.D. chemist, Frank Jirik. We were told that he had developed a small reactor that would help us produce polyvinyl acetate emulsion, a product used in the newer adhesives that were being developed from petroleum rather than from the traditional adhesive ingredients of corn, wheat, and tapioca.

We arrived in Costa Rica on the heels of a major earthquake and flood. Mud and rocks had roared down a mountain and had buried many things in San Jose, including the plant of Jirik's company, named Kativo after a tree that grows in coastal Costa Rica. We learned from Jirik's right-hand man, Walter Kissling, that their emulsifying reactor for polyvinyl acetate was a half-grown idea that was not ready for commercial application. But we were also told that Kativo had another plant, in Nicaragua, that was successfully producing paint, ink, plastics, and industrial chemicals. It was negotiating with a Mexican adhesive company called Resistal to get into the adhesive business. We quickly shifted gears and began to talk about a joint venture. That first day, after seeing the devastation in San Jose, we flew to Nicaragua. Before nightfall, we struck an agreement for a joint venture in adhesive manufacturing in Central America with Kativo. Three years later, Fuller acquired majority interest in Kativo Chemical Industries Ltd.

The minute I met Walter Kissling, I knew he was a man of unusual ability. He was capable, adaptable, and resourceful—a brilliant man. We worked together for years building up Kativo, until it became a $100-million Latin American company with sales throughout Central and South America and Mexico. Then Kissling came to Minnesota to become president and chief executive officer of H. B. Fuller Company. He has now retired and returned to Costa Rica, taking a fondness for Minnesota with him.

With all that occupied me at Fuller, the 1966 political year was fast upon me. It was then that I learned something I should have learned long before: In politics, nothing comes to you. You have to go and get it.

I felt that I had served well as governor. If the Republican Party appreciated what I had done and stood for, I thought, party people would want me to run again and reclaim the governorship from Karl Rolvaag. I waited for party leaders to approach me and initiate a campaign. I waited too long.

One good friend, Archie Jackson, chairman of the St. Paul Fire and Marine Insurance Company, did approach me about another run for governor not long after I left office. He recruited me in November 1963 to be the chairman of a $10-million capital campaign for Macalester College, Tony's alma mater. We worked closely through that effort. He said, "Elmer, people are so dissatisfied with what happened in the last election, you'd probably find it quite easy to get reelected." I agreed, but I waited to hear the same thing from others before declaring my candidacy and asking state convention delegates to support me.

I think if I had announced my candidacy early and worked hard to organize Republican convention delegates in 1965 and 1966, I could have been the party's nominee. Instead, I was a latecomer to the race and ran third in the convention's balloting, behind South St. Paul attorney Harold LeVander and insurance executive John Pillsbury. My old 1949 state senate rival William Randall was also a candidate. When continued ballots produced little movement and a stalemate seemed possible, I was approached and asked to withdraw, to accelerate the process of endorsing a candidate. I agreed. There was another mistake. You do not withdraw, even if it means that your party reaches no endorsement and the nomination is decided in the primary. That was the year the DFL state convention battled for three days before endorsing Lt. Gov. Sandy Keith over Rolvaag. A whale of a primary was brewing in that party. The Republican Party would not have been damaged by a gubernatorial primary of its own that year.

I tossed my support to LeVander, who became the Republican nominee and the next governor of Minnesota. I campaigned with him and cheered him on as he defeated Rolvaag in the general election. But I did so with no ill will toward the man who had unseated me. My friends in the DFL Party had told me that Rolvaag had opposed the use of falsehoods about Interstate 35 construction in the 1962 campaign. That information confirmed the impression I always had of Rolvaag—that he was basically a decent person. He fought a courageous battle in 1966 to win his party's nomination for governor in the primary, defeating Keith. Later, Rolvaag showed even greater courage by telling the public about his battle with the disease that had long plagued him, alcoholism. I was among those who helped him with the cost associated with chemical dependency treatment.

My tardy campaign in 1966 was my last hurrah in elective politics. After that year, I gave up the idea of being governor again. I had so much else to do.

Voyageurs Park

I AM TEMPTED TO SAY that Voyageurs National Park was born on a pristine June day in 1962, when a state and local delegation and I escorted Conrad Wirth, the director of the National Park Service, to Kabetogama Peninsula near International Falls. The sparkle of the water and brilliance of the sky matched the enthusiasm and promise of that day.

But decades of dreaming about a national park in Minnesota preceded that day. And two more decades of hard work were ahead for those of us who wanted this special slice of northern Minnesota preserved in the national park system.

The idea of a national park in northern Minnesota was by no means new. A legislator, G. J. Lomen of St. Paul, promoted the idea in the late 1800s, after the first national park was established at Yellowstone. He convinced the 1891 legislature to memorialize Congress to establish a Minnesota national park. The Federated Women's Clubs soon joined the call. Then, still in the 1890s, the Minnesota & Ontario Paper Company offered to trade lands that they owned on the Kabetogama Peninsula and surrounding area for timberland elsewhere, in order that land ownership could be consolidated and a national park established. I believe the motives of the M & O Company were laudable, but people at the time did not. M & O was accused of attempting to steal good forest land by giving worthless rock on an inaccessible island in exchange. The M & O owners were shocked at the hostile reaction to their proposal and quickly withdrew it.

A couple of generations later, the idea caught the imagination of a career conservationist in the state agency now called the Department of Natural Resources, U. W. "Judge" Hella. He was a quiet, dedicated worker who gave his whole life to environmental preservation. I worked with him on state parks legislation while I was in the Minnesota Senate, and was exposed to his sweeping vision for public parks throughout the state. The capstone in his vision was a national park in the northern wilderness. The idea appealed to me. Even before I was elected governor, we began to plot how to get it done.

While I was governor, by a happy coincidence a Minnesota native was in charge of the National Park Service. Conrad Wirth was the son of Theodore Wirth, the man remembered today as the father of the Minneapolis park system. Hella and I hatched the idea of inviting Conrad Wirth to come to Minnesota to speak at the dedication of Bear Head Lake State Park near Ely and to add a day for a tour of the Kabetogama area. Wirth accepted.

The tour group on June 27, 1962, included two outstanding promoters of wilderness and historical preservation, Russell Fridley of the Minnesota Historical Society, and Sigurd Olson, the acclaimed wilderness author. Their mission was to help Wirth see Kabetogama Peninsula as worthy of national park status. We toured the area in the morning, had a delicious fish luncheon at the little place at the end of the peninsula, the Kettle Falls Hotel, and then did a little fishing in the afternoon. Wirth caught a fish. It was perfect, just perfect. He was clearly impressed. In sales terms, we had our foot in the door.

But we also had in our midst that day one who would be our formidable, though worthy, opponent. George Amidon was land manager of the paper company that had by then taken the name Boise Cascade. That firm owned much of the land under consideration for the park and had been good stewards of the land for many years. Amidon could sense that his company was going to be against placing a national park so close to their operations in International Falls. He and I were good friends. He put me on notice early that Boise Cascade wanted to develop its Kabetogama land for profitable tourism, not lose it to the government. Boise's position was that a national park belonged in the Boundary Waters Canoe Area, not on Kabetogama. Their reasoning was understandable. It would be advantageous to have a national park maintained with public funds right next to your privately developed investment land.

I had lunch at one point with the president of Boise Cascade and found him polite but hard-nosed about what they intended to do with Kabetogama. He insisted that nothing was going to stop them. Later on, when their stock went from $54 to $28 a share, I was tempted to send him a wire that said, "I think the Lord has punished you enough."

It was not long before Amidon and I became something of a dog-and-pony act, debating the merits of the national park proposal for Rotary Clubs, Lions' Clubs, and service organizations of all kinds throughout the state. We used to say that we ought to change sides, just for fun. I told him, "I could give your speech as well as you give it, and so could you do mine."

Boise's position on the park changed eventually, when its investments in

tourism went sour. I was greatly satisfied when, in 1988, after Amidon retired and the park had been established, he wrote a lovely letter conceding
that the park was a good idea and expressing the hope that it would enjoy
broad support. George Amidon was a prince of a man.

But Boise Cascade was not the park's only opponent. Mistrust of the
federal government runs deep in northeastern Minnesota. A small but vocal
group of local resort owners and residents resisted the idea mightily. They
did not want any more government ownership of northern Minnesota land.
They did not want any new restriction on their opportunities to hunt, fish,
drive snowmobiles, or pursue other outdoor sports. The resort owners
claimed, erroneously, that national parks attract only backpackers who
spend little or no money in nearby communities. To overcome that opposition and convince Congress to authorize a park, we needed a major effort.

The first step in creating a national park is getting Congress to authorize
it. That is, in essence, a hunting license. With authorization in hand, land
can be secured. But authorization does not come without innumerable, in-
depth studies being made first. Every constituency involved must either
make a study or contribute to somebody else's study. The examination is
made in wearying detail. Meanwhile, political support in Congress must be
generated. Securing the backing of home-state representatives is crucial.
Almost nine years elapsed from that sunny day on Kabetogama Peninsula
in 1962 until President Richard Nixon signed the authorization bill in 1971.

It meant much to me that the first Minnesota congressman to support
the idea was Don Fraser, my ally in the Minnesota Senate. I took the proposal for Voyageurs to Fraser. "Don, if there's anybody in this state who can
afford to support a national park for Minnesota, you can," I told him.
"Your whole constituency wants to get out away from the city and get to a
park. Getting a national park in Minnesota, funded with national funds . . .
You ought to be head over heels for this." He was.

Fraser was the first of Minnesota's ten-member congressional delegation
to back Voyageurs Park. Rep. John Blatnik, whose district included the
park, was the last. Blatnik may have had the most politically secure seat in
the nation. But he always wanted to win with about 75 percent of the vote.
There would be no close deals for him. He waited and watched and waited
some more, until our Voyageurs National Park Association had built up
enough momentum to satisfy him that we had a decent chance to succeed.

The association was an organization assembled in April 1965 that brought
together a handful of vigorous proponents of the park from northern
Minnesota with some important forces in the Twin Cities. Martin Kellogg,

a businessman in St. Paul who is still active in the Minnesota Parks and Trails Council, was one. He was chairman then of a Minneapolis Chamber of Commerce task force that had been studying ways to promote regional tourism. He and chamber staff person Lloyd Brandt were instrumental in putting the Minneapolis Chamber on record for the park in the early going.

Fuller hired two public relations people, Archie Chelseth and Robert Watson, whom I assigned to work with me on Voyageurs. We set up a little office on University and Prior Avenues to get the association going. I tapped my friend Sam Morgan, a prominent St. Paul attorney, to organize us as a nonprofit organization. We found an important ally in Judge Ed Chapman of Minneapolis, an ardent conservationist and outdoorsman. He was eager to carry the case for the park to groups around the state. We made Chapman the association's first president, and soon he and Watson were traveling the state on nights and weekends, making presentations about the possibility of a new national park.

I served briefly as the association's president, but I also saw to it that the association's leadership positions were passed around. That was a way to recruit more talent to our cause. But I stayed heavily involved in the project, spending a great deal of time and quite a bit of expense to see it through. I had committed myself to establishing a national park, and I was going to do it. I am often reminded of the story of the flood, in which some men in a boat went to rescue a woman from atop her porch roof. As they looked down at the water, they saw a straw hat floating by. But when it got so far, it turned around and started moving back again. The men in the boat said to the woman, "Did you notice that? There's a straw hat down there going upstream." She said, "Oh, that's Pa. He said come hell or high water, he was mowing the lawn today."

We were a lean organization, but we needed some money. Wallace Dayton, of the department store family, and Wheelock Whitney agreed to let their names be used on a fundraising letter that had its intended effect. Meanwhile, in Duluth, a geologist named Jack Everett took up the cause. He decided that support in northern Minnesota would be easier to come by if the association were not centered in the Twin Cities. So he and a handful of others founded their own national park advocacy group, based in Duluth. We welcomed their contribution to the effort.

Lloyd Brandt remembers that once when he was speaking of the enormity of the task before us, I chuckled and said I had a secret weapon. That was Rita Shemesh. Fresh from her triumph with the taconite amendment, Rita was supercharged again and ready to rally public support for Voyageurs

Park. We made her the association's executive secretary. By the time we went to Washington to begin some serious lobbying, she had a list of fourteen hundred clubs and organizations in the state that had passed resolutions supporting the park.

Lobbying Congress is a daunting task, even when a proposal has little opposition. Ours had some active enemies. As a result, we experienced one crucial moment after another. At times Voyageurs Park seemed dead. Our perseverance was put to the test.

U.S. Rep. Roy Taylor of North Carolina headed the subcommittee of the House Interior Committee that handled park and environmental issues. He brought his subcommittee to International Falls for a public hearing on the Voyageurs proposal. He got a raucous reception from some resort owners. But in a dramatic moment, Ernest Oberholtzer, a legendary environmentalist and forestry researcher in the Kabetogama area, got to his feet and scolded the opposing resort owners for shortsightedness and bias against the people who would visit a national park. Ober, as Oberholtzer was familiarly known, had long championed the idea of an international park stretching from Grand Portage to Rainy Lake. Taylor was impressed. He became a friend of the project, and of mine.

Some years later, he called. "Elmer, I'm having a tough reelection campaign," he said. "You're a former Republican governor. Would you write a letter that I could use in the newspapers in my district? They think I spend too much time away from my district. I think I've been away because of important work, and I know you agree. You could testify to what it has meant." I was happy to help him in that way, and he was reelected.

The chair of the full committee, Rep. Wayne Aspinall of Colorado, was not our ally. He had given his word to Boise Cascade that there would be no Voyageurs National Park. Aspinall directed Taylor not to let the bill out of his subcommittee. But Taylor had an independent streak. He was not one to take orders. We plotted with Taylor about how to get around Aspinall.

As luck would have it, the voters in Maryland came to our aid. In a primary election in early 1970, the chairman of the House Public Works Committee was defeated. Minnesota's John Blatnik was next in line for the chairmanship and began to enjoy some of its perks. Suddenly everybody in Congress wanted to please the man whose committee was in the business of distributing political pork. By then, Blatnik was in our corner, and having gone public with his support, he was not to be denied.

Blatnik's administrative aide and eventual successor in Congress, Jim Oberstar, swung into action. Oberstar was indefatigable. He worked his

head off, helping us secure the needed votes in Taylor's subcommittee. With
the votes in hand, Taylor sent word to Aspinall, "Mr. Chairman, the bill is
coming out, and if necessary, it will be over your dead body."

I was part of a Minnesota delegation that testified before the subcommittee. The group also included then-Gov. Harold LeVander. His testimony came before mine. I am afraid he did our cause more harm than good.
He did not fully understand the difference between a national recreation
area and a national park. The difference is technical, but it is significant.
Everything he said argued for the designation of the Kabetogama Peninsula
as a national recreation area, not a park. I was beside myself listening to
what he said. I approached a committee aide and requested to be allowed to
testify next. I needed to undo quickly the damage LeVander had done our
cause. Taylor's people were helpful, and I hastened to the witness table to
try to turn the argument around. I apparently got the job done, because
Taylor said to me after my testimony, "I think you've saved the day."

Rep. Morris Udall from Arizona spoke up when I was finished. "Andersen, you have abilities that would serve you well in seeking public office,"
he said. I smiled. "I tried that," I said, " but I wasn't fully appreciated."

While we made our pitch in Congress, we also sought more public
awareness of our crusade. I carried that part of the campaign to the CBS
radio network studios in New York, where I was, briefly, a guest on the
popular Arthur Godfrey Show. Godfrey was sympathetic to environmental
causes. We appealed to that sympathy when we contacted him and asked
him for time on his program to explain our plan for Kabetogama Peninsula.

It was a heady experience for me to sit next to the genial, red-haired king
of daytime radio, and address a nationwide audience. But he quickly put
me at ease with his folksy manner. I was allowed only three or four minutes
to tell the Voyageur's story. That was not nearly enough, I thought. But I
had a strategy to try to win a few more minutes. I thought if I somehow tied
my remarks into his commercials, he would find me useful and allow me to
stay on the air longer. So, when he asked me a question, I would weave in
some remark about his sponsors. One was a nationally advertised bread that
we happened to buy at home, so I could give the product a testimonial.

It worked. He naturally responded to my interest in what he was trying
to sell, and would then return the favor by responding with interest in what
I was trying to sell—a new national park. As a result, I had enough time on
the air to give many people around the country their first inkling that a national park had been proposed for Minnesota. My debut on national radio
was a hit.

Partly through our efforts—but probably more by the members' desire to curry favor with Blatnik—the House Interior Committee was sold on Voyageurs. The bill came out of the committee and was passed by the House in early 1970. Normally, national park issues are decided in the House, and the Senate's approval is a matter of routine. But Boise Cascade had rushed over to the Senate and set up barriers there that were surprisingly tough. Jim Oberstar, Blatnik's aide, did what he could in the Senate, but we were hampered by a lack of strong support from Minnesota's two senators, Democrats Walter Mondale and Eugene McCarthy. They gave a little lip service. But to get something through the Senate over strong business opposition, one has to do more than that. It takes work.

The key to success in the Senate lay with the chairman of the Senate Interior Committee. He had the singular power to pass our bill, or kill it. The chair in 1970 was Henry M. "Scoop" Jackson of Washington. By fortunate coincidence, the committee's ranking Republican member was Sen. Gordon Allott from Colorado, with whom I was acquainted. I asked him, "Would you, please, get me an hour with Senator Jackson? It can't be fifteen minutes. I need an hour to present the Voyageurs National Park." He arranged the appointment. I arranged for Sigurd Olson, the noted environmental author, to go with me. I also enlisted my son Julian, by then a faculty member at Shoreline Community College in Seattle, to generate a little constituent mail to Jackson on behalf of the park. I thought, every little bit of persuasion helps.

Olson and I had a full hour with Jackson and his staff members, all of whom already had been lobbied heavily by Boise Cascade. Jackson wasted no time with small talk at the start of the meeting. "Go to it," he said.

I sure went to it. I poured out my heart for Voyageurs for the full hour, with Olson chiming in when he could. Jackson seemed swayed by our presentation. When we were finished, he turned to his staff and said, "What do you make of all of this?" Various staff members said, "I think we've been misled. I think this is ready to go. I think we should be for it." He said, "Let's do it." That settled it. One person settles things in Washington. I saw once again the difference a single person can make.

When the bill containing the authorization for Voyageurs Park passed the Senate, those of us who had been lobbying for the park were in Washington. We thought it would be fun to stay in Washington and witness the bill-signing ceremony. Then we received word that President Nixon was at his home in California, and the bill would be signed there, on January 8, 1971. We were too elated to let Nixon's whereabouts deny us a celebration.

We had a little party in Washington anyway. Rita Shemesh was on a family vacation trip in France but flew to Washington so she could be at that party. Even though we could not hover around Nixon as he signed the bill, we received the pens Nixon used. One of them became a prized possession for Ed Chapman and was thereafter on display in his living room.

But that was only the end of the first step, authorization. The next step is the actual establishment of the park. That took another five years of work, securing ownership of the land, negotiating agreements between the National Park Service and the state of Minnesota, making a huge array of auxiliary arrangements with affected parties. Only when all of that was done would Congress finally establish the park. Only then would federal money begin to flow and improvements such as a visitors' center be contemplated.

It was crucial in 1971, after Congress authorized the park, for the Minnesota Legislature to grant its blessing and direct state officials to take the requisite steps toward the park's establishment, including securing control of the land. Again, happenstance was in our favor. My brother-in-law, Stanley Holmquist of Grove City, was majority leader in the senate that year. He was helpful to us. So were several legislators from the region, including Reps. Irv Anderson of International Falls and Willard Munger from Duluth. Munger, whose record-breaking forty-three-year career in the house ended with his death in July 1999, was a stalwart on any proposal for preserving the natural environment.

Gaining control of the land we wanted was not easy. Land in the area was constantly being sold and resold. The Voyageurs National Park Association raised money in order to bid for desirable parcels, well before the park was established. We wanted to do what we could to hasten the land acquisition. Despite our efforts, the project seemed to barely crawl forward during some portions of the 1970s.

Some residents of the region continued to resist the park, even after it had been authorized. There was a fine woman named Brascugli who owned a resort with her husband. We had a connection through politics. She was dead against Voyageurs Park. I said, "Mrs. Brascugli, would you tell me something? Is there something that you enjoy about northern Minnesota that you'd be willing to give up, that you'd be willing to sacrifice, so that some generation one hundred years from now could have and enjoy it in the future? What would you be willing to give up if it was necessary to do so, in order to preserve it for some future generation?" I tried to phrase my question as delicately as I could. She looked me straight in the eye and said,

"Elmer, I don't see why I should be asked to give up anything." That is what we were up against. Self-preservation is a deep-seated human emotion.

I am reminded of a commercial that ran recently. It was in opposition to a United Nations plan for the United States to reduce its consumption of energy, to allow for an increase in energy consumption in Mexico, China, and other less developed countries. Of course, the fact of the matter is that the United States uses nearly half of all the energy in the world. We should be willing to give up some energy consumption to give other people a chance at a better life. But the forces in favor of selfishness are powerful indeed.

In June 1971, after the legislature had voted in favor of Voyageurs Park, the Park Service started things moving by appointing a project manager, Myrl Brooks. He set up an office in International Falls and began the painstaking tasks of land acquisition, master planning, and winning support for the park in the local community. There, the park continued to face resistance. Local efforts slowed down the state's transfer of land to the Park Service. Some area residents worked to exclude duck-hunting areas from the park and impede enforcement of federal waterway regulations. Even some staunch park supporters, including Gov. Wendell Anderson and state DNR Commissioner Robert Herbst, waffled on the hunting and water issues. For a time, it appeared that this wilderness enclave would be a paradise for attorneys.

Nevertheless, we forged ahead. Our hard work was rewarded in April 1975, when Congress voted to establish Voyageurs National Park. The lobbying was much easier for the park's establishment than for its authorization. This time, the National Park Service carried the ball. We had the Sierra Club, the Wilderness Society, and all the leading environmentalists in the country on our side.

But the work was not over. After the park was established, some people from the region pushed a bill through the legislature to create a Voyageurs National Park Advisory Commission. The motives of some of those behind the commission were less than friendly to the park. When I heard about the commission, I thought, I had better be on it. I arranged to get myself appointed. Willard Munger did the same. Soon the commission was talking about the performance of Myrl Brooks, who had become the first park director. He had a desperately hard time. He operated a little too close to the book and with not enough sympathy for the people who lived in the area. He did not make a sufficient attempt to understand their history and the reasons for some of their views. As a result, some of the local people treated him miserably. Moreover, they objected as I tried to argue for more environmental or zoning control over the land surrounding the park. I thought it would be a shame to surround a fine national park with overdeveloped land. Some resort owners agreed with me, but a fair number of advisory council members did not. We had some hard discussions.

The county commissioners of Koochiching County did not want any interference with their control. But it was not clear to me that they wanted to exert much, if any, control over land near the park. At one hearing, I asked one of the Koochiching commissioners, "How many requests for a land-use variance have you had in the last six months?" "Oh," he said, "we've had about twelve." "How did you handle them?" I asked. "We granted ten." I said, "What happened to the other two?" "One guy had already done it, so there was nothing we could do." I said, "What happened to the last one?" "We opposed it, but the fellow said, 'To hell with you guys,' and he went ahead and did it anyway." "You're not making a very strong case for control of the environment," I told him. That problem persists, I fear.

Controversy also persists over how much snowmobiling should be permitted in the park. I once had an agreement that I thought was going to settle that question. I have some sympathy with snowmobiling. I told some of those who wanted no snowmobiling, "You've got to recognize a few things. There are a lot of people who like to snowmobile. I wouldn't ride on one. I wouldn't have one. But I recognize that a lot of people like it. And a lot of the snowmobiles they drive are made in Minnesota. Thousands of people in Minnesota have jobs relating to snowmobiling. You just can't take a purist attitude that we're not going to have snowmobiling. Let's limit it. Let's limit the power of the snowmobile. Let's limit the trail that it can be on. Let's get snowmobiling under control. Then the drivers who cause trouble will go elsewhere where there is more freedom."

I thought that was the basis of an agreement that we had arranged with about ten groups. Snowmobiling would be allowed, but speed would be limited, and the size of motors would be limited. But the board of the Voyageurs Region National Park Association—the successor of our old organization—overruled its president, and the compromise fell apart. There is more work to be done on this question.

But the lingering issues at Voyageurs Park pale when compared to the joy the park brings each day to the people who visit it. I have known that joy myself. When I spoke on August 25, 1991, at the twentieth anniversary celebration of the park's authorization and the seventy-fifth anniversary of the establishment of the National Park Service, I spoke about what the natural wonders of the park mean to me. "Whatever my own future, I know that if I keep the lob pines in my mind's eye, I will stay on course, and when I hear the wild, free call of a loon, I'll know I am in paradise."

My experience with Voyageurs, perhaps more than any other, showed me the value of persistence. When you work at something and keep at it, you never lose. A person should not make a commitment easily. But once committed, do not let go. Stay with it, and your work will eventually come to a positive end. I did not let the end of the governorship or Boise Cascade opposition or local resistance or lobbying setbacks deter me. Today, there is a national park to show for it. In 1987, at the dedication of the park's visitors' center, I sat on the dock in the sun and thought, it took *twenty-five* years, but here it is, the park Judge Hella and I dreamed and schemed about in 1962. Bringing it to fruition was wonderfully interesting work.

The story of the park is also a story of common effort. It is flattering to have been called the father of Voyageurs Park. I think that I made a difference. But so did many, many other people, more than I could possibly name, who kept the dream alive until it came to fruition. Some of the real heroes were people in the region who opposed their friends or employers to support the park.

The park also had help from another real hero—Charles Lindbergh.

Charles A. Lindbergh

CHARLES A. LINDBERGH'S NAME deserves a prominent place in the annals of Voyageurs National Park. The man who did so much for the development of aviation also did much for his home state, for the cause of wilderness preservation—and for me.

My first meeting with Lindbergh was the result of my long relationship with Russell Fridley, who headed the Minnesota Historical Society at the time that I was its president. Fridley telephoned one day in the mid-1960s with news that Lindbergh was in the state and was going to be at his home that evening. The two of them had been collaborating on the renovation of Lindbergh's boyhood home in Little Falls, so that it could be opened to visitors.

Fridley informed me that at his home that evening, they would be joined by Bruce Larson of Mankato State College, who had an interest in writing a biography of the late Charles August Lindbergh, a Minnesota congressman and Lindbergh's father. He wanted me there, he said, because "you haven't had a chance to meet Charles." Further, he thought I might have a role to play in the biography Larson hoped to write. "Charles doesn't think it's appropriate for the family to finance a book on a family member. They may be looking for a little help," Fridley said. I did not hesitate. "I'll be over," I said.

We had a delightful evening. Lindbergh and I hit it off right away. It was a convivial time, rich with storytelling. One story Lindbergh told that first night concerned his connection with the famed rocket scientist Robert Hutchings Goddard. Charles first heard about Goddard, a professor at Clark University in Worcester, Massachusetts, in 1929. Goddard had an idea that a rocket could be shot into space beyond the control of gravity. Once it got into outer space, it could go to extraterrestrial destinations, such as the moon. That was Jules Verne stuff in the 1920s. Most people paid no attention to Goddard, and he found little financial support for his ideas. Lindbergh took an interest in him. He told how he went to Worcester in

November 1929 to meet with Goddard. An afternoon of conversation convinced him that Goddard had a feasible idea, and that the $25,000 a year for four years that Goddard said he needed would be money well spent. Lindbergh went to New York and met with Daniel Guggenheim, whose son Harry had been a friend of Lindbergh's even before his famous 1927 flight across the Atlantic Ocean. In fact, it was in Guggenheim's castlelike home on Long Island that Lindbergh wrote his first book, *We,* the summer after the flight to Paris. He went to Guggenheim and persuaded him to provide Goddard with $100,000 for rocket research. That was the birth of the American space program.

Goddard wrote a book describing those years, and Lindbergh wrote an introduction. Lindbergh sent me a copy of that book, inscribed to me. It is a precious part of our book collection.

Lindbergh and I became close friends quickly. Our bond was grounded in our shared belief that that there should be a balance between technology and nature. His ideas about that balance were appealing to me. That first night, we talked about how the advantages of technology always should coexist with the wisdom that can be found in wildness. He was eloquent on that point, and I was impressed.

Like most Americans of my generation, I knew some of the high points of Lindbergh's life. I was well aware of his historic 1927 solo flight from New York to Paris, his marriage to Anne Morrow two years later, the kidnapping and death of their first child in 1932, and his opposition to U.S. involvement in the war in Europe in the years leading up to World War II.

After meeting him, I made it a point to learn more about Lindbergh. He was the only child of C. A. Lindbergh's second marriage, to schoolteacher Evangeline Lodge Land. She went to her home in Detroit to give birth to her only child, named Charles Augustus, on February 4, 1902. He became a Minnesotan when he was five weeks old.

Minnesota was always home to Lindbergh, even though he left Little Falls as a young man and never lived there again. There was one time, in his last years, when we were together in Little Falls. As a child, he had made a birdbath. He built it in the ground. It was rough work, stones and cement, crudely smoothed out by hand. It was about four feet in diameter and saucer-shaped to give birds a place to bathe and drink. As an old man, he walked around the circumference of that birdbath, lost in memory. Plainly, it meant a great deal. He talked about sitting on the bank of the Mississippi River and dreaming of flying. I could see that his tie to Little Falls was deep.

After high school, Lindbergh went to the University of Wisconsin. He was there only one year. His mind was on flying, not studying. Some accounts say he flunked out. If he did, it was not for lack of intelligence. Then, he went to Lincoln Standard Aircraft, a flight school and airplane manufacturer in Nebraska, and learned how to fly. He graduated, but he left the school before he had been given the solo flight training the course entitled him to have. He found work as a stunt man with a barnstorming pilot and became adept as a skydiver.

Then, he went to a war-surplus supplier named John Wyche in Americus, Georgia, and bought a Curtiss JN4-D—a "Jenny"—for $500, half the asking price. The same day, he made his first solo flight. A fellow aviator named Henderson, from Birmingham, Alabama, was Lindbergh's volunteer tutor that day.

In 1982, the Lindbergh Foundation sponsored an exhibition at the Northwestern Bank in Minneapolis and displayed that first Lindbergh plane. It had been found in junk in Iowa. Some Lindbergh buffs on Long Island purchased it, brought it to Long Island, and restored it. Don Padilla, the Twin Cities publicist who had been instrumental in my 1960 campaign, was the heart and soul of the Lindbergh exhibit at the bank. Don always had ideas. He thought it would be great to get Lindbergh's Jenny, invite some of his family, and have a celebration in honor of what would have been Lindbergh's eightieth birthday. Mr. Henderson, by then old, feeble, and blind, came from Alabama for the event. We took great care in getting him here. He said again and again, "It is such a thrill to *see* that Jenny plane again." He could not see it, but he touched it, fifty-nine years after he taught Lindbergh to fly it.

The bank's Lindbergh commemoration was a great event that was followed by a close call. The Jenny was still in the old Northwestern Bank on Thanksgiving 1982, when the building burned. Probably because it was suspended from cables in midair, rather than perched on the floor, it was spared any damage.

Lindbergh flew his Jenny in barnstorming shows and transported his father as he campaigned for the U.S. Senate in a 1923 special election, the old congressman's last hurrah. After that, his love of flying led him to the U.S. Air Service Reserve at Brooks Field, near San Antonio, Texas. He graduated first in his group of 19 flying cadets—a group that originally contained 104 students. He got what was considered a plum job for a young aviator: flying the mail from St. Louis to Chicago.

In 1969, when Lindbergh was staying at our home one weekend, our son

Tony asked him if he had ever been afraid. Tony had in mind the famous solo flight across the Atlantic.

Lindbergh said, "No, everything there went smoothly and according to plan." But, he said, "I was afraid once." It was when he was flying the mail from St. Louis to Chicago in 1926. He got caught in a storm in a little makeshift plane that the postal service was using, and he had to bail out. His parachute opened. But the storm was so tempestuous that the parachute was swept in a big arc, and he was afraid it was going to collapse. "That was the time I was afraid."

In 1926, Raymond Orteig, a French-born American hotel owner, offered a $25,000 prize to any pilot who would fly the Atlantic nonstop. Lindbergh wanted to try for it. He had no plane. He had no money to buy a plane. He had nothing. But several incidents of daring-do in delivering the mail had given Lindbergh some notoriety in St. Louis. He was able to interest local businessmen in financing his ambition. That is how a crude plane manufactured in California and sold to a young man from Minnesota for $10,580 got the name *Spirit of St. Louis* and became the most famous aircraft of its age.

When the movie by the same name was made, two models of the plane were built, one to fly and one for camera shots on the ground. The one that did not fly was purchased by the Lindbergh Foundation, with which I was involved. It hangs today near the ticket counters of Minneapolis-St. Paul International Airport. The workmen who made the flying model tried to meticulously duplicate the original *Spirit of St. Louis,* but when they flew it, they thought they had failed. It was crude and hard to control. They were afraid of a negative reaction from Lindbergh when he visited the set of the movie, for they knew he wanted to fly their replica of his plane. They waited anxiously as he flew it. When he landed, he said to the men, "It's a sweet plane, isn't it?"

Lindbergh met Anne Morrow in Cuernavaca, Mexico. Her father was Dwight Morrow, a J. P. Morgan partner and by then the U.S. ambassador to Mexico, living there with his family. On a tour after the 1927 flight, Charles visited Mexico and was entertained in the ambassador's residence, where he met the Morrow family. The Morrows had three daughters, one of whom Lindbergh fancied a little before he centered on Anne.

He described his first real experience with romance in his posthumously published book, *Autobiography of Values.* Anne did not even know it had been written. When Lindbergh was dying, she asked him if there was anything he wanted to say or any messages he wanted to leave. He said, "I've taken care of that, Anne." He had the manuscript ready to be published upon word of his death. It is a lesser-known Lindbergh book, but it is among my favorites. It shows his spiritual side and describes his metamorphosis from thinking that technology is everything, to saying that if he had to choose between airplanes and birds, he would take birds.

He and Anne married after a short courtship. I admire her very much. She grew up in a protected atmosphere, yet married this dashing aviator who was flying over uncharted wastes, plotting routes for future commercial airlines. She flew with him, even when she was pregnant. She became a radio operator, a navigator, and Lindbergh's genuine partner. I once met a man who had been in charge of a Danish ship that supplied Lindbergh when he was charting routes for Pan American Airlines. He lived in Duluth at the end of his life, which is where I visited him. He recalled a flight when Anne was the radio operator. "She was a damned good radio operator," he said. From him, that was a great tribute. Nobody expected women to be doing things like that in his day—let alone pregnant women.

I asked Anne once, "Why did you become such a partner of Charles, and fly with him?" She said, "I was very much in love. I also felt that if anything was going to happen, I wanted to be there." I thought that was a wonderful expression. She did not always agree with him. Especially in later years, she was troubled by some of the things he said and the company he kept. Yet she was a devoted, wonderful partner, and a strong mother of their six children.

While Lindbergh had a clear bond with Minnesota, Anne and the children did not. Anne may have visited Little Falls only once or twice during her marriage. But in October 1976, two years after Lindbergh's death, Anne agreed to come to the Twin Cities for an event in her honor. And the following spring, three of the Lindbergh children—Jon, Land, and Reeve— were on hand in Little Falls for Minnesota's celebration of the fiftieth anniversary of Lindbergh's historic flight to Paris.

At a dinner at the governor's residence on October 28, 1976, Anne was seated at a table between Gov. Wendell Anderson and me. Anderson was busy playing official host, so I had Anne to myself during most of the dinner. That was the beginning of my friendship with her. She is a rather tiny person, but her size belies her strength. To have endured all she did in her marriage and in the loss of her first child, and then to write thirteen books, some of them classics, are marks of a powerful person.

Anne accompanied Lindbergh on a fateful trip to Germany in 1936, and a second one in 1938, at which he accepted the gift of the Service Cross of the German Eagle from Gen. Hermann Wilhelm Goering. Lindbergh thought nothing about how the world would view that gift, but Anne was shrewd enough to sense immediately that it was trouble. She reportedly called it "The Albatross" on first sight. Lindbergh was much criticized for making those trips to Germany. What was not known then, but what has been revealed since, is that Lindbergh was there at the urging of the U.S. military. They were, in essence, using him as a spy. The proud Germans revealed to Lindbergh much more about the development of the Luftwaffe than they likely would have to any other American citizen. Lindbergh never publicly discussed the full purpose of his trip, even in the face of bitter criticism. In personal conversations with me, he was open and seemed happy to convey his side of the story. But he was not inclined to wage personal battles in the press.

Lindbergh joined America First, the antiwar, isolationist organization, prior to World War II, and became its leading spokesman. In 1941, only a few months before Pearl Harbor, Lindbergh gave a speech that he hoped would be so powerful that it would slow or stop the nation's rush into war. The speech in Des Moines, titled "Who Are the War Agitators," named Jews, the British, and the Roosevelt administration as the three entities pushing the nation into the conflict in Europe. He said he could understand why Jewish Americans would want the United States to enter the fight, with their having many personal ties to the Jewish community being persecuted in Nazi Germany. But he described them in terms that suggested they were an alien force and enemies of the best interests of the United States. He was blasted with criticism.

As I came to know Lindbergh, I became convinced that he was not anti-Semitic. He was as wholesome and generous and outgoing a person as there could be. He maintained that he never meant anything anti-Semitic by what he said in Des Moines. He thought he was just reciting the facts. But the charge of anti-Semitism followed him for the rest of his life—and still does.

Soon after I met Lindbergh, we began to correspond. One handwritten letter I received was written while he was in the Philippine Islands, a place he visited often in the last years of his life, when he was an ardent environmentalist. It arrived after his plane was downed in the Philippines—though he never admitted to a crash, then or ever. He had a number of experiences that most pilots would call crashes, including a time when he broke a propeller. But to him, they were only forced landings. At one point while he was in the Philippines, the whole world was concerned about his whereabouts. He had landed somewhere in the islands, and the outside world did not know where. It turned out that he was holed up in a hut belonging to a primitive tribe he had befriended. He was writing letters to friends like me while the world was trying to find him. Lindbergh was remarkable in how he accepted whatever situation he encountered.

My growing friendship with Lindbergh coincided with the work I was doing to win congressional authorization of Voyageurs Park. When we reached the point when we needed an all-out push in Washington, I thought of him. His endorsement would be very helpful to us, I thought. Through correspondence, Russell Fridley and I told him about our plans for a national park, and how he could help. He responded that though he had grown up in Little Falls, he had never visited the northern border lakes. He wanted to spend a couple of days inspecting the area before taking a position.

His practice was never to give advance notice of when he was going to appear. He would tell us only that when he found a couple of days, he would fly to Wold Chamberlain Field in Minneapolis, as it was then called, and be ready to go north. We should be prepared to join him at a moment's notice. On October 3, 1969, the phone rang. It was Fridley: "Elmer, Charles is at the airport, ready to go." In thirty minutes, I was at the airport with a suitcase. We stopped first in Minneapolis to have a bite to eat. No one at the café recognized him. He had shielded himself from the public so thoroughly, and his appearance had changed so much in forty years, that people no longer knew what he looked like.

I drove as we headed north. We stopped in Little Falls so that he could visit his boyhood home and have a brief reunion with his half-sister, Eva Christie Spaeth, whom he had seldom seen since his father's death forty-five years earlier.

On our way to International Falls, we decided that we should rent a seaplane when we got there. Fridley called ahead to rent a plane from the manager of the International Falls airport, Francis Einarson, with whom he had served in the army. Lindbergh insisted that no one in International Falls be told in advance that we were coming, so Fridley's conversation with Einarson was a bit awkward. He said we had a special guest whom we could not identify, who would be our pilot. Einarson was skeptical, so Fridley turned the phone over to me. "We have our own pilot," I said. "I cannot tell you his name, but he's right here. I'll let you talk to him." I then gave the phone to Lindbergh. According to notes Fridley kept of that day's events, the conversation went like this:

EINARSON: Are you familiar with light aircraft on floats?

LINDBERGH: I've had some experience with a variety of planes.

EINARSON: Are you familiar with a controllable-pitch prop?

LINDBERGH: Yes, I've had some experience with it.

EINARSON: Have you had experience flying over water and this kind of
terrain?

LINDBERGH: Yes, I've had experience in that kind of flying.

Eventually, Lindbergh pulled out his pilot's license, showed it to me, and asked me to read it to Einarson. It was an "all-weather, all-nation" license. Einarson replied, "Hell, if he's got that, he can sure fly our floatplane." Of course, when we arrived, Einarson was astounded to discover that the pilot whose qualifications he had questioned was Charles Lindbergh.

A good friend in the Voyageurs Association, George Esslinger, met us in International Falls. He owned a resort in the area and was renowned for his dog team, which made appearances at local events. He was a beautiful person with a deep love for the north country. We asked him to join us for a couple of days. He made a boat available for our use around Kabetogama Peninsula. I told him we had someone special with us. "I can't tell you who it is, but you will be pleased to meet him."

When I finally introduced Esslinger to Lindbergh, Esslinger looked up at him and said, "Oh, my God!" The look on his face was absolute, unadulterated awe.

We had a couple of wonderful days at Kabetogama. I was impressed with Lindbergh's congenial, warmhearted, fun-loving nature. He was far from being the reserved recluse who was sometimes depicted in the press. We found him outgoing and expressive. He carried a little black book with him. It was not very thick, but it contained India paper, the thin, opaque, tough paper that was used in Bibles to keep them compact. He took notes often and kept an amazing amount of information with him. When we asked a question about a date or a fact, he would say, "I'd better check," and he would find the information in his book.

His great coat illustrated how orderly he was. It was his suitcase as well as his coat. Its many pockets contained everything he carried with him on a trip. He said, "One of the real troublesome things is that wherever I go, they want to have a formal dinner. I can't always politely avoid it. Yet, with my frame, I can't get a rented tuxedo, so I have to carry a tuxedo." He opened up his coat and showed me two big pockets inside the lining where he had stuffed a tuxedo. This same coat also served as a blanket and a portable office.

Lindbergh did not want to be bound by his mail. People sometimes sent him packages, which he did not open but sent to a charitable organization. It opened them, acknowledged them, and either appropriately used the contents or sent them to an organization that could. He only bothered with mail that he wanted. He told his personal correspondents, like me, how to mark their letters so they were not automatically thrown away, as much of his mail was. He was trying hard to preserve his freedom and live a simple life.

That day at Kabetogama, each of us was offered a ride with Lindbergh in the two-seat seaplane. I went first. When we got into the plane, he circled on the water many times before taking off, first thrusting the motor, then shutting it off. Just about the time I thought we would rise, we would not. I knew he was experimenting in some way. "Charles," I said, "I know there's a purpose in what you're doing, but could you explain to me just what you're about?" "There are a couple of things, Elmer. In the first place, every plane is different. If you're going to fly a new plane, you have to get acquainted with it. You have to know how it responds and the degree of its response. You have to know it individually, because every plane has a personality of its own. That's one thing. Then, the second thing: I've always had the practice that I never take off unless I have room to abort." He was testing how much space our plane would need to abort a takeoff. That is how careful he was.

When we were finally airborne, we had to shout over the engine's noise to converse, even though we were seated alongside each other. After a while, Lindbergh shouted, "Elmer, have you ever flown?" He meant, had I managed a plane. I said, "No, I sure have never flown." "You'll never have a better little plane to learn in. Why don't you try it? Put your feet up on the pedals and take hold of the stick. I'll guide it so you get a feel for it." He told me what each pedal did, and what the stick did. If you pulled it back, you went up; if you shoved it forward, you went down. He outlined how to fly the plane. Then he said, "I'd like to be excused for a little bit. I'd like to see a moose, and I can't very well fly the plane while I'm looking for a moose. It's really a simple plane to fly. Now, you fly it while I'm still here. You'll see how easy it is." I took the stick, and my gosh! I was flying! He said, "It comes naturally. You can do it. I'll be watching, but I'm going to look over the side of the plane now."

He looked for his moose, and I flew our plane through the heavens, reveling in what a glorious time I was having. All of a sudden, I realized I did not have the slightest idea where I was. It is easy enough to get lost in the wilderness in a canoe. From the air, it is one big map of sameness. I did not have any idea where I was—and I did not expect that Lindbergh did, since this was his first time in the area. I was becoming a little worried by the time he took back the controls of the plane. When he did, he just turned the plane around and flew right back to our landing place—one little spot of water in this great, immense area of land and water and trees.

It had been a beautiful day. Lindbergh was most impressed with Kabetogama. He said, "This is just glorious scenery. I don't know if there's any place in the world that rivals this. This would make a wonderful national park." We had won an important ally.

We started back to the Twin Cities on a Saturday morning. I had invited Lindbergh to spend the weekend at our home. I told him, "There's a great writer and naturalist, Charles, that you might enjoy meeting. His name is Sigurd Olson. He lives in Ely. If I could get him on the phone, he could meet us in Virginia, which is on our way back to the Cities, and you'd have a chance to meet him. I think you'd find it worthwhile." "Fine, that's agreeable," he said.

I called Olson and said we had Charles Lindbergh with us. Like many Americans of our generation, he was excited by the very mention of the Lone Eagle's name. I said, "We can meet at the Coates Hotel coffee shop in about an hour." "I'll be there."

That is how Fridley and I had the privilege of watching these two great Minnesotans explore each other, gently but persistently getting acquainted. Olson had brought two or three of his books to give to Lindbergh, which he graciously accepted and began reading the next night.

On the way home, Fridley and I did some contriving about how to bring Lindbergh's enthusiasm for the park to the attention of Congress. We knew that Lindbergh made it a practice never to do press conferences and interviews. We made this proposal to him: "We have to get an act of Congress. You can help us get attention in Washington. You can make this a national issue. If you say you think it ought to be done, that will give it incredible prestige. How you feel about this issue needs to be told to the people. We know you don't want a press conference, and we know you don't want to answer reporters' questions. But how would this format appeal to you? You and I sit together in our living room and visit. We talk about our trip, what you saw, and how you reacted to it. We talk about how wonderful it would be if Kabetogama Peninsula became a national park. Some newspaper people would be present, but they would say nothing. They would not ask any questions. They would just be observers, taking notes and recording what they hear. They get a story that way." He said, "I think I can do that, as long as I don't have to answer any questions. I want to keep my record consistent that I don't have press conferences."

That Saturday night and Sunday morning, I called some newspaper reporters. I said, "We have a special guest at our home. I can't tell you who it is, but I think you'd be interested to meet him. You're not going to be able to ask him any questions. He doesn't do press conferences, but we're going to be talking about a trip we've had to the Kabetogama area and the possibility of that becoming a national park. He'll express some reaction to it, and you can take all the notes you want to take. You can write whatever you want to write about the experience, but you have to come if it's going to happen."

They said, "Who is it, Elmer? Don't give us this stuff that you can't tell." I said, "Please, believe me, I can't tell you. I'd tell you if I could. You know that. I'll tell you this much: you wouldn't want to miss it. You better come. I'll promise you, you won't be disappointed."

About four or five reporters came, as did Gov. Harold LeVander. They were certainly not disappointed. Lindbergh was more than enthusiastic about the park proposal. He was eloquent. He had a deep sense about the connection between man and nature. One of the reporters present said later, upon his retirement, that the high spot of his experiences with famous people was that Sunday afternoon with Charles Lindbergh.

The next day, there were front-page headlines, "Lindy Endorses Voyageurs Park." We had a big local story, and the clippings we wanted to send to Washington.

Before Lindbergh left our home after his weekend visit, the two of us went for a walk in our St. Anthony Park neighborhood. We headed in the direction of the St. Paul campus of the University of Minnesota. We entered what was then something of a neighborhood war zone over the issue of parking. Student cars had become such a problem that the neighbors had obtained a two-hour limit on parking on the two streets adjoining Cleveland Avenue. The neighborhood did its own policing of the ordinance. Residents would be out each morning, marking car tires with chalk. In the afternoon, they would report the license numbers of the vehicles with chalk marks still visible.

As Lindbergh and I proceeded, we encountered Frank Paskewitz, a man I knew, marking cars. I thought, Frank is going to have a treat. So when we came near, I said, "We've had a special guest with us over the weekend. I'd like to have you meet Gen. Charles Lindbergh." Lindbergh said, "How do you do, Mr. Paskewitz." Paskewitz responded politely but quickly turned his attention back to the car whose tire he was about to mark. It was clear to me that Lindbergh's identity had not registered with him. We went on with our walk.

The name I had spoken must have clicked in Paskewitz's head after we passed. When I saw him again some days later, he struck his forehead with his palm to indicate his unhappiness with his response to Lindbergh. "Elmer, I've got to tell you, I've quit marking those damn cars," he said. Paskewitz had demonstrated how being caught up in trivial matters can cause one to miss bigger opportunities.

Lindbergh did more for the Voyageurs' cause. He wrote letters. One, written to me in longhand from Hong Kong, said, "What a beautiful and extraordinary area it is! With the combination of flora and fauna, islands, inland lakes, and forested hills, it would make one of the world's great national parks. It would be tragic to miss such an opportunity." He spent time in Washington, meeting with congressmen. He would telephone their offices and simply announce, "This is Charles Lindbergh. I'd like to come in and visit with you about a national park." Calendars would clear like magic when secretaries heard those words. Because Lindbergh was a national figure, he gave our project national status. That inclined many congressmen to support us before our bill ever reached them for a vote.

After the Voyageurs' authorization was won, I saw Lindbergh intermittently. He was traveling all over the world. When we got together, we indulged in long talks about many things. One night we discussed at length the comparative merits of two new planes, Boeing's B-57 and the French Concorde. He predicted—accurately—that the Boeing plane would become an industry standard because of its low cost of operation, while the Concorde was too expensive to make a big showing commercially.

Lindbergh used to say, "Elmer, one thing, they have never let me fly beyond Paris." By that, he meant that all that came later in his life was regarded as secondary to his achievement in 1927. For example, he was especially proud of helping the French surgeon Alexis Carrel develop the first heart perfusion pump, which made open heart surgery possible. Lindbergh and Carrel worked together in the 1930s, with Lindbergh a volunteer at the Rockefeller Institute, and became such good friends that the Lindberghs lived for a time in a home on the island of Illiec off the coast of France that the Carrels owned. Had anyone else been so instrumental in such an important medical advance, he probably would have received a Nobel Prize. Lindbergh's contribution to the pump was soon forgotten.

We discussed the pump's role in organ transplants during our long drive back to the Twin Cities from International Falls in October 1969. Transplants were still something of a novelty then, though Carrel and Lindbergh had foreshadowed them when they developed their pump. Yet Lindbergh said that day that if his organs failed, he would not be inclined to undergo a transplant. He wanted his own life to come to its natural conclusion without that kind of heroic medical intervention.

Few people know about Lindbergh's work at the Mayo Clinic beginning in 1942, testing how the human body reacts to travel at high altitudes and high levels of acceleration. He showed me pictures of those tests, which portray him with distorted features. As a result of his tests, the oxygen equipment used by high-altitude pilots was modified in a way that probably saved many lives.

In 1974, Lindbergh became ill with cancer. He was hospitalized in New York. When it became apparent that he would not recover, he arranged to be moved to Maui, Hawaii. The Lindberghs had built a home in a remote place called Kipahulu in 1969 on property they purchased from retired Pan Am executive Sam Pryor. It was not to there, but to the guest cottage of a friend that was closer to the local medical clinic, that Lindbergh retreated, and died on August 26. He was buried quickly, without embalming, in a little churchyard where Pryor's wife had been buried not long before.

I was aware that Lindbergh was ill, but I was not in contact with him in his final days. I later met Dr. Milton Howell, his physician at the end. Dr. Howell said that Lindbergh wanted to die and be buried in Hawaii because it was the one place where he was not pestered by curiosity seekers. He felt he was allowed to be himself.

I like to think he felt that way with me, too. We had a common mission: Voyageurs Park. But when we were together, we were just two people who liked each other. I never exploited our friendship. I did not want to impose on him in the slightest way. I loved him for the unique man that he was.

My association with Lindbergh did not end with his death. I became involved with the Charles A. Lindbergh Foundation, a group organized in New York in 1976 by Apollo 11 astronaut Neil Armstrong and World War II flying ace Jimmy Doolittle. The foundation was incorporated in 1977. Differences arose between the Lindbergh family and the group's early supporters, and the organization became relatively inactive for a time. When I became foundation president in 1982, I thought it belonged in Minnesota. I conducted foundation business out of my office for a time and then arranged for its headquarters to move to Minneapolis in 1985. It moved again in 1999, to Anoka. I was the foundation's president through 1985, then chairman of its board in 1986 and 1987.

The Lindbergh Foundation awarded grants to scientists seeking to discover a healthy balance between technology and nature, often through environmental research. The amount of the grant was uniformly $10,580—the price Lindbergh paid for the plane he flew to Paris in 1927. We thought that if Lindbergh could fly across the ocean on $10,580, scientists might rise to a challenge to do something great with the same amount. A grant from the Lindbergh Foundation became a badge of recognition, which enabled the recipients to attract other money. Once a year, the foundation had a meeting at which our grant recipients would report on their work. At the same event, we gave a Lindbergh Award to some noted person who had contributed something to advance Lindbergh's interests. Among the people we honored were environmentalist Russell Train, oceanographer Jacques Cousteau, anthropologist Thor Heyerdahl, and pilot Jimmy Doolittle.

I met Doolittle for the first time at a Lindbergh Foundation meeting in Houston. I sat with him at dinner. He said, "Andersen, there's one thing you should do with this Lindbergh Foundation. You've got to get out to Hawaii and see that Charles's grave is made available to serious people who want to visit it and pay their respects. When you get out there, you'll find out there is some difficulty. You ought to look into it." That seared into my mind.

The next year, I assembled Russell Fridley and Florida real estate developer Jim Newton, who met Lindbergh in the mid-1930s and became his closest friend thereafter. We went to Hawaii to visit Lindbergh's grave. We learned that the little congregation in Kipahulu in whose churchyard Lindbergh was buried was dwindling in number, and that the church's parent organization wanted to rent the building to some eleemosynary organization that would agree to keep up the building and let the congregation use it for worship services. I leaped at that opportunity. The Lindbergh Foundation became the lessees of the churchyard and the church, and undertook to maintain it.

We quickly learned that the local residents did not want tourists in their neighborhood. They sought to discourage the steady flow of people to Lindbergh's grave by refusing to repair the road from Maui down to their little seaside village. It was the worst patch of road I have ever been on. The local people preferred to suffer over it themselves rather than provide easy access for some unwanted tourist bus. Some local people would purposely misdirect visitors. Standing a few hundred feet from the cemetery, some local people would tell a stranger who asked about the grave, "It's about two miles down, and turn to your right and keep going." That would send people around the whole island.

The local conflict began to touch Anne Lindbergh. Her friend Sam Pryor wanted the graveyard kept open. Local residents began to write to her, complaining about the traffic Lindbergh's grave was generating. At one point, in frustration, Anne said, "If it gets to be so bad, we'll probably have to move the remains." Somebody wrote to her in response, "That's a good idea. Why don't you do it?" It was cruel.

Newton, Fridley, and I had a plan we thought would remedy the problem. We would have the Lindbergh Foundation buy some land contiguous to the churchyard, and use it for parking and for a heavily planted garden walkway leading to the gravesite. That would channel the traffic away from local homes and shield the tourist activity from view. We even had in mind a passage from the Psalms that we would have inscribed on an archway. Unfortunately, the land we wanted was owned by a former congressman from New Jersey, who was unwilling to sell it. Sadly, nothing came of our idea. The foundation's lease on the little church was allowed to expire, and the residents got their way. The churchyard was closed to public visitors.

Don Padilla succeeded me as Lindbergh Foundation president. He brought much vigor and many good ideas to the table. He thought that in 1987, for the sixtieth anniversary of the flight, our annual meeting should be in Paris and should include a reenactment of the flight of the *Spirit of St. Louis*. We proceeded with the idea, raising money and making the proper arrangements, when we received word that the Lindbergh family was unwilling to participate. The family thought of the Lindbergh Foundation as its affair and expected us to take directions from them. It was up to me to tell Lindbergh's daughter Reeve that whether the family approved or not, the Paris event would go forward. Jim Newton prevailed on a daughter of Jon Lindbergh to represent the family there. I was so pleased that she also came to my eightieth birthday party two years later.

The sixtieth anniversary of Lindbergh's flight was a glorious occasion. We had dinner at the American embassy in Paris. Then, at Le Bourget Field, the landing of that little plane was reenacted. Just as it was taxiing up, a Concorde, by prior arrangement, flew in, touched down, and flew off again to show the contrast between 1927 and 1987. I still shiver to think about the big, sleek Concorde, sailing out of nowhere at a huge speed, dipping down, touching the ground and taking off, in salute to Charles Lindbergh. A huge crowd witnessed the spectacle. We had worked hard and raised a lot of money to make that anniversary observance possible, and had run up a deficit. At that moment, I knew it was worth it. But the family was not pleased, and Padilla paid the price. He was not elevated to chairman, as was customary after serving as president. I was hurt for him. Gradually, I eased out of the Lindbergh Foundation.

Lindbergh has been gone for twenty-five years, but he lives in my memory as a treasured friend. A new Lindbergh biography by A. Scott Berg was published in 1998 and became a bestseller. I am not alone in remembering Charles Lindbergh.

Regent

I ABANDONED MY AMBITIONS for elective office in 1966. But I did not consider myself through with public service. One position in particular appealed to me: regent of the University of Minnesota. I think that outside of elective office, it is the single most significant public service post a Minnesotan can have.

I had learned painfully in 1966 that when one wants a position in public service, one must ask for it. In early 1967, I went to see my brother-in-law, Stanley Holmquist, the new majority leader of the Minnesota Senate. Years earlier, when I was in the state senate, I had helped him put one of his constituents on the Board of Regents. I was pleased that he was willing to return the favor by advancing my candidacy for the board.

Then, as now, eight of the twelve members of the Board of Regents were selected as representatives of the eight congressional districts. The remaining four are elected by the legislature at-large. For the eight congressional district seats, legislators from each district meet in caucus to approve a candidate. Then—with rare exceptions—the full legislature simply ratifies the district choice. For me to be one of the eight regents selected in this manner, I needed the support of the Ramsey County delegation in the legislature—a group that was dominated by DFLers. The situation was further complicated by the fact that George Lawson, who had held the so-called labor seat on the Board of Regents for several decades, was stepping down. By tradition, a spot on the Board of Regents is reserved for a leader of organized labor. The candidate to fill that seat was Neil Sherburne, secretary of the state AFL-CIO, a staunch DFLer—and a resident of Ramsey County. He was a fine man, whom I knew rather well.

I had a talk with Sherburne. I said, "Neil, I know you are a fair person. Isn't it a little unfair that one district should provide the labor seat? Anybody else in that district is forever sealed off from being on the Board of Regents. Shouldn't the labor representative be one of the at-large seats? If I can get the legislature to commit itself to appoint you as an at-large regent at the first opportunity, would you defer to me now and help me in the Fourth District?" He agreed. That speaks to the kind of man he was. So does the fact that I was able to get commitments to elect Sherburne as an at-large regent from both houses. Two years later, a Republican-dominated legislature elected DFL labor leader Neil Sherburne to the Board of Regents. Today, that would be considered a minor political miracle.

Stanley Holmquist deserves major credit for engineering both my election and Sherburne's. Stanley is a remarkable man who was much admired by his colleagues of both parties in the legislature. He comes from a long line of Swedish farmers. His family settled in Hallock, Minnesota, where he was one of eight or nine children. Stanley was inspired to get an education. He convinced his parents to let him attend high school at a little church academy in Wheaton, Illinois. After a few years, he transferred to Minnehaha Academy in Minneapolis. It was there, on the debating team, that he met Edith Johnson, Eleanor's sister. Stanley loves to make speeches and enter into debates and discussions, and he has always been a man of strong convictions. He made a lasting impression on young Edith.

After high school, Stanley went to work at Lund Press, a printing company in Minneapolis. He also enrolled at the University of Minnesota, working nights and going to class during the day. He not only got a bachelor's degree but also a master's degree in education. He got a teaching job in Grove City, in central Minnesota, and spent his whole career there, rising to become superintendent of schools. He followed me into the legislature, serving as a Conservative first in the house, then the senate. We used to have rousing discussions on legislative issues. I generally took the more liberal position. I was more willing to spend government money. But when it came to education, Stanley was no penny-pincher. He was a stalwart on the side of improving educational quality during the 1960s, when debates over consolidation of country schools into city districts rocked many rural areas. He also deserves a great deal of credit for convincing the senate to go along with DFL Gov. Wendell Anderson in dramatically increasing state funding of education in 1971.

Thanks in good measure to Stanley's efforts, I became a regent in 1967. The day after my election, I went to the university campus to walk the familiar pathways and contemplate my latest connection to Minnesota's premier institution of higher learning. My mind rolled over the almost continuous association I had enjoyed with the university since 1929. I met Eleanor there, almost immediately after becoming a student. I learned a little about political leadership by becoming president of the Board of Associated

Students of the School of Business. The debating team honed my speaking ability. I received wonderful training in business administration. The professors whose classes made me restive in 1930 imparted lessons that proved to be invaluable. The course in analysis of financial statements that I thought I would never use may have been the most useful class I took. When I was a legislator, I served on the committee that set the university appropriation and provided for its growth. As governor, I had a close relationship with university officials. Tears came to my eyes as I reflected on my new relationship, as a member of the Board of Regents. I think I may have been more thrilled at achieving that position than at being elected governor.

The university is an extremely complex institution. That is both its great strength and a handicap. The interconnectedness of myriad disciplines and the freedom afforded individual scholars are crucial to advancing human knowledge. But the same complexity makes the institution hard to understand, let alone manage. When I was governor, examining the university's budget, I thought, my goodness! I was in the state senate for ten years, approving university appropriations, and I am only now getting some view of it. When I was a regent, I had a similar revelation. I thought, only now, as a regent, am I beginning to understand what this university is.

One thing I learned is that the fabric that weaves thousands of scholars into one university is fragile. People think that the University of Minnesota is a powerful institution, and in certain aspects it is. But the threads that hold it together and make it a center of excellence are quite fragile. I believe Thomas Carlisle was right when he spoke of a university as a "community of scholars." The faculty forms the heart of the university. The faculty attracts the students, teaches the students, does the research. I thought that to be a good steward of the university, a regent must be attuned to the faculty. I made a point to become acquainted with the chair of the Faculty Consultative Committee, the faculty's elected committee concerned with university governance.

A university faculty includes scholars of two kinds. Some pursue their discipline with great vigor and go wherever their research leads. They make an academic contribution, but they are not institutionally loyal. The other kind settle in and make a career of an institution as well as a discipline. Those faculty members are to be treasured, for they make an institution strong. I think of a physicist who led the work in cracking the atom, Al Nier. Though he was a distinguished scientist with a national reputation, he devoted his whole career to the University of Minnesota and was dean of the Institute of Technology. I also admired Walter Johnson, whom I knew as "Corky" when he grew up in southeast Minneapolis, the son of our friends and fellow Grace Church parishioners Ruby and Walter Johnson. He was an outstanding teacher who had a chance to be the dean of the Institute of Technology but preferred to make his contribution in the classroom and his labs. He, too, spent his entire adult lifetime serving the University of Minnesota. There have been dozens, perhaps hundreds more who have done the same. Minnesota owes them a great debt of gratitude.

I came to know several faculty members well. Sam Krislov, chairman of the consultative committee and a distinguished professor of political science, was one. He deserves some of the credit for the new law school building that was built in 1978. Even though the old facilities were woefully inadequate, legislators were slow to authorize a new building. When Krislov and a group of students went to the legislature in 1974 to make the case for a new building, Krislov was absolutely eloquent. I always felt his testimony made the difference in securing the funding.

William G. "Gerry" Shepherd, an electrical engineering professor who went on to serve as academic vice president, was another faculty friend. He was a consultant in the development of the pacemaker at Medtronic. He also led the faculty portion of the university's $250 million capital fund drive, "The Minnesota Campaign," from 1986 to 1989. Faculty donations exceeded their quota by a substantial amount.

I was always an advocate for adequate compensation for the faculty. Talented people in any field deserve high salaries. If the university is going to attract top scholars, not just from other academic institutions but from private industry, they must pay accordingly. But in one part of the university, the compensation system for faculty was out of control and needed to be checked. That was in the Medical School. It was understood and accepted, then as now, that some Medical School faculty also practice medicine privately and are paid privately. But in those years, there was no limit on their earnings. Surgeons in particular were earning fabulous incomes. We thought there should be some limit on the amount of money a faculty member made doing work that the public might see as moonlighting. We decided that a faculty member's outside income should not exceed the amount of his or her salary. Earnings beyond that should go into a common departmental pool. Without attracting undue public notice, we brought our view to the faculty and gained acceptance. We thought we had resolved what could have been an embarrassing and difficult situation for the university, had it been given public scrutiny. Regrettably, it did not stay resolved in the 1980s. The embarrassing news stories we feared twenty years earlier were finally written in the early 1990s, and once again, the university had to establish new rules for the private-practice income of its medical school faculty.

We confronted another issue that would recur throughout the remainder of the century: the management of University Hospital. When I joined the Board of Regents, it also functioned as the hospital's governing board. I quickly saw the difficulty with that arrangement. The regents could not begin to give attention to all issues facing the hospital. The briefing papers sent to regents were so voluminous that I used to think the hospital was trying to intimidate us by giving us more material than we could absorb. I was determined not to sit silently, meek and unprepared, when hospital matters came before the board. It took a lot of time, but I waded through those reports. Nevertheless, I saw the value in creating a separate Board of Governors for University Hospitals and Clinics, subject to the Board of Regents. We did that in 1974. The first chair was Harry Atwood of Northwestern Life Insurance Company, a fine man. Immediately, he became one of the busiest people in town.

Dan Gainey, owner and president of Josten's Company in Owatonna, was the longest-serving member of the Board of Regents when I joined it. He was first elected to the board in 1939. Though he was not the board chairman, he was its dominant voice—and he was not much interested in change. I have often observed that people who are in positions of power for many years tend to lose their sense of stewardship and begin to think of the organization they serve as their own. Gainey was getting close to retirement, so no attempt was made to unseat him. But I allied myself with Les Malkerson, Otto Silha, Fred Hughes, and, later, Neil Sherburne to maintain that board members should not serve more than two six-year terms. That has been the usual pattern since then.

A new university president was also arriving in 1967. O. Meredith Wilson was departing, and the board had selected Malcolm Moos to replace him. I had known Moos, and his father before him, through politics. His father was an insurance man in St. Paul whose involvement in Republican politics had led to his appointment as postmaster. Malcolm had been a speechwriter for President Eisenhower and was the author of what may have been the most oft-quoted speech of Eisenhower's presidency, his warning in 1960 about the overweening power of the nation's military-industrial complex. Moos worked closely with the president's brother, Dr. Milton Eisenhower. I had lunch with Milton Eisenhower when he was president of Johns Hopkins University and asked him about Moos. He said, "He writes well, but Ike would send the speeches down to me to check over, and I frequently made some changes."

Moos served the university best in two ways. One was through his skill as a spokesman for the institution, and indeed for all of higher education. The other was in his concern for students—something that ought to be a prime responsibility of any president. He was excellent in that regard, as he showed with his handling of the students protesting the Vietnam War and other grievances between 1969 and 1972.

Board meetings were occasionally the scene of those protests. We chose an approach to the protesters that I thought of as resilient, as opposed to brittle. We did not bar protesters from our meetings. We decided that if the students wanted to have the microphone to say something, we would let them have it. We would give them a little time. We told them, "We want to hear your views. We understand some of your concerns, but you can't interfere with the education of others. If you want to interfere with us, we'll accept that. You come anytime you want, and we'll listen to you. But don't think you can stop the educational process of the university. We simply cannot permit that." We had that understanding with the protesters.

There were many good things about the student movement of those years. The students involved were bright. Their fundamental disagreement was with hypocrisy, against actions that were promoted with a false justification, and against edicts that were proclaimed and not followed. The students saw a lot of phoniness all around, and they wanted to clean it all out with a style of protest that would attract attention.

I was among those on the board who were sympathetic with the students' views, particularly about the war in Vietnam. I thought the war was a mistake. I am never sympathetic with violence of any kind. But neither did I approve of students attempting to take over a regents' meeting. Democracy provides a complicated but usable facility for societal change—the ballot box. I am for doing things through that channel.

The most vigorous antiwar demonstration occurred in May 1972. Students barricaded Washington Avenue and maintained a three-day siege. Gov. Wendell Anderson decided that the situation warranted the presence of the National Guard. I did not think that step was truly necessary. The protests had been largely peaceful. But Anderson was getting phone calls from worried people who would demand, "What's going on at the university? Why don't they crack down on those students?"

A state National Guard officer met with Moos to discuss the situation. Moos asked me to sit in on their conversation. I was never more proud of a university president than I was of Moos at that meeting. He said, "If the governor wishes and would feel more comfortable to have the National Guard here, and they'll take their instructions from you and you from us, we can live with that. But they cannot come on the campus armed." The Guard officer said, "There's no way they go anywhere without being armed. Our National Guard is always armed." Quietly, Moos said, "I have to tell you, they won't come on this campus armed. We're not going to have armed soldiers coming after our students. What do you want the students to do in response, get armed too?" It was a tense exchange, but Moos prevailed. The National Guard came to campus but as a quiet presence, not a threat.

One violent eruption occurred while the Guard was present, but it was a clash between students and the Minneapolis police, not the Guard. Former police officer Charlie Stenvig was mayor of Minneapolis in 1972, and he directed the Minneapolis police to take a hard line against protesters who had barricaded Washington Avenue near Coffman Union. A scuffle was the result, leading to several dozen injuries. Though the injuries were not life-threatening, the ugly incident showed how volatile the campus mood was. Only a handful of students were actively engaged in protests. But if those students had been mishandled in any way, literally thousands stood ready to come to their rescue. The day the police began to rough up student protesters, a crowd immediately gathered. If Moos had not taken the approach he did with the National Guard, Minnesota might have been the scene of the tragedy that befell Kent State in Ohio. He understood that the greatest damage to human relationships is often done when people assume a position that is too brittle. It is far better to be resilient and flexible, like grass in a windstorm that is bowed but never broken. It is to Moos's credit that the University of Minnesota got through the Vietnam-era protests without serious bloodshed.

But by the early 1970s, Moos's presidency was also facing mounting criticism, particularly from the faculty. Moos was behaving more and more as a figurehead rather than an actual manager of the university. He thought of the university presidency as a fine rostrum from which he could express his opinions on a wide range of educational issues. He was neglecting too many of his responsibilities internal to the institution. For example, a president is expected to preside at meetings of the Faculty Consultative Committee. That is the one place where elected representatives of the faculty consider issues that pertain to the university in general, not to one department or college. Serious matters of campus governance are discussed and decided in those meetings. Moos not only would not preside; he would not attend the meetings. It appeared that he did not want to be bothered. Neither did he want to have much to do with many other aspects of university life. He was so detached that he was not knowledgeable about some of what was happening on campus.

As the faculty's dissatisfaction mounted, agitation for change began to consume some of the university's best minds. Collegiate politics can be very harsh. I used to tell people that I had seen corporate politics, party politics, and governmental politics, and compared with them, collegiate politics is the toughest. When a faculty turns on a college president, his remaining tenure is likely to be brief. The Regents' Professors, a small group of people who are outstanding in both their scholarship and their dedication to the university, became spokespeople for the faculty and brought their concerns to the regents. Their message: Malcolm Moos was not being the manager that a university president must be. The board could not ignore such a strong message from such a respected group.

I became chairman of the board in 1971. That meant it fell primarily to me to carry official messages from the board to Moos. I talked with him about his relationship with the faculty and with the Consultative Committee in particular. He did not want to change anything he was doing, and he refused to believe that faculty unhappiness could in any way threaten his position. After more than one such conversation, I had to speak quite firmly. "Malcolm, I have to tell you that the majority of the board is very concerned. They are about of a mind to ask for your resignation. You are going to have to either function as a hands-on manager of this university, or leave." I had put him on notice.

This back-and-forth between Moos and me, speaking for the board, went on for months. Meanwhile, I had conversations with every member of the board. Politics had taught me that whenever you want to make a major change, you had better have the votes before you proceed. Fred Hughes, a regent from St. Cloud whom I had appointed to a vacancy on the board when I was governor, was sympathetic to Moos. He had known Moos for many years and admired his relations with students. He was reluctant to support any effort to ease Moos out. Hughes finally acquiesced, but he remained unhappy and did not stay on the board much longer.

I did not make a final move until I was sure that any board vote, should one become necessary, would be unanimous. Then, when no change in Moos's behavior came, it was clear that the board needed to act. Just before a decisive meeting of the board, I received a call from Dan Gainey, who by then had left the board. He had been much involved in Moos's selection as president. I suspected that he may have been calling at Moos's request, to very belatedly see if he could save his job. Gainey asked, "Elmer, how serious is this thing? Malcolm says that there's talk of his leaving." I did not want him to give Moos any illusions. We were past the point of negotiation. I said, "Dan, it's so serious that if he doesn't resign by the meeting this week, there's going to be a resolution offered calling for his resignation, and it will pass unanimously. That's where it is."

Gainey needed to ask, because the press had not reported any problem between Moos and the board. The board I headed believed strongly that any public display of difference between the president and the regents was unhealthy for the institution. We worked hard at resolving our differences before meetings, so that we would have unanimous votes in the public forum. We would have considered it a terrible breach of good conduct for any regent to run to the press with a tale about our dissatisfaction with Moos. There was a keen understanding on the board that our main purpose was to select a president, support him publicly as long as we could, and then replace him if and when we could not. The famous Harvard University president Charles William Eliot once said that there is only one motion that should ever be considered at a regents' meeting: Be it resolved that the president resign. If it fails, the board should adjourn and go home. That comment overstates the limits on a regent's role, but it pinpoints the proper focus of a university governing board.

The next day, August 9, 1973, Moos presented us with a letter of resignation. I told him, "Malcolm, there will be a good provision for your retirement. None of us are going to talk publicly about this. As far as we are concerned, you are resigning to pursue other interests. You've made your contribution, and you are simply moving on." That is how the resignation was presented to the press and the public. It was a graceful separation. Within a few weeks, Moos accepted the chairmanship of the Center for the Study of Democratic Institutions, based in Santa Barbara, California—a position that seemed a perfectly suitable next step for him. Leaving Minnesota was painful for him and his wife, and I regretted that. But a regent must recognize a limit in the extent to which one person's well-being can prevail over the university's best interests.

We turned immediately to finding a new president. As board chairman, I had a major hand in establishing a search process. I did not want to advertise for the position. I had long since learned that when people apply for an advertised job, there is often something wrong where they are—and usually it is with them. Instead, I wanted an aggressive effort at recruiting people we found desirable. Further, I wanted to visit those people personally, at their campuses, not begin by inviting them to Minnesota. I suggested that we have one regent and one faculty member make those visits jointly. That way, the faculty would be an integral part of the selection process. Those guidelines served us well.

My faculty partner, classics professor William McDonald, and I went to visit the young president of the University of New York at Binghamton, C. Peter Magrath, who we had heard was a promising comer. He had not applied for the Minnesota presidency, but that did not deter us in the slightest. We spent two days in Binghamton and gained a very favorable impression of Magrath. We met his wife and family, too. When we boarded the plane to come home, I did not want to make the first comment. I wanted to get the first comment from McDonald, whose opinion I had come to respect. For a long time, I just sat there—and he just sat there. Finally, he spoke up. "Do you realize, Elmer, that we were with that young man for two days, and he didn't make a single mistake?"

I made one other trip, with the university's acclaimed economist Walter Heller. He and I went to California to visit David S. Saxon, executive vice chancellor of the University of California at Los Angeles. Saxon seemed to have everything we were seeking. He was just superb. After two days with him, we had no doubt that we wanted him to come to Minnesota for a round of on-campus interviews. He initially refused. I argued with him, "The University of Minnesota is not an unimportant institution. The presidency there would put you in command of a situation, instead of in a secondary position. Maybe you will someday become president of the University of California, but maybe not. Maybe it would be easier if you were president somewhere else first, and they wanted you back in the worst way." I made the case that he practically owed it to higher education to come and visit Minnesota.

Saxon relented and agreed to come. He and his wife stayed at the governor's residence, then occupied by Gov. Wendell Anderson. Anderson was not there when we arrived. When he finally came, Mrs. Saxon looked up at Minnesota's handsome young governor and said, "I don't believe it!" He did not look anything like the politicians she knew in California.

The next day, we took Saxon to a private meeting downtown with a select group of civic leaders. Saxon made just one mistake that day, but it was a big one. I always thought afterward that his remark was a jab at me, because I had argued with him pretty vigorously about the fine situation he would find in Minnesota. He said, "There's one thing I know: Minnesota can't have two universities. If I were to come here, it would be one university. Everything else would be ancillary." He had the University of Minnesota-Duluth in mind, which he had learned I had helped to establish in new quarters when I was a legislator in the 1950s. He also knew of the ambitions of the Duluth faculty and northeastern Minnesota residents to add a medical school and law school to their campus. They wanted a full-blown university at Duluth, even though it would serve a rather limited population. We had not been out of the meeting two hours before my phone began to ring with calls from the Iron Range. Legislators, civic leaders, and friends from that area were all saying, "Don't hire that guy!" Duluth marshaled all its warriors, and Saxon's candidacy was sunk.

Something unfortunate also happened during Saxon's visit. He happened to be Jewish. One regent made an ill-advised anti-Semitic comment. Soon the word around town was that he was being passed over for the presidency because of his religion. That was untrue and terribly unfair.

Nevertheless, after his visit, Saxon was off our list. Several years later, he achieved his dream of becoming president of the California system. I wrote him a letter saying, "Congratulations. I think we helped a little to get you there." We showed California officials that they risked losing him if they did not promote him soon.

After the Saxon interview, our attention turned again to the president at Binghamton. He was bright, active, and full of ideas, and—perhaps most appealing of all—he was eager. We thought he would give the university vital, invigorating leadership. C. Peter Magrath became president of the University of Minnesota on November 26, 1974. He was forty-one years old.

Magrath's presidency came at the start of a long period of questioning and rethinking of the university's mission. The institution that had evolved somewhat haphazardly through the decades was suddenly being seen by some as too big, too costly, unfocused, and poorly managed. Legislators particularly were starting to ask hard questions about how the university was spending state money. Concern was growing that while Minnesota had built a big university, it had not built an excellent one. The questions about the university's mission and direction had little to do with Magrath's tenure. Yet it fell to him to respond, which he did with middling results. I think history will credit his presidency with more achievement than we who remember that period do today.

Magrath made Ken Keller, a professor of chemical engineering, his academic vice president. Together, the two of them worked to recast the university as a center of excellence, particularly in research, and to argue that educating the masses was more directly the responsibility of the state universities, community colleges, and technical colleges. That was the start of a twenty-year debate that was often framed as "access versus excellence"—an oversimplification but illustrative of the tension the university experienced as it sought to change. Magrath inspired a rethinking of the university's mission, but Keller was the workman who carried it through.

Magrath was such a young man when he became president that I did not expect him to end his career in Minnesota. I did not think that would be good for him, or for the university. In about 1980, I decided to share that opinion with him. I said, "Peter, this is going to come a little as a shock, maybe, but I think you've done about as much for the university as you can do. You're riding high, and you're doing well. There's no problem. There's no uprising. Everything is in good order. But I think that if you plan to stay in this field, now would be a good time to look around."

Magrath's wife was offended when Magrath relayed our conversation to her, so I had a separate visit with her. "I'm not trying to be hurtful," I explained. "I was only saying that there are advantages to making a move when you're on top, rather than waiting until things change. One thing is certain in life: Circumstances will change."

The view of Magrath's presidency then was reasonably positive but not enthusiastic. He did not create a strong public impression. He was active and creative, and he worked intensely hard. He set the tone for the changes that were to come.

A few years passed before he took my advice and sought the presidency of the University of Missouri at Columbia, Missouri. He left Minnesota in 1984. Keller was made acting president and then hired for the permanent position in 1985. I thought he was destined for a great presidency.

By that time, I had left the Board of Regents. I chose to depart in 1975, before the conclusion of my second six-year term. My successor in the Fourth Congressional District seat on the board was George Latimer, who four years later would become an able mayor of St. Paul. But I was still much engaged on campus as an officer and president of the University Foundation, the institution's fundraising arm. And my ally in Republican politics, David Lilly, was the dean of the university's School of Business Administration, and on his way to joining university administration as vice president of finance. He kept me connected to Morrill Hall as well.

I watched from that vantage point as Keller came under attack in a manner that I thought was quite unfair. He was faulted for extravagance in remodeling the president's residence, Eastcliff, and in refurnishing his office in Morrill Hall. I thought the only real mistake he made was buying a very expensive desk and credenza, when he could have gotten a wonderful desk from the Minnesota Historical Society for nothing. For example, when I was governor, I was allowed to use the desk that had belonged to Knute Nelson, who served Minnesota as both governor and a U.S. senator in the late nineteenth and early twentieth centuries.

Keller was right to try to upgrade Eastcliff. The place had been deteriorating for years. It had been given to the university for use as a president's residence a half century earlier. Like so many unsolicited gifts, it went unappreciated and uncared for. It was built as a private residence, but it was used as much as a reception hall. Yet it was never properly adapted to that use.

When Moos was president, the Board of Regents established a committee to examine what was needed to bring the place up to decent standards. We determined that the needed repairs would cost several hundred thousand dollars. When we came to Moos with the estimate of what it was going to cost, he said, "We can't do anything like that in this period of unrest and student concern. This is no time to be spending a lot of money on what will just be considered to be the president's residence. Forget it for now."

Then, along came Magrath, and we had another committee and another study. But he said, "We're not able to get faculty salary increases out of the legislature. I don't want to be a party to spending a lot of money on my residence when I can't get an increase in faculty salaries. Please, forget it for awhile." Keller came next. He bit the Eastcliff bullet—and it exploded in his face. Years later, when I related that history to him, he said, "That shows we had two smart presidents and one dumb one."

Keller resigned under fire in March 1988. Under the circumstances, he did the right thing. I felt then, and every other time when trouble befell the university, that the Board of Regents had a crucial role to play. They must communicate enough with each other and with the administration in private so that they can present a united front in public and help stabilize the institution. It is when the regents are divided that real trouble ensues. The regents are critical strands in that university fabric I often speak about— the fabric that is big and seems strong but is really quite delicate. It is ultimately a fabric of human relationships, and therefore must be treated tenderly. During the mid-1990s, when the regents seemed to be at war with the faculty and President Nils Hasselmo over tenure, I wrote an editorial headlined, "Nurture University, Don't Manage It." I was trying to make an important point about what the essence of a university is—its people. People respond better to care and nurture than to cold, dictatorial management.

President Urho Kekkonen awarded Elmer Andersen the Commander Cross of the Finnish Lion Order in Helsinki in 1963.

Elmer Andersen and Republican presidential candidate Barry Goldwater had a brief exchange at the 1964 Republican National Convention. Elmer worked hard for Goldwater's rival, New York Gov. Nelson Rockefeller, at the convention in San Francisco, to no avail.

Julian Andersen was joined by his parents as he graduated from Carleton College in June 1964.

Elmer Andersen and Charles Lindbergh visited Kabetogama Peninsula together on October 3 and 4, 1969.

Elmer Andersen and Charles Lindbergh walked and chatted outside the Andersens'
Hoyt Avenue home after Lindbergh's weekend stay there in October 1969.

On behalf of the Minnesota Historical Society, past president Elmer Andersen received a sketch of Fort Snelling by Seth Eastman, completed in 1866. It was given to the society in 1973 by W. A. Straus, chairman of Northern Natural Gas Company.

Four Minnesota governors and U.S. Rep. John Blatnik assembled in May 1971 for the signing of state legislation authorizing the creation of Voyageurs National Park. *From left:* Harold LeVander, Elmer L. Andersen, Wendell Anderson, Karl Rolvaag.

On August 7, 1971, the Voyageurs National Park Association transferred land it had acquired to the new park. The occasion was marked by a ceremony at Kettle Falls at which Elmer Andersen spoke. Behind him to the left is his longtime assistant Rita Shemesh.

Elmer and Eleanor Andersen with Bruce Larson, author of a biography of Charles Lindbergh's father, at the dedication of the Lindbergh Center at the aviator's boyhood home in Little Falls, Minnesota, September 1973.

Emily Andersen became her father's partner on environmental projects.

Regents' chair Elmer Andersen bids a fond farewell in November 1973 to fellow regent Josie Johnson, who served on the university's governing board for two years before a change in her husband's employment necessitated her departure from the state. Johnson had worked closely with Elmer on civil rights legislation when he was a legislator and governor.

Two governors flanked C. Peter Magrath at his inauguration as University of Minnesota president in November 1974. Former Gov. Elmer Andersen was chair of the Board of Regents; Wendell Anderson was Minnesota's sitting governor.

Eleanor and Elmer enjoy a quiet moment in the Andersen Horticultural Library at the Minnesota Landscape Arboretum on the day of its dedication, June 26, 1974.

Tony Andersen became president of H. B. Fuller Company in 1971, and succeeded his father as chief executive officer in 1974.

When in 1976 Elmer fulfilled his longtime dream of owning a newspaper, he decided he needed more training in journalism. So he enrolled in a two-week skills course sponsored by the Minnesota Newspaper Association. He worked especially hard at learning photojournalism skills.

Three CEOs of H. B. Fuller Company gathered for a portrait in the early 1990s. Elmer is flanked by his son Tony and Walter Kissling.

In 1989, Elmer and Eleanor presented their gift of an endowed chair in the Carlson School of Management to Nils Hasselmo, president of the University of Minnesota. Their gift is called the Elmer L. Andersen Chair of Corporate Responsibility.

Deer Lake Farm remained a family gathering spot, even after the dairy operation ceased. A mid-1990s summer weekend brought together, *from left,* Amy Andersen, her husband, Timothy Wilson, their daughter, Shelby, Tony, Elmer, Eleanor, Julian, Emily, and Julian's son Nathan.

Eleanor and Shelby visit Elizabeth Pond, named after Eleanor's mother, at Deer Lake Farm.

The Gustav A. and Elizabeth Johnson
Land Preserve

To honor the memory of Gustav A. and
Elizabeth Johnson of Minneapolis,
who purchased this land in 1934
and preserved its character.

Erected by family members
August 10, 1996

In 1996, the family placed a plaque on a large boulder at what had been Deer Lake Farm, honoring the vision and legacy of Eleanor's parents.

Emily, Julian, and Tony joined Elmer and Eleanor for the dedication of the plaque at Deer Lake Farm.

More than six hundred friends helped Elmer celebrate his ninetieth birthday on June 26, 1999. After Tom Swain's tribute to Eleanor, she stood to acknowledge the crowd's applause and her husband's kiss.

Keller's departure under fire gave new impetus to a proposal for chang-ing the selection process for regents. It was a proposal that originated in the mid-1980s within the University Alumni Association. I was a member of the alumni committee that recommended the creation of an advisory coun-cil, appointed by the legislature but not including legislators as members, that would recruit, screen, and nominate regents' candidates to the legisla-ture in advance of sessions occurring in odd-numbered years. The idea lan-guished for a while but suddenly looked good to legislators when they saw how a scandal at the university, such as the one that ended Keller's presiden-cy, could someday spatter them too. While legislators wanted to reserve the final selection of regents to themselves, they saw merit in sharing the screen-ing responsibility with someone else.

That is how the Regents Candidate Advisory Council was born in 1989. I was a founding member and served a six-year term. My colleagues on that initial council included Tom Swain, Kenneth Dayton, and other respected people from around the state. We were a group that the legislature could scarcely ignore. We struggled to reduce partisan considerations in the selec-tion of regents, going so far as to prohibit questioning would-be regents about their party affiliation when we screened them. But partisanship re-mains a problem in regents' selection.

I consider the advisory council an improvement over regents' selection controlled exclusively by the legislature. But no selection process is perfect. Mistakes have been made, particularly in the name of increasing diversity on the Board of Regents. That is why I have proposed the creation of a new body, a president's advisory council, of about thirty people from many places and walks of life in Minnesota, to advise both the university's presi-dent and regents about governance issues. A large advisory body would more easily reflect the state's diverse population and would ease the pressure on the legislature to elevate people to the Board of Regents for reasons other than good judgment and ability.

Making university governance as strong as it can be is well worth what-ever effort and sacrifice it takes, because no institution is more important to Minnesota's future than the University of Minnesota. Indeed, all of higher education in this state deserves more prominence and a higher level of stew-ardship from state government.

I have long believed that four years of liberal arts education today is comparable to what high school education was in the life of a person when it became free in the late nineteenth century. Public funding of education should include four years of tuition-free liberal arts education. No one should be expected to begin a career without ample general education in the world of ideas, history, languages, and the social sciences. American students study European and American history, but most of them complete their formal education having learned little about the history and culture of the rest of the world. In the global economy of the twenty-first century, that will not do. If we as a state and a nation are going to shine in the years ahead, it will be in direct proportion to the level of education we give our young people. And it will depend on the extent to which we cultivate in them the idea that the purpose of their education is to help them serve others. Service to humanity should be the ultimate goal of all education and of every life.

New Career

I TURNED SIXTY-FIVE in 1974. To me, that birthday did not mean retirement; it meant new opportunities. It was time to pass the leadership of H. B. Fuller Company to our son Tony and to begin something new.

I had been planning this change for some time. I was always more interested in Fuller as an institution of service to its customers and employees than in my relationship to it. I wanted to leave without causing so much as a quiver in Fuller's operations.

By the early 1970s, those operations were extensive. The little one-plant glue company I bought in 1941 had become an adhesives industry leader, with twenty-seven plants and offices in the United States and ten in foreign countries. The goal I set decades before of doubling our sales volume every five years was still before us and was still being met. In 1970, we had reached about $48 million in sales. At the Christmas party that year, I spoke to the assembled workers. "We have to stand by what we believe, and act on it. What we believe is that we're going to double every five years. If we're going to double in five years, that means it will be $100 million in 1975, and that means we'll need new plants and new territory."

After I finished speaking, I was told later, some people said, "Elmer's been smoking that stuff again." But I knew it was possible. Fuller was growing in Canada, Argentina, Nicaragua, Australia, Puerto Rico, Peru, Malaysia, and our newest territory, Germany. I admired the economy that Germany had developed after World War II. We learned about a wax factory that made a product used as a cheese coating. The technology involved was similar to something we were interested in developing, a combination of resin and wax called hot melt. While I was attending an international trade meeting in Belgium, I met with an official of the wax company, Gerrit Mol, to learn more. I was not exactly a suave business executive at that first meeting. I ordered a malted milk for lunch with Mol. It was thick, and as I lifted the glass to drink it, it oozed out over my mouth and down my chest. I thought, what a miserable way to make an impression on a potential business partner.

Fortunately, Mol was understanding. We cleaned up the mess and had our visit, and it went very well. He informed me that while the company was for sale, he was not its owner but its manager. The owner was a distributor of equipment for plants like the one he owned. Further, the owner was aging and eager to sell. The plant was in Lüneburg, but the owner lived in Hamburg. I made a second trip to Europe to meet the owner, and after an evening in his home, we had no trouble coming to an understanding. Our purchase in 1972 of the firm that was eventually called LW-Fuller gave us a base from which to sell adhesives and specialty chemicals to the European continent.

I took a great fancy to Lüneburg and to our new plant there. Lüneburg is an ancient city. It was a source of salt in medieval times and became part of the Hanseatic trading league of the twelfth through the seventeenth centuries. The city is a place of beautiful architecture and well-educated people, many of whom speak English. I was so impressed that I brought Eleanor to see Lüneburg at the earliest opportunity.

Fuller's performance was tracking well with the chart that I had made about twenty years before, showing the pace we would have to maintain to double our sales every five years. But overall growth in adhesive use by major industries was slowing in the early 1970s. It was time for Fuller to diversify. We began in 1971 with the acquisition of Multi-Clean Products of St. Paul and Sep-KO Chemicals, later Monarch Chemicals, of Minneapolis. We were on our way to becoming a developer and marketer of specialized chemicals.

I had always devoted a good deal of attention to the hiring of Fuller employees. But I may have given personnel matters even greater attention in the early 1970s as I made plans for a transition in company leadership. I tried to interview the two or three finalists for every position we filled. I do that still at ECM. I ask about personal preferences, what is important to them, what they value. I try to find out what makes each person tick. I look for evidence that work for them is not a means to an end but an end in itself. To love to work is a fine attribute. I like people who love what they are doing. And I look for the potential to grow and learn. I want to have the fun of helping employees grow.

One strong hire I made in 1971 was Dave Durenberger, who was fresh from several years as chief of staff for Gov. Harold LeVander. Durenberger became Fuller's corporate legal counsel and made a special project of bringing some structure to the company's philanthropic work. He headed Fuller's Community Affairs Council, a group of employees charged with deciding which local charitable organizations would receive the 5 percent of before-tax profits that Fuller was committed to returning to the community. Durenberger was elected to the U.S. Senate in 1978.

But the most important personnel change in 1971 was Tony's elevation to Fuller's presidency, at age thirty-five. I remained as chief executive officer. But as president, Tony had responsibility for all day-to-day activities and decisions. He was also the company's roving ambassador, scouring the world for new opportunities for Fuller. In a number of years in the 1970s, he was outside the United States more than two hundred days per year.

Devotion to Fuller was nothing new for Tony. I always say that he started with the company when he was about six. He loved coming to the Eagle Street plant as a boy, and as soon as he was able, he was doing odd jobs. He spent his adolescent summers lugging barrels, labeling packing crates, and learning to operate mixing machines. After he graduated from Macalester College in 1957, he went to work full-time at Fuller. He has never wanted to work anywhere else.

I thought it important that he start in sales. Selling is the heart of any business. If Tony could learn to associate with others and lead them to change their views, as a salesperson must do, those skills would aid him in every other effort he made. I feel strongly that the single greatest factor in the success of a person is the ability to get along with other people. It helps to be smart. It helps to be hardworking. It helps to be healthy. But if you do not get along with other people, you will never reach your potential. The first thing I would check when I examined someone's résumé was how many jobs the person had had in the past ten years. If he had one job, I liked him. If he had two or three, he was passable. If it got to be four or five, I strongly suspected that he was not able to get along with other people, and that he would claim it was always the other people's fault. I always counsel: "Stay with your job. If it isn't just what you thought it was going to be when you started, apply yourself to make something out of it. Don't flit from one job to another, thinking you're going to find some gracious people somewhere who will do everything the way you want it. You will never find such a situation."

Tony's sales career began in Nebraska and Kansas. After three years, he moved to Cornwall, New York, in the Hudson River valley, to open a large territory for Fuller, stretching from northern New Jersey up the Hudson River valley to Canada. He showed what an energetic, innovative fellow he can be when he parlayed one of his favorite hobbies, skiing, into a volunteer part-time job at West Point, as a ski instructor and coach of the West Point collegiate ski team.

He returned to Minnesota in 1963 and participated in the preparations to make Fuller a public company in 1968. Wheelock Whitney, the Dain-Kalman-Quayle officer who helped us take that step, took notice of Tony and became his advocate. Wheelock used to take me aside at Fuller board meetings and say, "That son of yours has got ability. You should push him along." I was hearing that from others at Fuller too. Some people in the company felt I did not give him managerial responsibility fast enough. I wanted him to learn by experience and earn his promotions. In 1968, he became operations manager; three years later, he was president.

Tony took the title chief executive officer on April 18, 1974. I retired two months later, though I continued as chairman of the board. I moved out of my office at Fuller headquarters, thinking that would solidify Tony's position. I wanted to be out of his way, and I did not want others at Fuller confused about who was in charge.

I need not have been concerned. Tony was his own man and already much respected by people both within and outside the company. He took H. B. Fuller Company from annual sales of just over $60 million in 1971 to Fortune 500 status in the 1980s. By 1992, total sales topped $940 million. Tony's years also saw the company gain national recognition as one of the one hundred best companies to work for, and as a leader in both environmental protection and customer service.

Tony not only maintained the impetus and the values he had inherited, but he built on them. We provided health care coverage for our retirees early on. Tony extended that coverage to retirees' spouses, an exceptional and generous benefit. A Variable Employment Benefit Association trust was established in 1991 to assure the funding of that benefit in the future, regardless of the company's ups and downs.

Meanwhile, I was on the loose, looking for a place from which to manage all my old ventures and launch some new ones. I set up shop in a little building on Emerald Street on the city limits of St. Paul and Minneapolis. As we had done so often at Fuller, we rented half the building but had an option to buy all of it, which we exercised. My secretary of thirty-three years, Donna Petersen, went with me. We were joined by a bookkeeper named Joyce Hedrick and an aide who ran errands. For a time, that was Greg Johnson, Eleanor's brother's son, who had left an ambitious program at Augsburg College and was working at a gas station when I asked him to join us. My arrangement with him was that he would work for me, and together we would plan a realistic college program, which he would enter as soon as he was ready to do so. We followed that plan, which led him to the University of Minnesota to study agricultural economics and eventually to a career in sales in South St. Paul.

Our four-person office on Emerald Street was a lively, happy place. Many a morning I would stop at a bakery and get apple turnovers or chocolate eclairs. The four of us would have coffee together. My schedule now permitted such luxuries. I would rent films, often educational ones, and we would have screening sessions. The office was small, but it included a "rare books department," a room that I had air-conditioned and properly humidified in which to store my growing collection of rare books.

The Emerald Street office eventually gave way to one on Como Avenue, then in the Rosedale Towers, and finally on the lower level of our home. From those offices, I managed a workload that included the affairs of the Board of Regents, the University Foundation, Voyageurs National Park, Deer Lake Farm, the Bush Foundation, the Lindbergh Foundation, and a number of other civic boards and special assignments.

I also had some new business. Eleanor and I bought a parcel of land along the southeastern shore of Lake Johanna in Arden Hills and started planning to build a new home. It was my quest for convenient office and book space that got us thinking about a new place to live. We liked our house on Hoyt Avenue, but when I began to think about spending more working hours at home, the Hoyt House seemed inadequate. Our search for building sites in St. Anthony Park proved fruitless. Then I heard that a ten-acre parcel on Lake Johanna was being platted for residential lots. That part of the lakeshore was originally divided into ten-acre summer home sites. The owner of the parcel in question had lived in an old frame house that was then being torn down. The location appealed to us—close to St. Anthony Park, close to a highway, close to good retail shopping, just a few minutes from both St. Paul and Minneapolis, and on a beautiful lake. In 1975, we bought two lots on Bussard Court.

We also tried to buy a part of the Lametti section, which was the next ten acres to the north. We could not quite negotiate a deal with Mr. Lametti. We thought he was asking too much, just to have a little woods next door. But we regretted that choice. Years later, after he died and we were negotiating with his family, we wound up paying a good deal more than he originally asked.

We did not build in Arden Hills right away. In fact, we kept watching for a suitable building site to become available in St. Anthony Park. Finally, in 1983, I said to Eleanor, "I'm 74 years old. If we're ever going to build another home for our later years, we'd better do it." We went through two architects—the first design was too small—before we actually began construction.

It was such fun to see the house rise from the ground that we visited the building site often, and became quite friendly with the building crew. They often remarked about the size of the sweeping horizontal design we had chosen. One of them approached me one day with a little smile. "Andersen, I've been wondering about something," he said. "Are you and your wife planning to start another family?"

Much as we enjoyed St. Anthony Park, we love our lakeside home. I still find it miraculous to come in the front door from a short trip to the city, walk across the living room, and be in the north woods. Once a business associate from Japan with whom we had become friendly came here. He was flabbergasted. "In Japan, a piece of land this large on a lake, hardly anybody in the country could afford," he said. We feel very fortunate.

I had other unfinished business on my agenda in 1975. When I left Fuller, I thought about the three goals I had set four decades before. I had achieved two of them: we owned and operated a farm, and I had served in the legislature. Perhaps, I thought, there was still time for the third goal, owning a weekly newspaper. It was an idea I had nursed through the years. I kept a file in my desk at Fuller on newspaper properties. I inquired once about the availability of the *Stillwater Gazette*—a daily, not a weekly, but a paper I admired. But when it finally went on the market, I was scared away by its $300,000 asking price. That seemed like too much money to spend on a new enterprise about which I knew very little. But even then, my newspaper dream did not die.

From my new perch on Emerald Street, I began to make a serious study of the weekly newspaper opportunities in the region. I got a map and circled all the towns that had weekly newspapers between St. Paul and St. Croix Falls, Wisconsin, where Deer Lake Farm was located. I often needed to make that trip and did not want to have to drive in the opposite direction to attend to a newspaper. Among the towns that I circled was Princeton.

I thought: Princeton. That is Bob Odegard's hometown. He was my colleague on the University Foundation and in Republican politics. In 1962, he ran for Congress against a Republican incumbent with some encouragement from me—and, regrettably, without success in November. I called Odegard. "What's the newspaper situation in Princeton?" I asked. "It's bad," he said. He filled me in. The *Princeton Union* was founded in the nineteenth century by Robert Dunn, who managed it for many years. He was the grandfather of state Sen. Robert Dunn of Princeton, who served in the legislature in the 1970s and 1980s. The elder Dunn had also been an unsuccessful candidate for governor in 1905, when John A. Johnson was elected. The family's love for the *Union* was so strong that when Dunn retired, his daughter Grace gave up her career as a Ph.D. biologist and came home to take over the newspaper. She was a formidable woman, possessed of strong opinions. I knew her while I was serving in the legislature. Her nephew Bob was in the business for a time too, but he was either put off by newspapering or by his aunt. He was established in the lumber business and politics by the time she was ready to step down.

The *Union* was sold and went through several hands. In 1972, it was taken over by the newspaper at Moose Lake, Minnesota. Those new owners made a serious mistake. They installed an outside person as editor, overlooking the talent and loyalty of the staff already in place. The staff was so upset that they bolted from the *Union* and started a rival paper, the *Princeton Eagle.* The *Union* had moved into new quarters, so the *Eagle* set up shop in the neat little place that had been home to the *Union* in Grace Dunn's day. Soon townspeople thought of the new *Eagle* as the hometown paper, and the *Union* as an outsider. The rivalry for advertising was fierce. Neither one thought the other would last six months.

Odegard said, "They are at each other's throats. I'm sure they're both losing money. They are tearing the town apart because the merchants are having to choose between them, or go with both papers. It's a bad situation. If somebody would come in and buy both papers, put them together and get on with things, he would do the town a great service."

I wanted to try to play that role. We called on the Moose Lake owners first. They were willing to sell the *Princeton Union.* It had been losing money. But they advised, "it would be unfair of us to sell to you unless you could get the other paper. You would just have the same situation we have." They took a dim view of our chances because they saw the *Eagle* owners as ogres. "Those people are impossible. You can't talk to them. You can't reason with them."

We went next to the *Eagle,* where we heard pretty much the same story and the same low assessment of the competition's character. Those *Union* people were horrid, the *Eagle* staff said. They were price-cutters, cheaters, and deceivers. The owner of the *Eagle* was Marian Manary, whose husband, Bob, was a cameraman for WCCO-TV. Her staff also included a fine young journalist, Luther Dorr, and a business manager, Tim Enger.

After hearing both litanies, I recognized two issues that had to be resolved before I could attempt to combine the papers. I had to decide which was going to be the surviving company, and I had to find a neutral location. I wanted the result to be one harmonious newspaper with one staff, formed by melding the two staffs into one. I knew it would be impossible for either group to move into the other's quarters. Fortunately, a furniture store had recently moved into a new building, and its old shop, which was quite spacious, was available at a reasonable price. Advantageously, it was located halfway between the two existing newspaper offices. It solved our location issue so nicely that I eventually bought the building.

As to which would be the surviving company, I decided to try to go with the local people. I negotiated to buy the assets of the Moose Lake owners and buy the corporation of the Manary group. After going back and forth with them all, I thought we had a deal. But when it came to the moment of signing legal papers with the Manarys in Princeton, Bob Manary raised questions. I said, "Bob, this was supposed to be a signing session. Everything was supposed to have been discussed and settled. All we're to do today is sign the papers. Is something bothering you?" He said, "We've been doing more thinking and talking." Then, he raised still more new conditions. I took it as a sign that I should back off and reconsider our arrangement. We negotiated anew to make the Princeton *Union* the surviving company.

The Princeton Publishing Company was born, and operations began. The new newspaper's name was the Princeton *Union-Eagle*. The first issue under Andersen ownership was published on June 17, 1976—my sixty-seventh birthday. We hosted a large luncheon in town to celebrate and get acquainted. I wanted to meet the advertisers, ministers, 4-H leaders, bankers, school officials—really anyone who was a community leader. I prepared a questionnaire that I wanted our luncheon guests to fill out to guide me. One of my questions was, "What is your reaction to a person coming from the outside to be the owner of your local newspaper?" I received many heartwarming replies to that question, but one stood out: "We all came from somewhere." How accepting, I thought.

Naturally, a few personnel issues arose immediately. One concerned bookkeeping. The *Eagle* had been operating on a cash basis. Money came in and money went out, and if there was any left over, they were ahead. If there was not, they had to borrow. I could not operate that way. Neither could I rely on the young woman who tried to keep track of the money, but who was not a trained bookkeeper. I have high standards for bookkeeping.

I called the young woman in for a talk. I said, "I'm going to need a trained bookkeeper. I'll have to try and find one. I wish you would stay with the company. We have another job here that would be suitable for your talent and ability. We'll pay you the same amount. We'll advance you just as rapidly. I hope you'll be willing to take the transition." I had done nothing, as yet, to find a new bookkeeper. I was trying to prepare this young woman for the coming change and ask her to be cooperative. Instead, she did not come to work the next day. She quit.

I hastened to advertise for a bookkeeper. Maxine Gift responded to the ad. She had been a bookkeeper for a feed mill in northwestern Minnesota before her husband's work as a police officer took them to Princeton. He then died, leaving her with a dead-end office job in a nursing home. I liked her character and style. Here is a person we can build on, I thought. I hired her.

At the end of her first day, she came into my office. "Elmer, I can't do this," she said. "This is way beyond me. It's such a mess. I haven't the slightest idea how to begin to get out of this." "Maxine, don't quit," I said. "You've got the ability. You have a real future here. Just let me get you some help."

I have always valued having good auditors and properly audited books. So I had already hired the firm Larson, Allen, Weishair, which specialized in auditing newspapers. Bob Weishair was the executive person assigned to us. I called him and said, "Bob, could you take a couple of weeks to come to Princeton, go through every bit of the bookkeeping procedure, set up a set of books, and help our new bookkeeper build up her confidence? I'm confident she has the ability, but she desperately needs some help getting started." Weishair did just that, so we solved our bookkeeping problem. Maxine Gift is now treasurer and director of accounting for all of ECM Publishing. As I predicted, she became a marvelous employee, and the supervisor of several others. It is a tremendous satisfaction to see how she has grown in a job that she nearly quit.

The first editor of the *Union-Eagle* was a man who had been the editor of the *Union* before the merger. Luther Dorr, the *Eagle's* young editor, may have been disappointed with that choice. But he stayed on as a reporter— and was on hand and ripe for promotion when the first *Union-Eagle* editor left a few years later. Dorr has been a stalwart editor for the paper ever since. Though we have not always agreed, our mutual respect has never flagged.

Writing editorials would eventually fall to me. But I held off at first. I wanted to better know the community before expressing any editorial opinions. Yet I could not resist the opportunity to write for a newspaper again.

Not long after we began publication, I started a column called "The Publisher's Notebook." It was based on observations I made as I submerged myself into small-town life—something I had never experienced before. I drove to Princeton nearly every weekday for many months. I carried around a little blue notebook and made notes constantly about the things I was seeing and learning. I noticed little things. When I saw baby ducks swimming on the waterworks pond, I wrote, "Don't miss going by the waterworks and seeing the ducks. They will brighten your day." Readers responded warmly to my comments about nature.

It was a joy to watch Princeton residents interact with each other. In that town, everybody knows everybody else. People speak to each other on the street. They show each day that they care about their town and each other. I wanted to be part of that.

I discovered early that there was a coffee klatch, a group of local businessmen and, in later years, some women, who met every morning for coffee, promptly at 10:00 A.M., in the K-Bob Café. I made a point to be there. Soon I felt that I was a part of that community. It was a group of friends who teased each other, remembered each other's birthdays, celebrated holidays with a fiddle performance, and generally enjoyed each other's company. It was a wonderful little institution.

I was so sensitive to everything. I did not want the newspaper to give offense—not unintentionally, anyway. One of the first summers, I wanted to bring a young man on board as a summer employee. He wanted to bring his companion along, and it was clear that they were unmarried. I wondered how the community would receive their arrangement. I asked Dorr, "How will the town react to that?" He said, "Elmer, we're not quite that far behind. There's a little stuff that goes on around here, too."

I joined the Minnesota Newspaper Association right away and learned about something they called the Skills Course. It is two weeks of intensive education in the basics of journalism. That is just what I need, I thought. The course was offered at Anoka Technical College in August and taught by Brent Norlem, a former Marine sergeant. My twenty-four fellow students were all bright, energetic, ambitious people—and all younger than I. I felt rather intimidated. To make matters worse, I had to qualify for the course by taking a test with three parts: typing, grammar, and current events. I had always been a two-finger typist, and not a fast one at that. I had not studied grammar for more than fifty years. I thought nervously that, maybe, I could get by on current events.

As it turned out, I did well on the test and loved the course. It was fun and beneficial. In addition to the work I did on my writing those two weeks, I had my first exposure to the darkroom side of photography. Our teacher said, "You've got to learn how to develop your own pictures, because that is the only way to get the picture you want." He gave us all an assignment, "Go out and take some pictures somewhere. Take difficult pictures. Then learn how to develop them, and come and show me the results." I got books on developing. We set up a darkroom. I went to the State Fair and took night pictures, something I thought would be sufficiently challenging. I took pictures of the Ferris wheels, sporting events, and prizewinning entries at the competitions, all colorful subject matter. The prints from the negatives turned out pretty well. My instructor was pleased. He said, "You're really good. I think you're going to make it."

The *Union-Eagle* was a financial drain at first. Every payday, Maxine Gift would tell me how much was needed to meet the payroll and pay the bills, and I would write a check. We paid our staff and our suppliers promptly, but I kept pouring money in and taking stock back. I knew that situation could not go on forever. And I had learned at Fuller that the imperative for any successful business is "grow or die." Little Princeton Publishing Company needed to do some growing.

ECM Publishers, Inc.

THE AVENUE TO GROWTH for Princeton Publishing Company was right in Princeton. We found it at the end of the route the *Union-Eagle* traveled each week to the plant of East Central Minnesota Printing Company, where eight of the region's weekly newspapers were printed.

In the early 1970s, eight newspaper owners joined forces to build a large, modern printing plant that could handle all their weekly printing needs. Linotype machines were on their way out, and the expense associated with modern offset printing was too great to be borne by small-town papers individually. The owners obtained financing from the First National Bank of Milaca, headed by Burton P. "Pete" Allen, a dedicated promoter of the region. The eight owners were organized into a sort of last-man's club: they all shared equally in the ownership of East Central Minnesota Printing. If any of them went out of the publishing business, they sold back their interest to the ones remaining. The plant had a strong manager in Richard Gossen, who knew how to attract outside customers as well as in-house business. The little plant was a moneymaker.

When we took over the *Princeton Union*, we acquired one-eighth interest in East Central Minnesota Printing. I became one of eight members of its board of directors and got acquainted with the other seven newspaper owners and their businesses.

Jere Craven, a third-generation owner of the *Mille Lacs County Times* in Milaca, was chair of the board. He was an able businessman, though some of his practices were illustrative of the casual financial management of some small newspapers. Every week, he would put a bundle of newspapers in local restaurants and stores for cash sales. When he came with a new stack of papers the following week, he would get the money for the previous week's copies that were sold. I once asked Jere, "How do you handle cash on your cash sales?" He said, "I make the rounds. I pick up the cash. I put it in my pocket, and that's where it stays."

Another third-generation owner on the East Central Minnesota Printing board was Charles Dare of the *Elk River Star News*. Both his grandfather and Craven's had founded their papers and devoted their lives to journalistic service to their communities. But in both cases, the grandsons were not very happy in the newspaper business. Dare was quite easily shaken by any threat of competition. He expressed interest in selling out. And that got me thinking: by buying these papers, I could eventually get control of East Central Printing.

I began negotiating with Dare. We were close to an understanding when Craven got wind of our talks. When he learned the price I was about to pay for *Elk River Star News,* he wanted to sell the *Mille Lacs County Times* to me, too. As things developed, we bought the Milaca paper first, in 1981, then the *Star News* a few months later. When Pete Allen, the banker who provided the initial financing for the East Central Printing plant, discovered how much I was proposing to pay, he said, "There's a lot of blue sky in this business, isn't there?" He was right. A newspaper's price has little relationship to its income. Rather, the price is based in part on the franchise—the brand name, one might say—that each small-town paper possesses. I quickly learned some newspaper economics. Concepts like multiples of sales and gross cash turnover became familiar to me.

The first thing I did as owner of the *Mille Lacs County Times* was remodel its ancient office. I thought it was a firetrap and a disgrace. I soon found that it was also typical of many weekly newspaper offices in the 1970s. Many still occupied the original buildings in which they had been founded at the turn of the century or earlier. I learned that in many cases, I had to figure the cost of remodeling into my initial investment when I acquired a newspaper.

My Lindbergh connections soon made me aware of another Central Printing newspaper that might be ripe for acquisition. Eva Lindbergh Christie Spaeth, Charles Lindbergh's older half-sister, had married into the newspaper business in Redwood Falls. Her son, George Christie, followed his father into journalism. She had helped him purchase the *Kanabec County Times* in Mora. By the late 1970s, Christie was thinking of retirement and wanted to sell. I investigated and decided not to buy the Mora paper. Its advertising base was too small, having been weakened by an aggressive independent printer who published an advertising-only "shopper." Instead of negotiating for a purchase, I arranged to buy out the *Times'* share in East Central Printing.

I made the same arrangement with Don and Carole Larson of the *Osseo Press*. I had my eye on that paper, but the Larsons did not want to sell.

Instead, we invited them to join the Princeton Publishing Company board, to keep a connection with them. The Larsons were hard-working business people who valued good journalism. Carole subsequently became president of the Minnesota Newspaper Association.

Eventually, every original participant in East Central Minnesota Printing became part of Princeton Publishing or sold their interest in the printing plant to us. Meanwhile, I set about finding some new clients for the plant.

I found one in George Johnson of Cambridge. Johnson had been in the furniture business, not journalism, when he became dissatisfied with the advertising offered him by his local paper. He started a little advertising bulletin called the *Scotsman.* It became popular with other local businessmen. In a short time, it was a profitable shopper, covering east-central Minnesota with about six zoned editions. Along the way, Johnson also acquired the little *Isanti County Times.* He obtained printing services from the *White Bear Lake Press* but did not have an entirely satisfactory arrangement there. He decided to give East Central Printing a try.

The relationship succeeded in part because of the efforts of our new manager at East Central Printing, Willard "Bill" Stang. He was an excellent printer with an instinctive business sense. He worked well with customers, managed the plant ably, and made money. He is one of the many people I have met who, had they been born into different circumstances, would have achieved vastly more with their professional lives than they did. I am always saddened when I encounter those situations because I regard the short-changing of human potential as a terrible loss. And I take great satisfaction from the thought that for a few of those people, I have provided some of the tutelage and encouragement they lacked.

The *Scotsman* and the *Isanti County Times* were our printing customers for a few years and then became part of the Princeton Publishing family. When it came time to sell his two products, Johnson was surprised that the Isanti paper, which was losing money, fetched a price that was a better multiple of its sales than that of his financially successful shopper. I tried to explain: "The difference is in the mission, George. There's a mission in publishing a newspaper. It may be an intangible thing sometimes, but it is worth working for and paying for." I was not in the newspaper business to make money. I was in it for the mission.

Yet we could not carry out the mission for long unless Princeton Publishing turned a profit. Growth was still imperative to make Princeton Publishing secure. We began to think that growth required a new corporate name, one less specific to one community. The initials of the name of our printing plant seemed appropriate. In 1987, Princeton Publishing became ECM Publishers, Inc.

We also decided to consolidate our holdings into a single corporate entity. Our initial pattern was to preserve the separate corporate identity of each newspaper. But that soon became cumbersome. And I had learned from my Fuller experience that if we ever wanted to make a public offering of ECM stock, we needed centralized control.

The leading papers near Princeton to the south were the ABC Newspapers of Arch Pease. ABC stood for Anoka, Blaine, and Coon Rapids. Pease was a third-generation publisher who had been active in his community and in politics. I had known him at least since 1952, when he was a delegate to the Republican National Convention, and we were friendly enough that we occasionally met for lunch after I became his fellow publisher. I just assumed that a family member would succeed him at ABC Newspapers, since some of his relatives were already involved in the business. But he told me that my assumption was mistaken. He had already tried to turn his business over to his son once, but the transition did not go well, and he had to come out of retirement to take charge again. His children now wanted nothing to do with the business. Plus, his health was beginning to fail. Further, he indicated that the business was not faring as well as it might. I was never slow to pick up on such information. I said, "Arch, if you ever get to a point where you want to sell your papers, we would certainly be interested."

It is interesting how politics and business intersect. Pease's lawyer was Robert Johnson of Anoka. He was the head of the state Municipal Commission, appointed by my predecessor, Gov. Orville Freeman, when I was governor. That was the body that oversaw mergers and acquisitions of territory by municipalities, which is always controversial. His term expired, and I had to decide whether to replace him. He had done a good job. It took a calm, steady hand to keep that commission functioning well—something he possessed. So, I reappointed him. His reappointment irritated my partisan Republican friends. "Elmer, don't you know that he's a friend of Freeman?" they said. "He was best man at Freeman's wedding." I said, "Yes, and furthermore, Freeman was best man at his wedding. What's that got to do with the Municipal Commission?" I came to know Johnson quite well. For many years, he served as Anoka county attorney. He was scrupulous about integrity. When he called some time after my conversation with Pease and announced that he was Pease's lawyer, I knew Pease was in good hands.

Johnson said, "Arch has decided to sell. He is negotiating with another party, but he would be glad to talk to you." I hastened to meet with Pease. He indicated that the potential buyer he had on the string was going to offer more than we would. I wanted to own ABC, but only if the terms made good business sense. I told Pease, "I have some ideas that might be useful to you. But I think you'd better proceed with the other people. I don't want to be in a bidding war with them. I think they are approaching it a little differently than I would."

A couple of weeks later, Johnson called again. Pease wanted me back in the picture, Johnson said. The other party was backpedaling and making Pease uncomfortable. I had rather expected the call. In fact, I had been studying the possible application of an employee stock option plan, or ESOP, to a merger with ABC. An ESOP provides a tax incentive to a proprietor for making stock available to his employees. It works this way: The proprietor sells stock to the ESOP. The ESOP pays for the stock by borrowing from a bank at preferred interest rates. Then, the company deposits money into the ESOP as debt service is due, so the company in effect buys the stock from the proprietor for the benefit of the employees. It is a little complicated, but it works like a charm. The money that the ESOP pays the owner for the stock is nontaxable if it is reinvested within a year in U.S. corporate stocks and bonds. Therein lies the incentive to the proprietor to make equity available to his employees.

My idea was to arrange a tax-free exchange of stock with Pease. That is called a pooled interest merger—the very thing Exxon and Mobile did in 1998. One firm gives its stock for the stock of the other firm. We gave ECM stock for ABC stock. Pease became a substantial holder of ECM stock, whereupon he was eligible to sell it to the ESOP and get cash for it at no tax liability.

I outlined all of this to Pease. Then I said, "Now, Arch, this is going to save you about $1 million in taxes—and you can't have it all. We are not going to offer you as much as the other bidder offered you. But we know each other. I think we can do business together better than you could do business with them." He was delighted with my idea. We began to negotiate on some of the details.

That led to one of the most gratifying experiences I had in my entire business career. I was sitting in Pease's office one day. He said, "Elmer, the people in the plant are kind of restless. They know something is going on. They are a little concerned that I'm going to make a deal with that other outfit, because they know they're tough on unions. They know that you might not be. I think we have an understanding of the basic parts of this. If we shook hands on an understanding today, we could work out the details later. The lawyers can work it out over the next couple of months. Then we could go out into the plant right now and tell the people that we have sold ABC to you. That would be such a relief to them." I said, "Arch, I have complete confidence that we'll have no difficulty whatever. If that's the way you feel, I can certainly go along." We shook hands. We had not signed a paper. We had not committed to any real detail. Yet then and there, we went into the plant and assembled the workers to announce that ECM was taking over ABC Newspapers. It was a happy moment. The employees were pleased.

When the lawyers got involved, the first thing we heard was that there had to be an exhaustive "due diligence" examination of each other's assets and liabilities. I thought that would disrupt the trust that Pease and I had developed. I said, "There's going to be no due diligence in this transaction. If Archie says he owns property, he owns it. If he says the accounts receivable are collectable, we accept that. Forget about due diligence. Just draw up the legal work, and let us handle the business details. We'll get along just fine." As we went forward, there was not a single point of difference. Pease was most pleased with the outcome. I think it was a comfort to him in what turned out to be his last years that his company was in our hands. He survived only about two more years. Our bond was such that we stay in regular contact with his widow, Amy, a lovely lady.

The deal was not only a personal pleasure for me but a boon to ECM. We spent no cash to acquire ABC. I have always been short of cash—and I have always gone ahead without regard to cash. The ESOP plan made it possible for us to acquire a business that was not only almost as big as ECM but also had a longer record and stronger reputation on which to build. And it finally provided the scale of operation ECM needed to be profitable. ABC brought with it three newspapers and a seventy-page shopper with a circulation of seventy thousand that was a strong income producer. And it established the principle of employee ownership of stock, which has grown so that it now reaches 40 percent of ECM employees. The merger served us well.

I had no question about whom to place as ECM's manager of the former ABC newspapers. We had a rising star in the company in whom I had great confidence—Jeff Athmann. Today, he is ECM's president and chief operating officer.

Athmann came to me in the early days of Princeton Publishing Company to succeed our nephew, Greg Johnson, as my aide. He came to my attention in an interesting way. Honeywell had closed a department and was laying off its employees, including a number of young people with computer skills. To assist those young people in their search for new employment, Honeywell issued a nice brochure containing the résumés of each one, attesting that each had been carefully selected and hired with intentions of a long stay. Honeywell earnestly recommended each one as a good worker. I was impressed that a company would go to that length for its laid-off workers. So, with no more interest than that, I looked through the booklet rather carefully, and I came upon Athmann, a young fellow from Stearns County who had graduated from technical college in computer science. He was a young man, probably twenty-one or twenty-two years old. He appealed to me, so I called him and offered him the position Greg had held, as a sort of personal assistant, and as someone who could advise us about computers.

Our auditor, Bob Weishair, came to know Athmann and spotted his ability. When we bought the newspaper in Cambridge, Weishair urged me to put Athmann in a management position there and let him grow into the job. He performed well, not only as a financial manager but as a kind and likable leader. He has excellent people skills. His climb to president and chief operating officer has been gratifying to me.

We were not through enlarging ECM nor done doing business with George Johnson. He not only founded a shopper but also created a separate delivery company to distribute it. That company kept growing even after he sold the *Scotsman* to us. Finally, we bought that, too, and put ECM in the delivery business.

We looked around next and spotted little Zimmerman, between Elk River and Princeton. It is right in the middle of our trade territory and did not have a newspaper. We thought, somebody is going to come along and put something into Zimmerman, unless we do it first. We started the *Zimmerman Frontier.* It was our first attempt to start a newspaper from scratch—an effort at which we may have been too ambitious. It was a skinny four-page thing. We finally made the *Zimmerman Frontier* a section of the *Elk River Star News.* But the *Frontier* is up to eight pages now, and Zimmerman is growing. It may make a name for itself yet.

In Zimmerman, we were able to help save a historic building. The Zimmerman City Council was trying to sell a nineteenth-century building that had once housed a bank and city offices. Its placement on the National Register of Historic Places limited its options for future use. We agreed to buy it as our office, while protecting its historic character. We later sold it to an accounting firm that was willing to undertake the responsibility of its proper maintenance.

In 1993, we added *The Times* of Forest Lake. Our decision to acquire *The Times* was somewhat defensive. The Cambridge-based *Scotsman* fanned out across east-central Minnesota. If a strong rival were to develop in Forest Lake, it would limit the *Scotsman's* territory. We knew the owner at Forest Lake was nearing retirement and decided to broach the subject of a purchase with him. "Maybe, in a couple or three years, but I'm not ready now," he said. We said, "We're ready now. We'd be willing to pay today what we'd pay a couple of years from now. We'll anticipate a little of the future to accommodate you." Our sales pitch worked. But acquiring *The Times* did not get us the protection we were seeking. The rival that we were concerned about, Gene Johnson from White Bear Lake, started a paper in Forest Lake after our move. We are worrying that out.

But ECM Publishing is big and strong enough now that our survival is no longer in question. At this writing, ECM includes eighteen newspapers and eight free-distribution shoppers. The newspapers' combined weekly circulation is in excess of 125,000. The communities ECM serves include Anoka, Blaine, Coon Rapids, Elk River, Princeton, Milaca, Zimmerman, Cambridge, Forest Lake, North Branch, Sauk Centre, Spring Lake Park, Caledonia, Burnsville, Lakeville, Apple Valley, Farmington, Eagan, and Rosemount. The acquisition of the *Caledonia Argus* in 1998 represented planting a seed in a new territory, southeastern Minnesota. Its owners sought us out. When a company consistently treats its customers and employees well, the word gets around. The Caledonia owners told us that they preferred to sell to us because they had confidence that we would be good to their employees. That pleased us very much.

The *Argus* is part of a group of papers that has a common, central printing plant. Our president, Jeff Athmann, said, "Elmer, I think we can do Princeton Publishing all over again. We'll get them one at a time." Time will tell.

If a new round of acquisitions is coming, it will be directed by another Andersen. For the second time in my life, I have been succeeded in business by a son. Julian, our second son, became the chief executive officer of ECM Publishing on January 1, 1998.

Julian has had a scholarly career. After majoring in mathematics at Carleton College and obtaining a master's degree at Wesleyan University in Middleton, Connecticut, he became a math teacher at a community college in Seattle. He later went into the administration of that same college. He was beginning to think about moving on when I approached him about ECM. He has been CEO for two years, all that while commuting from Seattle, spending half his time here and staying in touch the rest of the time with e-mail and the Internet. We talk often, day and night, about the business. He is doing well.

Since Julian's arrival, I have retired as chairman of the board. But I am still a board member, as are Eleanor and Tony. We introduced weighted voting preferred stock in ECM for the family, just as we did at Fuller, for the same reason: to make it possible to dilute our ownership without losing control. I believe strongly that a company cannot be run by a committee and run well. One person has to be in charge. For the foreseeable future, that person will be named Andersen.

Make no mistake—I have great confidence in the other people involved with ECM, starting with our president, Jeff Athmann. When we acquired the Forest Lake paper, we also obtained the services of Bob Cole, an advertising manager, who I quickly sensed had great potential. He is now marketing manager at ECM and is responsible for updating our marketing for the twenty-first century. Don Heinzman, who came to us from the *Sun* newspaper group, made an important contribution as editor and manager of the *Elk River Star News* and is remaining active though he has retired from that post. Tim Enger, whom we recruited twenty-three years ago from the *Princeton Eagle,* became ECM's secretary and general manager of printing and publication operations in Princeton.

I scored a great coup when I recruited Gene Merriam to be ECM's chief financial officer. Gene was a DFL state senator from the Coon Rapids area and the chairman of the senate's Finance Committee when, in 1996, he announced he would not seek reelection. The day he made his announcement, I called him. I knew him to be highly respected as the very soul of integrity and a wizard with numbers. The fact that he was a DFLer did not matter one particle to me. I considered him the ideal person for ECM. "Gene, I don't know what your plans are for the future," I said. "But if you have not committed yourself, would you, please, not do so until we've had a chance to visit?" We had that visit, and he joined the company soon thereafter.

Merriam and I visited again not long ago. I said, "Gene, other opportunities may come to you. I want to have an understanding with you. If something comes along that you feel you really want to do, don't feel that you'd betray ECM if you do it. We'd like to have you do what you want to do. We're going to do our darnedest to make ECM your choice." I think Merriam will excel at anything he chooses. I would be pleased if he would choose the Board of Regents as his next avenue of public service.

At ECM, we have continued the pattern we began at Fuller of offering our employees a benefit package that is more generous than the industry norm. Our parenting leave policy, adopted in 1998, is widely believed to be the most enlightened offered by any employer in the state. We allow parents of children under age three—mothers and fathers alike—up to a full year's leave of absence at 40 percent pay. An employee is eligible to take up to three parenting leaves during his or her career at ECM. The idea was mine—and in fact, I wanted to be even more generous. The recent discoveries about child development from birth to age three ought to change corporate thinking about parenting leave policies. It is incredibly important that children from zero to three get intensive, steady nurture of the sort a parent is most inclined to provide. Small children grow so fast. They learn so much. They obtain much of their physical structure and mental capacity during their first three years. Allowing parents to spend more time with their infants and toddlers may be the best investment for this nation's future that corporate America could make.

I believe that community newspapers have great potential to make a positive contribution to the communities they touch. For me, entering the community newspaper field twenty-three years ago has provided a pleasing kaleidoscope of personal relationships and experiences, including the satisfaction of expressing my opinions in writing. I have enjoyed the time I spent writing editorials about as much as any time I have spent doing anything.

Each ECM paper has always had an independent, local news staff under the direction of a local editor. But my editorials were shared and published in each paper. On Monday mornings, I used to make the rounds—Elk River to Princeton to Milaca to Cambridge—delivering copies of my editorial for that week's edition. Eventually, the fax machine made my long Monday drive unnecessary. But I enjoyed those weekly runs. They gave me a chance to visit with people in each office and each community.

Those Monday deliveries were the culmination of a weeklong process. I would find myself thinking about my next editorial almost continuously. I would have an idea or, often, several ideas. I would settle on one early in the week and develop it in my mind. I would gather some facts and often interview someone to get more information or a unique perspective. I would decide on an approach to the topic. A phrase or two would come to me. Then a few more. My pattern was to work that over thoroughly in my mind, so that the actual time I would spend at the keyboard was not long. I would rehearse it in my mind until I practically knew the whole thing by heart.

During my years in politics, I followed much the same routine when I prepared speeches. I hated to read from a manuscript. I wanted to talk to my listeners, watch for their reactions, and adapt to them. That was so much more satisfactory than preparing something in advance, without knowing the mood or the scene or what somebody else might have said just before I reached the rostrum. After I left elective office, I got some gratifying confirmation that my speech-making technique worked. I was one of about a dozen distinguished speakers who addressed a University of Minnesota graduate seminar on business management one quarter. The list included such luminaries as Rudy Boschwitz, then of Plywood Minnesota, soon to be a U.S. senator; Donald Nyrop, CEO of Northwest Airlines; and William Norris, head of Control Data. At the end of the quarter, the students were surveyed and asked to grade the speakers. My score topped the list.

Some editorial writers struggle to choose a topic. The choice was never difficult for me. Ideas were always popping into my head from current events, reading, thinking, dreaming—just living. I looked for topics that were current. I tried to vary them. I tried for a substantial number of serious political editorials, but I knew I would lose readers with a steady diet of weighty stuff. So I would add nature or literature to the mix.

I thought my knowledge of government and politics made the editorials on those topics my strongest. But others have told me they especially enjoyed the editorials I wrote about nature. John Parker, the retired librarian of the James Ford Bell Library at the University of Minnesota, once told me, "Elmer, you could have been a fine nature writer." I had to laugh, as I thought about my first newspaper column, "Birds of Muskegon." Maybe I should have stayed with the birds.

I also had a column—or, more accurately, two columns. I wrote "The Publisher's Notebook" almost from the start of the *Princeton Union-Eagle* in 1976. But it can now be revealed that I was also the author of a column about books and book collecting published under the name Arne Kjelsberg, my father's name in Norway. That column was short-lived and had a small but enlightened following—or so I thought, anyway. Arne Kjelsberg used to get some lovely letters from readers, occasionally from the same people who wrote to publisher Elmer Andersen. Once, a friend of mine pressed me for information about Arne. "He's a bashful, homebound friend of mine," I replied. A few weeks later, the same friend said, "I figured out who Arne is, you rascal."

I came to appreciate the difference between an editorial and a column. This difference is important, though it is lost on some readers. A column is a personal essay and can be quite freewheeling. An editorial speaks not only for its author but also for the paper. Ideally, if the writer is attuned to his readers, an editorial speaks for the community as well.

At ECM, as at most community newspapers, the publisher is a one-person editorial board. But I was conscious of speaking for my colleagues, and I would occasionally consult with them about an editorial. That is, I would consult, but never defer. I retained control of editorial policy. I took editorial writing rather seriously. It is no small thing to have the opportunity to be a voice for the community, to help it be at its best, to help it grow, to help its people be aware of common issues and concerns. I did not presume to know what is right on every matter I raised. But in every editorial, I attempted to stimulate thinking. I used to say, "I don't try to tell you what to think, but I would like to tell you to think."

When I started writing editorials, I tried to make them specific to each community. But as ECM grew, I could not keep in touch with them all. I asked each paper's editor to write local editorials, and I wrote on more state, national, and international issues. I loved writing about state politics, the domain in which I had spent so many years. And I found fascinating the development of issues. It is interesting to see how long it takes for an idea or proposal to advance from being controversial to becoming taken for granted—and rewarding to think that as an editorial writer, I had something to do with that progression.

Many years of living have given me a sense of confidence about the future that I hope was evident in my editorials. No matter how bad things seem to be on some front, they will change, usually for the better. When extremists come to the fore, moderate thinkers who might otherwise be inactive come to life and set things right. "Life goes on," as Robert Frost said at Kennedy's inaugural. Life goes on and comes out pretty good.

I found a more personal satisfaction in my newspaper work than in almost anything else I have done. Many people would consider reaching the governorship the apex of a career. But my time as governor was so short and such a whirlwind that it is a blur in my memory. I was much more deliberate and methodical about getting into the newspaper business. I made a point of enjoying small-town life, of appreciating the interrelationships of people, and of joining in those relationships myself. I relished writing editorials that I hoped would serve those communities. All these aspects added a great deal to my life experience.

I ended my editorial writing career in the summer of 1998 so that I could concentrate on writing this book. My increasing visual impairment made it difficult for me to do the reading that a good editorial writer must do. In my last few years of writing editorials, I could no longer type them myself.

Instead, I "wrote" them in my mind and then dictated them. That is how this book was written as well.

I was greatly pleased that in my final weeks as an editorial writer, I was the recipient of the David Graven Award for Achievement in Journalism, one of the Frank Premack Journalism Awards given each year to Minnesota's top public affairs journalists. The award is named after Frank Premack, who covered the state capitol for the *Minneapolis Tribune* in the 1960s, and died too soon, in 1975. It meant a great deal for me to be recognized as a journalist by other journalists.

Over the years, many people mentioned enjoying the editorials and asked about the possibility of reprints. But it was my old friend Russell Fridley, former director of the Minnesota Historical Society, who impressed me with the comment, "Elmer, there is some permanent worth in some of these editorials you're writing. I think you ought to put them into a book." I was skeptical because I have never favored an author publishing a book at his own expense. I wondered if any established publisher would be interested in a compilation of my editorials. I found one who was willing— Norton Stillman of Nodin Press. Russell was willing to be my editor. And we had help selecting the editorials for the book from a young friend, Jaime Becker, a disabled woman with a clean, sharp mind and a beautiful attitude toward life.

Views from the Publisher's Desk was published in 1997. It got reviews that made me blush. Dave Wood, the books editor for the *Star Tribune,* called it "a book for all seasons by a man who has weathered many of them."

A fitting send-off for the book, I thought, would be a reception in the capitol in the ornate governor's reception room. Though I knew then-Gov. Arne Carlson well, I decided not to approach him directly with such a bold request. I wanted to make it easy for him to turn me down, if he was so inclined. Instead, I called our mutual friend Wheelock Whitney and asked him to seek Carlson's approval. Carlson agreed. I thought that word was sufficient to pave the way for our book-signing party. But when Stillman arrived at the capitol at the appointed hour, loaded with boxes of books to be signed and sold, he was told by a building official that a book sale in the governor's office was out of the question. A distraught Stillman caught me at home before I left the house. "They're telling me I can't sell any books," he said. "I'll call the governor," I said. I reached one of Carlson's assistants, who went directly to his boss. Carlson told me afterward that he telephoned the building superintendent and said, "You're in charge of the building, but I'm in charge of my office, and I say that there are going to be books sold here today." After that exchange, we had a smooth event. It drew a big crowd—and I cannot resist trying to get a laugh from a big audience. When I stood up to speak, I said, "If a person had a choice as to when to die, this would be a pretty good time for me."

I am sometimes asked which editorials in the book are my personal favorites. I regard each of them as old friends—for I lived intimately with each one for a week or more. But one published on November 9, 1995, stands out. Its headline was "Traits of a Serious American Citizen." The text:

> There is no more complimentary title for a European businessman than for someone to refer to him as a "serious businessman." It means he pays attention to his affairs; he is informed; he studies; he thinks, he works. Restrained in his conversation and style, pleasant and polite but not aggressive, he has a quiet confidence that generates belief and trust.
>
> America needs more citizens who would generate the observation: "He or she is a serious American citizen." What would that mean? What would it signify? It would mean a citizen who was attentive to the government process as absolutely essential in a democracy. It would be one who knew his or her heritage through a broad-based education and continuous study. It would be a person who could converse clearly and disagree civilly. It would be someone who loved America's diversity, and was interested in and cared about other people, and wanted happy lives for them.
>
> It would be a person who knows and appreciates the incredible blessings of freedom, equality, opportunity and justice that are possible in a well-operating democracy. This means participating in elections, being active in the party of his or her choice, and believing that any individual can make a difference and have influence in the choosing of candidates and the determination of a party platform. A serious citizen would know something about public finance, the need to pay for what we enjoy and to divide that burden fairly.
>
> A serious American citizen would not be misled by hate mongers, by people or publications appealing to selfishness and greed, or offering programs that the citizen could sense were not in the long-range best interest of the nation or the world community. To be a serious American citizen would require time, attention and commitment. But it goes with being a part of a powerful nation, of seeking peace and prosperity for all people everywhere. It is a mission. It cannot be imposed. It must be spontaneous and self-generated. In a time when our wonderful country is plagued with many problems, our greatest need is for individuals to decide to so live that people would say, "Now, there's a serious American citizen."

Minnesota Historical Society

Whe n i came to minnesota in 1928, I brought with me a deep interest in history in general and Minnesota's history in particular. I soon learned where to go to satisfy my curiosity—the Minnesota Historical Society.

I have been a member of the society for more than a half century, and I was its president from 1966 to 1970. That assignment put me in exclusive company. Only one other person in the state's history, John S. Pillsbury, served in turn as governor, chairman of the Board of Regents of the University of Minnesota, and president of the Minnesota Historical Society.

Much about the Minnesota Historical Society appeals to me—its long service to the state, its dedication to historic preservation, its way of involving average citizens. The society's desire to found and nurture county historical societies was what first caught me up in its work.

In the mid-1940s, as the farms of rural Ramsey County were rapidly disappearing, my St. Anthony Park neighborhood experienced a surge of interest in its own history. A group began to meet at the local library to collect memorabilia and prepare modest exhibits of the area's history.

At about that time, the heirs to the Gibbs farm, just north of the St. Paul campus of the University of Minnesota, proposed to give the farm to the university. It appeared that not only would the land become part of the campus, but the old farmstead would be torn down. That prospect caught the attention of the little St. Anthony Park history club. The group mobilized to save the farm buildings and sought the advice of the Minnesota Historical Society. The state society advised the group to incorporate as a nonprofit organization and raise money to rescue and restore the Gibbs farmstead. That is how the Ramsey County Historical Society was born.

I was all for raising private funds for the Gibbs Farm project, and donating time, too. Eleanor was among the volunteers who labored to restore the farmhouse's interior. But I also thought that county taxpayers ought to help a little. As a new state senator in 1949, I urged the Ramsey County Board to dedicate a fraction of one mill levy to the county historical society, so that the society would have a permanent source of revenue. The dedicated tax was not forthcoming, but an annual appropriation was, and it has continued to this day. That made it possible for the Ramsey County Historical Society not only to endure but to flourish. Virginia Brainard Kunz was its director for twenty-five years, and the founder and editor still of its quarterly magazine, *Ramsey County History.*

Though my initial connection was with the county organization, my bond with the state society was sealed when I met Russell Fridley. He became the society's associate director in 1953, acting state director in 1954, and state director in 1955. He held that position for thirty-one years. Under his leadership the historical society had its renaissance and became one of the leading organizations of its kind in the country, if not the world.

I became acquainted with Russell in 1953, when I was a state senator and the historical society was looking for a legislative ally to sponsor bills that would aid its work. One such bill that session was to provide funds to microfilm the newspapers that had been piling up in the society's possession since territorial days. The society had raised some money privately for the project, beginning in 1949, but it was proceeding too slowly. Russell informed me that there were thousands of volumes of newspapers rotting away in the catacombs of the capitol. "We've got to save this fundamental record of our state," he said. "Elmer, I want to show them to you."

I never hesitated to learn more about the capitol, as well as about Minnesota history. So we were off to the subbasement of Cass Gilbert's grand building. You think you are in the basement—where the capitol press corps does its work—and then you open a door and find that there is another level below. Wandering around down in that dark, dank, cavernous space is like being in a ghost chamber. It is fascinating.

What I found there was an amazing sight—volumes and volumes of weekly newspapers that had accumulated over a one-hundred-year period. Most of them were not quite rotting, but they were deteriorating. The subbasement clearly did not afford ideal conditions for their preservation.

I became the sponsor of a bill to underwrite the microfilming of the society's newspaper collection. Part of my technique for winning votes was to offer selected colleagues a guided tour of the subbasement. I made it a point to take Sen. Bill Dahlquist of Thief River Falls into the catacombs. He was probably the most conservative member of the senate's Finance Committee. But he was also a newspaper editor. I knew that if I could get him to see the merit in microfilming, his consent would win over quite a few others. I appealed to him as a newspaper editor. Surely he could see the long-term value of newspapers. He and I had coffee together, down in the catacombs, and had a pleasant chat about the importance of community newspapers. That is how I got Dahlquist's vote.

Other legislators went along too. The legislature not only provided the money to start the microfilming that year but continued to fund the project for years to come. I teased Russell about asking for money long after all of the newspapers had been microfilmed, because the project had proven to be a surefire money raiser. "No, no," he would protest. "It's that more newspapers are always being published. They keep coming in, so we always have more to put on microfilm."

After that, for anything related to history that required some legislation, I was Russell's servant. He would call me before each session and tell me what he needed, and I would go to work on it. Russell set about an aggressive program of restoring Minnesota landmarks into highly educational and entertaining sites, open for public inspection. His first big achievement was the restoration of old Fort Snelling, beginning in the late 1950s. In 1969, the fort began its "living history" technique of displaying and interpreting life at the fort in 1827, using actors in period costume to tell the story. Russell applied the same technique to other sites too. The restoration and "living history" adaptation of the Oliver Kelly Farm, the Lindbergh House, the Northwest Company Fur Post, the Alexander Ramsey House, and more bear Russell's stamp.

We might have lost Russell to another state if the Minnesota Historical Society had not had its unique relationship with state government. Its genius is that it is independent, yet it receives state funds. It is a separate corporation with its own board, yet it is funded in part by the legislature. It is part of a funding category the legislature calls "semi-state" activities, independent endeavors that are deserving of state support. Russell had a chance to run the New York historical organization, but its status as a state agency made it much more subject to political whim and much less free to set its own agenda. Minnesota is lucky that he stayed.

My interest in books and my involvement in the Minnesota Historical Society created a pleasant synergy. I was eager to learn whatever the society had to teach about the role of books and publishing in the state's beginnings. Minnesota became a territory in 1849. Immediately thereafter, a printer named James Goodhue loaded a press on a flatboat and started for St. Paul. He knew that if there were to be any kind of government, there would be a need for printing. He printed the first journal of the Territorial

Assembly of Minnesota. That included Gov. Alexander Ramsey's famous 1849 inaugural address. Ramsey had some blemishes in his career, but he was a strong leader and a visionary speaker. His first inaugural address declared that the history of the area should forever be preserved—particularly its newspapers, which he called "the daybooks of history." He spoke about the creation of both the Minnesota Historical Society and the University of Minnesota. I much admired an expression he used in that speech: "I trust to be believed when I say . . ." I thought that was a graceful way to express confidence in public understanding—to acknowledge the public's awareness and engagement in the enterprise he was leading. Goodhue's inclusion of that speech added to the value of the journal of the Territorial Assembly, published in 1850. I was fortunate to put a copy in my collection.

Gaining statehood was Minnesota's overriding aim in the 1850s. That effort has always held particular fascination for me. We think of the modern era as highly charged with partisanship, but it is certainly no more so than Minnesota was in territorial days. On the first day when delegates to the statehood convention met, a fierce rivalry between factions developed over the election of convention officers. The losing group walked out and met in a rival convention. There was no real dispute between the groups over whether Minnesota should join the union, or even over the chief national issue of the day, slavery. The fight was over control, pure and simple. It was about who was going to be the boss.

Both conventions produced draft constitutions. The two conventions never got together, even when Congress sent word to Minnesota that it would only grant statehood if it were presented with a single constitution. Fortunately, the two rival constitutions were not very dissimilar. A clever writer made an amalgam of them, which was adopted by each convention independently and sent to Washington. Two volumes were produced documenting the dual proceedings—also by publisher Goodhue. Those volumes also found their way to my shelves.

I also took special interest in the history of the state capitol, where I spent so much time from 1949 to 1963. Minnesota had several capitol buildings from Territorial Assembly days through the 1890s. The building in use in the early 1890s was destroyed by fire. That is when Minnesotans began to talk about building something fine and permanent, a grand showplace for a young state with a bright future. The 1893 legislature did what I consider a tremendous thing. It appointed a commission to build a capitol. It appropriated $5 million—a royal sum in those years—and turned over to the commission full authority to design and build. The commission, in turn, was wise enough to hire Cass Gilbert as architect, perhaps the most distinguished designer of public buildings in the country at that time. He designed not only the capitol building but a whole complex of buildings around it, centered on a mall that would extend to downtown St. Paul and the Mississippi River. Already then, other, less worthy structures stood in the way of his plan. But the capitol commission managed to carve out a piece of ground atop a suitable hill and determined that there would be the capitol. It was a mammoth undertaking. Construction started in 1895, and the first governor to have an office in the new building was John A. Johnson in 1905.

What an achievement it was, within fifty years of achieving statehood, to build a noble building that to this day is a symbol of pride in our state. Who would have the courage today to provide taxpayer funds to put gold-adorned horses atop a public building? Likewise, if the St. Paul City Hall were built today, who would opt for a towering onyx sculpture in the lobby? *The God of Peace,* designed by Swedish artist Carl Milles, was started in about 1929, but it was completed with depression money. Both buildings are marks of Minnesota's visionary attitude about places that belong to everyone. Those buildings convey a message that Minnesotans favor doing things the way they ought to be done.

A characteristic of the early European settlers in this state was incredible vision. For example, I marvel at the likes of Jonathan Carver. He came here as a British soldier to represent his army and his country in the mid-1760s. He traveled by canoe and on foot, in primitive conditions, living off the land and with only the material he could carry with him. Yet he was never without writing material and paper. He kept a journal. When he returned to England, that journal was published in 1765. My collection includes a copy. It went into many editions because Carver's account was not only interesting, it was factual. He was not as learned as the good priest who also came in the first wave of European exploration, Father Louis Hennepin. Yet the journal of Carver, the soldier, is more highly regarded than that of Hennepin, the priest, because of its accuracy.

Many promotional books were published in the 1850s and sent to Europe to encourage immigrants to come here. I have several. They extolled the state's woods, lakes, game, and fish. They boasted about Minnesota's "invigorating" climate. Nothing was wrong with Minnesota, one said, save one thing: "The only shortage in Minnesota is cemeteries. Few people ever die." Those sales pitches did their job. Immigrants flowed in.

One early arrival was a young firebrand from Philadelphia named Ignatius Donnelly. He came to St. Paul in 1856 and embarked on one of the most varied and remarkable careers in early Minnesota history. He was a real-estate developer, newspaper editor and publisher, lieutenant governor, legislator and congressman, literary scholar, and political reformer—and that is but a partial list of his accomplishments. I am a great admirer of Donnelly, and so have never missed an opportunity to learn a little more about him.

In the 1950s, the society sponsored an exhibit of famous homes of Minnesota. One of the paintings in that exhibit depicted Donnelly's home in Nininger, the failed Utopian city he attempted to build. When I visited the exhibit, I noticed an older lady staring at that painting. I could not help myself. I approached her and said, "Please excuse me. I noticed your particular interest in the Donnelly home. I wonder if you'd be willing to tell me the nature of your interest, because I'm a great admirer of Donnelly." She said, "I'm his widow." "You're his widow?" I was astonished. Then, I remembered that in 1898, at age sixty-seven and less than two years before his death, Donnelly had married his twenty-year-old secretary, Marian Hanson. His first wife, Kate, had died some years earlier, and he confessed to his diary that he married the adoring young secretary because he was lonely. His children were outraged, and many other people were critical of the union. It quickly came to me that the lady standing before me, who said her name was now Mrs. Henry Woltman, was once Marian Hanson Donnelly. I stammered a bit before I said, "I'm so pleased to have the chance to meet you."

It then occurred to me that my colleagues in the senate might be just as surprised as I was to learn that Donnelly's widow was still living, and might be equally delighted to meet her. I said, "What I'd love to do is give the members of the senate a great surprise. If you'd be willing to come and sit in the well of the senate, I'd like to introduce you to the state senate. They'd just be overwhelmed to think that the widow of Ignatius Donnelly, who is an ancient character in their minds, is still living and part of the life of St. Paul." She agreed to come, and, after consulting with Majority Leader Archie Miller and Lt. Gov. Karl Rolvaag, who presided over senate sessions, we set a date.

When the moment came, I said, "I have a very special guest visiting us in the senate today. You'll find hard to believe what I am going to tell you. With us, today, is the widow of Ignatius Donnelly, the young secretary he married late in life. Here she is, Mrs. Marian Hanson Donnelly Woltman." The senate was agog and incredulous in the realization that here was a human link to a famous Minnesotan who died at the turn of the century.

I did not tell the senate that day that I had in my possession another link to Donnelly. Some years earlier, when our children were small, I wanted the family to see Donnelly's house at Nininger while it still stood. We made a family expedition to the site, near Hastings, seventeen miles south of St. Paul. The house was in shocking disrepair. Windowpanes were knocked out, and drapes were blowing out the window. A fine old grand piano stood exposed to the elements in the drafty living room. Law books were scattered on the floor. It was a scene of desolation. A few years later, the house finally, literally, collapsed.

Naturally, I was drawn to the books on the floor. Donnelly's literary library had already been retrieved by the society. The books still there were case law and statute books, of which many copies still exist. But I also noticed one black-bound book on the floor. I picked it up. It had Donnelly's name in gold inscribed on it. It was Jefferson's *Manual of Procedure,* the desk book issued to members of Congress. I quickly realized that this book had significance and should not be lost. After a few moments of consideration, I decided to take the book with me. I carefully explained to the family that we were not stealing, that we were taking this book to preserve and protect it. If we left it, it would just be lost to future generations, and that would be a shame. Donnelly's copy of *Manual of Procedure* will be part of the Andersen collection at the University of Minnesota.

I received a postcard once from a book dealer in California. Dealers often share the names of serious book collectors, along with information about their areas of interest. One of mine was Minnesota history. The card indicated that the dealer had a manuscript journal of a military person who had some connection with Minnesota. His name was Snelling, and the asking price was $100. Would I be interested? I was on the phone in a flash to the historical society. "Do you know of any journal that Colonel Snelling ever kept at Fort Snelling?" I asked. "Yes," was the reply. "Have you ever seen it?" "Yes." "Do you have a copy of it?" "Yes, we were permitted to make a copy of it. If you look in your collection of *Minnesota History* magazines, you'll find it referenced . . . Why are you so interested?" I said, "I'll tell you later."

I sent for the journal and learned its story. An Omaha woman descended from Snelling had obtained it from her family, and at one point, she had allowed the Minnesota Historical Society to borrow and copy it. She then moved to California and died there. Her books wound up in the hands of a dealer who knew neither what the journal was nor its significance. It is a manuscript journal that covers some or all of 1828 at the old fort. One of its passages speaks of Snelling's resolve to fight a pistol duel with an opponent. The duel likely never came about. I asked for a search of War Department records, and that investigation produced no record of it taking place. Nevertheless, Snelling's comments about it are fascinating: "In response to the bad passions of a bad man, I've agreed to meet Colonel . . . on the field of battle tomorrow at dawn . . ."—something to that effect. The part I found particularly revealing about Snelling's character came at the end: "There will be no reconciliation or shaking of hands. When I think a man a rascal, I never take his hand."

The journal also documents something historians used to debate: there was slavery in Minnesota. Snelling records that he bought a slave from William Bostwick of St. Louis for $500. Her name, Louisa, appears in his record. He also kept records of the accounts of men who died. In that simple day, it fell to him to look after the belongings of any soldier who died at the fort.

I used to put that book on display, along with the journals of Carver and Hennepin and a few other mementos of early Minnesota history, when I was invited to speak to civic organizations or schools. I prepared a talk for civic groups titled, "Adventures in Minnesota History." While I spoke, I would pass the books around for the audience to examine. Snelling's journal began to show a little wear.

One day, the society's curator of manuscripts looked at it. She said, "Elmer, you are not being a very good steward of this precious volume." Her words stung. I told her, "If you had tied me to the mast and hit me with ten lashes, it wouldn't have affected me any more." I wasted little time before taking the book to Lakeside Press, a division of R. R. Donnelly Company, the finest book-restoring laboratory in the country at that time. They kept it about six months and restored it meticulously. Then, I gave it to the Minnesota Historical Society and said, "Now, you take care of it."

Through the years, many other Minnesotans have had the same idea about their treasures. When they were ready to part with them, they thought, "Let the historical society take care of them." That, for example, was the idea of a couple of unmarried sisters who lived together in their family home, one of the older homes in St. Paul. When it was time for them to give up the house, they debated what to do about their attic, which was full of keepsakes. One of them had the idea to call the Minnesota Historical Society and ask them to take what they might want. Someone from the society came to the house and found some of the original maps of the Lewis and Clark expedition. The society was beside itself with delight in finding some of the original Lewis and Clark documentation. But Yale University, which has long arms and a long reach, heard of the discovery. Yale presented a claim that under a will of one of the people who had lived in that house, it was entitled to anything it wanted from the house in the way of books, manuscripts, and letters. The dispute over the Lewis and Clark map went to court, which ruled in favor of Yale. Though the episode did not end well for the Minnesota Historical Society, it showed how valuable the stuff of Minnesota's old attics and cellars can be.

By the time I was president of the society, storage space was already scarce. The society was crammed into a building adjacent to the capitol, the smallest building in the capitol complex. The capitol subbasement was also available, but it was hardly suitable for most of the collection. The society's Executive Council and Russell Fridley spent a lot of time seeking suitable additional space to rent and deciding how to cope when no space was readily available. Of course, Russell knew what the ultimate solution should be—a new building.

Behind the historical society building next to the capitol was the St. Paul Mechanic Arts High School. Our first idea was to acquire that building, which had outlasted its usefulness as a high school, and remodel it for our purposes. That plan included construction of a link between the original building, with its pleasant classical facade, and the school. But another force—namely, Appeals Court Chief Judge Peter Popovich—intervened to change our plan.

In 1983, Gov. Rudy Perpich appointed Popovich, my old friend and legislative colleague, to be the founding chief judge of the newly created Minnesota Court of Appeals, which started with twelve members and would soon grow to sixteen. Popovich saw immediately that a court that large needed a building. To him, only one location would do: it had to be next to the capitol. He set his sights on acquiring the historical society's building and garnered an important ally—the governor. Soon, a grandiose plan developed for a new judiciary building next to the capitol, and Russell was put to the task of finding another site for the society's expansion.

Fortunately, about that time, mergers in the hospital industry made an old hospital site near the capitol available for redevelopment. It was on a small rise overlooking both the capitol and downtown. Russell saw its potential and urged its acquisition, as did his successor, Nina Archabal. Governor Perpich was firmly on their side. But I think the History Center got its funding with relative ease from the legislature because Popovich was pushing for it too. Construction could not commence on a Judicial Building until the historical society got its building and could vacate its old quarters.

Nina Archabal succeeded Fridley in 1986 and has done a wonderful job. She is a worthy successor to my friend Russell: she is well organized, persistent, and strong. She built the building within budget and on schedule and has led its operation with great success.

At the groundbreaking ceremony for the Minnesota History Center, I sat next to Archabal and Governor Perpich, who was the speaker that day. I have a photo of the three of us together. I wondered that day whether I would be around to see the finished building. But in October 1992, at the building's dedication, I was there. The History Center turned out beautifully. One storage area is so immense that a railroad boxcar can sit in it and seem small by comparison to its surroundings. There is a boxcar there to this day.

In recent years, I had one disappointment with the Minnesota Historical Society—perhaps my only one during our long association. In the 1930s, Harvey Fuller introduced me to an artist named George Resler, whose specialty was etching. His work included some wonderful Minnesota landscapes and St. Paul street scenes that I thought made a real contribution to the state's culture. Much later, I began to collect his work and donate it to the society, and convinced others who owned his work to do the same. I arranged for Resler's widow, Dorothy Resler, to be interviewed on tape about his life as a Minnesota artist in the early years of this century. Sadly, the tape of that interview was lost. And when I was interested in working with the historical society to publish a collection of Resler's work in book form, the society turned me down. Art books were not their field, they said. Fortunately, I found a more enthusiastic response at the Minneapolis Institute of Arts. With our help, the institute published *George Earl Resler: Minnesota Etcher* in 1996, in conjunction with an exhibition of his work.

I left active service on the society's Executive Council in 1986 and joined an elders' club they call the "Honorary Council." From that post I have remained an enthusiastic booster of all the society does. I rank it second only to the University of Minnesota among Minnesota institutions devoted to the betterment of this state. It deserves the stewardship of Minnesota's best leaders.

University of Minnesota Landscape Arboretum

L IVING IN ST. ANTHONY PARK gave us interesting neighbors—many of them connected to the University of Minnesota. One who lived a block or two away was Leon Snyder, the head of the Department of Horticulture and an incredible font of knowledge about plants. He and his wife, Vera, were wonderful, down-to-earth people. Through Snyder we learned in the late 1950s that a major arboretum was being established west of Minneapolis.

My interest was immediately piqued. Since my boyhood days tramping around Michigan's Lake Mona with my friend Leroy Olson, I had loved nature. Here, I thought, was a project that merited our support.

The idea to create an arboretum did not originate with Snyder. It sprang first from the Lake Minnetonka Garden Club, an energetic group with a vision and the means to make it a reality. One of the grande dames of the organization was Mrs. John Pillsbury. An undeveloped tract of land became available west of Chanhassen, and the club had the idea of buying it and starting an arboretum. Soon after they made the purchase, they decided the arboretum should not be theirs, but the university's. The club donated the initial parcel of land to the university in 1958, and the Minnesota Landscape Arboretum was born.

When Mrs. Pillsbury was nearly one hundred, I arranged for the Board of Regents to present her with an award for her contribution to the arboretum and other generous gifts to the university through the years. Despite her age, she took the occasion to stand and dispense advice to the regents, wagging her finger at them as she spoke. She was thinking constructively and positively about things that should be done to make the university better. We were thoroughly delighted by her strength and spirit.

The Garden Club's gift connected the arboretum with Snyder. The connection was a strong one and lasted for the rest of his life. He loved gardening, loved the soil, and loved helping people have more success with their own gardens. He was remarkable in that he was a brilliant scientist, yet he never talked down to anybody. He was sympathetic with average gardeners, and that made him an ideal director of the arboretum. He saw it as a place whose mission was to serve the gardeners of Minnesota. It seemed he devoted all his time to developing the arboretum. Eventually, he moved to a home with a large garden near the arboretum. I used to tease him, "Leon, you amaze me. Regardless of what the conversation is or what anybody is talking about, in two sentences, you can relate it to the arboretum."

The arboretum was small and sparse at first, but Snyder's vision for it was not. His efforts to create something of horticultural significance west of Chanhassen coincided nicely with several developments in my life. After I left the governorship in 1963, I was ready to get involved in new avenues of public service. At the behest of my old friend at 3M, Cecil March, I joined the board of directors of the Bush Foundation in 1968. And in 1957, Eleanor and I had established the Elmer L. and Eleanor J. Andersen Foundation to commit our family firmly to philanthropy for the sake of community betterment. Our foundation made the first of many gifts to the arboretum in 1963.

At first, the arboretum's greatest need was for more land. But by the late 1960s, Snyder's attention had turned to the need for a building to serve arboretum visitors. A Development Fund was established in 1969 to amass $1 million for a visitor's center, and I became a member of the fund's executive committee. As I envisioned the building we aimed to build, I pictured a library in it.

I took the case for the arboretum to the Bush Foundation, which had been established in 1953 by Archibald and Edyth Bush. For years, Archie Bush was the top assistant to 3M's longtime chief executive William McKnight, and held the title executive vice president when he died in 1966. He was a fine, generous, outgoing man, much interested in the welfare of the state. The foundation he and his wife created had a giving capacity, even in its earliest days, of $10 million to $12 million a year, which now is up to $30 million to $40 million. Cecil March, my streetcar-commuting friend from 1934, had risen to a group vice presidency at 3M and was an early member of the foundation board.

After Archie Bush's death, a nasty fight broke out between the Minnesotans on the board and some unscrupulous attorneys who tried to gain control of the foundation and move it to Florida, where Edyth Bush lived. Cecil invited me to join the Bush board because he needed reinforcements on the Minnesota side. He said, "I've got a battle on my hands, and maybe you could help."

I joined on one condition. I told him: "It can't be a battle over whether you're going to control it or somebody else is going to control it. It has enough money to justify professional management. I'll come on the board if our first task will be to find a professional administrator." He agreed, and I came on the board in 1968.

Sadly, the Bush Foundation was in for a legal battle that would go on for years. Mrs. Bush established a second foundation in Florida, and the legal bills to defend the Minnesota-based foundation from those who sought to dissolve it and move its assets to Florida came to $400,000. But a Florida federal judge eventually dismissed the case of the Minnesota foundation's opponents, and Cecil made good on his commitment to hire a professional manager. It took diligent pursuit, but we got a gem, Humphrey Doermann, direct from being registrar of Harvard University.

The Bush Foundation continued to function philanthropically during those difficult years. Education was a particular focus of its giving, and the University of Minnesota benefited in a variety of ways from its annual gifts. The foundation set up a program and a series of qualifications for awarding capital grants to Minnesota private colleges, many of whom had difficulty meeting their need for new and improved facilities. The foundation has also been a major patron of the United Negro College Fund. Early childhood development was a particular interest of one board member, Irving Harris, and of Doermann. They arranged for the foundation to subsidize post-doctoral research on human development from birth to three years of age. Bush grant recipients have made an important contribution to our under-standing of this field.

We persuaded the foundation to pay the full cost of an addition to the Hill Monastic Manuscript Library, to have the satisfaction of providing that entire portion of an important work. The Little Sisters of the Poor came with an appeal for a large gift for a new building and were not disappointed. The Bush board was so impressed when the sisters made their appeal: "You know, we've been prudent over the years," they said in meek, modest tones. "We have accumulated about $1 million of our own."

Beginning shortly after I joined the board, the Minnesota Landscape Arboretum figured prominently on the Bush Foundation's giving list. Some years, the gift would be designated for land, other times, for building proj-ects. Acquiring land was not easy. Some landowners did not want to sell at a reasonable price—or at any price. Some parcels we tried to buy in the 1960s did not come into the arboretum's hands until decades later. It finally took a legislative appropriation to provide the large sums that land acquisition required in the 1990s.

Once it was under way, the effort to build an educational building produced quicker results. St. Paul architect Edwin Hugh Lundie was chosen to design a building that would include an auditorium, classrooms, a fireplace room, a tearoom, offices, a gift shop, and, of course, a library. I made a number of calls on potential donors to solicit contributions to the building. It was the first time many of them had been asked to support the arboretum. My pitch went something like this: "This is a fun project. You and I are often asked for contributions to alleviate hunger or poverty or desperate situations, and those causes certainly need support. But they aren't what you'd call fun projects. This is. You can get joy out of supporting this. You can go out and enjoy the arboretum, hike through the gardens that you help establish, or the grove of trees that you help get planted. You can memorialize your mother and father, and play there with your children and grandchildren." Nobody could resist a sales talk like that.

The pitch worked particularly well with the Bush Foundation. At my urging, it contributed nearly $175,000 to what would be called the Leon C. Snyder Building, earmarking a portion of its gift for the building's auditorium, which bears the Bush name. The Dayton family was also helpful. Kenneth Dayton still gives a substantial gift annually. The Pillsbury family took part, following their matriarch's lead. People were very generous.

Then I asked Eleanor, "Wouldn't it be fun if we could be identified with the library portion of the building?" She could not help but concur. I had already started collecting rare books about horticulture.

A library is not a building. A library is books. I did not wait for the construction of a building to start amassing the books to fill it. Beginning in the mid-1960s, we arranged to have horticultural books gathered at the St. Paul campus. The Andersen Foundation supplied a fund for book acquisition. In 1969, four years before the library wing of the Snyder Building was completed, we began the search for a librarian. On March 30, 1970, June Rogier started work as the first librarian of the Andersen Horticultural Library. She was an ideal choice: a trained librarian, an arboretum volunteer, and an avid gardener. Based at first on the St. Paul campus of the university, it was her job to select, purchase, and catalog the three thousand volumes we hoped to have on hand when the library opened.

A principle was established early: the Andersen Horticultural Library would be a noncirculating library. People would go there confident that the books that they wanted to see would be there. They would not be on loan to another patron or temporarily in some faculty office. One other thing: there would be no markings or stickers on the books. We had clear ideas from the start about the kind of library it should be, and to a great degree, those ideas have held fast through three decades.

We were more than donors to the library; we were intimately involved in its establishment. Eleanor deserves credit for connecting us with George Nakashima, the Pennsylvania woodworker whose beautiful black walnut furniture was chosen for the library. She spotted his work at an exhibition in Washington, D.C., in 1972 and immediately saw its potential for the library.

Shelving is always a question because it takes so much room. We learned of a new kind of shelving that is on rollers, so that only one aisle is needed for multiple rows of shelves. One could roll the shelves until an aisle appeared where you wanted to go in. That innovation allowed us to store many more books than can be accommodated with conventional shelves.

We took a great interest in the books that were to go on those shelves. I had the brainstorm to run ads in a national horticultural magazine. "A new, fine horticultural library is being established at the University of Minnesota," the ad announced. "Any donations to the library would be gratefully received." Responses came from all over the country and included some books of high quality. We offered to pick them up when we could, to save the donors the burden of shipping costs. By that time, the H. B. Fuller Company had salespeople all over the country. I would ask one of them to pick up the books and either ship them to me or hand-deliver them when we next met. Before long, at meetings, when the sales force compared notes, they were asking, "Have you had a directive from Elmer to go pick up some books?"

One by-product of our call for donations was a relationship with the American Hosta Society. The library acquired the papers of one of the most famous hosta cultivators in the country, Frances R. Williams of Winchester, Massachusetts. Then, in 1980, the Minnesota Landscape Arboretum became the national headquarters for the Hosta Society. Its national convention was in Golden Valley that year. The arboretum's lovely hosta glade was installed for that occasion, and it remains a popular attraction.

For our own purchases for the library, we sought rare, high-quality books on horticulture. Early herbals, that is, books describing herbs grown in the sixteenth century, are part of the collection. The earliest dates from 1542. They are as much works of art as they are historical reference books. We have a number of complete sets of serially produced garden books and periodicals published in the eighteenth and nineteenth centuries. The collection also includes some classics of botanical illustration. A number of the great illustrators of horticultural books from the seventeenth, eighteenth, and nineteenth centuries are represented. The most famous was a Parisian, Pierre Joseph Redouté. Redouté did work for Napoleon's wife, Josephine Bonaparte. He worked in Josephine's famous garden, Jardin de la Malmaison, making some of the most beautiful prints of flowers that have ever been made. Lilies and roses were two of his great works. At an auction, we were lucky enough to get one of the eight copies of Redouté's work with two sets of prints, one in black and white and one in color. There were only eight sets that had both. The Andersen library has several other volumes containing Redouté illustrations, making its collection of his work one of the largest and most significant anywhere in the world. Visitors to the library who are knowledgeable about botanical illustration often marvel at the range of what is available.

I just loved buying books for the library, and sometimes I bought a little beyond our means. Further, I was not always completely confiding to Eleanor what I was up to. Once a delivery person came to the door with some boxes of books from Sotheby's. I was not there at the moment, and Eleanor was at the door. As he set them down, he said, "I'm sure glad to get rid of these boxes. They are insured for $45,000."

So, Eleanor had to cope with some surprises along the way, but she has been wonderfully cooperative, understanding, and indulgent. We always bought books for a purpose or a goal. We have probably spent more on books destined for the Andersen Horticultural Library because we wanted it to be distinctive—and it is. We are still adding to the collection. It has grown to more than eleven thousand volumes.

I do not know how much we have spent over the thirty-five years or more that the collection has been growing. The money side of book collecting has never much interested me. When I buy something, I try to forget how much it costs. At one point, for insurance purposes, an appraisal was made of the library, and it was appraised at $3 million. I do know that either through personal gifts or the Andersen Foundation, we have supplied the majority of its books.

Once, librarian Richard Isaacson was giving a talk to the Friends of the Andersen Horticultural Library, a group of volunteers and contributors. He was comparing four copies of the same book, each a different edition, and explaining their subtle differences. When he called for questions from the audience, he was asked why it was necessary for the library to have four copies of the same book. He shot me a glance and said, "We have a patron who just loves to buy books." I had supplied all four copies.

The Andersen Horticultural Library was opened and dedicated on June 26, 1974. On that festive, memorable day, our guest speaker was George H. M. Lawrence, director emeritus of the Hunt Botanical Library at Carnegie-Mellon University in Pennsylvania. He was most impressed with the quality of the collection—and it was only beginning.

Our view was that the Andersen Horticultural Library should have a special area of excellence. We latched on to one early: its collection of nursery and seed catalogs would be the best in the nation. The library would be the place arboretum visitors could go to find out where to purchase any plant they saw on the grounds. A number of enthusiastic volunteers made that goal their own and worked diligently beginning a few months after the dedication. Within a short time, a nursery source was located for every arboretum plant that was available for purchase. By 1980, more than half of the questions posed to the library were requests for information about the purchase of plants.

This effort took on even greater importance in 1985 when Richard Isaacson succeeded June Rogier. He had been the librarian at the Eleanor Squire Library at the Garden Center of Greater Cleveland, Ohio. There, an attempt was made to establish a comprehensive, computerized encyclopedia of sources for plants and seeds. The project petered out, apparently, after he left, and the Squire Library offered it to him. He took it and made it a fabulous success. Today more than two thousand current seed and nursery catalogs are maintained. The computer has made the job of keeping track of material availability much easier than it used to be. There is constant change, so Isaacson reissues his "Source List of Plants and Seeds" periodically. A fifth edition is planned for release in 2000. It is now *the* reference book in libraries all over the country and has an international following too, including gardens in London, Paris, and Japan. Isaacson has lifted the Andersen Library to prominence in the horticultural field.

The library is fortunate to have had only two head librarians, both marvelously dedicated. June Rogier, now retired, is an active volunteer again, one of several who add a great deal to the library's service. Because of these unpaid but skillful people, the library can operate on a relatively small budget, compared to the significance that it is gaining. The university funds the librarian's salary, the Andersen Foundation provides a major portion of the annual operating funds, and the Arboretum Foundation picks up the remainder. That public-private funding arrangement is unique among libraries in the University of Minnesota system.

In 1987, after many years of planning, ground was broken on a research addition to the Andersen Library. I headed the fundraising campaign and enlisted the whole family to help, along with the Bush Foundation. Our combined efforts raised nearly $600,000 for the project, which was completed in 1988. The addition provided both suitable housing for the library's research collection and space for future growth. It offered climate-controlled, secured storage for our historical books. And it supplied some much-needed office space.

By then, I was a past president (later called chairman) and former board member of the Bush Foundation, having retired from the board in 1982. I headed the board from 1976 to 1981. My Bush Foundation experience was one reason I also became a member in 1971 of the board of the National Council on Foundations, a network that gave philanthropic foundations a single voice in Washington. That voice was much needed in the 1970s. In response to reports about greed and shoddy practices within some foundations, Congress began to dictate such things as the minimum disbursement of assets that a foundation must make in order to maintain its tax-exempt status. My service on the council board and its executive committee lasted through 1974.

Through years of focus on the arboretum, I became a gardener of a type—a management gardener. I lacked the time to nurture a garden myself, but we had plots for both flowers and vegetables at Deer Lake Farm, and we hired someone there to care for them. I would buy seeds and order plants each winter and early spring, in a quantity in keeping with my expansive but not always realistic vision for our garden. The amount was almost always more than we could use.

We planted hundreds of shrubs and plants to provide habitat and feed for birds and wildlife. We planted a profusion of flowers. And we planted vegetables, in varieties that I thought looked nice. I did not plant according to taste. For example, I never liked to eat eggplant. But I thought eggplant had the most beautiful purple color that I had ever encountered, so a lot of eggplant was grown. I do not know what we did with them. But at harvest time, I would hold the eggplant and admire its beautiful shape and marvelous color. Similarly, I was fond of growing kohlrabi because its stalks came out from a bulb that was above the ground. That made it an interesting looking plant. Only after I started growing it did I discover that raw kohlrabi makes a piquant addition to a salad.

I had a hard time satisfying Eleanor on zucchini. I tend to be expansive. I wanted our produce to be big and good-looking. I loved how fast zucchini grew and how long they could become. Eleanor would say, "I don't want great big zucchini. Zucchini should be about so long," indicating about eight inches. "But at that size, they've hardly started to grow," I would protest. "That's when you're supposed to eat them." I thought I was being unkind to the zucchini when I would cut a little beginning fruit to satisfy my dear wife. But as long as I provided her some small ones for eating, I was free to let some get big.

One of our farm workers, Mike Cotch, took particular interest in the flower garden. It included poppies, iris, snapdragons, and other colorful bloomers, which he worked carefully to nurture. I often brought him more bulbs and plants. On one such occasion, he stared at my bundle incredulously. "It's full," he said. "I couldn't plant another thing." I looked closely, and he was right. The garden patch was full of glorious blooming flowers. I said, "Mike, stand there and let me take your picture." Years later, when he was aged and confined to his home, I visited him. There, on the mantle, he had that photo by the garden that he had tended with great care. He told me he considered the day I praised his garden one of the great days of his life. He is in a nursing home now. My guess is that the photo is in his room.

At home, both at the Hoyt Avenue house and in the home we built in Arden Hills in 1985, Eleanor is the chief gardener. She had help with the landscape design in our new home from Jim Hagstrom of Savanna Designs, a fine landscape architecture firm. But Eleanor keeps changing things, to renew the appearance of the home and keep everything fresh. She has a green thumb. Once when we were going to be away from home for a few days, she asked me to help her put all her houseplants on the porch, where they could be accessed easily for watering. I counted when they were all moved, and was surprised to discover that we had more than seventy plants in the house. She approaches home gardening seriously. She studies each plant and experiments with different devices and concoctions to fertilize them. She is a real artist at horticulture, in the home and outside the home. Even at this advanced age of hers and mine, she is in charge of the yard.

The Minnesota Landscape Arboretum was a special and rewarding fundraising project for us. But it was just one of many causes that won grants from our family foundation. Rather than give one or two big gifts each year, as some foundations do, we have seen our foundation's role as assisting a large number of organizations and causes dedicated to community betterment. We see the foundation as a means for continuing to play a role in the life of the community after we are gone. In our personal philanthropy too, we have spread our gifts around.

Education, broadly defined, has always been a beneficiary of our giving. I headed Macalester College's $10-million campaign in 1964 and 1965. We contributed to the remodeling of the fine-arts facilities at Carleton College in Northfield. We were instrumental in securing a lovely site along the Rum River as the location for a new library in Princeton—and, of course, we contributed books to the new library, too.

And for many years, I served on the governing boards of either or both the Arboretum Foundation and the University Foundation, of which the Arboretum Foundation is a subdivision. Eleanor preceded me on the arboretum board in 1975; I joined in 1986 and served for nine years. I joined the University Foundation board of directors as the regents' representative in 1968 and remained for twenty years. I chaired the board from 1979 to 1981.

I thought when I joined the University Foundation board that I already knew a good deal about fund-raising and its importance to the university. But I was about to learn more. One of the foundation's delicate roles in those days was to connect underpaid professors and administrators with sources of supplemental income. The university's salary structure may seem generous to many people, but it does not compare favorably with what some of the university's top scientists, scholars, and executives could make in other activities. Some faculty members were aided in getting paid directorships on corporation boards. For example, service on the board of Northern States Power Company came with a handsome stipend. The foundation arranged for O. Meredith Wilson to serve on the Northern States Power board while he was president of the university in the 1960s. Making those connections was a sensitive matter that the University Foundation smoothed over, to the institution's benefit.

I served with a particularly able board member named Julius Davis, an attorney in Minneapolis. He taught the rest of the board the proper way to view our overhead costs. When he was a new member, he asked what it cost the University Foundation to raise money. The answer was 7 percent; that is, of the money raised in any one year, about 7 percent was consumed in fund-raising costs. He said, "My goodness me! If we can raise money at just 7 percent, we ought to be spending a whole lot more money to raise money." He showed us the merit in beefing up the whole organization. At his urging, we increased the number of solicitors and support staff members, and set higher goals. Davis's ideas and the capable management of a series of administrators were largely responsible for putting the foundation on a new level of activity and making a significant gain in its income. The current executive director, Gerald Fischer, has been a remarkable leader in the decade he has been with the foundation. He was chief financial officer at First Bank System before coming to the foundation. The University Foundation has been a national fund-raising leader among public universities and ranks high among all universities, including the prestigious Ivy League schools. In fiscal 1998, the foundation raised $134.5 million. A $1.3-billion campaign is in the works, with a public kickoff scheduled for 2000.

During the Minnesota Campaign, aimed at raising $250 million between 1986 to 1989, I had some revealing experiences asking for major donations. I discovered that while many people are inclined to give to special projects at the university, gifts for general university operations are hard to come by. The foundation has had to be creative in securing those funds. One technique they have used is to tap a small percentage from all gifts, even those with restricted purposes, for overall expenses. That approach raised Dave Lilly's ire when he became dean of the School of Business. He was an able money raiser, and he resented that every gift he brought in was nicked a little by the foundation. His objections led to further changes, including the placement of fund-raising personnel in each college to share that burden with the deans.

One generous donor was the late Jay Phillips. He was the head of Ed Phillips and Sons Liquor Company, and also of a successful aviation firm in Wisconsin. He was a shrewd, generous, kind man. The story goes that the University Foundation was actually conceived in his living room in a conversation among a number of major benefactors of the university. During the Minnesota Campaign, we decided to ask him to endow a professorial chair in the Department of Surgery for $1 million. Fund-raisers tend to go back to the people who have already done quite a bit. I was one of those who called on him to make the request. Not long into the conversation he said, "I think I could do that." I said, "You know, Jay, it's wonderful to be able to do what you can do, but it's much more wonderful that you do it." He looked at me and smiled. He said, "I never let anybody go out of here unhappy." I knew he was not exaggerating. His generosity was well known. He rarely declined to participate in anything. His wife, Rose, was equally generous. It was a privilege to know them.

About five of us called on the late Curt Carlson, chairman of Carlson Companies, to ask him to chair the $250-million campaign. The request entailed not only a bid for his time and service but also for a substantial lead gift. He asked directly what size gift we had in mind. We finally got out the word that we were thinking of $25 million. That staggered even Carlson, who was already then cited as the richest Minnesotan.

I said, "Curt, if you do this, you'll feel real good about yourself when you go home tonight." I saw that my comment registered with him. He liked to think well of himself, and he liked to be thought well of. Some people never lose a fresh, pleasant, adolescent-like genuineness, and he was one of them. He agreed to our request and became the drive's chairman and its leading contributor. I was not certain he would take an active role personally, but he worked hard. He attended campaign meetings and accepted his share of solicitation assignments. Before long, he was on the phone, reporting and discussing his experiences calling on people to solicit contributions. I can still hear him complaining about the hard time he was having with one potential donor in particular—Carl Pohlad, the banker and owner of the Minnesota Twins.

Russell Bennett of Bennett Lumber Company chaired the foundation's campaign committee. He set the example of commitment and hard work that Carlson and the rest of us tried to follow. With people of that caliber trying to outdo one another, it was no wonder that instead of raising $250 million, the Minnesota Campaign netted $362 million for the University of Minnesota.

My service on the boards of the University Foundation and the Arboretum Foundation has ended. Eleanor, too, left active duty on the Arboretum Foundation board in 1984 after nine years of service; she is now an honorary member of the board. But the family is still represented on the Arboretum Foundation board by our son Tony. And as long as we live, we will feel attached to those boards and committed to their missions.

Sugarloaf

OUR DAUGHTER, EMILY, telephoned one day in 1991, concerned about an area near property she owns on the North Shore of Lake Superior. She referred to Sugarloaf Cove, Beach, and Point, in Schroeder Township of Cook County, about seventy-three miles northeast of Duluth. It is a beautiful place with unusual geologic characteristics, including lava flow marks from several volcanic eruptions. That part of the state has some of the oldest exposed rock in the world, thrust to the earth's surface by prehistoric volcanic eruptions. Its name comes from the loaflike rocky point that projects into the lake. Early settlers said it reminded them of sugar, then sold in loaves in general stores. All of the North Shore has Precambrian rock, but Sugarloaf's outcropping is distinctive and has been much studied by geology professor John C. Green of the University of Minnesota-Duluth.

Emily's report was that Sugarloaf was in danger. The Minnesota Department of Natural Resources (DNR) had established a North Shore Management Board, made up mainly of township and city officials, to establish land-use plans for the North Shore. The North Shore Management Board hired a consultant from Michigan and assigned him to find and recommend the best locations for recreational safe harbors. The management board's emphasis was on making the area even more popular for fishing and boating. Fish tend to migrate in a pattern parallel to the shoreline. Good fishing conditions require easy access to fish migration waters by small boats, and a number of ports to shelter those boats and their occupants in the event of storm. Storms can come up on Lake Superior quickly. It is a wonderful lake when the water is calm, but its giant waves during storms make it treacherous for small boats.

The consultant from Michigan identified about nine possible locations for safe harbors. Number one on his list was Sugarloaf Cove. His report and the discussion of the management board evidenced little concern for Sugarloaf's geological importance, even though a separate advisory committee was at work at the same time on a recommendation that Sugarloaf be designated a state scientific and natural area. The state law governing the preservation of areas with that designation is quite strong.

I told Emily to relax. If a threat materialized quickly, I told her, we could go to court and obtain an injunction blocking it until an impact statement was prepared. With that tool at our disposal if we needed it, we could concentrate on making Sugarloaf safe from development for the long term.

We set to work. As a result, the threat to Sugarloaf is gone today. Its preservation is no longer in doubt, and its potential as a site for learning is great.

Sugarloaf has an interesting human as well as geological history. It was used from sometime near the turn of the century until 1971 as a landing and assembly area for rafts used in the logging and paper industries. The John Schroeder Company, after whose owner Schroeder Township was named, had a major logging operation along the Cross River near Sugarloaf in the first decade of the twentieth century. But the physical evidence that remains suggests that Sugarloaf did not come into heavy use by loggers until later, when Consolidated Paper Company made it a staging area and debarkation point for rafts hauling pulpwood to its mill across the lake in Ashland, Wisconsin. The giant rafts were held together by chains and pulled by tugboats at a painstaking one-mile-per-hour pace. (The story of the Schroeder Company, illustrative of the work done by a number of logging companies in the late nineteenth and early twentieth centuries, is nicely chronicled by Mary T. Bell in the 1999 book *Cutting across Time*. She credits me with persuading her to write it.)

In 1985, Consolidated Paper gave a sixty-five-acre parcel including Sugarloaf to the Nature Conservancy. Three years later, the Nature Conservancy did an unusual thing in disposing of it. They gave half of it to Cook County in exchange for another parcel on an island near Grand Marais. The other half was sold for $250,000 to the state of Minnesota. The DNR officials had no particular plan for the land when they acquired it. But soon after it was in their possession, John Green and his wife, Jan Green, a member of a DNR advisory committee, recommended that Sugarloaf be designated a state scientific and natural area. That designation came in February 1992 for the point, an area encompassing about three and a quarter acres of the parcel under DNR control.

Meanwhile, Cook County wanted to plat its acreage into lots and sell them, to put more property on its tax rolls. But DNR policy dictates that no additional Lake Superior frontage should go out of public ownership into private ownership. That policy blocked Cook County from selling the lots for a number of years—until another issue arose in the Hovland area concerning the county and the DNR, and a deal was struck that granted Cook County permission to proceed with a land sale at Sugarloaf. Five lots were platted and put up for auction. I was particularly anxious to get the lot that was contiguous to the Sugarloaf property that the state owned and that we were seeking to protect. I put in a bid and had a lawyer represent me at the auction. In that way, I acquired Lot 5, contiguous to Sugarloaf on the southwest side. Later, the owners of Lot 4 sold it to me too. I became the owner of about seven acres and 250 feet of lake frontage southwest of Sugarloaf. Emily's property is contiguous to Sugarloaf on the northeast. That created an Andersen family buffer from close-up development on either side.

I counseled Emily that it was not enough for us to simply oppose installing a safe harbor at Sugarloaf. We needed to present an alternative. There is a genuine need for small-craft harbors on the North Shore. We needed to be in a constructive position rather than solely in a position of opposition. We began to search for another harbor site.

Sugarloaf would indeed be a beautiful place for a harbor, if one disregards its geological uniqueness and the resulting flora and fauna. But making a small-craft harbor there would require the construction of a breakwater. A breakwater would change the natural wave pattern on the shore, and that in turn would alter the whole character of the shoreline. Over time, it would destroy it.

Strangely enough, nearby Taconite Harbor, where an enormous industrial harbor structure was built in the 1950s to load ore boats, had not been considered as a safe harbor site. That was partly because the Schroeder Township Board was not on good terms with LTV Steel Company and Cleveland Cliffs Iron Company, the owners of a taconite plant at Hoyt Lakes. That plant used Taconite Harbor as its outlet and loading point. The plant and harbor are connected by a seventy-four-mile railroad. I began talking to officials from the LTV Steel Company and Cleveland Cliffs Iron Company. After several conversations, they agreed to the installation of a recreational harbor on a portion of the site they owned and made a lease available. We had our alternative proposal.

Meanwhile, I also advised Emily that a not-for-profit vehicle was needed to engage more people in the cause of Sugarloaf protection. With the legal assistance of attorney Lori Stromme, we organized the Sugarloaf Interpretive Center Association in August 1992 as a tax-exempt corporation, which allowed us to raise money tax-free. Emily recruited some of her fellow property owners in the region. Though she lived in Duluth, where she attended the University of Minnesota-Duluth (UMD) as a graduate student, she had been an active environmentalist in Schroeder Township and was well acquainted with officials there. I was a founding member of the association's governing board and served for five years; Emily stayed on the board until 1998.

We recruited Robert Heller, the former chancellor of UMD, to be the association's first president. It was interesting that although he is a geologist, he took exception to the first version of the association's name that we proposed. We thought of calling it Sugarloaf Geological Interpretive Center Association, to emphasize the area's geological importance. But at Heller's urging, we dropped the word *geological* to signal a broader scope to our efforts. My idea was that an interpretive center at Sugarloaf might be established to explain to visitors and scientists not only about that one spot but also something about the entire North Shore's uniqueness and importance.

As I learned more about preservation issues on the North Shore, I found that the region lacked a single, comprehensive source of information and gathering point for citizen involvement in the cause. There were many fine county historical societies. There was a group whose focus was Split Rock Lighthouse. A number of concerned citizens lived in Two Harbors. But conservation efforts on the North Shore tended to be provincial and local in character. Silver Bay was not much interested in Two Harbors, and Two Harbors was not much interested in Grand Marais. Each community had its own focus. I thought there was a real opportunity for an organization that would address shorewide problems, especially the environmental risk posed by a growing population.

That is why we organized Shore Link in 1992. Its goal was to bring together representatives of various nonprofit and service organizations in the North Shore area and encourage them to share each other's problems and contribute to each other's activities. Shore Link quickly developed a life of its own, apart from Sugarloaf. It is not as active as I had hoped it would be, but it still has the potential to serve a useful purpose in generating communication and cooperation among like-minded people on the North Shore.

Meanwhile, the Sugarloaf Interpretive Center Association began to conduct public meetings and speak to civic organizations to build more awareness of Sugarloaf's geological value. People would come and hear about what Sugarloaf was and why it ought to be spared from harbor development. We had an uphill battle because Sugarloaf was simultaneously being touted as the number one priority of the North Shore Management Board.

Nevertheless, we began to make headway. A cadre of local citizens took up the cause.

Then we enlisted the aid of Gov. Arne Carlson. Through the good offices of our mutual friend Wheelock Whitney, I persuaded the governor of the validity of our case. He directed his chief of staff to work with Rodney Sando, commissioner of the DNR, to intervene in the matter. Sando had been the DNR's real estate expert before becoming commissioner. It was he who had acquired ownership of Sugarloaf for the state in the first place. I cringed when I heard that he had always thought it would make a wonderful harbor.

Fortunately, he was broad-minded enough to come around to our point of view. His conversion was nudged by Ed Stringer, then Carlson's chief of staff, now a justice of the Minnesota Supreme Court. Stringer was a sailor who cared about the future of the North Shore. He accompanied Sando on a trip to Sugarloaf that also included an inspection of Taconite Harbor, a few miles to the northeast. Stringer told me that he pressed our case: "Rod, how can you be for Sugarloaf when there is a possibility of a harbor at Taconite Harbor?" Taconite Harbor was well developed already, whereas much building would be needed at Sugarloaf. Plus, Stringer noted, Sugarloaf Point jutted into the lake from the southwest and took the brunt of storms from the northeast. Any structure on the point would take a beating.

With Sando and the state on our side, we took those same arguments to the Schroeder Township Board and the North Shore Management Board. Eventually, every agency involved gave up on putting a safe harbor at Sugarloaf and turned their focus on Taconite Harbor instead.

Our experience with the DNR reminded me anew of how unwieldy and inflexible a large state bureaucracy can be. The DNR has about ten thousand employees, with many levels of management and many agendas. There is a pervasive feeling that governors and commissioners come and go, but the DNR staff go on forever and can set their own agenda. I never could identify its point of origin, but within the DNR, there was always a preference for Sugarloaf over Taconite Harbor as a place to install a safe harbor.

In those years, Dorian Grilley represented the DNR on the North Shore. He has since become a good friend and the able executive of the Parks and Trails Council. Grilley attended a meeting of the Schroeder Township Board that I attended. I made a passionate appeal for Taconite Harbor and told them a Sugarloaf harbor was out of the question. But then Grilley indicated that the Sugarloaf site remained a possibility. After the meeting, I accosted him—that is the right word—and said, "Dorian, how can you tell that board what you did, to encourage them to have hope for Sugarloaf when you know—or you ought to know—that there's no way there's going to be a harbor at Sugarloaf? It just isn't going to be." He said, "All I know, Elmer, is that the people I work for and take orders from told me to keep Sugarloaf available." That was weeks after I had sat in on a meeting at which the governor told the commissioner in no uncertain terms that there was to be a harbor at Taconite Harbor, not Sugarloaf, even if it took eminent domain to accomplish it. Either the message had not filtered down to Grilley— or there were people somewhere within the department holding out for their own view.

The steel companies that owned the LTV plant in Hoyt Lakes were encouraging and cooperative. They were willing to let their property be used for a safe harbor rent free, though, reasonably, they expected the state to assume the local property tax burden on any land so used. We met in Duluth with lawyers from the corporate offices in Cleveland and with Ray Von Bidder, the wonderful manager of LTV Steel at Hoyt Lakes. They may have seen the safe harbor project as a way to build some good will among people in the area who have opposed Taconite Harbor since its construction. The harbor has been controversial from an environmental standpoint. It also is another point of contention in the old love/hate relationship people on the Iron Range have with the mining companies. From childhood, people there were taught to love the income from the mines and hate the mining companies. Von Bidder wanted to get past some of that feeling at Taconite Harbor. He has since been transferred to an operation in Trinidad and replaced by Jack Tuomi, a good man for that part of the world.

All this agreement between state and local officials and LTV executives did not settle how the harbor would be funded. The North Shore Management Board and its consultant concocted an elaborate, multisite $50-million harbor development scheme and approached Rep. Jim Oberstar to seek an appropriation of that size from Congress. He was ready to introduce a bill when local suspicion and opposition arose to a plan that large. People in northeastern Minnesota have come to associate federal money with federal control. Oberstar got an earful at a mass meeting on the safe harbor issue— at which I voiced my belief that a much smaller appropriation would get the job done at Taconite Harbor. The $50-million program was scuttled, and safe harbor development became a more deliberate, cautious business.

We began a two-pronged fund-raising effort for Taconite Harbor. One was with Oberstar and Congress, to get Taconite Harbor funded under the Safe Harbor Act. After several years of lobbying, the 1996 Congress appropriated $1.5 million. The other push was at the Minnesota Legislature. There, Taconite Harbor failed in one body or another, or in conference committee, through several sessions, despite the hard work of the late Rep. Willard Munger, Minnesota's lion of environmental protection. Finally he succeeded in 1998. Funding from the legislature came just in time. Our lease provided that we needed funding in hand by June 30, 1998, or it would be void. A complicating factor with the state was its policy not to use state bonds to pay for capital projects on leased land. At Taconite Harbor, the land was leased, and the seaway was state property. We had to get $400,000 from the general fund and $1.8 million in the 1998 bonding bill.

Construction of the safe harbor has been delayed because of another complication relating to the lease. With federal funding came a provision that the harbor would be built by the Army Corps of Engineers. The Corps will not proceed without a legal agreement in place specifying that if the lease is ever cancelled, the Corps will retain access to the harbor. That is a wrinkle that has taken time to iron out. The state Department of Transportation has also asked for a delay, until it can acquire more land for safe entrance and exit by motorists from the harbor to Highway 61. It is only a matter of time before both of these impediments are removed, and construction begins.

The source of the rock for the harbor is also yet to be determined. Von Bidder spoke to me about the possibility of rock from the mine at Hoyt Lakes being used for harbor construction. We are exploring that possibility with his successor, Tuomi.

Someday, anglers and boaters will ride in and out of Taconite Harbor and say, "Isn't this nice?" Little will they realize that large amounts of time, money, and effort went into getting it done. That is the nature of many public projects. There are so many people involved, so many levels of law and bureaucracy and constituencies to consider, that it takes enormous persistence to see things through. The preservation of Sugarloaf could have failed at any number of points, just as Voyageurs National Park could have been defeated at many points along the way. But I can attest that if you keep at a worthwhile project everlastingly, it does get done. I hope that I can attend the opening of Taconite Harbor and see the first boats come in to safety from a storm.

While we worked to deflect a safe harbor away from Sugarloaf, the Sugarloaf Interpretive Center Association also took steps to permanently protect the area around Sugarloaf Point and Cove.

At one point, Rod Sando said to me, "I know of your work on Taconite

Harbor and Sugarloaf. The interpretive center association may want to own Sugarloaf someday. You should know that we would not consider selling it to you outright. But if the association ever owned land that we wanted, we would consider a trade." I suspect he had in mind that we might be able to convince LTV Steel Company to transfer the land at Taconite Harbor to the Sugarloaf Interpretive Center Association, giving us trading stock for Sugarloaf. I also knew the thinking at LTV well enough to know that a trade involving them was highly unlikely.

But another option soon presented itself. Alden Lind, whose family owned Twin Points Resort between Split Rock Lighthouse and Gooseberry Falls, served notice that the family had always hoped the resort would become public property. But the resort was appraised at $845,000, and that was a much larger contribution to the state than the Lind family wanted to make. They were willing to make a gift of $95,000 of that appraised value if somebody would pay $750,000 for the resort and put it in public ownership. I asked Sando whether that property could be trading stock for Sugarloaf. "It sure could," he said. "In fact, we would help you with $210,000 to buy a part of it as soon as it is available, because there's a harbor possibility there that we'd like to develop."

So, in 1995, the Sugarloaf Interpretive Center Association entered into an option agreement with the Lind family that required our exercising it within one year—and I started raising money to purchase the Twin Points Resort. We found that when I could make personal calls on prospects, they were more likely to give. But I was eighty-six years old in 1995, and my physical condition made personal solicitation increasingly difficult. We had quite a struggle, but we succeeded. Twin Points Resort came into our hands in 1996, and we immediately sought a land exchange with the state of Minnesota.

Transferring land from the state to a private organization or a public foundation is not easily accomplished. It takes an action of the State Executive Board, which is made up of the governor, the state auditor, and the attorney general. Opposition from Lake County, which did not want the Twin Points Resort property to go off its tax rolls, complicated our proposed exchange. One of the Sugarloaf association board members, attorney Steve Pihlaja, led us through the complications and negotiated with the state, doing excellent work. Attorney General Hubert Humphrey and State Auditor Judi Dutcher were helpful too. The land in question was appraised, and it was determined that the resort property was worth $100,000 more than the Sugarloaf parcel we were to receive. We waved that as a contribution to the state, and the exchange was accomplished.

So, as of 1998, Sugarloaf is the property of the Sugarloaf Interpretive Center Association—all except for the small area on Sugarloaf Point originally designated as a scientific and natural area, which remains in state ownership. We successfully negotiated to increase the size of that designated parcel to give it a little more protection. We also arranged for a conservation easement on the Sugarloaf property we were acquiring, so at no time could it ever be used for commercial purposes. If the association ever goes out of business, the state is to have the first chance to buy the land. That should protect the scientific and natural area in perpetuity.

Whether an actual interpretive center will ever be built by the Sugarloaf Interpretive Center Association remains to be seen. I left the board in 1997. Today's board needs to decide whether it wants to provide a resource for study of the entire North Shore—something I envisioned—or confine its efforts to Sugarloaf itself. A building that remained on the property from Consolidated Paper's rafting days was recently removed. No building stands there today, but construction is expected to begin in 2000 on a pavilion where classes can meet and groups can gather.

Emily and I are no longer involved, but I have confidence in the people who continue in the association. All along, the effort has been blessed by the contributions of able, well-motivated citizens. I cannot name them all. But I want to salute our daughter, Emily, who sparked the whole effort and made us proud with her commitment and hard work. Progress is being made due to the wonderful effort of a professional director, Terri Port, who brings ability and enthusiasm to her task. Tjel Anderson, a marvelous biologist who lives on the North Shore, spoke at many public forums to help the association gain local acceptance. Attorneys Steve Pihlaja and Lori Stromme, a husband-wife team, contributed valuable legal services. Merlin Berg, now deceased, a relative of ours who was at one time in the Corps of Engineers, gave invaluable engineering service to the Sugarloaf board. Our old ally from the campaign for a taconite amendment, H. E. "Wes" Westmoreland, gave us sound public relations advice. Al France, a lobbyist whom I first knew when he was a young aide to Gov. Luther Youngdahl, chaired a committee of the board to prepare a long-range plan. It was so well done that Sando told me it was more complete than some plans presented for the establishment of state parks. We suffered a terrible loss when Bob Heller developed cancer and died suddenly. His widow, Geraldine, has remained loyal and helpful.

If I appear central in the Sugarloaf story, it is only because I am telling the story. Success in any public project takes a great deal of effort on the part of many people. So I felt it was on behalf of many that I accepted the Willard Munger Environmental Award in 1998, presented by the Minnesota Resources Foundation. I cherish this honor, as I do the memory of my friend Willard Munger, who died a year later. I am sure he would agree that the real measure of our success in environmental protection is the extent to which we were able to mobilize other people to make our cause their own.

Elder Statesman

WHEN I WAS ELECTED GOVERNOR in 1960, I also joined an exclusive fraternity—a governor's club. A bond of respect and affection links all of Minnesota's living governors, up to and including a man who will probably always be one of the club's more unconventional members, the state's current governor, Jesse Ventura. The governors are united in an understanding of what each other has experienced.

Minnesota has been fortunate in having a succession of honest, committed, helpful governors. I have known all of my predecessors going back to Harold Stassen, and each of my successors—though I am not yet well acquainted with Ventura. My connections with several of them have led to some interesting experiences and assignments.

Some very pleasant experiences involved former Gov. Wendell Anderson. Not long after he was inaugurated in 1971, he invited all the former governors and their wives to a dinner at the Alexander Ramsey House in the Seven Corners area of St. Paul. The evening was most enjoyable. I thought it was so considerate of a young new governor, with all of the demands that all of us knew he faced, to take time to meet socially with his predecessors. He called on some of us again and again for private counsel and support. Always, he was warm and considerate.

Anderson became quite friendly with Stanley Holmquist, my brother-in-law and, in 1971, the senate majority leader. The two of them had served together in the state senate in the 1960s. In 1971, the legislative session went into overtime because of a bitter dispute over whether to increase the share of K-12 education costs borne by the state. Though they were of opposite parties, Anderson and Holmquist were allies in supporting an increase in the state's share. Anderson never forgot that. Some years later, he asked me, "Where is Stan these days? I'd like to see him." "He's out in Edina, a resident there," I said. "I'd like to get together with him sometime." So, I arranged a luncheon for the three of us at the Minneapolis Club. He so appreciated the occasion that he reciprocated by arranging a luncheon involving a few other capitol friends from the 1960s and 1970s. One of them was Peter Popovich, by then the retired chief justice of the Minnesota Supreme Court. The comment afterwards was that Popovich did not look well. That was the last time I saw him. It was not long afterward that he died. I am grateful to Anderson for bringing us together that last time.

I liked the late Gov. Rudy Perpich from the beginning of our acquaintance in 1963, when I was serving my final months as governor and he was a new state senator from the Iron Range. I like genuine people, and he was genuine. There was no artifice about him. He said what he thought, and he worked hard for what he believed. He loved Minnesota. He was proud of his Croatian immigrant background and of the fact that he rose to the governorship from humble beginnings. He tried hard to improve education, health, and welfare and to make government a useful partner in economic development. He served for ten years—longer than any other governor did—and I believe history will record that he served well.

Perpich was the only governor to date whose service was interrupted. He was defeated in 1978, then reelected in 1982. I happened to be in the capitol the day after his 1978 defeat. I remembered my own experience in 1963— how the phones suddenly fell silent and the visitors stopped coming after I was no longer governor. I thought, I wonder if the governor is in his office. Maybe I will go in and say hello. So, I went into the governor's outer office and said, "By any chance, is Governor Perpich here?" He was in. He was free. I was invited in. We spent an hour and a half together reminiscing about our experiences and talking about the adjustment that is required when a governor has to leave office. There is an unavoidable residue of feeling about what you tried to do, what you did do, and what did not get done. I told Perpich my observation that when you make an effort for the public good, you never really lose. You make a contribution. You are part of the ongoing process of democracy. I tried to comfort him a little, because he took the loss hard.

Perpich was so appreciative of my visit that for years afterward whenever he would see me, even in an audience when he was speaking, he would make a reference to that day. He would say, "I'll never forget the one person who came to see me the day after the 1978 election when I was feeling pretty low. It was Gov. Elmer Andersen. I've never forgotten that."

In 1983, Perpich formed a commission to study the future of post-secondary education in Minnesota. He appointed me its chairman and made some staff available. One was Kathryn Roberts, who came from the Department of Administration as a management specialist to be our commission's director. She did a wonderful job. She went on to be the director of the Minnesota Zoo for twelve years and made it a great public asset. In 1999, she was appointed to head the Metropolitan Sports Facilities Commission.

The commission was Perpich's response to a rather widespread belief that Minnesota's higher education system was overbuilt and, hence, too costly. Further, some critics felt that by dividing state money among the more than sixty campuses then in existence, there was not enough concentration of effort to produce excellence at any of them. Some people complained that the state had too many community colleges; others thought seven state universities were too many. The state had experienced a severe revenue shortfall in the early 1980s, and economy in state government became the watchword. I think Perpich contrived to appoint a Republican to chair the commission because he wanted bipartisan cover for any controversial recommendations we might make.

We had an excellent commission, made up of people whose first loyalty was to education. Perpich chose the commissioners but allowed me to comment on each selection before he proceeded with it. He named fine people. Atherton Bean, chairman of International Multifoods Corporation, was one member. Cy Carpenter, president of the Minnesota Farmer's Union, was another. A third was the former mayor of Champlin, Josephine Nunn, the widow of an executive at the university. We had a strong staff, even though they were all volunteers because we were operating without an appropriation from the legislature.

We visited institutions that were likely to be recommended for closure should we conclude that Minnesota had too many campuses. One was a little community college in Pine City. I attended an evening class where some single mothers were receiving training to enter the job market for the first time. Many of them had been abandoned by their children's fathers. I saw how important that little school was to those women. If it were closed, those women could not transfer to another school farther away. They could not go and give up their responsibilities with their children. They were struggling as it was, and their struggle was crucial to their futures and their children's futures. I thought, it would be terrible to close this place.

That became the theme of our commission's deliberations. All of us saw real importance in every campus we visited. Instead of arguing that something should be shut down, we began to talk about a need for more two-year colleges, so every Minnesotan would have a community or technical college within commuting distance and could get at least some postsecondary education without having to leave home.

There was an expectation that our commission would recommend closing some institutions. As we neared the end of our work, word reached the
governor's office that we were leaning toward recommending quite the opposite. I got a call informing me that the governor wanted to have a meeting
with me before our commission completed its work. I knew that Perpich
was getting a lot of advice about fiscal restraint from his finance commissioner, Gus Donhowe. Gus was an able fellow but a little too money-minded
to suit me. I braced myself and trooped to the governor's office for a meeting with both of them.

Perpich wanted our conversation to be off the record. He made it his
policy that every meeting in his office was open to the press. Reporters
could sit in. But that meant that when he wanted to discuss a truly sensitive
matter with someone, they had to surreptitiously leave the office. We went
down to the catacombs of the capitol—where the Historical Society used to
store newspapers—so that not even the *Star Tribune's* Betty Wilson would
know we were meeting.

Donhowe had almost persuaded Rudy that a reduction in the number of
campuses was justified. They were thinking of proposing that Southwest
State University in Marshall should be closed. That stung. The establishment
of Southwest State was approved while I was governor, at my request. It had
never grown very large in Marshall. I thought at the time that it should have
been placed in Redwood Falls, a community that seemed to show more
promise in the 1960s. But Senate Majority Leader John Zwach and House
Majority Leader Aubrey Dirlam, both from the Redwood Falls area, were so
respectful of others that they bent over backwards not to seem to be trying
to get something for their districts. They let it go to Marshall.

Perpich and Donhowe peppered me with questions. What was the commission thinking? Was this really serving the public interest? I said, "Look,
Governor, you appointed this commission. They are good people, and you
had confidence in them. They are going to say what they believe. Education
isn't going to go downhill in this state. Enrollment isn't going to decrease.
There's going to be a greater need. You're going to need more community
colleges. It would be a mistake to close Southwest State." I did not buckle
under their questioning, or say what they wanted to hear. I refused to ask
the commission to reconsider and recommend campus closings.

We did not recommend a single closure. But we made many recommendations, including some that University of Minnesota President Ken Keller
picked up a few years later in his sweeping reform initiative called Commitment to Focus. Rick Heydinger, the university's able vice president for

institutional relations, drafted some of our proposals. We called for a new emphasis on graduate programs and research at the University of Minnesota, along with the realignment and consolidation of some of those programs. Doctoral programs are expensive because they require a low ratio of faculty to students, often one to three or even one to one. The university added a large number of doctoral programs after World War II and again after the Korean and Vietnam Wars, when the GI Bill of Rights kept students flowing onto campus in large numbers. But by the mid-1980s, the university had more than one hundred doctoral programs, many of them tiny, and more than a state the size of Minnesota could adequately support. Our commission's suggestions spurred the thinking that the university should concentrate on excellence rather than trying to do everything for everybody.

Though our report may not have satisfied Donhowe, in the end I think it satisfied Perpich. He was such a friend of education and such an optimist that he would have hated to close a campus. I think he was relieved when we did not thrust him into that kind of controversy. It is a terribly painful thing to close a college, as the University of Minnesota learned in 1992, when it closed its campus in Waseca. Despite decades of contention over whether Minnesota has too many campuses, the Waseca campus is the only one that has been closed.

Perpich was defeated for the second time in 1990 by Arne Carlson, in the weirdest campaign that one could imagine. Still the loyal Republican, I supported Carlson over Jon Grunseth in the Republican primary. Grunseth won, but he was soon in terrible trouble. A young woman went public with charges that he had gone swimming in the nude with teenaged girls at a Fourth of July party several years earlier. Soon other allegations of personal misconduct were flying, too. I was one who called for Grunseth to withdraw from the race. "You aren't going to win," I told him in mid-October. "You're just going to be a blight on the party and torture the state. You should withdraw." He did after more unsavory disclosures about his personal conduct, just nine days before the election. The state supreme court decided that the candidate who had come in second in the Republican primary—Arne Carlson—should take Grunseth's place on the ballot. That decision caused a lasting rift between Perpich and the longtime friend he had placed on the supreme court, A. M. "Sandy" Keith. Keith was too independent to let Perpich's desire not to face Carlson affect his thinking on the ballot question.

During those tense days before the supreme court ruled, I participated in a press conference urging a quick decision in favor of putting Carlson's name on the ballot. At that press conference, I had an encounter with a young DFL state representative from Minneapolis, Todd Otis. He is the son of James Otis, whom I had appointed to the state supreme court. Todd Otis thought he knew something about election law and the court and began to inject himself into the Republican press conference, offering counter-arguments to our case. I did not wait for the press conference to end to scold him. I said, "You shouldn't do it this way, Todd. I know you, and I know your family, and you're not behaving the way you should. You know better."

Apparently, I got the best of the exchange, because it silenced Otis. That night, TV news aired videotape of the moment. After the press conference, I walked out of the room with Eric Eskola of WCCO radio. He said to me, "You're still the champ."

I had known Arne Carlson for a long time. I first became aware of him during my 1962 reelection campaign, when he was a young campaign volunteer whose day job was at Control Data. In 1960, he had been a Democrat, employed as an organizer in several states by Hubert Humphrey's presidential campaign. But by 1962, he thought of himself as an independent. At some point, I had a conversation with him about his party affiliation.

"I think you ought to be a Republican," I told him. "I think you'd be more comfortable." I explained what I thought was the fundamental difference between Republicans and Democrats: Republicans would rather do things independently and privately. Liberal Republicans are fully willing to use the government when it is the only agent that can accomplish something, or when it can perform a task better or more to the people's liking than the private sector could. But Republicans do not turn to the government first. My view of Democrats is they expect government to have a solution to every problem. They have no qualms about letting government run everything. I told Carlson, "I think you'd be a better Republican, and happier as a Republican, because you tend to be conservative. Generally, Republicans are more conservative." I may have had some influence on Carlson, because later and on several occasions, he attributed his change of party affiliation to me. When he first ran for office in 1965, seeking a seat on the Minneapolis City Council, he ran as a Republican.

Carlson and I were never close friends, but our paths continued to cross through the years. I thought he had a wonderful name for a Minnesota politician—a short Scandinavian name that is distinctive and easy to remember. From the early days of his career, he stood out as someone who was somewhat pugnacious. He had a way of making an incident or a concern into a public issue. His excitable nature and forceful manner of speaking captured public attention. That is very important in politics.

When he was a new member of the Minnesota House in the 1970s, a dispute arose over whether the legislature should award itself a pay raise. Carlson opposed the raise so vigorously that he made it a public issue. When that happened, the raise was dead. That impressed me. I decided to invite him to breakfast at the old Holiday Inn near the capitol. I told him, "Arne, you could be governor of this state. You have a way of creating issues, and attracting attention to the issues you create. I don't know quite how you do it, but you do it. Maybe it's because you get excited. People like a fight, and you get into fights." I urged him to set his sights on statewide office. He ran first for state auditor, in 1978, and held that job for twelve years. I knew he would be a good auditor because he is a hawk on getting things right.

As governor, Carlson had some difficulties at first. The mistake that really affected the state was when he vetoed the reapportionment bill and failed to get the veto message back in time. A reapportionment plan that was heavily weighted toward the DFL became law as a result. His veto was not late by the tradition of things, but it was late under the letter of the law. Somebody was smart enough to exert the letter of the law and prevail in court. The reapportionment veto was thrown out, along with some others. That will likely be remembered as the greatest mistake Carlson made as governor. It assured DFL control of the legislature through most of the 1990s. The Republicans finally gained a house majority in the 1999 session.

Carlson was too independent to ask me for advice or help, but he gave me help when I turned to him. He generously supported our efforts to protect Sugarloaf Cove on the North Shore from the environmental damage that would be done by a proposed man-made harbor. He backed our plan to put the harbor at the already industrialized Taconite Harbor instead. He also aided in the release of my book of selected editorials, *Views from the Publisher's Desk,* by allowing his reception room to be used for a book-signing party.

Like most people associated with the Republican or the DFL parties, I have not had an acquaintance with Minnesota's first Reform Party governor, Jesse Ventura. Eleanor and I planned to attend his inauguration, but the extreme subzero cold that day made us change our plans.

I am assisting with an initiative that Governor Ventura is promoting heavily—a constitutional amendment to create a single-house, or unicameral, legislature. I am the honorary chairman of Minnesotans for a Single House, the committee seeking to get the amendment through the 2000 legislature and on the ballot. If Governor Ventura succeeds in making this change, that alone would signify importance to his administration for all time.

For fifty years or more, governors and legislators have been introducing bills, making speeches, and hosting conferences about a change to a unicameral legislature. The sheer fact is, a two-house legislature is unnecessary. The Supreme Court ordered in 1964 that both houses of state legislatures should be apportioned on a per-person basis, not on the basis of counties or other geographic jurisdictions. That means there is no difference in the selection of the senate and the house of representatives. They are duplicates in every respect, save for their size and the term length of their members.

Since the Supreme Court decision, many states have considered following Nebraska's lead, and abolishing one chamber of their legislatures. The next state to go for a single-house legislature, I think, will open a floodgate of other states making that change. Many students of legislative government see that having two houses elected on the basis of population is cumbersome. They recognize that many counties and school boards oversee big budgets and operate well without dual chambers. Some democratic nations do not have two legislative houses. A bicameral legislature is an anachronism that wastes money and leads to chicanery in playing one house against the other. Bad bills are passed in one body because legislators rely on the other body to kill them. Legislators are able to claim to be on both sides of an issue. Moreover, too much power and decision making gets concentrated in conference committees. A simpler single-house structure would be easier to understand. It would make following the progress of legislation easier for people.

The difficulty in getting a single-house amendment on the ballot lies with legislators who know full well that if it passes, many of them will be out of a job. It is always been difficult for the legislature to reform or renovate itself. Another way to amend the constitution is through the convening of a constitutional convention. If the legislature is not responsive to the many good arguments for placing a unicameral legislature amendment on the ballot, I think Minnesotans should seriously consider convening a constitutional convention. Minnesota is among about a half a dozen states that has never had but one constitutional convention, the one that preceded statehood. Many states have had several to periodically recast their government.

I am sometimes asked whether after all these years of supporting active government and writing occasional checks for DFL candidates, I still consider myself a Republican. My answer is the same as it was forty years ago. I am a liberal Republican. That is another way of saying that I am quite independent, or rather, I have become so as the Republican Party has moved steadily toward the right. I have always been much more interested in program than party—which may have been a weakness of mine as governor. It was a deficiency of Arne Carlson's governorship as well. Neither of us spent enough time building the Republican Party and making it reflect our own views. As a result, I lacked strong party support when I ran for reelection, and Carlson was not even endorsed by the Republican Party when he sought a second term—an incredible thing for a popular sitting governor to experience. I support candidates of both parties financially because I support a two-party system. I am well aware of the problem candidates have raising money. If you are for the system, you are for good candidates of both parties having the wherewithal to get their message to the people.

The abortion issue has done great damage to both political parties in Minnesota. It is unfortunate that a militant anti-abortion minority has held sway for two decades or more in the state Republican Party. My view is that abortion is best prevented by avoiding unwanted pregnancies, and by counseling and caring for young women who are unexpectedly pregnant. Simply outlawing abortion will only make criminals of young women and their doctors. It will subject the poor to the hazards of illegal abortion, while affluent women will be able to travel to other places where safe, legal abortion is available. I visited with young women about this issue when I was on the Board of Regents, and I am convinced that no woman enters into an abortion casually. It is a traumatic step that a woman takes only when she believes she has no other choice. We should not add to the plight of these desperate women by making criminals of them.

In the last two decades, the Republican Party nationally has preached an anti-federalism philosophy that I cannot support. In an effort to balance the federal budget, Republicans in Washington concocted the argument that the federal government is wasteful and inept. Those awful bureaucrats do not know anything, they claimed. Policies of all manner—including the basic needs of food and shelter for children—ought to be set at the local level. I disagree. This is one nation. One set of standards should apply to all fifty states, and to all Americans. Local governments can administer federal policies and can make decisions about purely local issues. But education, health, welfare, and defense are all proper responsibilities for the federal government. Americans know that instinctively. In an emergency, be it of natural or human cause, people automatically look to Washington for help. The first government the United States had was a confederation of sovereign states. It did not work because the states began to levy tariffs on each other and compete with each other. How different is that from today's tendency of states to compete for the lowest level of taxation, the lowest welfare benefits, the cheapest government, in order to attract industry from one another? That is what the Republican program of devolution has wrought.

The cheapest government is not necessarily the best government. It does not bother me that Minnesota ranks high among the states in taxation, because it also ranks high in its culture, education, health, life expectancy, and other positive measures. One reason Minnesota is economically strong and is growing today is that it has invested in good government, education, health and nutrition, environment, parks, and trails—in everything that makes for balanced, happy lives. I noted a recent report about rates of incarceration among the states. The state with the highest number of prisoners per one hundred thousand people is Louisiana. Texas ranks second. Minnesota and Maine are two of the lowest states in inmates per one hundred thousand citizens. That ranking is not coincidental to Minnesota's relatively high ranking in taxation.

The best investments Minnesotans have made have been the dollars they have paid in state and local taxes. The money Minnesota spends on government services compares favorably with what is spent on liquor, tobacco, cosmetics, spectator sports, and other entertainment—and brings a much greater long-term return. Government has an important function, and it should be properly financed.

I think Republicans here and in Washington have been pandering to a public desire for tax cuts that may not be nearly as strong as they perceive it to be. In 1996, Republican presidential candidate Robert Dole promised a big tax cut, and he was handily defeated. Today, while congressional Republicans push a tax cut so large it is sure to get a presidential veto, opinion polls show that a majority of Americans would rather pay down the national debt. The argument that a surplus in government revenues indicates that people are paying too much in taxes falls when it is pointed out that through thirty years of deficits, people were not paying enough. A surplus is an opportunity to begin to balance the books. Moreover, a tax cut now while the economy is strong will squander the nation's opportunity to cut taxes when the economy turns for the worse and needs stimulation.

I hate to hear Republicans demeaning public employees. My experience is that the people working for government are dedicated, learned, skillful people. We readily admit that a doctor knows more than the average person about health, and that a lawyer knows more about legal rights than the person on the street. Why should we not trust people who have been trained for careers in government and have put in years of service to know more about governance than the average person does?

It grieves me that my Republican Party, which has had so much good sense through the years, is so far off track right now. Unfortunately, I am not much impressed with their opponents either. Democrats cling to an overreliance on government that makes many people rightfully wary. It is no wonder that in 1998 Minnesota voters elected a governor from a third party. They were genuinely displeased with both the Republicans and the Democrats. *Washington Post* columnist David Broder had it right, I think, when he said that the importance of the 1998 Minnesota election was the warning it sent to the two political parties. Minnesota voters showed that if the parties do not begin to serve the people's interests, the whole country could be up for grabs by a new political force. So many people feel disenfranchised today. Ventura's election gives them the hope that they can still go to the polls and make a difference. They can choose somebody who is forthright, has common sense, and seems to represent them. Ventura was not the tool of any national party ideology or special interest money. That was his appeal. I am hoping that the Republican and Democratic parties take notice and mend their ways.

The Joy of Books

THROUGH A LONG LIFE, a number of constants have grown dearer with time. Among them is the joy I find in books. I have been a book collector my entire adult life.

My desire to own my own books began in childhood. In the home of my aunt Lillian Johnson, an unmarried teacher, I loved to touch, hold, and page through a set of books she owned. It was "Journeys through Book Land," a compilation of children's literature. Whenever I went to her home, I headed straight for her bookshelf to find some of my favorite stories. Our little home did not include such luxury. I went to the library and checked out a lot of books, and read a great deal. But the books always went back to the library again. How grand it would be, I thought, to own these precious objects and be able to hold and read them whenever I pleased.

The craving to own books, not just read them, did not pass with childhood. As a young traveling salesman in Minneapolis in the fall of 1928, I saved my loose change and then spent it on books. I always wanted nice books, but in those early years, I could not afford new ones. Instead, I scoured through Salvation Army or Goodwill Industries stores for high-quality secondhand books.

Boyd's Storage House on Lake Street was a wonderful place for my book-shopping excursions. It was where the possessions of affluent people from south Minneapolis would be stored when they were in transition. Some things would land there when a family broke up, an older person gave up housekeeping, or someone just got a notion to clear out unwanted clutter. Boyd's arrangement was that unless storage charges were kept current, stored items would be sold to cover the storage costs. Boyd's always had a shelf of books on sale for small prices. There were beautifully hardbound copies of fine books for 25 cents, 50 cents, or $1. One of my finds at Boyd's was a prized book illustrated by Arthur Rackham, *Undine.* His trademark illustrations were natural scenes that would include little urchins—*tomte,* they call them in Scandinavia—tucked away, almost hidden. That unique feature has made Rackham a much collected author and artist.

Even in my youth, I did not buy books casually. In my mind, I was building a library. My intention was to read my books, know them well, catalog them, and care for them. I still have the little book in which I recorded every book I bought. I would put a little red-bordered, numbered sticker in each book and then record the number in my little catalog, along with the book's name and author, how much I paid for it, and, sometimes, where I got it.

At first, I attempted to read every book I bought. Later, I bought books that I knew I could not read right away but expected to turn to at some later time. Some I bought for their value as reference material, should I want to research the topic they contained.

When my budget for books grew, I got to know bookstores and book catalogs. Paging through those catalogs became one of my favorite breaks in a busy day. I would give myself a fantasy buying spree, going through the catalog carefully and circling items that I would like to buy. When I was done, I would have a heavily marked-up catalog—and no new books, because the items I marked were much too expensive for me to buy. But by looking so intently at those catalogs, I was constantly learning about book collecting and about what I would like to do when my resources would allow.

I always sought out books of American and English literature and history. England deserves special appreciation by Americans because much of the law, tradition, and culture that we enjoy had its roots there. But in addition to those abiding interests, I developed particular book-collecting themes over time. For example, one theme I pursued early was the so-called lost generation of Britain following World War I. I sought out several authors, including Storm Jameson and Vera Brittain, who wrote about life in Britain following the war. The work of the women writers was particularly compelling because of their perspective on the enormous loss of young men in World War I. That disaster changed the course of their lives and their notion of what their lives would be. There were not enough men left to allow women to cling to dreams of marriage and motherhood. It was a poignant period of writing in England.

I also enjoyed reading inspirational poetry, so I collected that too. A favorite was James Whitcomb Riley, who wrote "Under the Spreading Chestnut Tree." It is so simple, but it is beautiful. In one's youth, particularly, it is wonderful to read.

When I came to Minnesota, I became interested in state history and wanted to buy books about early Minnesota. On a number of occasions, I had great good fortune in my pursuit of that topic. One was in the 1930s, when I received a book catalog from Swan Galleries, an auction house in New York. The catalog contained a book by Harriet Bishop titled *Floral Home*. Bishop was the first schoolteacher in Minnesota, arriving in 1849. *Floral Home* describes her experience as a Minnesota pioneer. She was a student in a girls' religious academy when the principal received a letter from a missionary in Minnesota asking him to send one of his students, upon her graduation, to teach in Minnesota. The letter reported that the children of French traders and Native Americans needed schooling. Bishop felt moved to respond. She came to Minnesota on a flatboat. Her book relates how the Indians presented their children to her in greeting. Every little face was put up to her to kiss. Her descriptions are vivid, for in addition to being a woman of courage and learning, she was a fine writer.

When *Floral Home* came up at auction at Swan Galleries, I agonized. I wanted the book badly, but I simply did not have much money then to spend on books. But, I told myself, nobody in New York is going to care about that book about Minnesota. The other bidders probably do not know who Harriet Bishop is. I put in a bid of $1.50 and crossed my fingers. I got it. Apparently, there was no other bid. I have treasured that first edition of Harriet Bishop for more than sixty years.

It was not long afterwards that I bought my first copies of books about Minnesota exploration by Father Louis Hennepin, who visited this region from 1680 to 1682, and Jonathan Carver, a British soldier who was in this region in 1766 and 1767. Hennepin, a French priest, had a dramatic story to tell of being held captive by Indians in Minnesota. He was released rather than executed on the advice of Daniel Greysolon, sieur Du Luth, a French trader and explorer whom the Indians knew well. Du Luth advised the Indians that holding a spiritual man was bad medicine. Carver's experiences with Minnesota's native people were much more positive. The natives ceded to him a large tract of land including Carver's Cave in St. Paul—leading to one of the longest-lived land claim disputes in Minnesota history. Their books are both gems of history, but of the two, Carver's has more value as a source of accurate information. Hennepin was a brave explorer but not a careful reporter of what he found.

I gradually began to spend more money on books and began to buy from the book catalogs I had only daydreamed over before. I soon learned the value of developing relationships with book dealers. Some collectors turn the responsibility for building a collection over to one trusted dealer. That was never my intention. I wanted to build my collection myself. But I wanted to get to know a few good dealers personally, so I could trust them and they could alert me to purchasing opportunities that I might otherwise miss.

I came to know James Ford Bell, the founder of the Bell Library at the University of Minnesota, who told me about Hans Kraus, a leading book dealer of the day in New York. He had everything from the Johannes Gutenberg Bible on down. When H. B. Fuller business brought me to New York in the 1940s, I ventured into Kraus's store and met him. He was most gracious and kind to a young impecunious book collector from the prairie.

After that meeting, Kraus's shop became a regular stop for me whenever I was in New York. We became friends. Kraus's personal attention to his regular customers and his deep love of fine books made him a superb book dealer. Sometimes people who should be called book investors, not book collectors, would come to his shop and want him to select some books for them that he thought would increase in value over time. Kraus refused to deal with them. He did not want to sell any books on that basis. He wanted the books he sold to go to people who truly wanted to own and care for them, for their own sake. That was the basis of my relationship with him. He knew that I never thought of selling my books for gain.

Kraus used to take me into his vault, where his treasures were securely stored, both to show off his latest finds and to make me offers that were difficult to refuse. His prices were reasonable. Anything I bought from him, I was forever grateful that I did. For example, I bought from Kraus a copy of Dante in Latin, printed in the nineteenth century on vellum by Ashendene Press, one of the world's great book publishers. Ashendene was operated by a man named Hornsby and his wife. They in turn had a key associate named Sidney Cockerell. Hornsby had inscribed this particular copy—one of only ten or twelve printed on vellum—to Cockerell. Cockerell, in turn, had written in the finest of writing on the inside front cover, "If you observe, you will find my initials have been woven into the vine in the border of the title page." Sure enough, there in the design of the title page is SCC, the initials of Sidney C. Cockerell. I shiver when I think of that beautiful work. Kraus told me, "Andersen, I haven't repriced this for ten years, at least. I've had it for quite awhile. I've been saving it for somebody, but I'll sell it to you at the price it's marked." I have forgotten what that price was—I generally forget the price of a book once it is bought—but I got it. I was so pleased that I did.

Another time, he showed me a copy on vellum of the Kelmscott edition of *The Works of Geoffrey Chaucer,* a huge book. It contained original etchings by Sir Edward Burne-Jones. It was priceless. I believe it to be one of the most beautiful books ever published. There were only eight or ten copies printed on vellum. A few others were printed on paper in 1896 and then bound in pigskin by the Dobes Press, another famous London institution. Kraus had priced the vellum copy fairly, at about $45,000 to $50,000. He said I should have it. "It would be the keystone of your collection," he said. "Actually, Andersen, I have another buyer. If you don't take it, it goes to England. It ought to stay in the United States, and it ought to be in your collection." He tempted me sorely, but I thought the price was beyond my reach. "I'm so sorry, I just can't," I told him. Today I wish I had mortgaged the house and bought it. If the same copy came on the market today, it would probably be priced at a minimum of $250,000.

As I came to know more about fine printing and fine printers, I learned that William Morris of the Kelmscott Press was among history's best. He was born in 1834 and died shortly before the turn of the century. He had more influence on printing in the world, not only in England but in Europe and in the United States, than anybody. He was a tremendously talented person—a gifted poet and elocutionist, an inventor, a furniture maker, a wallpaper designer. He was the inventor of the Morris chair. He went to Iceland, learned Icelandic, and translated Icelandic sagas. He became a socialist and was something of a political activist. In everything he did, he pursued the highest standard of quality.

Morris became a printer late in life and established the Kelmscott Press at Hammersmith, England, to print fine books. He sought throughout world for the finest ink. He wanted to use vellum, not paper, but he found that the Vatican had a corner on the vellum market for the Vatican libraries. Kelmscott Press printed 54 items, all of them classics. The Kelmscott *Chaucer* was *the* top work of these 54. At one time, I had a complete set of all 54, including *Chaucer*—not the vellum edition that I so badly wanted, but the pigskin-bound paper version that was published in 1896. An edition bound in paperboard was also produced, for a total of about 210 books in all. My edition also had a hand-embroidered cloth cover that may have been made by Mrs. Morris, and a beautifully hand-carved wooden box for safekeeping. It is a treasure of fine printing.

When I began to think about the next owner of my books, I checked with the University of Minnesota to see whether its collection included a Kelmscott *Chaucer*. I knew another Minnesota book collector, Frank Leslie of the Leslie Paper Company, had one—not bound in pigskin, as mine was, but in heavy board binding. I never told him I had a pigskin-bound copy, because I wanted to spare him the jealousy. I thought he intended to give his *Chaucer* to the university, but it went instead to the Minneapolis Institute of Arts. So, a few years ago, I surprised Austin McLean, then the university's curator of special collections, with a personal visit. I laid the Kelmscott *Chaucer* on his desk.

Excellence in book publication is not confined to the nineteenth century. Through a dealer named Jim Sitter, I became acquainted with the work of the Whittington Press in England. Whittington is operated by John and Rosalind Randle, a husband-wife team. I became their eager customer. Once, Jim Sitter told me, "The Randles need money to expand their press. They can't raise it in England. They've reached the point where they are willing to sell their archival collection, their own collection of their books, to raise the money." The archival collection included not only a copy of every book Whittington had published but a copy of every variation in binding and paper quality produced. The collection also included manuscript material and correspondence with authors. The Randles were willing to sell their archival records for $25,000. I bought the collection and gave it to the University of Minnesota.

That is how the University of Minnesota obtained the best collection of Whittington in existence. I further arranged to buy every Whittington publication in every variety published henceforward, to maintain a perfect, complete collection. But a few years ago, I revisited that arrangement with the university's head librarian, Thomas Shaughnessy. I said, "I've been buying the Whittington books and paying for them now for a number of years. I don't want the Whittington collection to quit when I quit. While I'm still here, I'd like to have you start buying them and paying for them." Tom said, "Our budget is tight." I said, "I know your budget is tight, but you have the finest collection of *the* outstanding press in the whole world, and you need to keep it complete." He agreed to squeeze the requisite sum out of his budget, so the collection is no longer dependent on me. When I saw Shaughnessy recently, I asked, "Are you still buying Whittington publications?" He said, "Elmer, we're getting every one."

Meanwhile, with the capital they raised by selling their archival collection, the Randles went on to become the acknowledged, preeminent fine-press publishers in the world. They have visited Minnesota on more than one occasion, giving lectures on fine printing and presswork. We hosted them at a most enjoyable dinner at our home a few years ago.

The University of California, which is active in book collecting, wants more copies of Whittington Press work. I have been told that the curators in California cannot understand why it is that whenever they inquire about a Whittington book, they are informed that the University of Minnesota has it.

Of course, I did not buy books only from dealers and catalogs. I looked for good books everywhere. Not long after I had begun substantial book buying, I was invited to visit a St. Paul law office. A lawyer had died and his legal practice had been sold, but his personal library remained in the office, and his heirs wanted to sell it. Somebody told them I bought books. I examined the library and found some choice selections in the mix.

"There are some really fine books here," I told the person representing the estate. "There are a number that I would like to have and would be willing to consider, if you'd put a price on them." "We don't want you to pick and choose," the person answered. "We want you to take the whole lot." "Oh, I couldn't take the whole lot. There are too many. There are about eight hundred books here." "We just want to get rid of them. Just bid anything you want. We have to get this job closed up today. Just name a price, and they're yours." Under that kind of pressure, I named a price, and I had eight hundred books. I called McAlpine Transfer Company, which served St. Anthony Park, and arranged for them to pick up the books and take them to 2188 Hendon Avenue.

Then, I faced the music of calling Eleanor. "I've been downtown and I bought some books," I said. "Oh, that's nice," she said. "What did you get?" "I got quite a few—maybe more than I can tell about right now. McAlpine Transfer is bringing them out." "What's McAlpine Transfer got to do with it?" "There are about eight hundred." *"Eight hundred!"*

Despite her shock that day, Eleanor has been wonderfully supportive of my bibliomania. She has lived in a home stocked with thousands of books for many years and has always done her part to give them proper care.

Some uninitiated people think book collecting is a rather dry, dull pursuit. For me, it has been anything but that. It has been a joyful part of life, a welcome diversion, and a source of excitement. The connection between people and their books is fascinating, and investigating that connection has given me some wonderful experiences.

One was born of my admiration for President Herbert Hoover, an honorable and decent man whose reputation was scorched by the flame of a world depression. I was interested to learn that he and his wife, Lou Henry Hoover, had translated a Latin classic. In 1536, Georgius Agricola wrote the book *De Re Metallica,* an account of mining practices up to that time. Both Hoover and his wife were mining engineers and Latin scholars. Agricola's work was a standard for about two hundred years but had never been translated into English. Early in their lives, as young engineers living in London, the Hoovers undertook the translation as a labor of love. They spent vacations, weekends, and holidays working on it and managed to get it published.

Once, I noticed a copy of their translation in an eastern book catalog. The description said that it was inscribed by Herbert Hoover. I ordered it. When it came, I was interested to see that Hoover's inscription was addressed to Albert and Marguerite Cole. I knew an Al Cole—an active and well-to-do Republican whom I had met on the Macalester College board. He was the man who convinced DeWitt Wallace that *Reader's Digest* could publish advertising and still be a magazine of integrity. They made him advertising manager, and he made *Reader's Digest* a fabulous economic success. Later, the Wallaces arranged for him to join the Macalester board and represent their interests at the college that they had made their legatee. During the capital campaign I chaired in 1964, Cole and I traveled to New York together and invited business people with *Reader's Digest* connections to attend fund-raising luncheons. He was good at delivering a direct message: "You will want to hire these nice farm-born college graduates out of the Midwest to run your big companies here in New York." Might he be the fellow in Hoover's inscription? What in the dickens was his wife's name?

I called Margaret Day, a longtime staff member at Macalester. "Margaret, what was Al Cole's wife's first name?" I asked. "Oh, Elmer," she said, "How can you ask me a question like that?" But Margaret did not let me down. "She didn't visit the campus very often, but she was here, and as I remember, she was called 'Peggy.'"

That helped a little, but it was not enough. I called *Reader's Digest* at Pleasantville, New York, and got a receptionist who did not want to spend much time on my inquiry. I said, "Please, be patient with me. It means quite a bit to me. Al Cole was an important part of your organization years ago. There must be an old-timer in your public relations department whom you could refer me to." She curtly said, "I think so," and transferred me.

I talked to a nice lady in the public relations department. She had my answer immediately. "Oh, of course, I knew her. Her name was Marguerite. She died, and Al remarried, and then he died, and his second wife is still living down in Florida." That satisfied me. So on my shelf today is a big white volume, the Hoover translation of *De Re Metallica,* inscribed by former President Herbert Hoover to my Macalester friend Al Cole. That book will go to Macalester College someday as a memento of Cole.

The matter of an inscription makes another item on my shelf special.

The Ampersand Club, a group of book lovers in the Twin Cities, invited journalist and scholar Christopher Morley to come to Minneapolis in 1940 and deliver the featured address at an event honoring Gratia Countryman, head librarian at the Minneapolis Public Library from 1903 to 1937. When he began his address, he said, "Friends, Romans," and then he bowed to Miss Countryman. I thought it was so clever. The speech was beautifully written and delivered, and the Ampersand Club printed about one hundred copies of it in a small bound volume. Club officials then wrote to Morley and asked him to autograph them. He replied with a two-page letter detailing his dislike of such requests and his unwillingness to write his name one hundred times. "It's a matter of time and commitment and just boredom," his letter said. The letter was quite a piece of writing in itself, so the club enclosed a photostatic copy of it when it distributed the books to club members.

I kept Morley in mind after that. Two or three years later, I wrote him a letter saying that I had a copy of that wonderful talk he had given in Miss Countryman's honor, printed by the Ampersand Club, and I would love to have it inscribed by him. I told him that I appreciated his work and had a number of his books in my library. I offered to send him the volume and provide postage and a suitable container for its return. I explained the ease he would have in complying with my request. And I enclosed a postcard for him to send back if I could be permitted to send it to him.

The postcard came back with three words on it, "Send it on." He did not even sign it. The card just said, "Send it on." I did, and he put in a nice inscription and sent it back. That is the kind of thing that warms the heart of a book lover. You have the book. You have the copy of the letter saying why he will not sign it. But *your* copy is signed.

I was eclectic in my interest in books. At times I grew fascinated by books of a particular type. Gift books were one such interest. Schools, particularly elite private schools, gave gift books to students of accomplishment. They were typically beautifully bound copies of classic works with the recipient's name inscribed on it and, sometimes, a notation of the recipient's academic achievement. The practice of giving gift books was quite common in the early part of this century. They did not often go on the market, because families regarded them as keepsakes.

When I saw one offered for sale in a New England book catalog, I sent for it. I was astonished to find that it had been given to John Cowles Jr., the son of the owner and publisher and, later, the publisher himself of the *Star* and *Tribune* in Minneapolis. It had been given to him as a high school student; it came to me more than forty years later. I kept it for awhile and enjoyed looking at it. Then, I sent it to Sage Cowles, John's wife. I said, "If you want to ever surprise your good husband, just wrap this up and give it to him as a gift. He'll wonder how in the world you ever came upon this gift book." Apparently, when he left school, he sold or gave away this book and most of the rest of his school possessions. It had been floating around New England ever since. Sage got a big kick out of it, and as I suggested, she gave it to John. He was flabbergasted as to how that book could have survived and found its way back to him.

Books have so many stories of that kind. They go on and on, passing from one pair of hands to another. They leave an imprint on human minds, and humans leave an imprint on their pages.

Sometimes the passage from one owner to another is a story in itself. I was involved in one such case when my friend and fellow book collector James Eckman died. Eckman was a public relations executive in charge of printing and publications at the Mayo Clinic in Rochester, Minnesota. He was a fine, witty writer, and he had an urge to become a publisher himself. In fact, he went so far as to remove a basement wall from his home in order to get a linotype machine into his basement and print books there. Not only did he print a number of things, but he was also a collector of many valuable books about printing. When I heard that he had died, I immediately wondered what would happen to his collection. I hesitated to inquire too soon. When I did, I learned that Mrs. Eckman was selling the collection and was close to closing a sale to a St. Paul book dealer, Rob Rulon-Miller, for $20,000.

Without even seeing the collection, I knew that $20,000 was a bargain. So I called Austin McLean, the special collection curator at the University of Minnesota, and said, "How would you like to go on a little mission with me down to Rochester to look at some books? James Eckman's collection is being sold." "Yes," he said, "I understand that Rob Rulon-Miller is buying it." "He thinks he is. That's what we want to change. Will you go with me?"

McLean joined me, and soon we were looking at Eckman's collection. We found some prizes—a copy of Samuel Johnson's *Dictionary of the English Language* and a leaf of the Gutenberg Bible published by A. Edward Newton that I have always wanted, to name two. I made a proposal to Mrs. Eckman. "I wonder whether this would appeal to you: I buy your collection for the $20,000 that I understand you're willing to sell it for, but I give it to the university to select whatever they want from it to have as an Eckman Collection at the university. Your husband was talented. His work ought to be remembered. His writing ought to be retained. It just shouldn't be dispersed to book collectors. It ought to be kept as a collection. Whatever the university doesn't think appropriate to keep, we'll sell. Now, I know you've had dealings with Rob Rulon-Miller, and there are two works you have that the university already has. So, we suggest you sell Rob Rulon-Miller the Johnson dictionary and the Gutenberg leaf, at the price he has offered. We'll give you $20,000 for everything else for the purpose of establishing the collection at the university."

She thought that was a fine idea. I said, "You certainly have had a lawyer working with you." She did. I said, "Would you call your lawyer and tell him there is an urgent matter, and would he, please, come down right away while we're here?"

She sent for her lawyer. I went over my plan carefully with him. I said, "I want it clearly understood what we're doing, why we're doing it, how it's going to be done, and have your approval and your recommendation to Mrs. Eckman." He listened carefully. Finally, he said, "It sounds like a wonderful way to handle it, Mrs. Eckman. I certainly recommend that you go ahead." She agreed. McLean and I went home the legal owners of Eckman's collection.

McLean and his staff went through the collection and selected a great deal of material that they wanted to keep. Those selections comprise the James Eckman Collection at the university. But the librarians chose not to include a fair amount of material. I was free to sell those items. McLean asked, "How shall we go about that?" I said, "We'll offer it to Rob Rulon-Miller. He wanted to buy it in the first place." "How much?" "$20,000." He said, "Elmer, $20,000 for what's left?" "It's worth it, and he'll pay it. You watch. He knows the value of these books. He really was quite low in his offer to Mrs. Eckman."

We called Rulon-Miller, who was a little upset with us for snatching a nice transaction in Rochester away from him. But Rulon-Miller and I are good friends. I told him, "Now, Rob, I'm not trying to do anything to you. I'm not trying to do anything for myself. I'm just trying to do something for the university, that you will agree, as a bookman, ought to be done. There ought to be a James Eckman Collection." I told him that after the university had made its selections, a lot of material remained. "You know it's worth quite a lot, Rob." "How much do you want for what's left?" he asked. I said, "$20,000." "Oh, Elmer! You've taken the heart out of the collection, and still you want $20,000?" I said, "Now, Rob, you've got the Gutenberg Bible leaf and you've got the Johnson dictionary. I know you did well on those two purchases. I know that you will do well on this at

$20,000. Furthermore, you'll be having a share in something that you can feel good about." I like to tell people that I am giving them an opportunity to feel good about something that they have done. Rulon-Miller bought the remnants of the Eckman Collection for $20,000.

McLean marveled at the entire transaction. He said, "Elmer, anytime you have any projects like this, you can count me in." We got a wonderful collection for the university at no cost to the institution, and no cost to me. In fact, I picked out a few of the books that remained, so I came out a few volumes ahead on the deal. And we had a very good time.

Rob Rulon-Miller truly is a distinguished bookman, one of the leading rare book dealers in the country. His office is in the former Ordway residence on Summit Avenue in St. Paul. He has been head of the American Antiquarian Book Dealers Association and is scheduled to become president of the International Antiquarian Book Dealers Association. I have bought many books from him and sold some through him.

Our book buying has been intimately connected with book giving. Eleanor and I have been buying books to fill the Andersen Horticultural Library at the Minnesota Landscape Arboretum for more than thirty years. Either personally or through our family foundation, we have purchased a majority of its eleven thousand volumes.

In 1998, I had occasion to visit the state's new Judiciary Building, on the site of the old Minnesota Historical Society building adjacent to the capitol. I particularly wanted to see the Minnesota Law Library. I learned that in planning the building, my old friend Peter Popovich, the chief judge of the Court of Appeals and, later, the state supreme court, had proposed the establishment of a rare book room. I was pleased to visit that room, where precious documents collected for 150 years are stored, and to think of Popovich as having planned it.

It occurred to me that a fitting memorial to Popovich might be the creation of a Peter Popovich Rare Book Fund, to provide for the care of the rare books already in that room and allow for more to be added. I took that up with the court, and the idea gained approval. I made an initial $10,000 contribution to start it and invited other friends of Popovich to contribute. So many people loved and admired him that I know the fund bearing his name will grow.

The University of Minnesota has long been a preferred next stop for books on my shelves. For example, I have been a collector for some years of Limited Edition Club books. A man named Jack Macy started the Limited Edition Club in 1929. He selected classic works, about eight or nine each year until his death in 1965, and had them beautifully bound and illustrated by top artists. He published just fifteen hundred copies of each book. When possible, he would arrange for them to be signed by the author and the illustrator. The collection that developed includes some wonderful works. One was the complete works of Shakespeare in twenty-six volumes, each illustrated by a different artist, and designed by Bruce Rogers, who was a preeminent book designer. Another was one volume of Aristophanes, illustrated and signed by Pablo Picasso. A novel by James Joyce was illustrated by Henri Matisse. The club's *Alice in Wonderland* was signed by the original Alice, Alice Hargraves.

An auction house in California proved quite fruitful as a source of Limited Edition Club books. I set out to get a complete collection through 1965. The club continued after Macy's death but did not adhere to the high standards he set. Frequently the California auction house, and other sources too, would offer two or three of the books as a single item. I had to bid on all three in order to get the one I did not have. In that way, I wound up with quite a few dozen duplicates of Limited Edition Club books in order to get a nearly complete set. The duplicates quickly found their way to the university.

One day a few years ago, Tom Shaughnessy, the university's head librarian, sent me a letter inquiring whether I had made any long-range plans for my library. If I had not, he said, he would welcome a chance to discuss its future with me. I was not sure what to expect from the conversation. There was a period when the university was cool toward fine printing. Many universities have departments dedicated to the book and book art. I was helpful in starting the Minnesota Center for Book Arts, something I hoped might eventually be located at the university, but it has not happened. The university even closed its School of Library Science. I once said, "The trouble with university librarians is that they are experts on information retrieval, instead of being book lovers."

That was a somewhat flippant observation, but a serious point lies behind it. I have felt that the university has been a little lax in owning up to only three central missions, teaching, research, and community service. They overlook a fourth mission—an archival one. It falls to the universities in our culture—and specifically to university libraries—to preserve information, knowledge, and culture so it can be found and passed on. There is nothing like the original form of information. A first-edition book signed by an author is more worthy of preservation than a $6.95 paperback because it is the book the author wanted it to be, not revised by a later rendering.

I had indeed begun to think about my library's future. I thought that maybe some of my rarest books should be placed where they were truly wanted, rather than dumped on an indifferent recipient. So, through the catalogs of Rob Rulon-Miller, we had already sold some of the rarest books in my library.

Nevertheless, I invited Shaughnessy to Bussard Court for coffee and took him downstairs to our book room. There, about a dozen giant floor-to-ceiling, double-sided shelves were stacked with more than twelve thousand books. Shaughnessy was amazed—and I was pleasantly surprised at his enthusiasm. "This is tremendous," he said. "You've got everything. It's so diverse. It's ornithology and Greek mythology and . . ." He rattled off examples of the variety of books he had seen. "There isn't a university or a college in the country that wouldn't be delighted to have this collection. We'd like to have it and maintain it as a named special collection, instead of dispersing it into the books of the university."

Eleanor and I talked it over, and we decided we would like that too. No one in the family was prepared to take over the maintenance of a library so extensive. All of our children and grandchildren are book lovers. But they are readers and scholars, not addicts. We decided to invite the family to help themselves to a few volumes that are special to them, as mementos. We would keep a few sentimental favorites and the children's books, so that they could entertain our grandchildren and young visitors. But the rest would become the Elmer L. and Eleanor J. Andersen Collection at the University of Minnesota.

On March 31, 1999, four moving trucks pulled up to our curb. A crew loaded with packing crates invaded our book room. So did a *Star Tribune* reporter and photographer. By the day's end, they were gone, and so were 12,500 books. I struggled to hold back tears as I watched them go. But as I had promised so many people from whom I solicited donations to good causes through the years, I felt good about myself that night.

Then, two wonderful things happened. One occurred on May 14, 1999. University President Mark Yudof and University Foundation executive director Gerald Fischer came to inform me that on the recommendation of the Honors Committee and by action of the Board of Regents, the new library and archive center at the university would be named the Elmer L. Andersen Library. The massive facility is carved into the sandstone river bluffs on the university's West Bank campus. It is intended to be the home of the university's archival collections—including the Andersen collection—and to be the headquarters of efforts to digitalize and preserve historically significant material. Two underground caverns have been excavated into the riverbank for storage. The site is large enough to allow for as many as eighteen caverns someday, as the university's needs grow. The public announcement that the library would bear my name was made at my ninetieth birthday party, in the company of six hundred friends, at the St. Paul Radisson Hotel on June 26.

The other wonderful thing occurred on June 17, the day I turned ninety. I had been thinking my book-buying days were done. But a wonderful auction catalog arrived in early June from an auction house in San Francisco, and I could not resist. As a birthday lark, I bid on forty-one books. Mine was the winning bid on twenty of them—far more than I expected.

I took that as an omen. The bulk of the Elmer L. and Eleanor J. Andersen Collection may already reside at the University of Minnesota, but it is not complete. More books belong in the collection—books we may not even know about yet. Macular degeneration may keep me from reading the books I love, but not from buying them. Each year henceforward, I intend to summon Tom Shaughnessy and a few others to a harvest celebration, to send that year's harvest of books on their way to join the rest of the collection.

A few days after Eleanor and I decided to give our collection to the university, I was looking at a book catalog and saw the name Boethius. It rang a bell. Boethius was a Roman who lived in about A.D. 500. He was the last of the great Romans, a good, kindly, and learned man. Degradation came after him. He was, finally, put to death after a long imprisonment on charges of treason. But he had a fundamental philosophy that is not subject to decay. The last year he was in prison, he wrote a book called the *Consolation of Philosophy*, which has been admired through the centuries. I bought the book with the hope that it could be a kind of foundation book for the collection, for it states what Eleanor and I believe. Boethius articulated a philosophy of goodness. He believed in the power of love. There is a universality about his ideas. He was thinking, reflecting, and analyzing life, and the process of doing so enriched his life, even when he was in prison and confronting death. We are not philosophers on par with Boethius. But we want our collection to stand for the belief that when people read and think and reflect, when they study the past, when they believe in the power of goodness and love, they too will find a richer life.

Life Goes On

AGING IS A WONDERFUL THING—despite its bad reputation. It is an extension of life. Early in life, a man seldom thinks about mortality. As he grows older, he begins to realize that life has a limit. But if he is in reasonably good health and has adequate financial resources, his older years can be a satisfying time.

I have often said that if a man can avoid heart problems in his fifties, cancer in his sixties, and prostate trouble in his seventies, he can go on indefinitely. Having just celebrated my ninetieth birthday, I am well past those danger zones. My heart is not strong, but I go easy on it. I have no cancer, and the little bit of prostate trouble I once had cleared up nicely. So, I am going on indefinitely.

Some interesting changes come about with age. My philosophy has always been to look for a good side to every development and not to let any turn of events get me down. I think age has made me even more adaptable. I am better able to accept what comes and be satisfied with conditions as they are. But I am also highly conscious of the opportunities I still have and much intent on taking advantage of them.

Aging tends to reduce one's level of activity. It is a chance to move from a world of activity to a world of thought. I have the luxury of being able to just sit and think for more than a fleeting moment. I need not feel guilty about taking time away from a business obligation or children who need attention. The opportunity for prolonged reflection is a pleasurable thing. I am able to relive experiences and rethink views and enjoy many things in contemplation and reverie. For example, I probably will not visit Australia again, but I have been there enough to know Australia fairly well. As a result, I can close my eyes and go to Australia anytime I wish, without the hassle of air travel. I sometimes get so caught up in my mental excursions while doing things that take me awhile—like trying to get up from a chair—that I forget that I am supposed to be moving!

I do not miss a life of scheduling and running about. That kind of activity seemed important once, but I now understand that ideas are what really build a life. Ideas are inspired by the thoughts and work of other people, and fueled by quiet, uninterrupted reflection. I believe the saying that "the kingdom of heaven is within you" is true. There is much in the mind that is undeveloped. There is much to know. There is much to think about. There is much to try to resolve. There is much to try to reach out to and touch for good.

Of course, aging deprives one of physical abilities. Through macular degeneration, I have largely lost the ability to read. That has been a major loss, though a gradual one. The deterioration in my eyesight began a decade ago, and it is progressing still. At first, it did not bother me much, because there were magnifying glasses and there was a television-like reading device that would magnify printed material to any size I wanted. But when tremor began to accompany macular degeneration, I could no longer hold a magnifying glass steady or easily insert a sheet of paper into a reader. As a result, I do not read as much as I would like. But I listen more.

The tremor I experience is related to post-polio syndrome, the late-in-life aftereffect of having polio as a child. The syndrome causes loss of muscle mass. Weakness and impaired mobility result. I must take great care to avoid a fall, because in my weakened condition, a broken bone would heal very slowly and could be life threatening. That is why I keep my "Swedish Jaguar"—a sleek, strong walker designed in Malmö, Sweden—close at hand as I move about. My great-granddaughter Shelby provided its accoutrements—a beeper to warn traffic of my approach, a quilted pad to cushion my baggage, and a cup holder for in-transit refreshment. In recent months, I have also added an electric wheelchair to my transportation fleet.

It is heartening to realize how much thought modern society has put into making life pleasant and endurable for older people. We live at a wonderful time. Medical technology has always seemed to stay just ahead of me. About the time I have needed a new remedy or drug, it has been there for me, often newly developed. The devices and special services available for visually impaired people are exploding in number. Books on audiotape, read by excellent readers, are quite readily available. The special tape deck for books on tape allows for adjustment of the speed of reading, and for repetition. I am told that the Library of Congress has 155,000 books on tape— enough to keep me going for quite a while. I also take advantage of a special twenty-four-hour-a-day radio station that reads books, newspapers, and magazines to the visually impaired.

In my home office, I have an easy chair designed to assist people with mobility challenges. It is incredible. When I sit down, it adjusts from almost a standing position to a sitting position, to a reclining position if I wish. When I want to get up, it reverses the motion and practically disgorges me.

Despite weakening eyesight and muscles, I enjoy generally good health. I attribute it to marrying Eleanor, who has made sure I have had proper nutrition for sixty-seven years. I was a meat-and-potatoes guy until I married. Eleanor saw to it that my diet included salad, fruits, and vegetables. She is disciplined about preparing balanced meals.

I was a smoker during my early adult years, but I wanted to quit as soon as I heard the first warnings from the U.S. Surgeon General about the hazard smoking posed to one's health. So, I studied why I smoked. I discovered it was a habit connected with certain activities. When I answered the telephone, I would light a cigarette. If someone came to my office to see me, I would light a cigarette. Quitting, I concluded, had to involve changing those habits. I would start while on a two-week family vacation, away from telephones, away from the office. My plan worked, until we got to Newark, New Jersey, where Fuller had an office. I called on the manager, and he offered me a cigarette. Before I thought about it, I lit it. But after my two-week hiatus from tobacco, that cigarette tasted awful. It was the last one I ever smoked, but it made me aware of how easily I could have fallen back into the habit again. If smokers analyze when they smoke and then change their habits for a time, they will find that quitting is possible.

Good physical health is also the result of an active life. There is no end to things that need doing by willing people, no matter their age. It is good to have projects. It is good to have a reason to get up in the morning, a task or a challenge that you want to get at. Complaining about all that is wrong in the world does not promote good health, but doing something about a situation that needs rectifying does. Selfless action is a great road to satisfaction and good health. Older people sometimes think that any contribution they could make would be too small to be meaningful. But the important thing is to do what you can, wherever you are. Grains of sand are what make a beautiful beach.

I also think people do well when they refuse to dwell on the past, and look ahead. When I think today about losing the governorship in 1963, I do not think about what-ifs or might-have-beens for my own career. But I am mindful of the agenda that I left unfinished and that is still unfinished. Minnesota does not do as well with its natural resources of timber and water as it should. There is an enormous subterranean body of water in northwestern Minnesota that has never been tapped. Someday, somebody is going to come up with an ingenious way of using that water, hopefully without squandering it. Water is going to be one of the greatest critical needs of the future, and Minnesota has it in abundance. Minnesotans should be thinking about managing that resource for the long haul. What should we be doing now, so that in one hundred years, not only is life better in Minnesota, but the state is an important contributor to the rest of the world? I like to think in terms of one hundred years. Five years, ten years, or even twenty-five years is a short interval in the history of a state. A one-hundred-year resource management plan allows enough time to get things done.

An abiding love of learning is another asset in one's later years. I studied business administration in college and learned many valuable things. But today I have a great hunger to know more about the liberal arts—philosophy, literature, history, the social sciences. American education pays too little homage to the scholars of antiquity. That may be why we tend to think that anything that is more than twenty-five years old has little to teach us. In fact, things said and done 2,500 years ago have great relevance to today's problems—and they are a largely untapped resource. I relish the chance I have now to learn about them.

When I indulge in the opportunity age affords to sit and think, my thoughts often turn to religion. The Christian faith taught by the Lutheran Church was crucially formative in my life. Grace University Lutheran Church in southeast Minneapolis reshaped my life when it introduced me to Eleanor and to the mentoring friendship of the Rev. Claus August Wendell. He provided a marvelous example of living the Christian spirit. He was not always right on target with the dogma of the church. He was more of a humanitarian who adapted Christian principles to life in a way that people could understand. He elevated people's aspirations. That is a wonderful thing to do. Sometimes the true value of an effort does not lie in what is accomplished but in what one aspires to do. It is the reaching that counts.

As Robert Browning wrote, "A man's reach should exceed his grasp, or what's a heaven for?" I am convinced that the reaching and grasping Browning refers to have nothing to do with money. They have to do with the human spirit, with wisdom, generosity, and love. The heaven he speaks of is not some afterlife destination. It is the here-and-now result of a life that is spent always striving for that which is good.

My faith and theology have evolved through the years. But they come to this: one should attempt to put into practice the essential teachings of

Christ. They are about grace, forgiveness, love, caring, and selflessness. They are wonderfully evident in the parable of the Good Samaritan, who cared for his natural enemy without concern for personal gain. As the Old Testament prophet Micah says, what more is required of a person but to act justly and love mercy, and walk humbly through life? All of the contests and speculations about an afterlife do not mean as much to me as life itself, how it is lived, and how it affects the lives of others.

Religious tolerance has always been in short supply in the human race, and the lack of it remains one of the world's most pressing problems. Unless and until the Judeo-Christian nations come to an accommodation with Islam, world peace will be elusive. Even a slight study of Islam reveals its great depth of faith and hope. But the dogma that Islam, or any religion, has the entire truth is unfortunate. It is bound to lead to a clash. All religions have at their heart a spirit of love beyond oneself. Any religion is sadly debased when people use it to justify cruelty, torture, or killing. Any religion is twisted when it is used to justify punishment without mercy or forgiveness. What ought to matter is not which religion one practices or studies. What should matter is that the message of religion—the message of love for one's fellow human creatures—somehow finds its way into one's heart.

The thing that puzzles me the most is why more people do not catch the idea that reaching out to others is the way to achieve a life that is glowing and growing. The very act of getting is restrictive. The very act of giving is expansive. Giving expands the spirit. It expands the mind. It expands one's health and, I would argue, one's years.

I used to struggle trying to believe every story I had been taught in Sunday school. Then, I remembered the passage in St. Paul's letter to the Corinthians that says that when you are a child, you think as a child, and when you grow up, you put away childish things. The yearning and search for truth never ends.

Eleanor and I did not have much under our first Christmas tree in 1932. But at least we had a tree, and we had fun finding, borrowing, and making decorations to make it festive. When we finished, it did not seem complete. It lacked a star on top. A store-bought star was an extravagance. But we had a silver-lined cardboard box. From it, we cut out a star and then fashioned a little hinge on its back with which to attach it to the tree.

Sixty-six Christmases have come and gone with that same star—or a duplicate, made one year in the temporary panic of thinking the original was lost—perched atop the Andersen family tree. It has become a cherished symbol to Eleanor and me of constancy and family and abiding love.

Christmas in the Andersen home has been a big event, built around family, church, food, music, and tradition. The celebration is almost always in our home, with as many of the children, grandchildren, and great-grandchildren as possible gathered around. It begins in the late afternoon on Christmas Eve.

The Christmas Eve dinner varies a little from year to year, but it always includes a few traditional dishes. One is Swedish sausage, a potato and pork sausage. When it is homemade by someone who knows how, it is the most delicious treat, one Scandinavians reserve for Christmas. My friend Reuben Thoreen of Stillwater—the man whose stuffed loon resided in the governor's office for a time—made wonderful Swedish sausage and personally delivered a package to me for many years. I cannot eat Swedish sausage on Christmas Eve today without remembering Reuben. The feast also includes ham, roast turkey, or chicken, and Swedish meatballs. Eleanor's Swedish meatballs are something to look forward to. There is something about the combination of meat, breadcrumbs, and seasonings that gives them a special flavor and texture. A delectable Scandinavian treat we often include is rice pudding with a lump of butter in the middle of each portion, and cinnamon on top.

Our holiday fare also includes an abundance of Christmas cookies, some of which Eleanor makes from recipes her mother used. The preparation of a variety of cookies begins weeks in advance. I always look forward to the butter cookies called *Berliner Kranser,* made in the shape of a wreath. Rosettes are another treat. They are so delicate and crisp that they practically explode when you eat them. We used to dust them with powdered sugar, but we discovered that granulated sugar was not quite as messy. I have never been much involved in the baking, but I am generally quite involved in the eating.

After our Christmas Eve dinner, we go into the living room for a family program. We read the Christmas story in the Gospel of Luke, and sing carols. We have a family prayer, ending with the Lord's Prayer. We want the children to register that behind all of the fun and the food and the gifts, there is a tremendous message to the holiday.

Only after that sacred moment has passed are gifts opened. Usually, the youngest person is assigned to retrieve the presents from under the tree and distribute them. Every gift is distributed before the opening begins.

We end the evening by going to our church service. That is always a beautiful, moving service that makes a strong impact, almost as if the worshippers are reliving the birth of Jesus.

Tradition guides us even after midnight. After church, before we go to bed, the children hang their stockings and prepare a little treat for Santa Claus. For a number of years, Rotarians at the St. Paul Rotary Club's Christmas party received large canvas stockings, courtesy of a member who was in the awning business. Those stockings have been much in demand by children in our family through the years. In the morning, the children find them stuffed with oranges and other special treats. It takes some bulky items to make an impression in those big Rotary stockings!

Christmas is a glorious time, filled with generosity, the warmth of human relationships, and the inspiration of a powerful religious message. When our old cardboard star goes atop the tree each year, it is hard for me not to get misty-eyed thinking of all these years of tradition and togetherness.

Tony never misses our Christmas celebration because he lives in the Twin Cities. He has just retired as chairman of the board of H. B. Fuller Company, having retired as chief executive officer in 1992 after providing twenty-one years of outstanding leadership. I retired from the Fuller board myself in 1994, after sixty years of association with the company. I thought I ought to retire before Tony did! Tony is still active in the community, serving on a number of industrial and philanthropic boards. One in the latter category is the Wilder Foundation in St. Paul, which does wonderful work to improve the lot of children, the elderly, the mentally ill, and the handicapped. Tony is still an outdoorsman, still a vintage sports car racer, and still a devoted son.

Tony is single. His only child is Amy Andersen, our beloved granddaughter. The love of the outdoors that her father instilled in her has had a big influence in her life. It inspired her to attend the National Outdoor Leadership Training School in Lander, Wyoming, in hopes of starting a career in outdoor experiential education. Instead, she took a job offered at the school, and met Timothy Wilson, another staff member. They were married in an outdoor setting in Wyoming. They have two adorable children, Shelby Katherine Wilson, born in 1991, and Caleb James Wilson, born in 1997.

Julian, our second son, is the new CEO and publisher of the ECM newspapers, though he continues to live in Seattle, Washington. He concluded a successful career teaching mathematics and computer science at Shoreline Community College in a suburb of Seattle, Washington, where he spent twenty-nine years. Julian is an active Democrat. He was chairman of the negotiating committee of the faculty union for a number of years.

One of the nicest letters we ever received arrived in connection with Julian's retirement from Shoreline College. Some of his coworkers, all of them strangers to us, wrote us a letter to congratulate us on raising such a fine son. We were so moved by their praise for Julian, and their gesture in writing to us.

Julian is married to Jamie McIntyre, and they have two sons, Nathan Lee and Benjamin Lee. Quite a few Andersens have my middle name, Lee, as their middle name. Nathan, born in 1982, is bright and studious. He wrote us a note last year about his excitement at getting his driver's license. We predict a career in some area of scientific research for him. He has the thoughtful, deliberate nature of a careful researcher. Benjamin was born in 1985. He is an artistic lad. He impressed me once when I was interested in developing a logo for the publications of the Sugarloaf Interpretive Center Association. I told Benjamin what was on my mind. He agreed to try to come up with something, and, with the help of his mother, found a page of Egyptian hieroglyphics. With that page beside him, he began to work. I was so surprised and pleased with what he designed. It was the letters SICA in an Egyptian style, along with a tree and a bowl to represent water.

Our daughter, Emily, has submitted a proposal for a doctorate in education while teaching seventh-grade English. She has undergraduate and master's degrees, and the doctorate would document language use and acquisition by children. As our effort to preserve Sugarloaf Point and Cove demonstrates, Emily is interested in environmental preservation. Additionally, she has been active in the Schroeder Area Historical Society and its renovation of a historic building. Recently she participated in the publication of a book about flowers on the North Shore, a book written by Sandra Bennett and Tom Sullivan. It is an exquisite example of the art of bookmaking as well as a source of reliable information. Always active in the out-of-doors, Emily is a scuba diver and at one point was an instructor in marine biology for children and in scuba diving. She is a model of life-long learning and devotion to public service.

My own three siblings have all left this life, Marvin first, in 1960, then Arnold in 1980, and Caroline in 1997. Caroline was a registered nurse and then a graduate health professional, before marrying a labor lawyer in Detroit and raising three children. One of her sons became a Ph.D. in psychology, and the other a rock musician; her daughter, Eve, is a mother and nursery worker in Detroit.

Arnold became a business leader in Muskegon. He owned several companies, served on the governing board of a bank, and was an officer in the

Chamber of Commerce. He was a fine man, one I always looked up to. He and his wife, Eunice, had two children. One carried on his father's business; the other married a person who had a business background and has become a successful investment counselor.

Marvin and his wife, Ella, moved from Muskegon to White Plains, New York, where Marvin worked for a manufacturer of scientific supplies. When he died in 1960, Ella took the loss hard, and within a year, she was gone too. They had two children. One is married to a professor of journalism in a state university in Marysmith, New York, and the other became an obstetrician in Wilmington, Delaware.

We are so proud of the large and productive family that sprang from the four Andersen siblings on Muskegon's Smith Street. We are trying to encourage the later generations to recognize their connection as one family, and remain in touch with one another. Our son Julian and Arnold's daughter-in-law, Marilyn Andersen in Muskegon, are publishing a periodic newsletter called the *Andersentinel*—a name we first used for Tony's birth announcement in 1935.

I marvel at Eleanor. Now in her eighty-ninth year, she remains very much the manager of our household. She is the same marvelous cook and homemaker she has always been, though she has consented to a bit more household help in recent years. She stays faithfully in contact with a large circle of family and friends. Her work with the Schubert Club continues, though she recently left the board of the Children's Home Society in St. Paul after many years of service. Thankfully, her eyesight and voice remain strong enough for her to read to me. That is how we pass many pleasant hours together.

When my great-grandson, Caleb, was born in 1997 and I first held this little child, I could not help but wonder at four generations. How marvelous life is, in the mysteries of its creation, in the talents a human being develops, in his or her capacity to think and care and feel and work and serve. Life is just as remarkable at age ninety as it is for a baby. It is an abundant experience. It comes through families. It comes through traditions like Christmas. It comes through connection and service to others. It is boundless and wonderful. Whatever impairment may come with age does not amount to anything compared to all the joys that life still can hold.

About three years before I turned eighty, my friend Wheelock Whitney said, "Elmer, when you turn eighty, your friends want to have a party for you. All we want you to do is to agree to the idea, and be there. We'll do the rest." I gave my consent, so for three years, a little luncheon club met to plan a tremendous party. I was elated with their grand production. I told the crowd that evening, "For my ninetieth birthday party, I'll invite you all back as our guests."

I made good on the promise on June 26, 1999. We had another glorious evening, with six hundred friends gathered around Eleanor and me at the St. Paul Radisson Hotel. Wheelock and Tom Swain spoke. The Plymouth Ensemble sang, as did my grand-niece Mollie Dustin; my nephew Marvin Andersen played the trumpet. My grandchildren, great-grandchildren, and some young friends brought in the cake. And University of Minnesota President Mark Yudof topped it off with the announcement of the new university library's name: the Elmer L. Andersen Library. It was a night to relive in memory for years to come.

We are beginning to give some thought to another occasion. What in the world do you do when you turn one hundred?!

Epilogue
The View from 2000

AWONDERFUL NEW CENTURY has dawned, and I am glad to be among those who greet it. There is so much to live for. The twentieth century produced enormous advances, and the twenty-first century has the potential to bring greater things still. Just ahead are fabulous developments and important challenges for our state, our nation, and all of humanity.

The United States enters the twenty-first century in a strong position. The twentieth century ended with an unequalled surge of business activity, giving the nation a historic run of economic expansion. But prosperity is not enjoyed equally by all segments of the American population. Farmers are having a difficult time due to overproduction, diminished world demand, and discrimination against genetically modified grain. Small businesses continue to struggle with the onslaught of merger after merger, and the takeover of whole industries by monolithic corporations.

America and the rest of the world need to face up more directly to the problem of poverty. Every American—indeed, everyone in the world—should know freedom, justice, and opportunity. Those should be the greatest goals of the twenty-first century: freedom, justice, and opportunity, so that every human being has a chance to survive and flourish.

We are blessed with new tools that should make those goals attainable. One is the Internet. Its prospects are awesome. It is amazing to think that all the people of the world can be in communication, and that anyone anywhere can be a market for anyone else. Today we see only the earliest stages of the Internet's development, but it is clear already that the Internet will change the world for the better.

Similarly, the explosion of knowledge in the biological sciences should greatly enhance the prospects of humankind. The twenty-first century may be known as the biological century, as compared to the mechanical twentieth century. Genetic research has made substantial gains, but it is still at an early stage of development. Yet one has the sense that the cures to maladies that have afflicted humanity through the ages—disease, hunger, even mental illness—will soon be within our grasp.

I hope that particular attention is given to mental and emotional illness. Already we are beginning to recognize that such disorders can be controlled or even cured with proper therapies. We have also come to understand that mental illness can be a brief passing thing, in contrast to the early-twentieth-century concept of mental illness as a lifelong affliction. But much, much more must be understood about the workings of the human psyche. This field is ripe for research in our new century.

For Americans, the twenty-first century will likely be a time of discovery of parts of the world that held little interest for them before. It could be the century of Asia, with China having great potential, India ready to emerge, Russia with at least the potential of reestablishment, and Japan still a strong economic power. Those nations have large, impatient populations and economies that may not grow fast enough to keep pace with citizens' demands. Asia will present a challenge to the United States as we strive to maintain a position of leadership while balancing power so as to avoid war. We must make war appear to be a losing rather than a winning proposition to ambitious nations.

That was the great achievement of some of the best statesmen of earlier ages: they understood how to establish and preserve a balance of power that prevented war. That was the aim of Klemens Metternich of Austria, who dominated political thought in Europe in the early nineteenth century. In the seventeenth century, Cardinal Richelieu positioned France to balance the power of the Habsburgs, and stabilized Europe.

Individual leadership of that caliber is needed in the twenty-first century, to balance power in such a way that war is avoided and individual human potential is free to develop. History teaches that able individual leaders characterize periods of achievement. As much as ever, gains for humanity depend on the rise of wise, visionary leaders who know how to capture imagination and inspire new ventures.

In the new century more than ever, the individual is vitally important. Individuals are going to have more opportunities than ever before. That will put enormous pressure on individuals to have the knowledge, stability, and values to cope with rapid change. No education will be satisfactory in the future unless it instills openness to change and confidence that new skills can be mastered.

In Minnesota, in the United States, and throughout the world, we also need to inculcate in more individuals a sense of desire and obligation to play a role in governance. Today, too many people avoid government service. The unfortunate result is that government becomes a place for self-seekers. We need our best intellects and high ethicists to deal with state, national, and world problems. One example of intellectual leadership is that of Václav Havel, who became president of Czechoslovakia when Communism fell in 1989, and is now president of the Czech Republic. He is a writer and a person of great intellectual achievement, and has given his country inspiring leadership. Both in his writings and in his example, he has shown the way for others.

Minnesota has a tradition of citizen involvement that has served us well. It is something Minnesota can teach the nation and the world. Despite the great success of American democracy, far too many Americans are dissatisfied with their own government. The growing feeling that people want to have their own way within the American framework, instead of accepting the American framework, should summon those who value unity in this country to a larger, greater citizenship. In the early twentieth century, Americans marched off to a challenge as great as a world war with songs and high spirits. That spirit of joy to be an American is lacking today. It should be rekindled.

Minnesota is not without problems, but they tend to be less severe than in the rest of the nation. For example, Louisiana and Texas have the highest percentage of incarcerations per one hundred thousand of population. Minnesota has one of the lowest, but its criminal justice system still needs improvement. I would like to see an experiment in something that might be called restorative justice, based on sentences that aim to restore people to right thinking and good standing in society, rather than to punish them and then turn them loose without treatment.

Education in Minnesota has been a great strength, but it too can be improved. We are not using programs that work well to the maximum. For example, we know that Head Start and other early education programs are helpful, but they are not available to all children. We need to infuse modern education with more of the great thinking of the last 2,500 years, to give today's citizens a sense that their mission is to build on the work of those who have come before. We need to invest in architecture, art, and music, things that will enrich the lives of people, rather than concentrating solely on utility and profit.

I have one concern about a danger for the whole United States that has particular application to Minnesota. We must guard against the balkanization of the United States. We should have one language and one education system. We should respect ethnic differences without letting them become ethnic divisions. We should welcome legal immigrants, not resent them, and encourage them to adopt American customs and culture. People come to America today to establish a new base for themselves, just as immigrants have come for several centuries. Some of Minnesota's more recent arrivals did not want to come. They were forced out of their homelands. Some seek to reestablish in this country much of what they left behind. While some aspects of a culture can be transplanted and sustained, it is not good for the long-range health of this nation for citizens to be divided into separate enclaves.

Similarly, it will not be possible in the long run to sustain nations within a nation. I refer to Native Americans having many sovereign nations, several of them in Minnesota. It just is not possible for people to live side by side with some under one rule of law and others under another. There has to be unity. It has to be achieved with justice, fairness, generosity, and compensation for the shortcomings of the past, but we need a unified America. Minnesotans of all races should work toward that goal.

I foresee a wonderful century. It is certain to be marred by individual failures and terrible examples of inhumanity. But I am confident that the century will bring glorious examples of the triumph of the human spirit in poetry, art, architecture, music, and ideas of governance. I believe that, gradually but unrelentingly, the universal consciousness is moving us toward higher achievement. If we aim to release and encourage the creative powers of the people, great things are possible. I hope I will be around to see some of them.

February 7, 2000

Professional Positions, Activities, and Honors of Elmer L. Andersen

BUSINESS POSITIONS

President, chairman, and CEO, ECM Publishers, Inc., Princeton, Minnesota, 1976–97

President, chairman, and CEO, H. B. Fuller Company, 1941–74

Board member, H. B. Fuller Company, 1974–94

ACTIVITIES

Governor of Minnesota, 1961–63

Minnesota state senator, 1949–58

Member, Board of Regents, University of Minnesota, 1967–75

Chairman, Board of Regents, University of Minnesota, 1972–75

Treasurer, University of Minnesota Foundation, 1975–78

Chairman, University of Minnesota Foundation, 1979–81

Member and president, Executive Council, Minnesota Historical Society

Director and president, Voyageurs National Park Association

Member, Governor's Voyageurs National Park Advisory Committee

Member, National Parks Centennial Commission

Director, University of Minnesota Arboretum Foundation

President and director, Child Welfare League of America

Director, president, and chairman, The Bush Foundation, St. Paul, Minnesota

Chairman, Executive Committee, Council on Foundations, New York, New York

President, St. Paul Rotary Club

District Governor, Rotary International

Trustee, Augsburg College

Member, Minnesota Higher Education Coordinating Commission

Member, Regent Selection Advisory Council, University of
Minnesota

Director, Association of Governing Boards of Colleges and
Universities

Chairman, Minnesota Constitutional Study Commission

Member, Minnesota Judicial Planning Committee

Founding director, Minnesota Center for Book Arts

Founding director, Sugarloaf Interpretive Center Association

Chairman, Charles A. Lindbergh Foundation

Chairman, Alliss Educational Foundation

Director, Minnesota Orchestral Association

Director, Minneapolis Society of Fine Arts

Director, First Trust Company, St. Paul, Minnesota

Director, Minnesota Mutual Life Insurance Company

Director, George A. Hormel & Company, Austin, Minnesota

President, Adhesive Association of America

Director, National Association of Manufacturers

MEMBERSHIPS

American Antiquarian Society, Worcester, Massachusetts

Grolier Club, New York, New York

Minneapolis Club, Minneapolis, Minnesota

Rotary Club of St. Paul, St. Paul, Minnesota

Rowfant Club, Cleveland, Ohio

HONORS

LL.D., Macalester College, St. Paul, Minnesota

Doctorate of Humane Letters, Carleton College, Northfield,
Minnesota

Honorary Doctorate of Management, School of Management, University of Minnesota

Honorary Doctorate of Laws, St. John's University, Collegeville, Minnesota

University of Minnesota Regents' Award

University of Minnesota Outstanding Achievement Award

Alpha Kappa Psi Award, Twin Cities Alumni Chapter

National Phi Kappa Phi Award (Honor Society), presented by the University of Minnesota

Order of the Lion, Finland

Twin Cities Business Monthly, honored as founding member, Business Hall of Fame, 1999

Izaak Walton League, Award of Merit

St. Paul Chamber's Great Living Saint Paulite Award

Distinguished Minnesotan and Rotarian, honored at the Rotary International District Conference, 1980

Silver Beaver and Silver Antelope Award, Boy Scouts of America

Minneapolis Junior Chamber Conservation Award

Taconite Award, Public Service Recognition Award of the American Institute of Mining Engineers of America, Minnesota Chapter

ASC Award, first award presented by the Adhesive & Sealant Council for contribution to the adhesive industry and for distinguished public service, 1980

1981 Packaging Man of the Year, Packaging Education Foundation, Philadelphia, Pennsylvania

1982 Brotherhood Award, National Conference of Christians and Jews

David W. Preus Leadership Award

Minnesota Library Association Distinguished Achievement Award

MEA Friend of Education Award

Kay Sexton Award, Minnesota Annual Book Awards, 1997

Reuel Harmon Award, Minnesota Parks & Trails Council

AAA Service to Motoring Award

David Graven Award for Journalistic Achievement, the Frank Premack Awards, 1998

Index

Created by Eileen Quam

ELMER L. ANDERSEN has been described as Minnesota's leading citizen. His political service included legislative leadership in civil rights, special education, and welfare, and culminated in his election as governor in 1960, an office he held for one term. He was chairman of the Board of Regents of the University of Minnesota, his alma mater, and president of the University Foundation. His role in the creation of Voyageurs National Park, several state parks, and the Sugarloaf Interpretative Center Association has earned him distinction as an environmentalist. He built a small adhesives company, H. B. Fuller Company, into a world leader, and founded a weekly newspaper company that now includes twenty-five publications. He has been an award-winning dairy farmer, journalist, and philanthropist.

LORI STURDEVANT is an editorial writer for the *Minneapolis Star Tribune,* specializing in the coverage of state government, politics, and higher education.